National Theatre Connections
2014

PLAYS FOR YOUNG PEOPLE

Same

Horizon

The Wardrobe

Heritage

A Letter to Lacey

A Shop Selling Speech

Angels

Hearts

Pronoun

Tomorrow

with an introduction by
ANTHONY BANKS

B L O O M S B U R Y
LONDON · NEW DELHI · NEW YORK · SYDNEY

Bloomsbury Methuen Drama
An imprint of Bloomsbury Publishing Plc

50 Bedford Square   1385 Broadway
London   New York
WC1B 3DP   NY 10018
UK   USA

www.bloomsbury.com

Bloomsbury is a registered trade mark of Bloomsbury Publishing Plc

This collection first published in 2014

British Library Cataloguing-in-Publication Data
A catalogue record for this book is available from the British Library

ISBN: PB: 978-1-4725-7143-4
ePub: 978-1-4725-7145-8
ePDF: 978-1-4725-7144-1

Library of Congress Cataloging-in-Publication Data
A catalog record for this book is available from the Library of Congress.

Typeset by Country Setting, Kingsdown, Kent CT14 8ES
Printed and bound in Great Britain

Contents

Introduction

Connections has been at the heart of the National Theatre's work for young people for the last two decades. The formula is simple: established playwrights create short plays for young actors to perform. Ten new plays are launched each year, building up a repertoire for young theatre companies to produce in schools, colleges and youth theatres. Each year more than 200 youth theatres and school groups from across the UK and beyond take up the challenge of staging a brand new play. Young people are involved not just as actors but as stage managers, designers, lighting and sound technicians – all the roles required for a professional theatre production.

At the beginning of the rehearsal process, the NT hosts a weekend in our Studio in London for the directors of the youth theatre companies in the Connections programme. Here the directors get the chance to spend a day with the playwright, discussing the new play they're about to direct. When the plays are performed in the companies' home venues, a director from the National travels to see the performance, and provides detailed feedback in the form of a show report. All productions then transfer to a Connections festival held at professional theatres across the UK. One version of each play is invited to the final festival of the season which is held at the National Theatre.

The first collection of plays was published in 1995. The project was originally sponsored by British Telecom, who created the name 'Connections'. It has since enjoyed sponsorship from Accenture, Bank of America Merrill Lynch and Shell UK, and is now supported by a consortium of individual donors and from the NT's own core funds. Originally running bi-annually, Connections now runs every year, and since 1995 over 150 new plays have been commissioned, developed and performed by thousands of young actors across the country.

For more information and to get involved:
www.nationaltheatre.org.uk/connections

Connections 2014

Each year the National Theatre invites playwrights whose work excites us to write new plays for Connections. Playwrights take many different approaches to the commission but all Connections writers have the opportunity to test their ideas with young people through research, rehearsed readings and workshops. The ten plays in the 2014 collection were developed with young people across the UK.

DEBORAH BRUCE is an acclaimed theatre director of new writing, who has led sessions at the Connections Directors Weekend, and has recently started writing plays herself. Her idea for her Connections play had been brewing for a while. It is a story which came about partly through her experience of the death of her own grandmother but also an experiment to see if she could create a scene in which young actors play the elders who reside in a care home. Deborah workshopped it with young actors at the National Theatre.

MATT HARTLEY won the under-25s Bruntwood Prize with his play *65 Miles* which is about two brothers and was produced by Paines Plough in Hull, where Matt went to university. He had the idea for his Connections play while sitting in a shopping centre in Hull and decided he wanted to research the theme of youth unemployment. He went to Newcastle upon Tyne to workshop his idea with over a hundred young people around the city – Year 9s in Whickham School in Gateshead, young actors from Live Theatre Company by the quayside and The Young People's Theatre in Heaton. Several months later, when Matt had written the play, he went back to the People's Theatre in Newcastle and they did a reading of the script and discussed the play. His Connections play is about two sisters, one who is losing her job in a shop and the other who has a place at university but can't afford to go.

SAM HOLCROFT is currently writer-in-residence at the National Theatre Studio. A few years ago Sam created a play for the National Theatre of Scotland called *Cockroach* which presents an extraordinary scenario in which a classroom full of unruly schoolchildren slowly morphs into a horrific battlefield of contemporary warfare. For Connections, Sam has conjured a bold vision of a big Tudor wardrobe in which lots of different groups of young people through centuries of British history are hiding from danger – each group in very different circumstances to the last, but in turn guarded by the same wooden walls. The play was developed with the help of the young company at the Tricycle Theatre in Kilburn. Sam embraced the Connections play brief by deciding to write more scenes than any production would require, meaning that each production will be unique, as each company must choose the scenes they want to include and the order they play them in.

DAFYDD JAMES writes in both Welsh and English. He had two very successful shows in 2010: his acclaimed play about identity, *Llwyth* (*Tribe*), which began in Cardiff and then toured internationally, and a national tour of *My Name is Sue*, which had won a Total Theatre Award at the Edinburgh Festival in 2009. Daf wanted to write a play which explored what it meant to preserve cultural traditions. Over the course of two years, he wrote several drafts of his play, which had several titles along the way as he discovered what his play was about. He workshopped his ideas with several youth theatre companies in Wales. The play ends with an anthem which Dafydd has composed, and which the characters come together to sing as a choir.

CATHERINE JOHNSON wrote a short play, in the form of a monologue, about a young woman who was being physically and psychologically abused by her boyfriend which was workshopped and performed by The Meriton school in Bristol, facilitated by Myrtle Theatre Company. The following year Catherine developed the monologue into this full-length Connections play, in which the characters the girl talked about in the shorter piece came to life. Her play also contains about half a dozen songs which give some light relief to the serious subject matter of partner abuse.

SABRINA MAHFOUZ creates highly poetic plays which she sometimes also performs. Sabrina is half-Egyptian, her father still lives and works in Cairo, and she travelled to Egypt to research her Connections play by interviewing many young people who had been involved in protests in and around Cairo during the last few years. The information and stories they told her sparked the creation of her play which is about freedom of speech. The play is set in present-day Cairo, although the portrayal is far from naturalistic – it's a stylised world which could easily be any imagined place where there has recently been acute political unrest. When Sabrina returned to London, she workshopped her play with some young actors and the idea of a shop being held up by robbers who are wanting speech tokens gradually took shape. Director Hettie Macdonald gave some fantastic notes on the script in the final stages of its development.

PAULINE MCLYNN is known to millions as Ireland's much loved legendary housekeeper Mrs Doyle in the television comedy *Father Ted*. As well as appearing in several other television dramas, Pauline also writes novels, both for adults and for young readers: her *Jenny Q* series celebrates teen-obsessions with unbridled hilarity. During her acclaimed performance as Winnie in Samuel Beckett's *Happy Days* at the Sheffield Crucible, she came up with an idea to write a play for Connections. She created a magical graveyard in which a group of young people are carrying out community service. She wrote a few drafts of the play and did a workshop reading of it at the National Theatre Studio, after which she wrote the final version, settling on the order of events in the story and sharpening up the jokes. Although the heart of Pauline's play contains big themes like life and death, poverty and loneliness, it's a very warm-hearted play, with about a dozen characters, a few songs and carved stone angels who come to life.

LUKE NORRIS is a writer and an actor who has played leading roles in *War Horse*, *Antigone* and *The Habit of Art* at the National Theatre and most recently *Hamlet* and *As You Like It* for the

Royal Shakespeare Company. His writing debut came through the Royal Court Young Writers Programme in which he wrote *Goodbye to All That* which was produced at the Royal Court Upstairs in 2012. Luke was keen to write a play about football, but knew it would be tricky to write a play about the game itself and would be more dramatic to write about the people who play it and the people who support them. He explored the stories of the play with a group of Year Nine girls at Haverstock School in Camden, and discussed the characters and script with Year 10s at St Edward's School Stratford and with sixth formers at Stratford-upon-Avon College. His play is set in a changing room of a local youth football club, and is divided into three scenes. The first scene includes all the boys before a match; the middle scene their girl friends; and the final scene has everyone together on the night of the club's end-of-season party. It's a light-hearted rom-com and should be played as fast and furious as the game itself.

EVAN PLACEY wrote a play for Hampstead Theatre's Heat & Light youth theatre programme called *Banana Boys* which was a comedy with serious themes. He went on to write the award-winning *Mother of Him* and for Synergy Theatre *Holloway Jones*. For Connections, he brought the idea of investigating a story about a young transgender person. He carried out detailed research with the organisation Gendered Intelligence, who introduced Evan to some young trans people who very generously shared their stories with him. Evan then wrote a couple of drafts of the play and did readings at the National Theatre Studio, to which a few members of Gendered Intelligence were invited, and then discussed the play with Evan before he wrote the final version.

SIMON VINNICOMBE wrote an angry and exhilarating play called *Year 10* in 2006 which was produced at the Finborough and Battersea Arts Centre, followed by *Turf*, a piece of youth theatre at the Bush Theatre. When thinking about his play for Connections, Simon was interested in public examinations and the expectations they set up. He was also interested in setting the play in a location which suggested small-town suburban life. He spent his childhood in Berrylands which is situated just outside London, and he returned there, to his old school Holyfield, to research his play with a group of Year 11 students. Simon talked several times with this group of exam candidates over a period of six months: just before their mocks, at their school production of *Annie*, after their final day at school at their prom night, and finally on GCSE exam results day in August when he had a long discussion with them about what they were going to do next. He then wrote the play which takes place in a school hall during three potent dramatic episodes: final day of school, prom night and GCSE results day.

ANTHONY BANKS
National Theatre, March 2014

Same

by Deborah Bruce

For my grandmothers,
Pru Bruce and Paula Barnett,
and their great grandchildren,
Barney and Nell Herrin.

Deborah Bruce is a theatre director and writer from London. Her first play, *Godchild*, was staged at Hampstead Theatre in October 2013, and her play *The Distance* was shortlisted for the Susan Smith Blackburn Award 2013. She is currently under commission from the National Theatre and the Royal Court.

Characters

Emma, *sixteen*
Fay, *Emma's sister, fifteen*
Harry, *Emma's brother, thirteen (Young Harry)*
Sarah, *Emma's cousin, fourteen*
Callum, *Sarah's brother, twelve*
Jo-Jo, *Emma's cousin, thirteen*
Clare, *late seventies*
Sadie, *late seventies*
Alf, *eighties*
Eddie, *eighties*
Marion, *Clare's sister, eighty*
Grace, *seventies*
Josie
Harry

The action takes place in an old people's home in a small town in 2014.

Depending on the number of actors, there can be doubling between the young and old characters. Or not.

The older characters are written to be played by teenagers with the intention that it enables the audience to see the young person inside the old. I strongly encourage actors and directors to steer well clear of any 'old person' acting.

A forward slash (/) in the middle of a line denotes an overlap in dialogue, so that the next character starts speaking before the first has finished.

Scene One

A bedroom in an old people's home. Half packed up. Boxes on the floor, some of the pictures taken down and leaning against the wall. No sheets on the bed.

There are six teenagers in the room.

Emma, **Fay** *and* **Harry** *sit on the bed.* **Sarah** *stands by the door.* **Callum** *sits on the floor playing on a Nintendo DS, and* **Jo-Jo** *sits on a stool at a dressing table.*

They are all looking at screens except **Harry**.

Silence.

Fay   Aaaw, thanks for liking my picture, Jo-Jo.

Jo-Jo   You're welcome. Thank you for liking mine.

Emma   Have you changed your profile picture?

Jo-Jo   No –

Fay   Is it that one with your hair tonged?

Jo-Jo   The one with my friend's puppy.

Fay *and* **Emma**   Aaaw –

Fay   Oh my God, that was so sweet.

Harry   Get off Facebook.

Fay   Sarah. Are you logged in?

Sarah   I'm talking to my friend.

Fay   On Facebook?

Sarah   On What'sApp.

Fay   I've just sent you a message on Facebook.

Sarah   Saying what?

Fay   Go on it.

Sarah   OK.

Pause.

Sarah   Aaaw. Sweet.

Emma   What is it?

Harry   What'd you send her a message for? She's right there.

Sarah   I've liked it.

Emma   Let's see.

Fay *shows* **Emma** *her phone screen.*

Harry   Get off fucking Facebook.

Emma *slaps* **Harry** *round the head.*

Emma   Oh My God, I cannot believe you just swore in Nan's room. Oh My God, Harry, I am not joking.

Harry   So? She can't hear me, can she?

Fay   Harry!

Emma   Oh My God, Harry, you are so disrespectful.

Harry   What?

Emma   Sorry, Sarah. Sorry, Callum.

Fay   Oh My God, I am so embarrassed for you.

Harry   What?

Fay   Sorry, everyone, for my disrespectful brother.

Emma *looks up and puts her hand on her heart.*

Emma   Sorry, Nanna.

Fay (*looks up too, puts her hand on her heart too*)   Yeah, sorry, Nanna.

Silence.

Harry   What though? She can't hear me can she?

No one says anything. **Fay** *and* **Emma** *give him a look.*

Harry   Well she can't, can she?

Fay *glares at him.*

Harry   You're all on Facebook. That's not very respectful is it?

Fay   I'm putting that Nan's died actually. I'm writing a whole thing about her, thank you very much.

Harry   Putting it all over Facebook, what's respectful about that?

Pause.

She wasn't even on Facebook.

Emma   Shut up or I'm going to tell Mum that you said the f-word in Nan's room.

Fay   Just because you've had your phone confiscated. You wouldn't even be speaking to us now if you had your phone. God!

Silence

Sarah   Aaah, that's so sweet, Fay.

Fay   Thanks.

Sarah   Shall I like it?

Fay   How many likes has it got?

Harry   'How many likes has it got?'

Sarah   Three –

Harry   Who cares?

Jo-Jo   Don't like it. It's like you're liking that Nan's died –

Fay   Who's liked it?

Sarah   Oh yeah! Oh I pressed it, just as you said that! I've liked it!

Jo-Jo   Unlike it! Press unlike!

Sarah   There's no unlike!

Emma   Press like again. It unlikes it.

Sarah   Oh My God! I can't believe I liked it! Oh I hope she doesn't . . . What if she . . . ? Sorry, Nanna! Oh no!

She starts to cry.

Emma *goes to her.*

Emma   Oh no, don't. Come on. Harry, get up and let Sarah sit on the bed.

Harry *gets up.*

Emma   Come on, sit with me and Fay. Do you want Harry to go and get your dad?

Sarah   No, it's OK.

Emma   It's OK to cry, we've all been crying.

Jo-Jo   Nan would have wanted us to cry. That sounds weird, but do you know what I mean?

Fay   I know what you mean –

Jo-Jo   She would have been like, 'Let it all out, come on, have a hanky.'

Harry   Shall I go and get Uncle Andrew?

Fay   She said no.

Jo-Jo   She'd have been like, 'Better out than in.'

Harry   That's for if you belched –

Sarah   I just feel so bad, I hadn't seen her since Easter. You all saw her all the time, me and Callum didn't.

Harry *belches.*

Fay   Oh My God, Harry, what are you doing? / Fay's *crying.*

Emma   Well, you see your other Nan, don't you, like loads and stuff.

Fay (*to* **Harry**)   What are you *like*?

Harry   I can't help it, can I?

Fay (*to* **Harry**)   Yes you *can*.

Sarah   I know. But, I really miss seeing her, and now I can't. Do you know what I mean?

Emma   I know.

Fay   I know.

Harry   Shall I go and get Uncle Andrew?

Emma   Be quiet.

Sarah   And I'm not being funny, I know she loved us all the same and all of that.

Harry   I think she loved me just a little bit more than all of you actually.

Fay   Oh My *God*, Harry, are you for actual real?

Harry   I'm joking! Gosh! Chill *out*.

Sarah   It's just, you lot all saw her loads before she died, and me and Callum, well we didn't, kind of thing.

Emma   She wasn't herself, Sarah, honestly, you are better off not having seen that.

Fay   She was like demented and stuff –

Emma   Not demented –

Harry   I was going to say! Bit rude.

Emma   Yeah, she had dementia, obviously, so she got confused about who people were, sometimes.

Jo-Jo   Saying strange things, things that didn't make like total sense.

Harry   It's not like she was frothing at the mouth.

Fay   Oh My *God*, why don't you like – (*Mouths.*) *Fuck off.*

Sarah   Did she know who Mel and Alison were?

Harry   I am going to text Mum and tell her that you said fuck off.

Fay   Yeah? Really? You haven't got your phone, so good luck with that.

Harry   Jo-Jo, can I borrow your phone please?

Jo-Jo   No.

Emma   She kind of did know Mum, mostly.

Fay   Yeah she knew Mum, and she knew Auntie Alison, and she knew us, didn't she?

Harry   Sarah, can I borrow your phone please?

Sarah   I bet she wouldn't have known me and Callum, she hadn't seen us since Easter/ I hate my Dad.

Emma   Of course she would have known you, Oh My *God*.

Fay   Oh My God Sarah, she *so* would have known you, wouldn't she Emma?

Emma   Of course.

Sarah   Why didn't my dad bring us over here? I hate him.

Pause.

Emma   Are you alright, Callum?

Callum   Yeh.

Emma   What are you playing?

Callum   Super Mario.

Emma   That's good.

The girls all sit on the bed.

Emma   Are you alright, Sarah?

Sarah   I can't believe I 'liked' that post.

Fay   It wasn't that you liked that she was dead though, it wasn't like that.

Sarah   I know. I just wanted to. Support the sentiment.

Fay   Yes.

Sarah   I just wanted to be part of it.

Emma   Oh My God, you are.

Pause. **Emma**, **Fay** *and* **Jo-Jo** *all look at each other.*

Sarah   What was it like when you last saw her? Did she know you were there?

Jo-Jo   Kind of.

Emma   Not really.

Jo-Jo   Yeah, not really.

Emma   She was very confused the last time.

Sarah   What did she say to you?

Emma   Nothing really, I can't remember exactly.

Jo-Jo   No, I can't remember exactly.

Harry   You weren't there.

Jo-Jo   I was.

Harry   It was just me and Emma and Fay the last time, you were at a sleepover.

Jo-Jo   I *was* there, I was there the last time we saw her.

Harry   You were probably there the last time *you* saw her, but you weren't there the last time *we* saw her, when she was going on about Grandad and asking for Uncle Andrew.

Emma   Harry.

Harry   What? I'm just saying.

Sarah   Did Nanna ask for my dad?

Emma   Sort of, but she wasn't awake. She hadn't been properly awake for two days.

Sarah   What did she say?

Emma   Just like, 'Is Andrew here? Where's Andrew?' That kind of thing. But like talking in her sleep.

Fay   'I want Andrew,' she said that as well.

Sarah   Oh My God.

Emma   But she knew that he was like really busy with work and stuff, she knew that he would come when he could.

Sarah   Oh My God.

Emma   It's alright. Honestly, Sarah, I can't explain, it wasn't like being with Nanna. We were there and stuff but she wasn't like there, it was like she was in a really deep sleep. Your dad saw her loads before she was ill. That's the main thing.

Sarah   Shit.

Pause.

Fay   Oh My God! I can't believe it's got like, thirteen likes. I only posted it, like ten minutes ago. I'm so popular! Jokes.

Harry   Yeah you're so popular, everyone's really happy your nan's dead.

Fay   I wish you were dead.

Jo-Jo   Oh My God, I can't believe you said that!

Emma   You don't understand, Jo-Jo, because you're an only child.

Sarah   I don't know what's going on, I'm all over the place.

Emma   Everyone is. Mum locked her car keys in the car before we drove over this morning. Then she banged her knee on the table in the hall and started crying. / She's a nervous wreck.

Harry   That was funny.

Fay   You're a tosser.

Harry   Dad laughed.

Fay   Dad wasn't even there so that just shows what a liar you are. Why don't you shut up if you haven't got anything useful to say. Go and sit in the TV room, that Barbara woman said we could.

Harry   I'm not going in there, have you seen them? It's like *Shaun of the Dead*.

Emma   You are so disrespectful.

Harry   They're all dribbling and shitting themselves.

Jo-Jo   Who's Rachel Charlie?

Fay   A girl in my year. Why?

Jo-Jo   She's liked your post about Nanny.

Fay   Oh My God, what's she liking my post for? She's such an idiot. She was the one who said about America –

Emma   Oh My God, you have to tell them that, that was so funny –

Fay   She was like, 'Ya, I've been to three places in America, New York, LA and Paris.' We were like, 'Uh?' Oh My God, so funny.

Jo-Jo   Paris isn't in America.

Harry   We're in the company of a genius –

Fay   I know, that's like the whole point. Aaw, Jo-Jo, you're so sweet.

Pause.

Sarah   I feel so bad.

Emma   Why didn't your dad bring you over, do you think?

Sarah   He's gone weird.

Jo-Jo   Didn't he want to come and see Nanna?

Sarah   I don't know. Everything's gone weird.

Callum *looks at her.*

Sarah   Mum's sort of, in a relationship.

Beat.

Emma   Seriously?

Fay   What, with like a boyfriend?

Harry   No, with like a unicorn –

Emma   Oh My God, Sarah, seriously?

Callum   What do you have to tell them that for?

Sarah   Of course I'm going to tell them, they're our family.

Fay   Oh My God, I can't believe your mum's got a boyfriend.

Callum   Just shut up about it.

Jo-Jo   Does he live at your house?

Sarah   No, he's got his own house, near the retail park.

Fay   Does he like stay over and stuff?

Callum   What are you telling them for?

Fay   Has he got his stuff at your house?

Sarah   I can tell them what I like.

Callum   No you can't.

Sarah   Yes I can. He's called David, he's a history teacher.

Fay   Oh. My. God.

Sarah   Not like in a school, like in a university type thing, like a college.

Fay   I was going to say, what if he was like your history teacher –

Sarah   He's got dyed hair.

Fay   Oh My God, fail. / Epic fail.

Emma   Is he nice though?

Harry   He *dyes* his hair.

Sarah   He's alright. He wears Converse and stuff.

Callum   Stop talking about it.

Sarah   Why?

Callum   Because.

Pause.

Nan's dead.

Silence.

Jo-Jo   There's a packet of wine gums in this drawer.

Harry   Awkward. Change the subject.

Jo-Jo   Shall I open them?

Emma   Your mum said not to touch anything, so / don't look in the drawers, Jo-Jo.

Harry   Not wine gums, she was talking about like letters and stuff. Not like wine gums and shit. / Give us one.

Fay   Stop swearing!

Harry   She'll of bought them for us anyway. They'll be for us. She'd of wanted us to eat them.

Emma   Auntie Alison said leave everything as it is, they haven't done the inventory. They have to go through everything with the manager. Then we can have stuff.

Harry   Not wine gums!

Fay   They haven't done the inventory.

Harry   You don't put bloody wine gums on an inventory. / She means like jewellery, valuable stuff.

Fay   Harry!

Jo-Jo   Oh My God, did you hear, my mum had to get Nan's wedding rings off?

Harry   One packet of wine gums, unopened. Check.

Emma   I know.

Sarah   When?

Jo-Jo   After it happened. She had to twist them off, she had to get hand cream and rub it in, to make it slippery. They wouldn't come off.

Fay   Oh My God, that's so sad.

Harry   One screwed-up tissue and half a packet of Polos. Check.

Emma   She never took her wedding ring off. She never took her engagement ring off even when she went into hospital. They said she had to and she refused. She said they'd have to cut her finger off.

Sarah   Oh My God. So did your mum have to rub the cream in?

Jo-Jo   Yeh. She had to twist them. She had to pull really hard. She said Auntie Mel said maybe they should leave them on. They felt bad. They would have left them on if she was going to be buried, my mum said. It seemed a waste just to burn them.

Harry   Hey! That's sick.

Fay   Shut up.

Harry   If I'd said that you'd have done your nut.

Fay   Yeah, because you're an idiot and you'd have just said it to shock everyone and to show off.

Harry   No I wouldn't –

Fay   Jo-Jo's actually telling us something, we are having A Conversation.

Callum   Isn't Nan going to be buried?

Jo-Jo   She's being cremated.

Callum   Why isn't she going to be buried?

Jo-Jo   Because she's being cremated. Cremation's more environmentally friendly.

Callum   She has to be buried. She wanted to be buried.

Harry   Nan didn't do recycling. She covered her recycling crate thing in wrapping paper and put her Christmas tree on it.

Callum   Who said she was going to be cremated?

Harry   Nan wouldn't be bothered about being recycled.

Emma   Your dad was on about the crematorium to Mum.

Callum   What does he know about it? He's a dickhead.

Pause.

Harry   How come he's allowed to say that?

Fay   Because Uncle Andrew and Helen have split up and he's upset.

Harry   Yeah, what if I'm upset as well?

Fay   Aaaw, diddums. What about?

Harry   Nan. Obviously.

Fay We all are. Obviously.

Pause.

Emma OK, let's all go round and say something we remember about Nan.

Harry Everything, obviously. She only died on Thursday.

Fay She doesn't *mean* it like that.

Emma I mean, the real Nanna, before she got dementia, the Nanna *before*.

Jo-Jo 'Go and sit in the sunshine and untangle your knickers.'

Sarah 'If you can't say something nice – '

Emma Wait, let's all go round one by one. Let's do it properly. Harry, get in the circle. Callum, put your DS down for a minute. Let's all do it together.

Fay The cousins!

Emma Aaaw.

Jo-Jo The Wombles, like Grandad called us.

Sarah Oh My God, yes! And things about Grandad as well. (*She starts to cry.*) I can't believe they've both gone!

Jo-Jo Grandad used to dance like he was walking but standing still.

Sarah He called me his little princess –

Jo-Jo And me! –

Harry And me!

Fay Shut *up*, Harry.

Harry Oh no, hang on, he called me his little soldier –

Fay Oh My God, that is so sexist! Sorry Grandad, but Oh My God –

Emma He used to say to Nanna, 'Oh Josie, do you remember when I could climb a ladder? Do you remember when I could run round to the shop and back in a commercial break?'

Fay 'Do you remember when I?' All the time, he used to say that!

Emma Say stuff about Nanna as well –

Sarah 'Oh well, we'll never run out!'

Fay Oh My God, all the tins and tea bags in the garage. Oh, I miss that house so much. Do you remember?

Harry No, I've got Alzheimer's –

Fay Shut up, you're not funny, why do you spoil everything?

Callum The toilet was in the garden.

Sarah Not the only toilet, there were two in the house –

Callum It had mould in it –

Fay There were flower fairies in the shed, they left sweets for us –

Harry That was Nanna –

Fay Durr, I *know* –

Jo-Jo *sings the opening lines of 'My Girl Josephine' by Fats Domino.*

Jo-Jo/Emma/Sarah/Fay *sing the next few lines together, until:*

Jo-Jo *(forgetting the lyric)*
Something about an umbrella, la la la la la
'It was a crying shame', or something!

Emma Go on –

Jo-Jo I don't remember the rest of it.

Fay *remembers, sings the line about the umbrella uncertainly.*

Jo-Jo I can't remember the words.

Fay Try. You do.

Jo-Jo   I'll Google the lyrics.

They sit in silence for a bit.

Sarah   Nanna and Grandad had such a perfect marriage, didn't they? I feel bad for them that their children didn't, you know, follow in their footsteps.

Harry   Our mum and dad are still together –

Sarah   Yeah, apart from them –

Emma   Only just –

Harry   What do you mean?

Fay   Don't say that. / They're fine.

Harry   What do you mean, 'only just'?

Emma   Nothing, they're fine.

Sarah   I just meant our parents. And Auntie Alison and your dad.

Jo-Jo   Nanna said it wasn't Mum's fault.

Sarah   I'm not saying it's anyone's fault

Callum   Shut up about it then.

Harry   Why did you say 'only just'? Are Mum and Dad going to split up?

Fay   I know what you mean, marriage is different now, it doesn't mean what it used to mean in Nanny and Grandad's day, does it? They didn't have like loads of ways of finding out about each other before marriage, like Facebook and checking out people's profiles and looking at photos of their ex-girlfriends and stuff. They just had to get on with it. They had to get to know each other on their own and work things out on their own.

Harry   Are Mum and Dad going to split up?

Emma/Fay   No! Shut up!

Sarah   They couldn't, like, text each other to say sorry if one of them stropped off, they had to work much harder, I think. I think their relationships were much stronger, do you?

Fay   Yeah, I think their generation were more respectful to each other, I think they took the wedding vows much more seriously, because they'd had to work so hard already, and like getting divorced was really bad.

Jo-Jo   For richer for poorer, till death do us part, for as long as us both shall live, and stuff.

Fay   People make up our own vows now, they're obviously not going to be as good.

Emma   They are, it's better not to have to say all that stuff, I think, it's better to be more realistic, more specific about what you want your relationship to be like.

Harry   What's the point of getting married anyway if you can just get a divorce?

Fay   Shut up, we're not talking about that.

Harry   You can get a Happy Divorce cake in Tesco, it says like Happy Divorce, and there's like a groom falling off a building –

Emma   It's a pedestal.

Harry   And he's cracked his head open and there's like blood everywhere –

Emma   There's not –

Fay   Shut up, you can't get a cake of it –

Emma   You can. / There isn't blood though.

Harry   You can.

Sarah   I bet Nanna and Grandad were disappointed when Dad left Mum. I bet they thought he hadn't worked hard enough at their relationship.

Jo-Jo   My mum worked really hard at her relationship with my dad but he moved to Totnes so there wasn't really any point.

Sarah   Mum said Grandad drove all the way to where Dad was staying with his friend, to try and get him to change his mind, but he pretended not to be in and Grandad had to come all the way back in the rush hour. Mum said Grandad was really angry and banged his fist and broke the little window in the washroom. There's still a crack in it. I can't believe Dad didn't come and see Nanna. I can't believe he left it too late.

Fay   Let's remember nice things.

Jo-Jo   Let's talk about Christmas.

Harry   Let's talk about fluffy bunnies and hairclips.

Fay   Shut up, you moron –

Emma   Do you remember when Nanna went to bed on Christmas Day when she was ill and she said, 'I don't want to hear any one of you trying to be quiet.' Oh, lovely Nanny.

Sarah   Were we there that Christmas?

Emma   No, I don't think you were.

Fay   I remember playing solitaire on the patio, and going to the bring and buy sales at the church –

Jo-Jo   Choc ices –

Emma   'I hope you've got your vest on' –

Fay   When we all danced to *The Muppets* with the mop.

Emma   When Harry was born and Nanna said he looked like Grandad and Grandad said 'Poor sod', and then Mum called him Harry and Nanna cried.

Sarah   I wish she was here.

Emma   She is in a way, she's in all of us.

Jo-Jo I've got her name.

Sarah You're so lucky.

Jo-Jo *comes over to* **Fay** *and* **Emma** *with her phone and shows them the screen.*

Fay *and* **Emma** *sing the first few lines of 'My Girl Josephine' by Fats Domino.*

Pause.

Sarah Who sings that?

Emma Fats Domino.

Jo-Jo *sings the next line.*

Fay Fats?

Sarah *and* **Jo-Jo** *sing the next line together.*

Fay You can't call him Fats.

Emma That's his name.

Fay What? His parents called him Fats?

Emma Not his parents / probably.

Fay Oh My God, that's so un-PC.

Emma It's like a nickname –

Fay Was he fat?

Emma I don't know what he looked like – Nanny played the record, do you remember a picture on the cover, Jo-Jo?

Jo-Jo No. He sounds, a bit fat. I'll Google images.

Fay Sorry, but that is so wrong, that is so bad for his self-esteem, he could have been so damaged by that, God!

Pause.

Callum I remember when I was sick off school one day just before Mum and Dad split up and Dad was supposed to

be looking after me but he couldn't so he drove me to
Nanny's house and I was watching a *Simpsons* DVD.

Harry   Was it *Simpsons the Movie?*

Callum   No, just the series.

Harry   That's mine.

Callum   And Dad and Nan went into the garage –

Harry   But you can watch it.

Callum   And they had a massive row.

Sarah   No, Callum.

Callum   And I could hear them while I was watching the
DVD. And Dad said fuck, and Nanny said she was glad he
wasn't her real son, and then she cried and said she was sorry
and Dad drove off without saying goodbye to me, and she
was saying that she would never forgive herself and that she
would take her sorryness to her grave with her.

Sarah   What did you have to tell them that for?

Callum   I'm just saying. That's how I know she definitely
wanted to be buried.

Blackout.

Scene Two

*A large sitting room in an old people's home with high-backed chairs in
almost a semicircle.*

Clare, **Sadie**, **Alf** *and* **Eddie** *sit in the chairs.*

Marion *stands with her coat on, beside* **Clare***'s chair.*

Marion   Well, I didn't know. No one said.

Clare   It was last-minute. They didn't tell us it was going to
be held here till this morning.

Marion   I called to say I was coming as normal. I always come on a Wednesday. No one said not to.

Clare   Who did you speak to?

Marion   I don't know. Not Barbara.

Clare   Wasn't it Barbara?

Marion   No, it wasn't Barbara. Barbara would've said.

Sadie   It could have been Sally.

Clare   Sally, that's right. It would have been her. Now, you see she's new, she might not have thought to say.

Marion   She should have said.

Clare   She's new.

Marion   I wouldn't have come. Or at least I could have come later. Or earlier. I could have come yesterday. Well, not yesterday because I had Pilates, but I could have come Monday. After Spanish.

Clare   Well, you're here now, eh?

Marion   All the black cars outside. It's very morbid.

Clare   Well. You're here now.

Silence.

Marion   So is no one allowed in the dining room then?

Clare   It's for the funeral guests. They have their tea in there. Only half an hour or so. You can go in if you want to go to the funeral. Everyone's welcome, Barbara said.

Alf   I'm not going in there.

Clare   Do you want to go in there?

Marion   Whose is it?

Alf   I'm not going in there.

Clare   Josie Fowler. Lung cancer and dementia. Room 4, next to the airing cupboard. I only saw her once in the whole time she was here so I'm not going in.

Alf   Death tramping through the lounge, they should hold the funeral at the house.

Sadie   They sold her house to pay for the home.

Alf   What about the daughter's house? What about the son? Haven't they got a house? What do we want reminding of dying in here? We can't forget it long enough to need reminding of it. Piling the wreaths up in the hall. Do you want some flowers in your room, Mr Barratt? No thank you very much, I know where they've come from and I know where you can stick them.

Laughter.

Sadie   Those lillies get their pollen all over your sleeve every time you brush past, they're a terror.

Pause.

Marion   Well, I'm going to see if I can get a chair from somewhere. Anybody need anything while I'm going walkabouts?

Sadie/Clare   No.

Marion *exits.*

Alf   You wouldn't catch me going in there, I tell you.

Pause.

I wouldn't go in there if you paid me.

Pause.

Eddie   Because in its heyday of course, you know, there were twenty-five thousand dockers working on the Mersey. That's how it was. Up and down Great Homer Street, you'd get the smells, the fresh food being cooked up, from the markets. And we supported each other, the core of the society we were. None of your scroungers and your wasters sitting around on their backsides waiting to be given something for nothing. We earned a good wage, we knew our manners, always well turned out. I never heard my father swear, not once. Never owed a penny to anyone in his life. Not like these days. Not like the banks these days, messing it all up for everyone, throwing money around then wanting it back bigger.

Clare   She'll need to get a chair from the activities room, she won't be able to lift the ones in the hall.

Sadie   What?

Clare   She won't be able to lift the chairs in the hall. She'll need to get a chair from the activities room, one of the plastic ones.

Sadie   Who?

Clare   My sister. My sister's gone to get a chair.

Alf   They better be quick about it, that's all I can say. Standing round talking. Where were they when she was alive? Hadn't got so much to say then, had they?

Eddie   Langton, Brocklebank, Carrier, Canada, Huskisson, Sandon, Sandon Half Tide, Wellington.

Marion *returns with a chair. She places it next to* **Clare**.

Clare   Did you get that from the activities room?

Marion   I don't know, a nice young man found it for me –

Clare   He'll of got it from the activities room, didn't I say that?

Sadie   Yes.

Eddie   Because most of them are filled in now of course.

Marion   Pardon?

Eddie   But in the forties, 1947, I started. Yes, it was a going concern then, well over three-quarters of us were dailies mind, not until the strike, and they guaranteed our working hours, didn't they, it was a good wage.

Marion   Oh, yes, well that's good.

Eddie   My father, honest to God, now, he never owed a penny to anyone in his life, not a penny. He was a gentleman. And his father, and *his* father. Settled in Scotland Road, he did, over from Ireland, eleven of them there were, 1845 it was. Worked on the docks since then we all have. Just four hundred of them now. That's it. Four hundred left out of twenty-five thousand. One hundred and fifty of them in the terminal. There's not the loyalty now, not the solidarity. There was Seaforth, Gladstone, Hornby, Alexandra, Langton, Brocklebank, it was next along.

Marion   Is that right, oh!

Clare   I said to Sadie, I said, 'She'll have to get one from the activities room because she won't be able to lift one of the heavy ones from the hall.'

Marion   My arthritis, I can't lift the kettle some mornings.

Clare   You should go back to Dr Monk, I'm sick of saying it.

Marion   Well, I will, when I get round to it. I've got too much on! I'm in and out of here every five minutes, aren't I? And that bus timetable's a fiction. Had to wait nearly three-quarters of an hour when I left last week. The dogs were beside themselves when I eventually got home.

Eddie   But God's watching over me. 'Eddie,' He said, 'Eddie, you listen to me. You have to let it go, nothing lasts for ever, you're an old man now, and those days have gone.' I can see it, clear as you like, from the north side to the south, sun coming up first thing. 'Alright Ed!' It went Huskisson, Sandon, Sandon Half Tide, Wellington, Bramley-Moore. 'Alright Ed!' 'Alright Robbie!' We looked out for each other, always watching my back, Robbie.

Marion   Oh really? Well.

Clare You don't have to keep interacting with him, he doesn't need you to, he's happy enough talking to himself.

Marion Oh. It seems a bit rude to ignore him.

Clare We all do, he doesn't mind.

Marion Well, it'll be what he's used to, won't it, so understaffed they are in here. No time to turn round, most of them. Let alone talk to people.

Clare Sadie and I have put our names down for the memory box project, haven't we, Sadie?

Sadie Yes.

Clare So we've got that coming up.

Marion That's nice.

Clare Yes. I might need some things bringing from home.

Marion Like what? I've got that nightie, remind me to leave it at the desk before I go. It's a twelve, they didn't have a ten. You've lost so much weight.

Clare Can you bring my school reports, and some photographs from the purple album, just bring the album. And the keyring I bought in Tenerife, and the Spanish postcard with the Spanish dress stuck on that Mum and Auntie Phyllis sent us –

Marion What? / Hang on.

Clare And Bruce Forsyth's autograph, it's in the wicker box on my window sill –

Marion What are you going to do with all that nonsense?

Clare Put it in my memory box. Me and Sadie have put our names down.

Alf I'm not having anything to do with that bollocks. What do you need to put memories in a shitting box for? They're in your head, aren't they? That not a good enough box for you?

Clare   I'm not talking to you, I'm having a private conversation with my visitor.

Alf   Nothing's private unless you're sitting with the deaf ones.

Clare   So can you bring those things in please, Marion? And a box.

Marion   What kind of box?

Sadie   I think they provide a box.

Marion   Well, I should think so, what kind of project is this, you have to provide all the materials yourself!

Clare   It's a very prestigious organisation actually, they are a nationwide –

Marion   What do they actually do?

Clare   They are a nationwide organisation. There were limited places.

Marion   I see. What's it *for*?

Alf   Nowt.

Clare   It's for your self-esteem.

Alf   Ha! I've heard it all now!

Clare   It's so you can assemble all your memories in one place –

Alf   They're in one place already! Your head!

Clare   – and then you can decorate the box with personal things about your personality, newspaper cuttings and recipes they said. And then you leave it outside your door so that any new members of the team, or if you need a nurse or anyone comes to interact with you, they can look in the box and learn all about you before they meet you.

Pause.

Marion I see.

Clare What are you saying it like that for?

Marion I'm not saying it like anything.

Clare So can you bring me the bits when you come next week?

Marion Well, if I remember.

Clare Can't you write yourself a note or something?

Marion Well, yes, I'll have to. I've got my watercolours class on Friday, and the fund-raiser for Mozambique on the Monday. I've got a dental appointment on the Tuesday so –

Clare What's wrong?

Marion Just the hygienist, but I'll need to remember that, so.

Sadie You're keeping yourself busy, aren't you?

Marion Yes I am. I'm going to nip this nightie over to the desk before I forget, actually. Just like me to end up taking it all the way back home again!

She exits with the nightie.

Sadie She's keeping herself busy, isn't she, Clare?

Clare Yes.

Pause.

Sadie My granddaughter's sending me my bits and pieces in a Jiffy bag registered delivery. Barbara helped me send her an email about it.

Clare Oh well, that's good, isn't it?

Sadie Yes. it is.

Pause.

Alf   You'll be in a box soon enough I say, a bloody coffin!
That's the only memory box I'll be doing. And no one'll be
rifling through that before they meet me, thank you very much.

Eddie   George's Basin, George's Dock, Manchester,
Canning –

Alf   It's worse than the shitting shipping forecast sitting next
to him –

Eddie   Old Dock, Canning Half Tide, Albert. All the way
down, mostly filled in now, of course. Twenty-five thousand
dockers we were, never took a day off work sick, never owed
a penny to anyone in his life, my father. Went to see Everton
play every other weekend, like a religion it was, singing all the
songs, talking about it all week, seeing us through.

Marion *re-enters pushing* **Grace** *in a wheelchair.*

Marion   Look who I found sitting all by herself in the hall.
No one at the desk. No one anywhere. It's like the, um, the
um –

Alf   They'll all be eating biscuits and talking shite, couldn't
give a toss about us. We could all have had a stroke, they
wouldn't care. Sitting here with blood trickling out our ears.
'Blah blah blah.'

Marion   It's like the um –

Sadie   Are you alright, Grace?

Marion   She's alright now, aren't you? You're alright now,
you're back in the gang! All on your own out there! No one
around. It's like the, you know.

Sadie   You OK, Grace?

She's very frail, she gets anxious easily.

Marion   There you are, OK now, aren't you?

Grace   Is it nearly time?

Marion   Time for what, love?

Grace   Are they here?

Marion   Who?

Grace   The people for Harry's wife.

Clare   Harry who?

Grace   Harry Fowler. Are they here?

Clare   I don't know what she means, I think you better get Barbara –

Marion   Do you want me to get Barbara, Grace? Do you need your inhaler?

Grace   Who?

Sadie   Do you need someone to see to you? Shall I call?

Marion   I can go.

Clare   You're supposed to be visiting me, not running around the place!

Marion   Well, I know!

Clare   I was telling you about the memory project, wasn't I?

Marion   Shall I get you a cup of tea, Grace? / It's no trouble.

Clare   I think it's a lovely thing to do. I've been really looking forward to it. Sadie and I were the first to put our names down, weren't we?

Sadie   Yes.

Clare   I said, 'Let's get our names down pronto' didn't I? 'That looks like a lovely thing to do.'

Josie Fowler had her name on the list as well, but. Well. they Tippexed it out.

Pause.

Marion   They'll be nearly done in there surely! No one at the desk! Anyone could walk in. (*To* **Grace**.) Now, I'm just going to park you here, OK?

Alf   A load of clueless teenagers traipsing through earlier –

Marion   Teenagers? / What were they doing?

Alf   Trousers hanging halfway down their backsides.

Clare   For Josie. / Grandchildren probably.

Alf   Gawping at us, like they were on safari. They think we were born old.

Sadie   It's not their fault, you were the same when you were their age, how can you know? My granddaughter and her friends, they all think the world will wait for them, we were the same.

Alf   Head full of wire wool half of them. They've got nothing about them, I was never as gormless as the teenagers now.

Sadie   That's what you think. I was two years below you at Mannington Grammar, we all called you Alfie Two-Tries because you always tried it on twice.

Alf (*laughter*)   That'll be right! Oh dear me, that's made my day! Two-Tries! Yes, that was me. Oh dear God.

Marion   Ooh, I know what I was going to ask you. How have you got on with those support tights I brought in last week?

Clare   I haven't had a chance yet. They're in my bedside drawer still. I'm waiting for Barbara or someone to give me a hand with them.

Alf   I can give you a hand with them if you like. (*Laughs.*)

Clare (*to* **Marion**)   Just ignore him.

Alf (*to* **Sadie**)   You were two years below me at Mannington were you? Well, I say.

Sadie   You've already tried it on twice with me so don't waste your time.

Alf (*laughter*)   Oh, that's made my day, that really has. Two-Tries Barratt, you're absolutely right. Well, stick that in your pipe and smoke it. You couldn't fit that in your memory box. Well I never.

Clare   I think someone will be free to help me with the tights this week, they've been rushed off their feet with Josie Fowler passing away. It'll calm down now.

Marion   Until the next one.

Clare   Marion!

Marion   Well.

Clare   What a terrible thing to say.

Marion   Yes, sorry. I didn't think.

Clare   Well, you should think. How would you like it, stuck in here –

Marion   It's hard for me too, I'm older than you!

Clare   You're not stuck in here though, are you?

Marion   It's very stressful for me, on my own at the house, walking the dogs twice a day, keeping on top of it all. It's difficult. I'm just waiting to fall over and not be able to get up. On my own.

Clare   Well at least you can get around. I'm a hostage to my hip.

Marion   I know.

Clare   My hip's never going to be the same as it was.

Marion   I know.

She tries not to cry.

Clare   Come on now. Chin up.

Marion   Yes. I am.

Clare   And Penny and Phil are around, aren't they, they'll pop in if you need anything, won't they?

Marion   They're away. The car hasn't been in the drive since Sunday night. I'm fine! I'm too busy to be lonely!

Clare   It might be in the garage. It might need an MOT.

Marion   No, I'm pretty sure they're away, it's very quiet.

Pause.

I'm fine! I've got a hundred and thirty mobile phone covers to run up on the machine for the school's table-top sale. They rang me up! 'Miss Jessop,' they said, 'I hope you're not going to let us down!' / Too busy to feel sorry for myself!

Clare   I don't know why you say yes to all these things!

Marion   I know! They raised nearly three hundred pounds on that stall last year, they said. 'We're relying on you!' I don't know how I ever had time to work, honestly, I can't fit it all in!

Grace *starts to agitate in her chair.*

Marion   Alright there, Grace?

Grace   Is Josie in there? Is Josie in there with them?

Clare   Josie's dead, Grace. She died last week, didn't she? That's why we can't go into the dining room.

Grace   Is Harry there with her?

Clare   Don't you remember, the End of Life team came in, first thing Tuesday I think it was. A week last Tuesday. (*To* **Marion**.) She's got no one. Not a single visitor, she's been here eighteen months, and no one's been in. Isn't it terrible?

Marion   Terrible. (*To* **Grace**.) Can I get anything for you, Grace? Would you like me to find the tea trolley?

Clare   Do you want my sister to get you a cup of tea?

Grace   No! I don't want tea.

Clare   OK. Well, that's alright.

Grace   I want to see the baby.

Clare   What baby?

Grace   Harry's baby. My baby. I want to hold the baby!

Clare (*to* **Marion**)   The sense gets lost, you see. No one knows what anyone's talking about half the time.

Marion (*to* **Grace**)   There's no baby here. You'll be allowed back in the dining room soon, so all back to normal in no time, don't you worry, Grace. (*To* **Clare** *and* **Sadie**.) I'm doing their job now, it's like I work here! We're the lucky ones really. It's just a tiny bit of arthritis with me, I'm fine apart from that, still got my mind, lucky really.

Sadie   We are lucky really.

Marion   This is ridiculous! I'm going to see what's going on.

She exits.

Eddie *starts singing soulfully. He has a lovely voice.*

Eddie (*sings*)
    It's a grand old team to play for
    It's a grand old team to support
    And if you know your history
    It's enough to make your heart go ooo
    We don't care what the red side say
    What the heck do we care
    'Cause we only know there's going to be a show
    When the Everton boys are there.

Sadie   My granddaughter says to me, the world's different now, Gran. It's not like when you were young, it's all changed. She says I'm better off not having to deal with things, I get so confused, you see. She says, 'You're better off in Sea View, Gran, they can cater to your needs in there.' But what she can't understand is, I still feel the same, the world might have changed, you might have your cappuccinos and your internet shopping and what have you, but has it really changed that much? We're all still people aren't we? I still feel like I did when I was sixteen. Stepping off the bus in my new skirt and heels, feeling like a proper lady on my way in to my first day at work. No more school! I remember it like it was just the other day. The first time I saw my Ray, with his collar up and his dad's smart coat, waiting for me on the corner so he could pretend he was just passing. Oh, the butterflies in my stomach as I walked towards him! I thought my legs would give way beneath me.

Alf   Old Alfie Two-Tries! That's very good. That's tickled me that has.

Sadie   My granddaughter's moving to York in the new year, got a teaching post at the university there. She got a first-class degree, you see.

Marion *re-enters with a tea towel drying a cup.*

Marion   Right, ladies and gentlemen, all clear now.

The urn's on. Now who wants what?

Alf   All clear now, is it?

Marion   Yes. Barbara's just taking Mrs Webster back to her room for a lie down. She said, if you want to use the dining room it's all yours.

Alf   All the stragglers gone now, have they?

Marion   Yes, all gone. I said to Barbara, 'It's like I work here! I'm doing your job now!' She said, 'Oh lovely, thanks ever so much, we could do with an extra pair of hands!'

Sadie   A good send-off was it? Did Barbara say?

Marion   She didn't say. I expect so though.

Sadie   I should have gone in. I didn't feel up to it really.

Marion   There's half a tray of sandwiches left in there!

Marion   I said to Barbara, 'I'll nab these, shall I?' She said, 'Go ahead, why not?' Salmon some of them.

Sadie   I say my goodbyes in my own way.

God rest her soul.

Marion   The tea trolley's in there, we're just waiting for the urn. So it's all back to normal. Business as usual! Everyone alright?

All (*except* **Grace** *and* **Eddie**)   Yes.

Marion   You alright Mr – um?

Clare/Sadie   Pope.

Marion   You alright there, Mr Pope?

Eddie   And of course Morpeth, Egerton, Wallascy, Alfred, Great Float, Vittoria and Bidston Docks, they were on the opposite bank you see. All gone now.

Marion   Yes, that's such a shame, isn't it?

Eddie (*looks at* **Marion**, *meets her eye*)   It is a shame. It breaks your heart.

Marion   Yes.

Pause.

And Grace, OK is she?

She goes over to **Grace** *and takes her hand.*

Marion   Would you like me to bring you a nice cup of tea, Grace, in your special cup?

Grace   Josie?

Marion   No, love. It's Miss Jessop's sister. I'm going to bring you a nice cup of tea, OK?

Grace   I want to talk to Josie. I'm ready to talk to Josie now.

Marion *looks at* **Clare** *and* **Sadie**, *a bit panicked*

Clare   It's OK, Grace.

Sadie   There we are, now. Yes.

Marion *stays and strokes* **Grace**'s *hand for a while. Then she gets up and goes to the door.*

Marion   Let's see about this urn.

Alf   Hey, Miss Jessop's sister! How about you and me? Where do you fancy going? A club? A slap-up meal?

Marion   Oh, well! I don't know!

Alf   Come on, it's on me, I'll treat you, get your glad rags on, let's hit the town!

Marion   Oh no, I'm at my choir practice tonight.

Alf   They won't miss you just this once will they? It's two for one up the Legion tonight!

Marion   Don't tempt me!

Alf *and* **Marion** *laugh.*

Lights fade.

Scene Three

Two weeks earlier. In **Josie**'s *room in the home.*

Josie *lies in bed, very still.*

Emma *sits on a chair doing some homework on her laptop.* **Fay** *sits on the floor looking at her phone.*

In the corner of the room stands a young man in fifties army uniform, **Josie**'s *husband* **Harry**. **Emma** *and* **Fay** *are unaware of his presence, and cannot hear the conversation between him and* **Josie**. *The only lines they can hear are noted.*

Silence apart from a clock ticking and the occasional sounds from the corridor outside.

Harry (*soft*)   Josie.

Josephine.

He moves to the edge of the bed.

Josie.

Gently he sits on the edge of the bed. He takes out a packet of cigarettes and a lighter, goes to light up.

Josie   You can't smoke in here.

Harry   Who says?

Josie   Put them away, you can't smoke in here.

Harry   Why not?

Josie   You can't smoke in hospital, there's signs all over.

Harry   We're not in a hospital, this a hospital?

Josie   Isn't it? I thought it was. I don't know.

She sits up a bit.

What are you wearing that for?

Harry   What?

Josie   That get up. / Your uniform!

Harry   It's my uniform. / What's up with it?

Pause.

Josie (*heard by the others*)   Oh Harry. (*Unheard.*) It's good to see you again.

Emma and **Fay** *look up.*

Emma   Are you alright, Nanny?

Silence.

Fay   Did she say 'Harry'?

Emma   I think so. (*To* **Josie**.) It's me and Fay, Nanny.
Harry's at Tai Kwondo. Mum's gone to pick him up.

Silence.

Fay   Shall I text Mum? See where they are?

Emma   No, she'll be here in a minute.

Emma *and* **Fay** *go back to what they were doing.*

After a moment:

Harry   I walked round the back way, the long way round.
I wanted to see if the daffs were out in the field at the top.
The sun was coming up, the light was bouncing off the
yellow, I wanted to climb up on to the stone wall and shout
your name at the top of my voice.

Josie   You better not have done.

Harry   I wanted to.

Josie   You didn't, did you? / Making an exhibition of
yourself.

Harry   I don't care who hears me.

Josie   Scaring everyone awake with your nonsense.

Harry   Are you going to come with me now, Josie?

Josie   I don't know if I'm coming or going.

Harry   You're coming *and* going. It pulls you all ways.

Josie   Ever such a funny feeling.

Harry   Go with it, I've got you.

Pause.

Josie   I don't know which is the top and which is the
bottom. There's splinters of me scattered all over the place.
Am I in bed, Harry?

Harry   Yes and no.

Josie   What kind of an answer is that? You're no help.

Harry (*soft*)   Josie.

Josie   Yes.

Harry (*soft*)   Josie.

Josie   What?

Harry   Come on, girl. It's getting late. Let's go.

Pause.

Emma *stands and stretches her legs.*

Fay   Where are you going?

Emma   Nowhere. My leg's gone to sleep.

Fay   Liam keeps texting me to see if I'm going to Billy's.

Emma   Have you texted back?

Fay   Do you think I should?

Emma   If you want to. Have you got those crisps Mum gave us?

Fay *hands* **Emma** *a packet of crisps.*

Emma *goes over to* **Josie**, *smoothes her sheet. Kisses her face.*

Emma   Love you, Nanny.

She sits back down and carries on with her work.

Harry *watches* **Emma** *and* **Fay** *for a moment, then looks back to* **Josie**.

Harry (*soft*)   Josie.

Josie *sits up in bed.*

Josie   Did we make a mess of things, Harry?

Harry   We did well. We made the best of it.

Josie   We tried our best, didn't we? Tried to get it right.

Harry   We did.

Josie   I worry about Andrew. He's never found his way.

Harry   You took him into your heart like he was your own. You brought him up like he was your own flesh and blood, there's not many women who would have done what you did.

Josie   My mother said I should leave you. Pack a bag, take Melanie, up and off. I could have gone full-time at Wickhams you know, they said I could. My mother would have had Mel.

Harry   She never liked me.

Josie   No, and she liked you even less when you went with that slapper.

Harry   We're going to rake over all this now, are we? I just said, there's not many women would've done what you did, I know what it took you.

Josie   It was so humiliating, the way they all looked at me.

Harry   I just said, didn't I?

Josie   Gracie's brothers all giving us daggers every time we stepped foot out the house. Like I'd stolen something that was theirs. I wanted to say, 'She would've killed this baby if it was up to her. I've saved a life, not taken one, so you can stop with the evil stares.'

Harry   It's all in the past now, Josie, What good does it do to dig it all up?

Josie   And she couldn't have looked after him! Couldn't look after a sock in a box that one. Useless she was. All that rouge she used to slather on, what were you thinking!

Harry   I wasn't myself. I'd lost my mother, I was chucked out the army, wasn't I? I had lost sight of it all.

Pause.

Young Harry *enters the room tentatively.*

Young Harry   Hi.

Emma   Hi.

Young Harry   Mum's talking to someone in the office. Have you got my crisps?

Fay *hands him his crisps.*

Emma   Nanny said your name.

Young Harry   Did she?

Fay   Oh yeah.

Young Harry   What did she say?

Emma   Just Harry. 'Oh Harry.'

Young Harry   What else?

Emma   Nothing.

Young Harry   Cool.

Young Harry *goes to* **Josie**. *He stands awkwardly beside the bed for a while.*

Young Harry   Hi Nanna. I'm here. I'm back from Tai Kwondo.

Pause.

It was good.

Young Harry *goes and sits on the windowsill and eats his crisps.* **Emma** *and* **Fay** *go back to what they were doing.*

Emma   Did you text Liam?

Fay   Yeah. I just said 'Dunno'.

Emma   Has he texted back?

Fay   Not yet, no.

Young Harry   Keep us posted.

Josie   Who's talking? Is that my voice, Harry?

Harry   You're shouting the place down.

Josie   It's me doing all that talking, is it?

Harry   I've got you.

Josie (*heard by the others*)   Is it Andrew? I want Andrew.

Young Harry *looks up.*

Young Harry   Did you hear that? She wants Uncle Andrew.

Fay   Oh My God, get Mum.

Is Uncle Andrew here?

Emma   I don't think he's coming till the weekend.

She talks to **Josie**

Emma   Uncle Andrew's coming at the weekend, Nanny.

Harry *takes her hand.*

Josie   Get off me, what are you doing here anyway?

Harry   Sitting with you aren't I.

Josie   I don't know if I'm coming or going.

Harry   Hold my hand then.

Josie   I can't hold your hand, I don't know where my hand is, I've gone small, I can't get myself back in the right places. (*Heard by the others.*) Where's Andrew?

Emma   He's coming at the weekend, Nanny.

(*To* **Young Harry**.) Get Mum.

Harry *sings, softly, the first few lines of 'My Girl Josephine'.*

Josie (*heard by the others*)   Give over, I'm not in the mood for singing.

Emma (*laughs*)   You don't have to sing, Nanny!

Fay   Maybe she wants us to sing, do you think?

Young Harry   Sing what?

Fay *sings the first line of 'My Girl Josephine'.*

Emma   Go and get Mum, Harry. Those crisps stink.

Young Harry *exits.*

Fay *and* **Emma** *sing the next two lines of the song together.*

Harry, **Fay** *and* **Emma** *sing the fourth line of the song together.*

Fay   Oh My God, my voice is so rubbish!

Emma   I bet Harry tries to get Mum to buy him a drink from that machine by the lifts.

Fay   I can't tell if she likes it or not. She's probably like, shut up!

She checks her phone. **Emma** *arranges things on the bedside table. Reads a card.*

Harry *sits on the edge of the bed.*

He sings the next three lines of the song.

Josie   What are you doing here, you fool.

Harry   Singing to you, aren't I, like I used to do.

Josie   Give over.

Emma   Mel's coming, Nanny. (*To* **Fay**.) She knows we're here.

Fay   Do you want us to sing to you, Nanny? Harry's gone to get Mum. Mum's coming.

Emma   Mel's coming, Nanny. It's OK.

Fay   Shall we keep singing to her?

Emma   No. Wait till Mum gets here.

Emma *and* **Fay** *hover at the foot of the bed.*

Harry *takes* **Josie***'s hand. She lets him.*

The clock in the room is ticking louder than usual.

Harry   Come on, Josie, that's right.

Pause.

I've got you.

Pause.

Let me walk you home.

Josie *looks at* **Harry** *as . . .*

Lights fade.

Same

BY DEBORAH BRUCE

*Notes on rehearsal and staging, drawn from a workshop
with the writer held at the National Theatre, November 2013*

Workshop led by Raz Shaw with notes by Laura Keefe

How the writer came to write the play

Deborah Bruce explained how important youth theatre was to
her as a young person. She believes that the ability to imagine
what it is like to be someone other than ourselves is so valuable;
she wanted to write something that allowed young people to
gain some insight into the lives and feelings of a group of
people they may not have seen as having much in common
with before.

She wrote the play shortly after her grandmother's death.
Deborah says the play is about how we are all fundamentally
the same, only some of us have had thirteen years of experience
and some of us have had seventy-two. She wanted to look at
the enormous strangeness of death juxtaposed with the
normality of it, how life goes on around it.

She would like to free up actors by encouraging them to look
at the older characters as people, rather than at their age.

Her starting point for writing the play was finding Josie and
Harry's song. This is the song by Fats Domino which is sung
in the play.

Approaching the play

Director Raz Shaw believes you can't direct by just talking: it
is a two-way interaction between the actors and the director.
There must be input from the actors. Don't go into the
rehearsal room with all the answers, go in with a lot of
questions. This will provoke thought and response from the
actors. Remember that there are no right or wrong answers at

the early stages of making a play. The most powerful thing you can ever say is 'I don't know'. This is the driving point to an answer. Actors will often think you have all the answers. When they realise you don't they will try to find the answers themselves.

He also believes that it is important that you have a strong personal connection to the play you wish to direct. Raz would encourage directors to try to distil what they think the play is about into one sentence. When you are lost in rehearsals go back to what initially drew you to the play. Your ownership of a play as a director will come from your personal connection with the piece.

In preparing to direct a play the most important thing you can do is read it, keep reading it and read it without worrying about finding all the answers. Raz reads a play in this way about five or six times before reading it with the intention of planning his production.

'Always approach a classic play like a new play and a new play like a classic' (*George Devine, founder of the Royal Court*).

Themes

The play addresses how we see age as a boundary when we should see the person.

It is important for the actors to understand the world in which the play takes place. Raz suggests that it may be helpful for actors to carry out some research into old people's homes in order for them to fully understand and engage with the world of the play. If possible, he suggests arranging a trip to an old people's home or watching video footage or documentaries. Actors could also look at photographs on the internet, or ask friends and family who have experience of old people's homes for insight.

Language

The writer is happy for you to come up with alternatives to the swear words within the play if it would cause offence or be awkward in performance. You may change Nanna to Nanny or Gran or another term for grandmother that would suit the region the piece is being performed in. Other than this, she says, do not add or take out any other words or change them. When an actor says 'My character wouldn't say this', respond 'Your character does say this, so make it work – create a character that would say this.'

Characters and characterisation

Raz doesn't have fully formed ideas about characters at the early stages of rehearsal, so he uses the exercises below to further explore and develop them. All the exercises are intended to act as triggers or keys to unlocking characters. Raz spoke about 'the penny dropping' for an actor, when their character comes into focus. This can happen at any point of the rehearsal process. The exercises act as tools to help 'the penny drop'. Character work becomes more important when working with young people as you are giving them the tools they need to do it independently in the future.

THE FAMILY TREE

Josie (1943–2014) *married* Harry

Their children:
Mel *(married)*
Andy *(just separated from his wife)*
Alison *(single parent whose husband has moved away)*

Mel's children:
Emma, *sixteen*   Fay, *fifteen*   Harry, *thirteen*

Andy's children:
Sarah, *fourteen*   Callum, *twelve*

Alison's child:
Jo-Jo, *thirteen*

GRACE   Although Grace doesn't have much stage time, there is a lot of information about her within the script from what other characters say. Deborah suggests getting the actor playing Grace to do the four lists exercise (on page 54) and then fill in the gaps with their imagination.

ALFIE   How you physically feel about yourself is affected by your surroundings and company. How does it change Alfie's physicality when Sadie recognises him from school? Does he revert back to the schoolchild she once knew?

HARRY   Harry probably died within the last few years that the play takes place. When we meet Harry in the final scene Deborah says he is 'in no man's land'.

Actors playing married couples should agree on significant dates and events. Raz suggested improvising the significant events that we don't see in the play as part of creating character back story. This will give the actors joint memory. Deborah thinks it would be very useful to improvise Harry and Grace meeting, as well as Harry and Josie meeting.

Another suggestion for finding character is to get an older person to read an actor's lines for them so they can hear their speech pattern, tone and personality. They may wish to record the older person doing this so they can practise and create their character's voice from the recording.

Deborah is keen to avoid young actors doing caricatured old people. Urge performers to find the truth within the characters. The play is written to be seen and performed by teenagers and the writer encourages directors to find the teenager within the older characters. Equally, if a girl is playing a male role or a boy is playing a female role encourage them to play the truth not the gender.

Most importantly, approach who a character is first, their age and gender last. Don't start with the stoop! The writer doesn't see a distinction between an actor playing a character the same age as themselves and an actor playing a character forty years their senior. They are both characters that the actor is not. She says play the kernel of the person.

Casting

The writer tried to keep the casting as open as possible. Double cast or change genders – whatever you need to do to tell the story in the best way you can. She deliberately wrote the play so it can be played by fourteen or more different actors, or doubled up to be played by a smaller cast. She doesn't have a preference which way it is cast and believes it will work as well either way.

If you have a large cast the writer suggested several ways in which you could use additional bodies. In Scene Three you could entirely create the world young Harry is in – extra actors could become soldiers, for example. In other scenes there is the opportunity to expand the world in which the play takes place with nurses or additional nursing-home residents.

Production, staging and design

The most creative 'aspect of a rehearsal is time management. Raz counts pages and schedules adequate time per page. He says be strict with your time management. If Scene One is amazing but Scenes Two and Three aren't, you don't have a play. Have a schedule for all rehearsals and aims of where you want to be at the end of each rehearsal.

Deborah explained her decision to have Harry in a uniform in the final scene. She wanted to find a way that instantly identified that he was not in the same space and time as the rest of the play. In the final scene he probably resembles the man that Josie first met.

In the last scene the characters go back in time. The first scene is set in a packed-up room and the last scene is the same room unpacked. Think about how you can show that quickly and efficiently. Scene changes can be scenes within themselves. If you have costume changes in between scenes think about how allowing these to happen onstage may enhance the production.

In Scene Two the writer has written 'high-back chairs' into the stage directions as it easily signifies an old people's home to an audience, but any chairs may be used.

Deborah spoke about how in pre-production and rehearsals, finding solutions to obstacles that are presented to us can often generate our most creative and innovative ideas.

It might be helpful to rehearse the last scene in two sections: one which exists in the reality of the room and one which exists in Josie's head. You could then fit the two sections of the scene together.

Style and technique

Embrace the humour that comes from the reality and truthfulness of the situation. Deborah has written a very truthful play that should be played within the realms of naturalism, with a sensitivity to the way in which we portray old people on stage.

Exercises for use in rehearsals

Raz began the session by asking the following questions. Directors may find it helpful to answer these questions for themselves before directing the play and/or asking their actors.

- What do you think the play is about in one sentence? (Try to answer this emotionally and not just with the plot.)
- How do you connect with what the play is about in one word?

Character exercises

FOUR LISTS

Once you have allocated parts, ask your actors to create the following four lists:

- All the facts about my character in the play from stage directions and dialogue.
- What other characters say about my character.
- What my character says about other characters.
- What I say about myself.

These should be direct quotes from the script. Try to avoid summarising.

Once the actors have compiled the four lists ask them to read them out loud. Hopefully this will provoke discussion. Set this task on day one so you immediately have something to talk about.

THREE WEIRD QUESTIONS

Raz would then ask his actors to answer the following 'weird' questions. These should be informed by the information they have gathered about their characters through the four lists exercise.

MIND PRINT

What are you afraid of about yourself which is actually true? What is your character most vulnerable about? It's an active drive inside you (which is what character work is all about – trying to find out what drives your character).

Example: A boxer's mind print is 'I'm a coward', therefore it spurs him on to fight.

YOUR SHAME EVENT

The thing you did once, that you have told no one about, that you are most ashamed of. This may be particularly helpful for an actor who has to build the character back story of an older person. How long have they been carrying that shame? How does that manifest itself now? Shame events make people less frightening and can give insight into a character's behaviour. To help own their character, actors may not wish to share their shame event with the rest of the company.

YOUR DAY OF RECKONING

In your character's last day on the earth who do they want to spend it with – their mother or their father?

Actors can make these answers up, but encourage them to keep it relevant to the character and the play.

SEVEN UP

Inspired by the television documentary that filmed a group of people every seven years of theirs lives, Raz does an exercise with actors that he calls 'Seven Up'.

Ask two actors in character to think about how their character was at seven and ask them to interact with each other. After some interaction ask them to turn away from each other and think through the next seven years of their lives until they reach fourteen. At this point they can turn around to face each other and interact again. The exercise continues until you reach the desired age. You don't have to go up in multiples of seven. You may jump to more significant ages in the character's life. Emphasise that actors go through each year in detail in their heads.

You could also do the same exercise with a larger group – so actors feel less exposed, or to occupy large groups and get through the work in less time. The characters can also project into the future. So if an actor is playing a young character they can go through the entire exercise too.

Deborah likes this exercise as an alternative to hot-seating, as it takes the pressure off the actors having to make instant decisions. It will also help to find the teenager within the older characters, as you actually allow the actors to meet their character at that age.

TACTICS

Raz spoke about using tactics in scenes to get what a character wants within a scene. Below is a quick and simple exercise to demonstrate tactics.

One actor stands either side of a chair. Both want to sit on the chair. When you say 'Go' they both try to sit on the chair. Whoever doesn't manage to sit on the chair must try to get what they want through whatever means they can. This exercise is a good way to demonstrate wants and objectives and the tactics one will use to achieve them.

This can be applied to scenes. What does your character want from other characters in the scene and what tactics do they use to achieve this?

STAGING EXERCISES

Set an empty chair on stage. What story does it tell the audience? When the chair is placed in a different position, how does the story change?

Ask an actor to sit on the chair. Give other actors in the group a piece of paper with a relationship written on it (e.g. jealous lover, overprotective friend, spy, brother). The actors must then place themselves onstage in a still position that conveys that relationship. What image does this create? Ask the audience what story is being told.

If the initial actor changes their focus, how does who they are looking at change the story? If you change the position of the audience how does that change the story of the image?

Deborah says this exercise can act as an important lesson in ensemble work and storytelling. It will help the director and cast to be aware of what pictures they are painting and what story is being conveyed to the audience. You could try taking a photo of the image you have created and showing it to the actors, asking them to tell the story of the photo.

Suggested reading and viewing list

BOOKS
Different Every Night by Mike Alfreds
The Director's Craft by Katie Mitchell
Actions: The Actors Thesaurus by Marina Caldarone

DOCUMENTARIES
The UP Series, Channel 4
Harrow: A Very British School, Sky

PLAY
London Road by Alecky Blythe

MUSIC
'My Girl Josephine' by Fats Domino

Horizon

by Matt Hartley

For Dave Wilson

Ackowledgements
Anthony Banks and the entire NT Connections team.
All the students and staff who generously gave
their time and energy to help inspire and develop this script.
Helen Perry, for the insights into the Connections experience.
And, of course, to all those who take part in the productions
of this play, I wish you all the best for the future.

Matt Hartley is originally from the Peak District and studied Drama at the University of Hull. His work includes *Sixty Five Miles* (Paines Plough/Hull Truck; Bruntwood Award); *The Bee* (Edinburgh Festival); *Trolls, Epic* and *Life for Beginners* for Theatre 503; *Punch* (Hampstead Theatre); *The Pursuit* (Radio 4), and *Hollyoaks* (Lime Pictures/Channel 4). He is currently under commission to the Old Vic Theatre and Royal Shakespeare Company, and his play *Microcosm* will be produced at the Soho Theatre in spring 2014.

Characters

Holly Ranson, *nineteen years old*
Sally Ranson, *fifteen years old*
Jake Ranson, *eleven years old*

Becky French, *fifteen years old*
Max Jones, *fifteen years old*
Carl Scott, *fifteen years old*

Simon Peters, *seventeen years old*
Kelly Francis, *fifteen years old*

Beth Howells, *eighteen years old*
Tom Armitage, *eighteen years old*

Joey Barnes, *thirteen years old*
Scott Hayes, *thirteen years old*

Setting

A town in the UK. Horizon Shopping Centre.

A water feature which doubles up as a wishing well is prominent. Around this are several benches. Two lonely-looking palm trees stand in front of a wall painted with images of city skylines from across the globe. A clock is also visible.

Summer. The last day before school restarts.

Note on punctuation

A forward slash (/) indicates that the character continues on to their next line.

A dash (–) indicates an abrupt stop.

Scene One

Nine a.m.

Sally *runs in, checks the coast is clear. She quickly dashes and grabs a seat. She is pleased with herself. She takes out a packet of crisps from her bag and starts to eat. Shortly after* **Becky** *dashes in from another entrance. She stops dead when she sees* **Sally**.

Becky   No way. Seriously!

Sally   First.

Becky   No, no, no! Can't be true!

Sally   Is.

Becky   But like I ran, like, literally really ran /

Sally   Time even to get crisps out.

Becky   / got aches, stitches to prove it.

Sally   You're slow.

Becky   No, no, no, no!

Sally   Are. Woah, don't come near me!

Becky   What?

Sally   Sweaty. Can see it, you've got pearls streaming down your face.

Becky   Told you I ran.

Sally   Gonna stink.

Becky   Nah.

Sally   Are.

Becky   I am motion sensed to the max. See, my pits are dry.

Sally   Don't point them pits at me.

Becky   Can't believe this. So unfair. I woke up first thing, yeah, didn't even set no alarm – just first bit of light coming through curtains, that's how early. Could have been real mean and like woke Casey but didn't, let her hog it in bed – Then like I had a quick wash – got dressed – tried to eat cereal, milk was off though, well grim, felt a bit sick, not enough for a mini-vom but had to rinse my mouth out and this is like all before like Mum even gone to work! And she works well early – Thought yeah, save bus fare, walk, can get a can of fizz instead on way – so I stroll along sipping my Coke – arrive outside at eight-seventeen. Eight-seventeen, Sal! No one else even thinking about coming in. No one – so like, I just have a wait, not even a text to say I'm here, not to you, to Carl, no one – not giving my game away, no way! Totally get you sweating, doubting about whether I'll be here like you asked – Turns nine. Security guard like he opens doors and like a flash I'm on it. Boom! Barge past him – full pace – not gonna let you down, Sal, show you I can be on time. Like run past Boots – past H&M – past Carphone Warehouse before they're all like even open! And after all that, like what do I get, yeah? You. You, that's what. Joker.

Sally   Should of come in through Marks. Always first open.

Becky   Duh.

Sally   Duh?

Becky   Opposite side to bus station. Time efficiency, yeah.

Sally   Duh.

Becky   Duh?

Sally   Didn't come on bus, did you, Becks, like you just said that. Walked, didn't you. Said eight-seventeen you arrived. Could of walked round to Marks in no time.

Becky   Shut up.

Sally   You shut up.

Becky   Wanted to be first.

Sally   Unlucky.

Becky *plonks herself down. Swings her feet.*

Becky   Whatever. Going to totally beat you to school tomorrow, Sal, telling you. No way you going to be first.

Sally   Fine.

Becky   Fine?

Sally   Not bothered.

Becky   Er, it's like first day back, Sal.

Sally   Yeah.

Becky   Well, first day back means new form room, yeah: L5, like gotta bagsy best desk, yeah, not gonna let Mel Munday get in there, grab best seat. No way.

Sally   Don't care.

Becky   You what? Don't care?

Sally   No.

Becky   You ill?

Sally   No.

Becky   Got a fever?

She tries to touch **Sally**'s *head.*

Sally   Leave it out –

Becky   Talking like you're burning up.

Sally   – seriously.

Becky *withdraws her hand.*

Becky   Not caring. Mad.

Sally   Just school.

Becky   Just?

Sally   Yeah, *just.*

Becky *watches* **Sally***, momentarily bemused by her tone.*

Becky   So when they launching it?

Sally   What?

Becky   I want my tester. Better do it in bright pink.

Sally   Better not be going on about Carl all day.

Becky   He loves big lips. And Maybelene make my lips huge.

Sally   It's been cancelled.

Becky   Cancelled?

Sally   Yeah.

Becky   Like stopped?

Sally   Yeah.

Becky   But what about my lips?

Sally   God, Becks, there'll be other free stuff.

An announcement comes on over the Tannoy.

Tannoy *(voice-over)*   Good morning and welcome to Horizon Shopping Centre, for all your shopping needs and beyond. Please remember that to help you enjoy your experience with us, Horizon is a smoke-free zone.

Becky *starts to swing her feet.*

Becky   O.M.G. You like cannot be serious.

Sally   No need drama queen.

Becky   Scuffed, look at that, my trainers are totally scuffed, Sal. Must like be polish they use on these floors. Stupid floors, these were new shoes. Brand new. Properly new.

Sally   Weren't.

Becky   What?

Sally   Not brand new. They were Kelly's. Kelly gave you them. She was gonna throw them away.

Becky   No.

Sally   They've got holes in the bottom.

Pause.

Here.

Becky   No way.

Sally *passes* **Becky** *some lipstick.*

Becky *happily begins to apply it. She runs across to look at her reflection in a shop window.*

Becky   Seriously. Witness. The fitness. Think my skirt's too short, Sal?

Sally   I know what colour your pants are.

Becky   Thought I'd give Carl a treat. Says he loves my legs. You not think about treating Max? Look like a nun.

Pause.

Holly working today?

Sally   Yeah.

Becky   She still get discount?

Sally   Yeah.

Becky   Go in later then, yeah. Thought might get new top. Got this one with sequins in window.

Sally   Only thirty per cent. All she gets.

Becky   Oh. Thought it were like. More.

Sally   No.

Pause.

Becky   They crisps? What flavour are they? I can see they're like the browny purple packet, but can't remember if that means they're like prawn or smokey bacon – Like I know they've both got brown in them, those flavours.

Sally   Smokey bacon.

Becky   Course, breakfast, yeah. (*Pause.*) I like smokey bacon. Nice flavour.

Sally   You want one?

Becky   Well like if you're offering. Yeah.

She takes one.

She eats.

She takes two.

She eats.

She takes more.

Sally   Not eat breakfast?

Becky   Told you, milk was off.

Sally   Toast. Could have had toast.

Becky *shakes her head.*

Sally   It's just bread. Nah?

Becky   Covered in green.

She takes another crisp.

Sally   Finish them.

Becky   What?

Sally   Have the rest.

Becky   Yeah?

She eats, hungrily.

Sally   Got an apple as well if you want it.

Becky   Apple?

Sally *opens up her bag.*

Becky   What's that?

Sally   Don't laugh, Holly gave me all this.

Becky   That like a lunch box?

Sally   It's cling film.

Becky   She make you lunch? What are they?

Sally   Just sandwiches. Cheese and crisps.

Becky   No way, cheese and crisps? What flavour?

Sally   I dunno what flavour.

Becky   Oh.

Sally   They're all wrapped.

Becky   I love cheese and crisps sandwiches. Beef is so the best flavour. Telling you, Holly is such a better sister than like Casey is.

Sally   Not.

Becky   Is.

Sally   She thinks she's my mum.

Becky   Casey does nothing like that for me.

Sally   Casey is eleven, Holly's nineteen.

Becky   Would so swap them.

Sally   You wanna be talked to like you're some sort of baby?

Becky   Not a baby.

Sally   Well, that's what she does. Patronising me. What does she know? Not like she's been anywhere but here.

Becky   She works in Topshop.

Sally   So?

Becky   She knows loads a' stuff. Like how to work the tills. Fashion. Like loads. And she got like well good A-levels.

Sally   Like that matters.

Becky   All 'A's. Well smart.

Sally   Now she works on tills in Topshop.

Becky   I'd totally work in Topshop. Be so cool. Discount. I'd just be like so buying all the clothes.

Sally   Yeah, great for someone who wants to be a vet.

Becky   I don't wanna be a vet.

Beat.

Sally   You going to take the apple?

Becky   Can I save it?

Sally *nods.* **Becky** *puts the apple in her pocket.*

Becky *looks in the wishing pond.*

Becky   Teachers were back today. Have to go back in day earlier. Teacher training. Better give Mr Osborne some. He is soooo rubbish. Never listens, does he?

Sally   Dunno.

Becky   Dunno?

Sally   Doesn't teach my set.

Becky   Oh yeah, only teaches thickos, Mr Osborne. You get all the good ones. Ones that don't have food on their shirts. Tell you what I am so not looking forward to – Physics. Or Chemistry. Or like Maths. Or English. Or History. Or French. Or Biology, sooo boring.

Sally   Stop with all the talk of school, will you.

Pause.

Becky *sees something in the pond.*

Becky Yes!

She fishes it out. It's some money.

Ah – only twenty p. Thought it were fifty. Used to get loads
more out.

She counts out her money.

How much is cinema?

Sally More than that.

Becky It's alright, Carl will pay for me. (*Pause.*) Proper old
fashioned, like. (*Pause.*) Max do the same for you? (*Pause.*) Bet
he will. (*Pause.*) Minted. (*Pause.*) Two pounds. (*Pause.*) Ninety.
(*Pause.*) Get a milkshake later maybe. Strawberry. Yeah?

Sally Maybe.

Pause.

Becky Chips. If I got some change left. (*Pause.*) Barbecue
sauce with them. (*Pause.*) Best sauce barbecue, yeah. (*Pause.*)
Just talking to myself, am I?

Sally Like I want to talk about barbecue sauce.

Becky God, got blob on or what, Sal.

Sally No.

Becky Acting like it. Proper sulk.

Sally *goes to speak. Before she gets a chance* **Becky** *spots* **Holly**
entering.

Becky Oh my God, is that Holly, Sal? Oh it is. No, that's
not Jake with her, is it? Ah man. Not going to have to babysit,
are we?

Sally Shut up.

Becky No way, no way, Max and Carl be here soon. He's
gonna totally ruin it.

Sally Don't believe this.

Becky   That's it, isn't it? Why you wanted to meet early, avoid your duties?

Sally   Not my duties.

Becky   Maybelline never giving freebies, were they?

Sally   Shut up, will you.

Holly *enters. She drags* **Jake** *with her.*

Jake   Ah that's my ear, Hol.

Holly   That's what you get when you slow me down.

Jake   Hol, Hol, get off will you. Please. Look, Sally is there with –

Holly   You better stay here. Seriously, if you make me chase you.

Jake   Won't.

Holly   Right. There.

Holly *approaches* **Sally** *and* **Becky**. **Jake** *waits.*

Holly   Very mature.

Sally   What you saying?

Holly   Very mature, Sally. Really mature. Running away from me, like you're how old?

Sally   Know how old I am.

Holly   Seven.

Sally   Not seven.

Holly   That's what I think looking at you right now, seven-year-old. Sulky little baby.

Becky   She's fifteen.

Holly   I know she's fifteen, Becky, think I don't know that?!

Becky   Dunno.

Sally   Don't speak to her like that.

Holly   Never asked her to stick her nose in.

Sally   Did. She's got rights.

Holly   Rights is it?

Sally   Yeah it is, not just me you're trying to dump him on, it's her as well, can say what she wants.

Becky   Yeah.

Sally   This is our last day, last day of summer –

Becky   Is, last day.

Sally   – and we're not looking after him. Full stop.

Becky   Not a creche.

Sally   Exactly.

Pause.

Holly   What do you think I should do then, Sal? What you think I should do with him?

Sally   Whatever.

Holly   Take him to work with me. Start him young?

Sally   Works in China.

Beat.

Holly   Seriously. Help me out here. I've tried everyone else. You know he can't be left by himself.

Sally   Must be somewhere else.

Holly   Name it. Go on, name somewhere.

Becky   What about Pepys?

Sally   Closed.

Becky   No way?!

Sally   You know that.

Becky   But when we were little that was like where we spent all our summers.

Sally   Becks, shut up will you.

Holly   See, can't just drop him off at some club. Can't do that, they don't exist any more. Think I want to ask you? Think I want to ruin your busy day? Sat on your arse all day, round a fountain, think that's my plan?

Sally   Such a bitch.

Holly   Now come the big words.

Sally   Just cos your life –

Holly   What, cos what? My life is what?

Sally   You know.

Holly   Yeah, I do.

Silence.

Not asking the world, Sal, just till Mum finishes work. Six, maybe, seven hours max.

Silence.

Sally   Today is going to be so crap.

Holly   Yeah, well, welcome to my world. (*Beat.*) Jake, come here.

Jake *approaches. Hovers. Looks at the floor.*

Holly   You're going to sit here with Sally and Becky. Right?

Jake   Yes.

Holly   Give them no trouble.

Jake   Yes.

Holly   You've got your sandwiches. Yeah?

Jake   Yes.

Holly   What?

Jake   Yes.

Holly   So that's your lunch sorted. And Mum gave you money to buy some new stationery. Yes?

Jake   Yes. (*Beat.*) Fifteen pounds.

Holly   Yeah, well, you got that. And that's for stationery, not food.

Jake   Yes.

Holly   Not to buy any fast food.

Jake   Yes.

Holly   Know what that does to you.

Jake   . . . Holly

Holly   You make sure he doesn't buy any.

Sally   Think I want him yakking everywhere.

Holly   Remember it's for stationery, that money.

Jake   God, Hol, yes.

Holly   They'll take you to buy some.

Sally   What?

Jake   I can buy my own.

Holly   Make sure he buys what's on the list. He's got a copy of the list. Sally?

Sally   Fine.

Beat.

Holly   I'm late. Right, I get a break just after eleven, then lunch at two. I will be coming back to check on you. Try not to –

Beat.

Sally   What?

Holly   Just keep an eye on him, yeah.

Sally   Go already.

Holly *goes to exit.*

Becky   Holly?

Holly   What?

Becky   Sal says you get like thirty per cent off, is that right or is it like more? Must be amazing.

Holly *stares at* **Becky** *and then exits.*

Becky   It's totally more. So obvious. More like sixty. Seventy maybe. Free even.

Pause.

Becky   What? So he just stands there?

Sally   No. (*Pause.*) Sit then.

Jake *goes to sit near them.*

Sally   God, not there. There.

Sally *points at a bench which is facing the other way, a short distance from them.*

Sally   And Jake, so you know. Three things. One: never speak. Two: you try and listen to me –

Becky   – to us –

Sally   – talking about anything, you're dead. And three: don't cry. At any point. Or be sick. Understand?

Jake *nods.*

Becky   Play a game on your phone or something.

Pause.

Sally   Bench hasn't got legs, Jake.

Jake *looks at them both, resigns himself to his day and then goes and sits on the other bench. He pulls out a Sudoku book and starts to do it.*

Becky *gets her phone out. Nothing.*

Becky   You got reception?

Sally   Always get it here.

Becky   Check though.

Looking at **Becky***'s phone.*

Sally   What's that, Becks? What are they?

Becky   Bars.

Sally   You've got three of them. Nothing to do with signal. He's just not texted you. (*Beat.*) Yet. Like it's early.

Becky   Yeah. He's probably sleeping.

Sally   Yeah.

Becky   I'll text him to text me when he wakes up. Not like he was gonna be here now anyway, is it? Have to set off well early. He says it takes him and Max over an hour just to get here on the bus.

Sally   I know.

Becky   An hour.

Sally   Hill Park is miles away.

Becky   Showed me pictures of how green it is. Trees and rivers. Said he'll take me there. Take me to a pub where he can get served. Buy me some wine. But I said 'I prefer Vodka Orange', he said that's fine, get me that. Be amazing. Like you and Max can come with us too. Have you smelt him, Carl? I think he smells like heaven must smell.

Sally   It's not heaven, it's Instinct by David Beckham. Costs a tenner from Boots.

Becky   You're being so ratty today.

Sally   And you're being so annoying.

Becky   Er, not the one who brought her baby brother.

Sally   Er. didn't bring him.

Becky   Did.

Sally   Summer ends today.

Becky   What?

Sally   Tomorrow we go back to school. Our school. They go back to their school. Miles away.

Becky   So?

Sally   After today it's over. You. Carl. Gone.

Becky   No.

Sally   Yeah.

Becky   No way. Takes them an hour on the bus just to like come meet us. They do that. Carl says they'll keep doing that. Honestly they will, they so will.

Sally   Won't.

Becky   Totally will. Carl, says we're different to the girls at his school.

Sally   Easy.

Becky   No. Not easy.

Sally   Yeah. Both of them were virgins before we met them. Just using us.

Becky   We're in a relationship.

Sally   On Facebook? Single, it says.

Becky   He just never changed it. Posts pictures of us up.

Sally   Maybe not tomorrow, or day after, but you'll be blocked. De-friended.

Silence.

Becky   Really hate you right now.

Silence.

So mean.

Sally *gets up.*

Becky   Walking away from me, is it?

Sally   Want me to piss on the bench, do you?

Becky   Sort of thing a tramp would do.

Sally   Coming from the girl with her wang out.

Becky   Think I'm just going to sit here and look after your little brother? Think I'm going to do that?

Sally   Nah, think you're the one that needs looking after.

She goes.

Becky *tries to compose herself.*

Jake *stands and goes and sits next to* **Becky**.

Becky   You hear that?

Jake *offers* **Becky** *a tissue from a pack of tissues.*

Becky   Don't need it.

Jake *fails to withdraw the offer.*

Jake   Look like a panda.

Becky   Sister's mean.

Jake   Sometimes.

Becky *takes the tissue.*

Jake   Want a go on Sudoku?

Becky   No, Jake.

Jake   OK. That was my last tissue.

Becky   That's OK.

Jake   Sally was crying all last night.

Becky   Was she?

Jake   Heard her in their room.

Becky   Not making this up?

Jake   No. Her and Holly screaming at each other.

Becky   About what?

Jake   Don't know. Put my headphones in. Listened to Beyonce.

Becky   I like Beyonce.

Jake   Yeah. Saw you do the dance once. Round ours. In front of MTV. That's why I've got no tissues left, sorry. Put them under their door. Don't tell her I said this.

Becky   OK.

Jake   Promise.

Becky   Promise.

Jake   Becky, it's twenty-five.

Becky   What is?

Jake   Holly's discount. Not thirty.

Becky   Really, you sure, Jake?

Jake   I like playing with numbers. Holly tests me.

Becky   Oh.

Jake   Sorry.

Pause.

Becky   Is my skirt too short, Jake?

Jake *stares at her legs.*

Shakes his head.

Becky   You better go and sit back over there, yeah. People meant to be like arriving soon.

Jake *nods. Stands and goes and sits round the other side of the bench. They wait.*

Lights fade.

Noon.

Jake *is sitting in the same place. He's reading a book. Occasionally he draws in his notebook.*

Becky *and* **Sally** *are sitting with* **Kelly** *and* **Simon**.

Simon *is using his phone.*

Kelly *is sipping on a large coffee from Starbucks.*

Becky   That a Frappuccino?

Kelly   Caramel.

Becky   Venti?

Kelly (*nods*)   Only paid for Grandi.

Becky   No way?

Kelly   Ronaldo served me.

Simon *tuts.*

Becky   He didn't.

Kelly   Gave him a smile like this.

Becky   No way, like that?

Kelly   Yeah.

Becky   Behave, licking your lips.

Kelly   Asked if I wanted extra sauce.

Becky   He said that? And what did you say?

Kelly   'I love sauce.'

Simon   Tart.

Becky   OMG. Really?

Kelly   Worked, didn't it?

Simon   He's a sleaze.

Kelly   He's jealous.

Becky   Defo.

Simon   Of that? No way – so greasy.

Kelly   Looks like Ronaldo.

Simon   Does not. He's just greasy.

Becky   His arms are like massive.

Kelly   Well fancies me.

Simon   Proper paedo.

Kelly   Not.

Simon   Is. He's at least twenty-four.

Becky   Si is well jeal. Should be careful, Si, Kel could so easily have him. Leave yer for dead.

Simon   Whatever.

He goes back to his phone. **Kelly** *tries to brush off* **Simon**'s *lack of interest.*

Becky   So that was like how much?

Kelly   Shouldah been three-ninety. Did it for two-seventy.

Becky   Oh my God he so fancies you. Sal, you hear this? You hear what Ronaldo did with Kel. Did you?

Sally   Yes.

Becky   So amazing. I like love caramel Frappuccinos. (*Pause.*) Love them.

Kelly   Er. God. Tomorrow, have to have like those machine coffees.

Becky   Grim, don't even do mocha.

Kelly   The cappuccinos taste of sock.

Simon   When you drunk a sock?

Kelly   No, like what socks would taste like –

Becky   – like feet.

Kelly   – yeah, like feet –

Becky   – so grim.

Simon   Not for me.

Kelly   No.

Simon   No machine coffee. No teachers. No stupid uniform. Get to stay in bed. Get to like play on X-Box when you're in a room listening to Harrison bang on.

Kelly   Oh not Mr Harrison.

Simon   Square root. Pythag-whatever, blah-blah, like I need to know any of that, but you've still gotta listen.

Kelly   Shut up, Si.

Simon   Going to be proper mint. Tell you.

Becky   Can't wait to leave.

Sally   That right?

Becky   Totally. one more year, bye-bye.

Sally   Then?

Becky   Then?

Sally   Yeah, then?

Becky   Dunno.

Kelly   Go cookery college with Si.

Simon   No way, not having that come near me.

Becky   Like I'd want to go near you.

Kelly   Probably be kicked out anyway.

Simon   No.

Becky   Bet he does, be hanging outside school at lunchtime.

Kelly   Going to come take me for a ride, are you?

Simon   As if.

Becky   Cos he won't have a car!

Kelly   Shame!

Simon   Yeah, like the world's going to be biting your hand off when you leave school.

Becky   Will.

Sally   Got to do something, Becky.

Becky   What, I gotta decide now? Fine, tell you what, I'll go work in Topshop with Holly, get a discount. Be sick.

Kelly   Yeah, yeah, then I can use your discount!

Becky   Course. Or tell you what, could get a job down Starbucks, work with Ronaldo, look at his arms!

Kelly   Carl would get well jealous!

Becky   Yeah, yeah. Could drink as many Frappuccinos as I like, even give Si a discount.

Sally   Know how many calories in that?

Kelly   Don't care.

Sally   Five hundred. Plus. Shouldn't drink it.

Kelly   Taste so good though.

Becky   It does, totally, doesn't it . . .

Sally   Shouldn't drink anything from there. Shouldn't want to work for them. Treat workers like crap.

Becky   How do you know?

Sally   It's in the news. Starbucks. Bad company. Don't pay tax.

Becky   Er, neither does my dad.

Sally   Your dad's not got a job.

Becky   Duh, I know.

Sally   Maybe if they paid tax he might.

Becky   Doing what? Making coffee? Doubt it.

Sally *goes to explain, decides it's not worth the bother.*

Simon   Owned.

Sally   What?

Simon   Owned.

Becky   OWNED.

Sally   No.

Becky   Yes.

Sally   No, just no point explaining to her.

Becky   Why, cos you think I'm thick?

Sally   Yeah.

Simon   Cold.

Kelly   God, Sal, that's so mean. Becky, you're totally not thick.

Becky   She's just in a mood. Proper raj. Been like this all morning.

Kelly   Yeah?

Becky   Yeah.

Kelly   Bet she just wants some Frappuccino, yeah?

Becky   Probs.

Sally   No way do I.

Kelly *jokingly puts the Frappuccino near **Becky**'s face.*

Kelly   She does.

Simon   So does.

Becky   Yeah, you do.

*She pushes it into **Sally**'s face.*

It spills.

Silence.

Didn't mean that.

Simon   That's quality.

Kelly   Er, shut up, that was my drink.

Simon   Got to get a photo, stay still.

Sally *stands up, looks at the mess on her clothes.*

Becky   Sal . . .

Simon   Smile. Uh-oh. Proper Grinch face.

Sally *sticks her fingers up at **Simon** and exits.*

Becky   Sal, Sal, wait up.

She follows her.

Simon   This phone is proper mint. Look how sick that picture is. Kel, look. Quality.

Kelly *doesn't.*

Kelly   Waste. Total waste. Had like not even half of it. Like no way near half.

Simon   Good thing.

Kelly   What?

Simon   Heard how many calories it's got?

Kelly   You saying?

Simon   Saying makes you fat.

Kelly   What is your problem? Calling me fat. Simon, you calling me fat?

Simon   Skinny now, but give it time.

Kelly   Never getting fat.

Simon   Seen your mum?

Kelly   Not like my mum.

Simon   Course, course.

Kelly   I'm going to order two more of those and a muffin, chocolate muffin, wolf them down, prove you wrong.

Simon   Do it. Go pump up your tits. Flash them over the counter. Greaseball give you anything.

Kelly   Yeah. Will. (*Pause.*) Will do.

Simon   Go on then.

Pause.

Kelly   Am.

Simon   Well. Waiting.

Pause.

Kelly   Not meant to say that. Meant to want me just for yourself.

Pause.

Ignore me is it?

Pause.

Fine.

Pause.

Just sit here.

Pause.

Be a hater.

Pause.

Just play with your phone, yeah.

Simon   Not playing

Kelly   Little toy.

Simon   Giving Parsons some grief.

Kelly   Mr Parsons?

Simon   Found him on Twitter, didn't I. Telling him he's gay.

Kelly   He is gay.

Simon   Yeah, telling him. Used to give me so much grief. No respect. Now I'll show him.

Kelly   He'll just block you.

Simon   Prove my point then, yeah. Not just going to sit here take it, you know. Giving it out loads.

Kelly   Si, what else you done?

Simon   George Linekar retweeted me. Told him he was a maggot. That he should have died.

Kelly   You said that?

Simon   Big-eared prick. Living off his dad. Giving it large. Think's he's top lad. Deserves it.

Pause.

Getting loads a' grief now.

Kelly   Well stop, then.

Simon   Stop? You like mad? Funny.

Pause.

Kelly   This like cos of Ronaldo?

Simon   Don't flatter yourself.

Pause.

Kelly   Parsons takes me for English.

Simon   So?

Kelly   So, he teaches me English.

Simon   Not me. Never teaching me again. Never have to set foot in school again.

Kelly   Knows we're together.

Simon   So?

Kelly   He'll think I said that.

Pause.

Kelly   Such a –

Simon   What?

Pause.

Kelly   Wanted to buy a top.

Simon   Buy a top then.

Pause.

Kelly   Said you'd do that with me.

Pause.

You coming?

Pause.

Fine.

Pause.

Sit there.

She gets up and goes.

Simon *considers. Follows.*

Jake *is left by himself.*

He looks around.

Gathers his things. Goes.

Becky *enters.*

She sits.

She takes her phone out.

Nothing.

She weighs up her options.

Makes the call. Rings out. Answerphone.

Erm, yeah, well, like I'm up Horizons, and you said, well, like I'm sure we agreed. You'd come up. That we'd do stuff. Here. So. Like call me back. It's Becky.

She hangs up. Stares at the phone. Puts it in her pocket.

She looks round. Stares at the pictures of far-away cities.

She takes a coin out of her pocket. Makes a wish. Chucks it in the water.

Holly *enters.*

She watches **Becky**.

Holly   What you wish for?

Becky   Oh heh, Holly.

Holly   Store discount or something.

Becky   If I say it won't come true, will it?

Holly   Yeah, well, think you might have to chuck a fair few more coins in to give it a chance.

Becky   Only got thirty p.

Holly   Well, wishes don't come cheap. Where are they?

Becky   Where are they?

Holly   Er, I asked that.

Becky   Yeah. Sorry.

Holly   Is she getting Jake his stationery.

Becky   Yeah. Like loads of it.

Holly   Doesn't need loads, just what's on the list.

Beat.

You tell her I came by.

Becky   Yeah.

Holly   And that Jake's got to eat his fruit.

Becky   Yeah.

Holly   Becky, you asked earlier. It's twenty-five. That's what it is.

Becky   Yeah. Jake said.

Holly   Little know-it-all.

Becky   Yeah.

Holly   My lunch break's at two. I'll come back then.

She exits.

Becky *looks to see if she can see* **Jake**.

Joey Barnes *and* **Scott Hayes** *enter. They are eating chips.* **Joey** *is cramming in as many as possible. They go and sit where*

Becky *was.* **Joey** *has a football top – referred to as Chelsea in script, but please use what feels appropriate for the area.*

Joey   Twenty!

Scott   No.

Joey   Is!

Scott   No way!

Joey   Yes way – and ketchup.

Scott   Massive gob!

Joey   Can fit more.

Scott   Grim.

Becky *notices.* **Joey** *spits his words out through his chips.*

Becky   What you doing?

Joey   Eating chips.

Scott   Got twenty in.

Joey   Twenty-two!

Becky   Does it look like that's free?

Scott   What?

Becky   There. Where you're sat, does it?

Scott   Yeah.

Becky   Well, it's not.

Scott   Nobody sat here.

Becky   Did I give you permission? Did I? Did I?!

Scott   Don't need your permission.

Joey   No permission needed.

Becky   That's my bench. Get your own.

Joey   Mental.

Becky   What did you say?

Joey   MENTAL!

Becky *grabs* **Joey** *by the nose.*

Becky   Better swallow those chips if you wanta breath.

Scott   Get off him.

Becky   Get off my bench then.

They do.

Give me those chips.

She snatches the chips off them.

Never sit on my bench, never.

Scott   Gonna regret that.

Joey   Seriously.

Becky *swings out at them. They run off.* **Becky** *looks around. Eats some chips.*

Sally *enters. She has washed her top. It's still dark from the water. A moment.*

Sally   Way to go, Becky, real way to go. Stinks. Going to stain. Such a div.

Beat.

Becky   Jake's not with you?

Sally   What?

Becky   Thought he might be with you.

Sally   Been in the girls' toilets, course he's not with me. What you telling me? Telling me Jake's not here?

Becky   Maybe he's with Simon and Kelly.

Sally   I just saw Simon and Kelly arguing outside Starbucks.

Becky   So he's not like with them?

Sally   No. No he's not.

Becky   Right, maybe he's just . . .

Sally   What?

Becky   Like he must have just gone to the toilet. Buy his stationery.

Sally   Better hope. Better hope so.

They stare at each other. They look round the centre.

Fade.

Ten past two.

Simon *and* **Kelly**.

Kelly *has a couple of shopping bags by her feet.*

She's drinking another Starbucks.

She has another empty Starbucks container by her feet.

She enjoys it.

Simon *ignores her.*

Kelly   That gulp. So was at least eighty calories.

Pause.

Minimum.

Pause.

Oh no, oh no, look what it's doing. Getting so fat.

Pause.

Barely fit in my jeans.

Pause.

Simon   How much you spend on that?

Kelly   Worth every penny.

Simon   Three pounds seventy. Both a' them. No discount.

Kelly   Like –

Simon   Full price. Seven pounds forty you just spent. Not even finished the first. Ten minutes later back in. Looked desperate. Other girl, fit one, working with Ronaldo, laughed at you as you walked out second time.

Kelly   Didn't.

Simon   Put her hand on Ronaldo's arm. Whispered about you. Both of them laughed.

Pause.

Just a little girl to him.

Pause.

Should drink that. Got at least another three hundred left in it.

Kelly *doesn't drink it.*

Holly *enters.*

Simon   Alright, Hol?

Holly   Seen my sister?

Simon   Yeah. She's around.

Holly   Around?

Kelly   Yeah.

Simon   Looking out for your Jake.

Holly   Out?

Kelly   After. He means after.

Simon   Yeah. After.

Holly   Tell her to come see me. Tell her that.

Kelly   Yeah.

Simon   You working?

Holly   No, I dress like this for fun.

Simon   Right. (*Beat.*) Bet you're like me, Hol.

Holly   Like you?

Simon   Yeah.

Holly   How's that?

Simon   Glad you don't have to go school tomorrow.

Holly   They not let you back?

Simon   No. Too old. Going cooking college, aren't I.

Holly   Is that a question?

Simon   Yeah, no, I am, going. Not like her. Back at school.

Holly   Just tell Sally that Mum's got to work late, will you? That she's stuck with Jake for longer. If she's got a problem, tough.

She goes to exit.

As she does so she bumps into **Tom Armitage**.

Tom   Holly?

Holly   Oh hi. Hi, Tom.

They awkwardly embrace.

Tom   Good to see you.

Holly   Yeah.

Tom   You look –

Holly   Hanging.

Tom   No.

Holly   Kind of you, but, yes.

Tom   And me . . . ?

Holly   Yeah, you look, look, like you always do.

Tom   What are you doing here?

Holly   Erm, I'm working.

Tom   Right, course, yeah.

Holly   Don't wear my name badge for fun.

Tom   Thought you were just getting forgetful.

Holly   No, sadly not, no, I remember everything, this is just part of the job.

Beat.

Tom   Hol, I really wanted to –

Holly   Oh, it's OK –

Tom   No, no, it's not –

Holly   Honestly, it is –

Tom   Just with uni I'm hardly here, I thought, really wanted to stay in touch, you –

Holly   Can we not, can we not do this? You know I never got back to you as well, it works two ways.

They look around. **Tom** *points at the New York landscape.*

Tom   . . . Start spreadin' the news . . . I'm leaving today . . . I want to be a part of it . . .

Holly   Yeah.

Tom   . . . New York, New York.

Holly   I'm still here though, Tom.

Tom   Sorry. Was that, that was, wrong of me, I . . . ?

Holly   No, no, just we're not fifteen, sat there any more, are we?

Tom   . . . Hol . . .

Holly   Fucking Horizon, of all the names.

She turns to **Simon** *and* **Kelly**, *who have been gawping at them.*

Holly   Ironic, isn't it? Horizon?

Kelly   What?

Holly   Mind your own business.

Beat.

Holly   What you doing here anyway, Tom? Not fifteen any more.

Tom   No, no reason. Just, bits . . .

Holly   Bits?

Tom   Stuff. Clothes. A few things.

Holly   That's nice. Really nice.

Beat.

Tom   And you?

Holly *points at her name badge.*

Tom   Course, course, yeah, being stupid, proper thick. (*Beat.*) Nottingham not hap –

Holly   Don't. Don't. Tom.

Beth Howells *enters.*

Beth   God, there you are, Tom – Holly, oh my God.

Holly   Beth.

Beth *hugs* **Holly**.

Beth   So good to see you. What you doing here? You've got your name on your shirt.

Holly   Yes, I have.

Beth   That's so random.

Holly   Not really.

Beth   Oi, you, why you running away from me? Left him for literally one second, and he's off, like zoom. Go on, let's hear it then, let's hear your excuse, go on then.

Tom   Thought I'd check the times.

Beth   And?

Tom   Well, I bumped into Holly.

Beth   Hear that Holly, hear that?

Holly   Yes.

Beth   So you don't even know what time it's on?

Tom   No.

Beth   Typical. What are you like? Totally dragging me to see some film, not even sure what it's called or about but we're just like trying to spend as much time together before we both go back to uni, you know. Cos I tell you what, it is such a totally mental time when you're there. Time, just goes, like goes. Like, every night, Hol, like every night I'm out, so many parties, barely went to a lecture, mad, gonna come out with a degree in partying, I swear, by the end. My dad keeps going, knuckle down girl, but I'm like, whatever, keep paying the bills but I suppose you know all about that, don't you?

Holly   I'm not at uni, Beth.

Beth   God, yeah, sorry my bad, stupid. Going to now, though, aren't you, got it all to look forward to, haven't you?

Tom   Beth, we should –

Holly   It's OK, Tom. No, Beth, I don't have it all to look forward to.

Beth   But you got a place to do Vet Studies, right?

Holly   Veterinary Medicine, Beth. Vet Studies would be something very different.

Beth   Totally. Looking after animals, though, yeah?

Holly   I did, but it doesn't . . . well, that's not happening.

Tom   No?

Holly   No.

Tom   Thought you'd just deferred?

Holly   Yeah, only so long you can defer for though.

Tom   You've always wanted to be a vet.

Holly   Nothing's changed.

Tom   Can't not . . .

Holly   What? What, Tom?

Tom   You have to go.

Holly   Easy for you to say.

Beth   Holly, you can't just operate on animals without training, not fair on the animals – tell her, Tom.

Tom   I think she knows that.

Beth   You do?

Holly   Yes.

Beth   Then Tom's right, you have to go. Doesn't she? So got to.

Holly *takes a moment, weighs up whether or not to say anything. She chooses not to.*

Holly   You should go and check your film times.

Beth   Totally. You just like hanging about with them?

Holly   No, no, I'm going back to work. At Topshop.

Beth   Oh, you're like still working at Topshop?

Holly   Oh yeah, can't keep me away.

Beth   Ah that's . . . nice.

Holly   Thanks, Beth. Thank you. Thank you.

Beth   Oh, is that like why you've got a name badge on?

Holly   Yes.

Tom   Beth, we really should go.

Beth   Eager beaver. Like Hol, just saying, it may be like fun all the clothes and stuff, but like you should totally quit and go to uni though. Don't want to work in a shop for ever, do you?

Tom   Beth.

Beth   Yeah, yeah, coming. So lovely to see you.

Beth *and* **Tom** *go.*

Simon *stares at* **Holly**.

Simon   She's got warts like as big as conkers. Down there.

Kelly   How do you know?

Simon   Everyone knows.

Kelly   Obviously he doesn't.

Simon   Hear that, Hol? Big as conkers.

Holly   I heard.

She goes to exit.

Kelly   Hol, if I come in later, will you let me use your discount? Really want loads a' stuff.

Beat.

Holly   Tell Sally and Jake to come and see me.

She exits.

Kelly   That was totally a yes, wasn't it?

Joey *and* **Scott** *enter. They are carrying and drinking milkshakes. They creep up on* **Kelly** *and* **Simon**.

Simon   Like you need more things.

Kelly   Always need more.

Simon   Such a girl.

Kelly   Yeah.

Simon   Spoilt girl.

Kelly   No.

Simon   Proper Daddy's girl.

He notices **Joey** *and* **Scott**, *who were just about to tip the milkshake over* **Kelly**.

Simon   You want something?

Joey   It's not her.

Scott   Not her!

They run off. **Kelly** *remains oblivious to what nearly happened.*

Tannoy (*voice-over*)   Horizon Shopping Centre: For all your shopping needs and beyond. Today why not join us in the Food Court where you can be transported from the East to West with an array of culinary delights. Horizon Shopping Centre, taking you away from it all.

Kelly   So mean to me today.

Simon   Kiss me.

Kelly   No.

Simon   Yes.

She does.

Becky *storms in.*

Becky   Like way to go, Kel, way to go.

Kelly   What?

Becky   Rubbing it in my face. Tongue down his throat.

Simon   Carl stood you up, has he?

Becky   Shut up, Si.

Simon   Oh he has. Denied!

Kelly   Stop picking on her.

Becky   Like today, yeah, not fair, so not fair. Don't need you, Si, don't need that, Si.

Kelly   You found Jake?

Becky   Last day, last day before we go back and I get stuck with this. Do I look like a babysitter?

Kelly   You've not found him?

Becky   Tell you this is so not my fault, if this ends up on *Crimewatch*, they are not getting some massive div to play me, no way.

Simon   Don't need another massive div, can just play yourself.

Becky   Yeah, yeah, I would, like, do that, show it wasn't my fault.

Kelly   So, no?

Becky   Duh, does it look like it? Looked everywhere. Jake's such a little prick, can't believe this.

Kelly   Holly were just here.

Becky   What?

Kelly   Seriously, she was like looking for Sal and Jake. Told me to tell Sal to go see her. She was like, well, not messing about.

Simon   Fierce.

Becky   You didn't say, you said nothing about –

Kelly   Er, not mental.

Sally *enters.*

Kelly   Nothing?

Sally   Not giving gold star for stupid comments, Kel. Not funny, Si, may be twice as clever as you but Jake's only eleven years old.

Simon   Scared he's paedo-bait, yeah?

Sally   What did you just say?

Kelly   You tried calling him?

Sally   No, no, no, I haven't.

Kelly   Maybe you should

Sally   *Idiot.* Course I have. Just rings out.

Simon   Sister was looking for you both.

Sally   Course she was. Oh my God you got another Frappuccino!

Simon   Charged her full price.

Kelly   Shut up.

Sally   Greedy bitch.

Simon   Oi, watch your mouth, yeah.

Sally   If you had never got that, if you'd never been stupid and pushed it in my face and you egging her on and then you pushing it so it spilt, I would never have run off and this would have never happened.

Kelly   No.

Sally   YES.

Pause.

Becky   That's like not fair. Like he's your brother.

Simon *and* **Kelly**   Yeah.

Becky   Don't try like and blame us.

Simon *and* **Kelly**   Yeah.

Sally   Not trying. I do.

Pause.

Becky   You were fighting last night. You and Holly. Jake told me. Sounded like an old person when he talked about it. Like he was tired. Like it happened a lot. If he's run off. Gotta think why. Why he ran away from you.

Pause.

Sally   You have no clue. Literally no clue what you're talking about.

Becky   He passed you tissues under the door.

Pause.

A text message. **Becky**'s *phone. She looks at it.*

Becky   Oh my God.

Kelly   Is it –

Becky   Carl. He wants to meet. Him and Max are coming. (*Beat.*) What?

Simon   Not smart, Becky, not smart at all.

Sally *steps towards* **Becky**.

Kelly   Now, Sal, don't do anything stupid, yeah.

Sally *keeps walking towards* **Becky**.

Sally's *phone rings.*

She hesitates.

She looks at the phone.

Anxious looks all round.

She answers it quickly.

Sally Jake? Where – what? You're what?

Blackout.

Six-fifty p.m.

Becky *is draped over* **Carl**.

Carl *is wearing very brightly coloured trousers.*

Max *is sitting by the fountain.*

Becky Twenty p, that's what it cost me. I wished and I wished and splash and now here you are.

Carl Am I worth it?

Becky Totally. (*Beat.*) Totally. (*Beat.*) Though like, if that fountain was a like a swearbox it would be chocka, words you were making me say.

Carl Told you, my mum and dad they were like what, what you doing? Horizons? Not a chance, you have got to be ready for school tomorrow.

Becky Could have texted.

Carl Never been to the countryside have you?

Becky No.

Carl Can't appreciate how hard it is to get reception then. Non-existent.

Becky Yeah, right. Really?

Carl Impossible. Had to go to the bottom of the garden to get any. Wave my arms like a right nutter. Then it's not like we've got loads of buses to choose from. One every two hours.

Becky Such bumpkins, you two.

Carl I'm so dead if they find out.

Max Not just you.

Becky   Such a rebel.

Carl   Worth it.

Becky   You like my skirt? Put it on especially for you.

Carl   I like what's under it.

Becky   Behave. (*Beat.*) No, don't.

Max   Yes, do.

Becky   GRINCH.

Max   People are watching.

Becky   Yeah, pervs like you.

Max   No, old-age pensioners.

Becky   Like I care.

Carl   Don't be jealous, Max, it really isn't cool.

Max   Is Sally actually coming?

Becky   Told you. She doesn't want to see you.

Max   Yeah, yeah, you said that. But you also said she would be back here at seven.

Becky   That's when Jake said he'd be back here. He said seven. Here.

Max   Why did he run off?

Becky   I don't know. I'm not like ten.

Max   He's eleven.

Becky   Well duh, I'm not that either. And you know like we're both in the same boat here, she totally hates both of us right now, so like you should be like me and not care about her.

Max   Well, I do. It's ten to seven now, so I'm going to wait here until she comes.

Becky   Well, she hates you and we're going to do some snogging. So stop being such a dogger, Max, and go somewhere else.

Carl   Snogging? Here?

Becky   You don't want to?

Carl   Hundred per cent do want to. Just, thought, you know.

Becky   What?

Carl   Well, like I want to stay with you, you know that, for hours, upon hours but we haven't got long, the last bus is in nearly an hour. So, I thought we should go somewhere more private.

Becky   You mean like the disabled toilets?

Carl   You like it there, don't you?

Becky   With you, yeah.

Becky *and* **Carl** *get up to go.*

Scott *and* **Joey** *enter.*

Scott *has something behind his back.*

They approach **Becky**.

Scott   It's her.

Joey   It is.

Becky   Get out my way.

Scott   Defo is.

Joey   Go on.

Carl   Hello. Yes, can we help you?

Scott   Nice trousers.

Joey   Boyfriend buy you them?

Carl   What?

Becky   Calling you gay. He's not gay. He's my boyfriend.

Scott   Urrr, that's worse.

Joey   She's minging.

Carl   What?

Joey   You heard.

Carl   Know them, do you?

Becky   Carl, say something.

Carl   What?

Scott   Knows it's true!

Max   That's enough. Go away.

Joey   That your boyfriend?

Scott   Is!

Max   Ignore them.

Becky   No, put them right.

Carl   They're just little scrotes.

Scott   Scrotes, hear that.

Joey   Did.

Scott   Told you you'd regret it.

Joey   Do it.

Scott *takes out a bottle from his behind his back and throws the contents in* **Becky***'s face.*

Joey   Bullseye!

Becky *recoils in shock.* **Carl** *freezes.* **Max** *approaches but hesitates.*

Becky   Oh my God, oh my God, oh my God, that's my face, that's my face, that's acid, it's burning,

Carl   Becky? Becky, are you OK?

Becky   It's in my eyes.

Joey   It's in her eyes!

Scott   Pissy eyes!

Max   WHAT?

Scott   Yeah, it was mine –

Joey   – and mine.

Scott   We pissed in a bottle –

Joey   – and threw it in her face –

Scott   – in your face!

Becky   CARL!

Carl   You're . . . so . . . dead . . .

Joey   What you gonna do?

Scott   Yeah, rent boy, what you gonna do? Nothing.

Joey   We're just gonna walk away.

Scott   And you'll do nothing.

A beat.

They walk away. Then they run off laughing.

Carl   You OK?

Becky   Am I OK? Am I OK? Am I OK? Am I OK? Am I OK? Am I OK?

Carl   Bad question.

Becky   NO, I AM NOT OK! I'm covered in piss and you did nothing, Carl, nothing.

Carl   Happened so fast.

Becky   Let them like walk away. What sort of man are you?

Carl   They were –

Becky   Twelve. Babies. You were scared of a pair of babies.

Carl   No.

Becky   Wimp. Wet. Gay boy.

Max   Should I call security?

Becky   Meant to be your girlfriend and you let them, just like walk away, walk away having covered me in piss.

Max   They'll have CCTV.

Becky   Think I wanna see that, see me getting covered in piss?

Max   Might help identify them.

Becky   I don't know like what's tears and what's piss. I put this on for you.

Carl   Becky . . .

Becky *runs off.*

Max   Hero.

Carl   Shut up. What could I have done? If they're throwing bottles of their own slash around, who knows what else are they capable of doing?

Max   They were half your size.

Carl   Probably carrying knives. Not getting stabbed for the sake of –

Max   What?

Carl   For the sake of anyone. Let alone her.

Max   Well, you're definitely not getting laid now.

Carl   Shall we just go?

Max   Some piece of work you are.

Carl   What? All I'm going to get is grief. Like she looked a state beforehand but now she's covered head to toe in whaz, so there's no way I want to have to actually touch her, and you heard her, Sally wants nothing to do with you.

Max   And I need to know why.

Carl   Come on, summer's over. Never have to come here again. See their faces. Served their purpose, didn't they?

Max   Whatever.

Carl   Know it's true.

Max   No, you may think that about Becky, but I actually really –

Carl   Like. That what you gonna say, really like Sally?

Max   Yeah, I was. I do. I think she's amazing and –

Kelly *and* **Simon** *enter.* **Kelly** *has even more bags. One from Topshop.*

Kelly   Er, why's Becky run past screaming at me like a proper mad banshee?

Carl   Some kids just chucked a bottle of whaz all over her.

Kelly   What?

Carl   In her face. Whaz. Piss.

Max   Completely soaked her.

Simon   Who did it?

Carl   These two kids

Simon   What? Not two little kids, Chelsea top?

Carl   Yes, couldn't be more than twelve, thirteen. Little chavs. Quite funny really.

Simon   What's that?

Carl   If you'd seen it you'd have found it hard not to laugh. Her make-up was all smudged and you couldn't tell if it was tears or, you know, piss.

Simon   Laugh when they did it, did you?

Carl   Managed to contain it.

Simon   Prick.

Carl   Sorry?

Simon   PRICK. That's your bird, mate, you're laughing at.

Carl   Well –

Simon   My friend. You just let them do that to Becky, did you?

Max   I think Carl has –

Simon   Shut up, Roland.

Max   Max.

Simon   Whatever, posh name. Talking to Rupert the Bear. (*Beat.*) I want to wipe that smile off your face, I really do.

Carl   Not smiling, honest.

Simon   Don't move. Tell you this, if some little kid had chucked piss over my Kel I wouldn't be laughing, I would be inflicting some serious hurt on them. Kel, Becky's going to need some clean clothes.

Kelly   She can like wear this top, I can put one of these new things on.

Simon   Yeah, you go do that.

Kelly *exits with shopping bags.*

A moment.

Carl   I think our bus is going pretty soon, heh, Max.

Simon   Sit.

Carl   If we miss it . . .

Simon   Mummy or Daddy will come pick you up.

Max   They don't know we're here.

Simon   That's one of those tragedies you only ever hear about on the news.

Beat.

Sit. And you, Hugo.

They do.

When Becky comes back. Gonna tell her she looks beautiful.

Carl   Si . . .

Simon   And that you're a prick. Gutless. Posh. Prick.

Holly *enters.*

She looks tired, on the cusp of breaking down.

Simon   Wanna hear what posh boys been laughing at?

Max   We're not posh.

Simon   Hol?

Holly   Don't talk to me.

Max   Holly, have you seen Sally? I really need to speak to her.

Holly   Barking up the wrong tree, Max. She's not coming out to play with you.

Max   Don't know what I've done.

Holly   Says it all.

Max   I know she's had a tough day.

Holly   Oh she has, has she?

Max   I'm sorry about Jake, I can't like imagine how stressful that must be for you both –

Simon   Wrong words, Tarquin.

Max   – but I really like your sister and –

Holly   What's that about Jake?

Simon   Real smooth. She doesn't know.

Holly   Know what?

Carl   He went missing.

Holly   Missing?

Max   But it's OK now, he phoned and said he will be back here at seven.

Holly *tries to comprehend what she is hearing.*

Carl   That's a couple of minutes.

Max   Holly can tell the time, Carl.

Holly *approaches the fountain. She takes out a pile of change from her pocket. She hurls it into the fountain.*

Max   Holly?

Holly   Not even gonna make a dent.

Max   Are you OK?

Sally *enters.*

Holly   One thing I asked of you. One thing.

Sally   Don't start, not my fault.

Holly   Never is.

Sally   Becky threw a Frappuccino in my face. I went to wash it off and he was gone. Didn't just leave him and run off. Simon was still there.

Simon   Don't drag me into this.

Holly   Simon, he still finds velcro shoes complicated, why would you trust him?

Simon   Yeah, not my fault, not a babysitter.

Holly   Where's Jake?

Sally Just get off my back, always on at me, he's not dead, he's just walked off, and he's alive, and I spoke to him, wouldn't say where he was and I'm going to belt him, so just shut up, Hol. (*To* **Max**.) And I don't even know why you're here, told you to not call me, text me, even try and see me ever again.

Max I want to talk.

Sally Oh leave it out, it's over. You've got what you want. Go back to your tower and your pearl-wearing, inbred daddy-I-wanna-pony bitches.

Max Why you talking like this?

Sally It's how it is.

Max No.

Sally Max, wake up, you're posh, not blind.

Max I'M NOT POSH. WHY DOES EVERYONE KEEP SAYING I'M POSH?

Sally You're parents took you to Cuba on holiday, to help you understand politics.

Max Think I wanted to go?!

Sally Cry me a river.

Max Please, that sounded terrible, I didn't mean that to come out like that. What can I do? It's not my fault if they took me there. My parents work really hard and I don't tell them how to spend their money. If that's what they want to do with it then what can I do? Say no?

Sally I don't want to talk to you.

Max Well, I want to talk to you.

Sally Tell him, Hol.

Max Don't bring others into this, like this –

Holly Not the time, Sal.

Sally   Listen to him. Boo-hoo. His parents work hard.

Beat.

Holly   Our mum works three jobs. She does over a hundred hours a week. She walks to work. She had to sell our car, it cost too much.

Sally   Summer has been amazing, Max, but today, yeah it ends. Tomorrow, yeah, we go different ways. You go upwards, you just keep going that way, up and up and I just move along. Steady, flat. It's not your fault.

Max   Not true.

Sally   Go home – you too, Carl, just let us be.

Carl   I think Sally's right.

Simon   Nah, nah, he's not going anywhere.

Sally   What?

Simon   Long story.

Max   Sal, come on, where has this come from? All we've talked about this summer is things we'll do tomorrow, haven't we? About – please will you stop gawping and give us some privacy!

Simon   Sorry, Edward, you don't own this land, we're staying.

Max   Can we go somewhere and talk away from –

Sally   No.

Max   Sal, I'm not letting this go: we did, we sat here, talked about everything. Uni, travelling, looked at those buildings, those skylines, and said how we'd see them for real. About moving away, jobs, we did that together. We did, remember? We sat here, holding hands. That's been my summer. You and me.

Simon   Gay.

Max   Sally.

Sally   Max, I'm sure you will do all those things.

Max   And so will you.

Sally   No.

Max   Come on, you're far brighter than I could ever wish to be.

Sally   True. But I'm still half as clever as Holly. And look where dreaming and chucking coins in fountains got her.

A moment.

Sally   Not got a clue, Max.

She hugs **Holly**.

Kelly *enters wearing a sparkly top.*

Kelly   Becky wouldn't even let me see her. Ended up like having to just chuck the clothes over the cubicle. She's a proper mess. (*To* **Carl**.) Prick. (*Beat.*) What have I missed? Not little Jake, is it? Is he alright?

A loud chime is heard through the Tannoy system.

Sally   He said seven. I swear.

A moment, they all look round. An announcement comes over the Tannoy system.

Tannoy (*voice-over*)   Thank you for taking the time to visit Horizon Shopping Centre. The stores are now closed for today. If you could make your way to the nearest exit as Horizons will shortly be closing. We look forward to welcoming you again soon. Horizon Shopping Centre, taking you beyond it all.

Beth *and* **Tom** *enter.*

Beth   Oh my God, it's like time stood still. We were all just here literally a minute ago. Well, virtually all of us.

Holly   Not a good time, Beth.

Beth   Oh no what's wrong? Tough day at work? Rude customers? Swear, some people have no idea. Rather have been you though than sit through that film, tell you, *boring*, nothing could be more like dull.

Holly   Tom –

Tom   Holly, doesn't want to hear about the film, Beth.

Beth   She's not the one that had to sit through it.

Tom   Are you OK, Hol?

Holly *shakes her head.*

Holly   My brother is missing and she's banging on about a film.

Tom   Jake? Holly, he's there.

Holly   What?

Tom   There.

Jake *walks in.* **Holly** *and* **Sally** *rush up to him.*

Beth   Bit dramatic.

Tom   *Don't.*

Beth   What? She said I was banging on. Just being nice.

Simon   There he is.

Holly   Where have you been?

Sally   We were worried sick.

Kelly   Scared us to death.

Jake   Said I would be back at seven.

Sally   Don't be clever, where have you been?

Jake   I went for a walk. I was bored. Just sitting here. Boring. So I went.

Holly   A walk?

Simon   Walk, what you like?

He ruffles **Jake***'s hair.* **Jake** *brushes him off.* **Simon** *goes and sits back down.*

Holly   Where?

Jake   Places.

Holly   Which places?

Jake   Lots of places.

Sally   Don't be funny. Where?

Jake   I drew them.

Sally   What?

Jake   I drew them. See. I bought more pens, my stationery, then I went and drew things in my book. Loads of really good things.

Beth   He's so sweet.

Jake   Not sweet, brave.

Beth   Of course.

Jake   I can look after myself.

Max   You really scared your sister, Jake.

Sally   Stay out of this.

Carl   Our bus, Max . . .

Simon   Sit.

Jake *rushes over to* **Tom**.

Jake   Hi, Tom.

Tom   Hi, Jake.

Jake   You don't come for tea any more.

Tom   No.

Jake   Or play in Holly and Sally's room.

Holly   Jake, enough.

Jake   Want to see what I drew, Tom?

Holly   He doesn't.

Jake   Can I show Tom?

Tom   I don't think that's –

Beth   No, go on, we'd love to see.

Jake   Loads of amazing things. So many. Drew loads.

Beth   They're well beautiful, Jake.

Max   Looks like Jake's stolen your optimism.

Sally   Yeah, well, what does he know, he's eleven.

Beth   Amazing colours. So bright.

Tom   They're really good, Jake.

Beth   Should look at them, Holly.

Holly *takes the book.*

She gets upset.

She shows them to **Sally***.*

Sally *stares at them. Flicks through them.*

She looks at **Jake***, so full of hope.*

Sally *stares out at everyone, at all the pictures on the wall, the shops, her future . . .*

She starts to rip up a drawing.

Gasps from all round.

Jake   My picture?!

Holly   What are you doing?

Chorus of disapproval from everyone else.

Holly   Sally? You hear me?

Sally I don't . . .

Holly *grabs the book off* **Sally**. **Jake** *tries to put the paper back together.* **Tom** *attempts to help him.*

Beth That's the cruellest thing I have ever seen. And I was like in Guides.

Holly They were just so hopeful, and that's not true. Sal it's not true, is it? Jake, I don't want you to dream, it's not . . .

Beth You're a monster. You should apologise to him.

Holly Oh, mind your own.

Beth She should.

Holly Beth, walk away.

Beth Not till I hear that girl apologise to him. Go on, apologise now.

Holly DON'T YOU TELL MY SISTER WHAT TO DO!

Beth What's your problem?

Holly My problem? My problem?

Beth Yeah.

Tom I think we should go.

Holly Yeah, I think you should too.

Beth No, I've said I'm not going anywhere till I hear an apology.

Holly Sal, do not apologise.

Beth Oh, how mature.

Tom *puts his hand on* **Beth**'s *arm.*

Beth Get off me, Tom. You know what? You may be able to bully your sister and your little brother but you can't bully me.

Holly No?

Beth No.

Beat.

Holly What set were you in for Maths at school, Beth?

Beat.

Beth Third. But I hate Maths.

Holly English?

Beth Second.

Holly Science?

Beth Third.

Simon I was in third.

Holly What did you get in your A-levels?

Tom Don't do this.

Beth It's fine. Two 'C's and a 'D'.

Holly I was in the top set for everything. And I got two 'A plus' and Two 'A's. Yet, you're at uni and I'm working in a shop.

Beth And why is that? Because –

Holly Tell you why, because your daddy pays for you. Because you don't have to worry about paying rent, about student loans, buying bread, taking a summer off to intern, and then the two years when you graduate doing things for free to help get on the career ladder.

Beth Vets don't have to intern.

Holly Is that right? Five years I'd have to study. Each of those summers everyone has to do placements. Everyone. Unpaid. Nothing. Just to stay with the course. And then more. More. Two years after, placements hardly paid at all. One year I was meant to take out, save up, do a bit of volunteering, give me a base to start with.

Beth   There are grants, loans, for people like you.

Holly   What, clever?

Beth   Poor.

Holly   That's nice. Seven years, you got any idea how much that would cost, got any idea? Well, best case it would be a hundred thousand, worse case hundred and fifty.

Beth   There're ways to make it cheaper.

Holly   Like what, go on, what?

Beth   You could live at home.

Tom   Beth, don't – only five places do the course in the country.

Holly   Well, actually seven. But why should that even be an issue? You get to go where?

Beth   Brighton.

Holly   See you get to go there and just get drunk /

Beth   I do study.

Holly   / Why shouldn't I get to go to the best place for me to do the course? Why? Because my mum doesn't have money.

Beth   You'd have a good job at the end of it.

Holly   Get out of my sight. Tom, take your airhead away.

Beth   I'm not an airhead.

Holly   Beth, you were stupid all the way through school, you will continue to be stupid throughout your whole life, but sadly you will get a job in which you have to make decisions, decisions that will affect other people's lives, and you'll make stupid ones, which will have consequences, because it's people like you who had the ability to wait it out until a job came up, and –

Max Are you just going to stand there and let her rip her to shreds, Sally?

Simon Oi, don't stop it.

Sally Why? She's right.

Max It's not fair, I totally know. You should be able to go to university, you should, but –

Holly He's got lovely hair, hasn't he?

Sally His mum buys him Kangaroo Shampoo and Conditioner.

Holly That's nice.

Max Why are you trying to turn this like it's into two sides?

Sally Cos that's what it is.

Becky *enters.*

Becky Don't anyone come near me.

Jake Becky.

Becky Jake, you're – honestly, don't hug.

Too late. He has.

Becky You OK?

Jake I drew something for you.

He shows her a picture.

Becky Oh. What is it?

Jake It's you.

Becky Oh.

Jake You're wearing different clothes to earlier.

Becky Yeah.

Simon Got something to say, Carl?

Carl   Becky –

Becky   Drop dead. (*Beat.*) Kelly, when did you get that top?

Kelly   Earlier. Nice isn't it?

Becky   . . . Yeah.

Tom *starts to move away with* **Beth**.

Holly   Going are you, Tom?

Tom   Yes.

Jake   Sally ripped up one of my pictures.

Becky   Did she?

Jake   Yeah.

Becky   Why?

Jake   I don't know.

Becky   What's going on?

Holly   Tom and Beth were just leaving.

Sally   So were Max and Carl.

Carl   Thank God.

Beth   No, we're not.

Max   Not going anywhere.

Beth *approaches* **Holly**.

Beth   Tom told me you were really frigid. That you were like a starfish in bed.

Tom   Hol –

Beth   If you really wanted it, Holly, deep down, if your life depended on being a vet, you could find a way.

Holly *stares at* **Beth**.

Beth   You could, Holly.

A moment.

Holly *walks away.*

Beth   Always a way.

Sally *punches* **Beth** *in the face.*

Beth *falls to the floor.*

Sally *goes to attack her again but is pulled off by everyone.*

Sally   Get off me, get off me!

Holly   She's not worth it.

Sally   That's my sister, my sister, you bitch, my sister!

Max   Sally, Sally, heh, come on.

They manage to get **Sally** *to stop her attack. She is wild though and can't stay still.*

Sally   Don't touch me! Get off me!

Tom *helps* **Beth** *to her feet.*

Sally   That's it, run away. You trout. Tom, you obviously know nothing about sex if you hadn't noticed she's got warts the size of conkers on her –

Beth   I'm going to have you arrested.

Sally   Yeah, go on. Do it, like I care. Like it matters. DO IT!

Max   Sally, stop this.

Sally   No, I'm not stopping, what's the point?! There's none. Should just not bother with anything. School, anything. Why care? Nobody cares back.

Max   I care.

Sally   Oh shut up, Max, you care with only one thing.

Max   Now that's not true.

Sally   Look at Holly, look at her, look what's she doing. She's the brightest here by a mile, she worked every hour, every single hour and look at her. Here. Trapped. Look at her and tell me what's the point in going to school tomorrow. Tell me?

Max   You're being stupid, of course there is –

Sally   Am I? Study hard, work my socks off, want to go places, places that just won't happen. So then what am I going to do? Work in Topshop all my life?

Becky   Nothing with wrong that.

Sally   No, for you there's not. But do you not get it, Becky, do you not see it? If Holly ends up working there, if Holly does that, somebody as bright and as clever as her, what's going to happen to you? You so can't compete with her. You need her, you like need me to leave, you need us to go to uni to fill jobs up the food chain, to be like that, cos if we don't what will happen to you? No job, it ripples down, look how your dad lives, look how they treat him, take his job away give him nothing in return, make him feel guilty, cut his benefits, blame him for not having a job that doesn't exist, blame him for making you hungry and live on hand-me-downs, cos that's what will happen and I want to see you work. I want to see you happy in that shop, buying those things you always wanted but it's not gonna happen, it will happen to people like her, like Kelly, always splashing her dad's cash, they're fine, go about spending money in shops that don't ever pay tax, places that just take and never give back, that mean that my chances get ripped in two because greedy people won't help me and you out, like there's no point and I say we might as well just start smashing places up, smashing them up. Topshop, Vodafone, all of them, because we're doomed, there's nothing here for us, no future no nothing, just might as well fight it, rip up Starbucks, rip it all up, here, there, everywhere, because, they don't care about us, about our futures, they don't, otherwise they'd say it's not fair, you deserve better futures, it should be easy for you to go to uni, it should be easy for you to want to dream big. But they don't. And if this is my future then I'm not going to go there lying down. No way. I am going to fight, I am going to shout and I want to do it loudly and I want to do it now and I want to know who of you are with me? Want to know who wants to smash this stupid skyline? Who wants to tear it down? Who wants to do that? Who wants to burn this place to the ground? Who wants to do that? Who? Who? Who wants to join me?

She stares at them all.

Blackout.

Horizon

BY MATT HARTLEY

*Notes on rehearsal and staging, drawn from a workshop
with the writer held at the National Theatre, November 2013*

Workshop led by Lorne Campbell with notes by Cheryl Gallagher

How the writer came to write the play

Matt Hartley was inspired by the experience of sitting in a
shopping centre in Hull and seeing two young people push
each other into a fire alarm. The scene provoked him to ask
questions about young people's options and choices, boredom,
and how they fill their time.

Matt spoke about the fact that the play explores key moments
in a day and it is therefore up to each production to decide
how the characters behave when they are not in the play and
how they might inhabit spaces that are not in the play.

Approaching the text

Before you start your rehearsal process find a way to describe
the play in twenty words or less. This will help you focus and
structure your rehearsals.

Your rehearsal room can create a space for possibility, in
which actors feel safe to explore and research without the
pressure to create a performance. To do this, you need to
think carefully about:

- What you as the director are in control of, and what you
  are not in control of.

- What you are responsible for as the director, and what you
  are not responsible for.

- What the text is already doing, and trusting in that.

Lorne Campbell offered a process that can empower actors to
take responsibility for playing, exploring and being available to
the other actors. Instead of regarding the text as literature, you
can introduce the text as action at the beginning of this process.

Starting the process

Here is an example of how you can start this process with your actors involved in *Horizon*:

Select a scene or a section of the play. Ask the actors playing each character to stand up with their script – they are the 'feeders'. Then ask for some volunteers from the rest of the cast to be the 'instrument' for each feeder (one instrument per feeder). They do not need a script. The feeders stand behind their instrument.

Run the scene, with the feeders feeding their character's lines to their instruments in front of them and the instruments saying the lines fed to them to each other. The instruments are asked to not invent anything, but to communicate the content of the line and make contact with the other instruments.

Run the exercise through once and observe how much the actors/feeders are watching and listening to the instruments in front of them; the temptation is to feed lines quickly to maintain the pace of the dialogue rather than using the opportunity to observe what is happening. As the director, you have the responsibility to ask the actors to slow down. If they take their time to watch what is going on between the instruments in the space, they can use this exercise as a period of research about what is really being communicated in the text.

Do the exercise again and ensure that the actors feeding the line are watching and exploring what is going on in the scene.

Lorne advises going through the whole play in this way from the start, discussing what is happening with the feeders as you go. This is useful because the feeders are absolved of feeling worried about making choices and are free to just hear the text.

The second stage to this process is to ask the feeders to feed their instruments with the objective truth of the line. The feeders begin the line with their character's name. This enables the actors not to invent what isn't in the text. For example, the first line of scene two might be fed to the instrument as follows:

'Becky asks what coffee Sally has.'

The instrument then repeats this line to Sally, playing with the quality of the line. The next line might be fed to the instrument as follows:

'Kelly tells her what coffee she has.'

Follow this process through until the end of the section. If the actors are observing what their instruments are doing, there will be so many choices available they will have to make an interesting choice later on in the process.

The third stage of this process is to ask the feeders and the instruments to swap over. Remind those who are now instruments that they are responsible for playing and being available to receive, and that the feeders need to watch the interactions between the instruments, rather than getting ready to read the next line.

In this way, rehearsal is research rather than a space to practise answers. This process also describes to your actors what you expect the performance to be like. Rather than doing a read-through at the beginning of the process, you could run this exercise as a way to encourage the actors to remain active and available. You could also cast after you've run this exercise, to get the actors working together and not worrying about 'owning' their part and making decisions too soon.

This process can be made bespoke to suit the way you want to work, and you will need to be pragmatic about how often you do it – perhaps spending a day at the beginning of the process or even asking groups to go away into a different room and explore a scene in this way.

The action

Lorne spoke about how describing the result you want can be closing and disempowering for an actor. We looked at how actions can be used to further research and experiment with the options available to actors, exposing possibilities. Lorne addressed the fact that everyone means something different when they say 'action', but it is typically a verb that *does something* to another person.

Lorne spoke about the fact that the danger with 'actioning' is that performers and directors believe they have solved the play or solved the drama with the action, as if all the work has already been done. The action describes what you do, not how you do it. For example, the action 'I hug you' can lead to wide possibilities about how the actor does this. To encourage detailed acting, the actor must be encouraged to explore the possibilities of how they do their action. You can put this into practice by trying the following exercise:

Choose a section of the play (we looked at the beginning of the play). Two people are the instruments, and two the feeders, feeding Sally and Becky's lines. Choose two conflicting actions to play; for example, we chose 'to hug' (embracing, comforting) and 'to flick' (aggressive, playful), but you can choose any action. Then, using a pack of cards, decide that the highest cards would mean the instrument would play lots of 'hugs' with a hint of a 'flick', and the lowest cards were all 'flick' with a dusting of a 'hug'.

Each instrument is shown a card and is asked to play the quality of the action that the card corresponds to on the lines fed to them by the feeders. The instruments should not literalise their action (for instance, by actually hugging the other character) but play the quality of the action on the text.

Observe the exercise and assess whether the actors are just playing one tactic. The playing of an action does not mean that it is successful; for example, the action 'to intimidate' might not mean that the other actor is intimidated all the time. In fact, it might be more interesting if the other actor is not intimidated at all, forcing the actor with the action to find new ways of varying how they play 'to intimidate'.

Run the exercise again, with the actors trying to vary the tactics they use to play their actions. You can then give the instruments a different card to play a completely different action.

As a director, you have to make some compositional choices in terms of how you decide on which actions the actors play. The obvious version involves the characters playing an action that matches what the text is already doing, while the counter-intuitive version can be more interesting. 'We trust the writing to deliver the story', Lorne said.

As an example of this, we looked at the exchange between Simon and Kelly in Scene Two that starts with Kelly's line, 'Waste. Total waste. Had like not even half of it. Like no way near half.' Two people acted as the feeders for Simon and Kelly, and two people stood in front as the instruments. This time, Lorne told the actor playing Simon that the higher the card, the more he wanted to make Kelly laugh. The lower the card, the more the actor wanted to protect Kelly from herself. Lorne then told the actor playing Kelly that the higher the card, the more she wanted to bring Simon to heel. The lower the card, the more she wanted to bring him awe. If either actor drew a card that was in the middle, the two actions had to exist together. We then ran the exercise a few times with the actors choosing different cards on the scale, playing actions that conflicted or clashed. We observed the discoveries, discussing how often the counter-intuitive action was more interesting. Lorne then asked the actors to play different actions: the actor playing Simon was told that the higher the card, the more he wants to correct Kelly, and the lower the card, the more he wants to agree with Kelly. The actor playing Kelly was told that the higher the card, the more she wanted to help him to be a better boyfriend. The lower the card, the more she wanted to stop him from becoming worse. Again we ran the scene a few more times, with each actor playing a different action on the scale. The more obvious actions for each character sometimes matched what the text was already doing, while the more counter-intuitive options sometimes offered more interesting possibilities. To run this exercise, you can suggest different actions to the ones we tried for the exercise. Ensure you are mixing and matching the actions, and the actors are listening to each other and continuing to try different tactics to play their actions.

After going through this process, Lorne spoke about how the second phase of the rehearsal process is about guiding and steering towards the choices you like, and allowing things that aren't working to fade away. The actors are always encouraged to be responsible for remaining open, active and available.

Tempo

In this play, the rhythm and tempo of boredom is something you might want to explore. How do the young people in the play deal with it? Are they bursting to escape it? Or dissolving into it? Is the production marking this? We explored how you might look at this in performance with the following exercise:

Choose a section from the play in which one character is speaking. Ask for volunteers to be the instrument and the feeder (as before, with the feeder standing behind the instrument with the script). Ask for a further two volunteers to stand either side of the instrument. These two must feed the instrument with a two-digit number each, at the same time as the feeder feeds a line. The instrument must add the two two-digit numbers together in their head before saying the line. Run this exercise through once, discussing with the group how it puts a tension on the text. To explore how playing a few notes at the same time might colour the scene in an interesting way, ask for another volunteer to stand opposite the actor. This time give the actor an action to play which might conflict with the task of adding up two two-digit numbers. In our exercise, the actor was told to try to conceal from the other actor that there was any difficulty going on in their head. Run the exercise again, discussing the discoveries.

Structure

Lorne spoke about the importance of exploring the structure of the whole play before rehearsal. Sometimes directors can get lost in sections of the play and forget that audiences experience the whole piece, so it is useful to return to your thoughts about the play's structure as you journey through the rehearsal process. The structure informs everything: the design, the music, the performances. Does the structure of your production match the text? Or if it does not match the text, does it do so in an interesting way?

A useful exercise to understand the structure is to draw or create a graphic version of of the play. Your graphic might chart any number of themes and ideas. In terms of *Horizon*, we explored how the graphic version of the play's structure might chart ideas about hope, or crisis, or time (and sometimes all these things at once).

Whichever ideas you seize on to create your structure will impact upon how the characters in the play experience the whole piece. For example, if your take on the structure of the play focuses on time and the running out of time throughout the play, then this will affect the design, the music – everything. And then in terms of boredom, what happens when time is going slowly? How might the characters experience the whole structure? For Sally, is the shopping centre everything for her? It explains why she gets there so early and why the last few moments before closing are like the candle being snuffed out.

Lorne also flagged up how there is a danger in production that the last fifteen minutes are really shouty and there's nowhere for Sally to go with her final monologue, so it is a director's job to navigate how you build to this.

Throughout the rehearsal process, return to this graphic drawing and begin to perceive how the structure is acting on the characters or against them.

Casting

In terms of gender-swapping, both Joey and Scott can be played as girls if required. Their names can be changed or they can remain the same (Joey can pass for a female name and Scott could be the character's surname, for example). However, it was advised that the other male characters should be played as male in order for the text to make sense.

There was a question about whether the strongest female actor in a company should play Becky or Sally. It was suggested that the director finds the actors who can deliver the very different qualities of each character. For example, Sally needs to be able to hold, absorb and ensure that the momentum is not lost by the end. Becky, meanwhile, needs to be firing energy throughout.

Characters

There was a question about the social and economic class of the characters. Matt said that he sees all the characters as being from the same class except for Max and Carl, who are probably from a different world and go to a different school. Sally is the same class as the social context and sees herself as lower class to Max and Carl.

If the actors feel that the characters are different from them in terms of class or wealth, they need to find a way of being truthful to those characters' impulses and not stereotyping their performances.

Note on location

Directors should feel free to change and adapt colloquialisms in the play to make their production specific to their region. For example, the word 'hanging' can be changed to whatever young people in that region might use to say hungover. 'Don't set the play in London if your young people are from Belfast', Matt said. 'Make it specific to their world.'

Other resources

Matt was listening to The Kills and The Jezabels (specifically 'Deep Wide Ocean' and 'Prisoner') as he wrote the play – artists with strong female voices.

The Wardrobe

by Sam Holcroft

Sam wishes to thank all who helped develop,
edit and support the writing of this play,
including Anthony Banks, Rob Watt, Lucy Deere,
Tom Lyons, Matthew Poxon, Alastair Muriel,
Richard and Katherine Polson, Mel Kenyon
and all at Methuen Drama. Thanks also
to the Tricycle Theatre's Young Company
for their help to workshop the play during
the early stages of development.

Sam Holcroft is currently Writer-in-Residence at the National Theatre Studio. In 2009–10 she was the Pearson Playwright in Residence at the Traverse Theatre and in 2009 won the Tom Erhardt Award for up-and-coming writers. Theatre plays include *Edgar & Annabel* (part of *Double Feature 1* for the National Theatre); *Dancing Bears* (part of the 'Charged' season for Clean Break at Soho Theatre and Latitude Festival); *While You Lie* (Traverse Theatre); *Pink* (part of the 'Women, Power and Politics' season at the Tricycle Theatre); *Vanya*, adapted from Chekhov (Gate Theatre); and *Cockroach* (co-produced by the National Theatre of Scotland and the Traverse Theatre; nominated for Best New Play 2008 by the Critics' Awards for Theatre in Scotland and shortlisted for the John Whiting Award, 2009). In 2013 Sam Holcroft wrote the libretto for Vasco Mendonça's opera *The House Taken Over* for the Festival International d'Art Lyric d'Aix en Provence. She is currently under commission from the National Theatre, the Royal Court and the Traverse Theatre.

Characters

There are twenty-eight characters in this play. Some are female; some are male; some haven't been assigned to either gender. Please feel free to change the sex of characters where appropriate to suit availability. The characters can be played by individuals or by a company of actors who play several parts each. All characters are between the ages of eleven and twenty.

In order of appearance:

Elizabeth	**William**
Cecily	**Jaffrey**
Benjamin	**Martin** (*or* **Agnes**)
Daniel	**Robert** (*or* **Beth**)
Henry	**Tom**
Mathilda	**Archie**
Tobias	**Hugo**
Caryl	**James**
Anne	**Nell**
Mary	**Anthony**
Sarah	**A**
One	**B**
Two	
	Friend One
Dido	**Friend Two**

Setting

The entire play is set within one wardrobe. We travel through time visiting this wardrobe at specific moments throughout its history.

Scenes

Guidance for National Theatre Connections participants 2014:

Only nine of the total twelve scenes can be performed. Participanats are free to choose their preferred scenes.

This rule can also be applied to subsequent productions of the play.

Prologue

In view is a huge and imposing wardrobe dating from the late fifteenth century. The effect is of hand-made solid oak, with detailed carving and beautifully panelled double doors, with ornamental holes which allow in the light. It is an impressive presence.

The wardrobe rotates revealing to the audience its rear side. The back of the wardrobe has no wall, allowing the audience to see its contents. We are privy to anything that takes place within the confines of its walls. The inside of this wardrobe is our stage. The wardrobe is large enough to fit at least four people at any one time.

Scene One

The bedchamber of Elizabeth of York, the royal court, London, 27 October 1485, afternoon.

We can hear Tudor court music or similar sounds of the time and place.

The Wars of the Roses for the English throne have raged for thirty years between the houses of York and Lancaster (whose heraldic symbols were the white and red rose respectively).

Following the defeat and death of the Yorkist King Richard III at the Battle of Bosworth, the conquering hero and Lancastrian heir Henry Tudor ascends to the throne as King Henry VII of England. Nieces of the defeated King Richard III, Elizabeth of York, and her younger sister, Cecily of York, reside at court in anticipation of the coronation of their new king.

The door of the wardrobe opens. **Cecily**, *sixteen years old, climbs inside. She closes the door behind her, pushes aside the hanging robes and sits. She scowls. After a moment, the door opens and* **Elizabeth**, *eighteen years old, enters and closes the door behind her. Bright daylight filters through the ornamental holes dappling them with light.*

Elizabeth   There you are. Move aside.

She sinks down beside **Cecily**.

Elizabeth   Well, 'tis official: a letter from the King was published in the Parliament house just this morn. Shall I read it to you? (*Holding the parchment up to candlelight and reciting.*) 'Henry, by the grace of God, King of England and France, Prince of Wales, and Lord of Ireland, ascertaineth you that Richard Duke of Gloucester, lately called King Richard, was slain at a place called Sandeford and there laid openly that every man might look upon him: God have mercy on his soul. And, moreover, the King, our Sovereign Lord, shall wed the lady Elizabeth of York to the pleasure of Almighty God, the wealth, prosperity and surety of this Realm of England.' (*With sarcasm.*) Oh Cecily, how it puts to shame the greatest love poems!

Cecily *giggles.*

Elizabeth   He has no intention to share power, thus his coronation will occur afore marriage. Can you believe your ears, Cecily? I've eaten partridges with a stronger royal lineage. Besides, he's so old.

Cecily   He's thirty.

Elizabeth   Exactly, he's *ancient*. And he has such a long face. I do not care to look at my husband and think of my horse. Henry Tudor. He'll insist we name our firstborn son after him. What shall that make him? Henry . . . the Eighth. How tedious! No, I shan't have that. I'll start a new fashion: Barnaby the First.

Cecily   We cannot have King Barnaby.

Elizabeth   Why not?

Cecily   It sounds absurd.

Elizabeth   Humphrey.

Cecily   No.

Elizabeth   Arthur, then.

Cecily   King Arthur?

Elizabeth   In honour of the legendary King Arthur and his Knights of the Round Table. On this I shan't negotiate. I am the daughter of King Edward the Fourth; sister to King Edward the Fifth – if I weren't a woman, Cecily, no one would question my right to rule my country. But because I have a womb and breasts he'll not share his crown with me, only his bed. I've half a mind to deny him.

Cecily   He'd confine you to the Tower.

Elizabeth   So be it.

Cecily   Oh, hush your ridiculous brabbling! You know not how lucky you are. One day they will write books about you, plays about you: Elizabeth of York, the White Princess who married the Red King and thus ended the Wars of the Roses. But what of her sister, Cecily? Who ever heard of her? I expect she died alone in a convent!

She attempts to exit the wardrobe. **Elizabeth** *stops her and produces a silver spoon.*

Elizabeth   I have found a spoon. I think it is silver. Six points?

Cecily *snatches the spoon and gnaws at it with her teeth.*

Elizabeth   Cecily!

Her gnawing reveals some other metal underneath: it is only silver-plated.

Elizabeth   Oh. Three points? One point.

Cecily   Half a point.

Elizabeth   Half a point! Fine. Have you done any better?

Cecily *digs in her pocket and retrieves a jewelled dagger.*

Elizabeth   Wherever did you find that!

Cecily   The courtyard.

She unsheathes the dagger. She cuts the air with it. The light glints off the blade.

Elizabeth   Well. Ten points?

Cecily   Ten? These are rubies. One hundred. At least.

Elizabeth   Very well then.

She prises open a board in the base of the wardrobe and hunts underneath.

Oh yes. He said something else. If I die, he intends to marry you.

Cecily *looks at the dagger in her hand and then at her sister's exposed back.* **Elizabeth** *retrieves a box from the base of the wardrobe and opens it. She takes out a scorecard and a stick of charcoal. She writes.*

Elizabeth   Half a point to me. One hundred points to you.

Cecily *looks between her sister's back and the dagger.*

Elizabeth (*still with her back to her sister*)   He had Uncle Richard's body stripped naked and tied to the side of his horse. They paraded the horse in town. Richard killed Edward; Henry kills Richard; who will kill Henry? It is a game of death, Cecily, and we have no choice but to play it. They thought nothing of killing our brothers. We, too, must be prepared to do things of which we never thought ourselves capable.

Again, **Elizabeth** *rummages in the base of the wardrobe.* **Cecily** *raises the dagger to plunge it into her sister's back. Suddenly* **Elizabeth** *swings into view a short-handled axe. The girls face each other with their weapons.*

Elizabeth   I do not know what I would do without you. You are my best friend. I will see that you are always provided for. You will marry a gentleman and have many babies. I promise you this: you will never die alone in a convent, not while I am alive and we are sisters.

She uses the edge of her axe to slice her own hand and spill some blood.

And while the same blood courses our veins, I solemnly swear, here and now, that I will do everything in my power to see that you never come to any harm.

She offers her hand to her sister for shaking.

Cecily *slices her own hand on the blade of the dagger. She cries out in pain.* **Elizabeth** *quickly presses her bloodied hand to her sister's mouth to silence her and unintentionally smears blood all over her face.* **Cecily** *pulls* **Elizabeth***'s hand away.*

Cecily   Urgh!

She spits **Elizabeth***'s blood from her mouth.*

Elizabeth   Oh frothy boggarts, I am sorry!

Cecily   Urgh, your blood!

Elizabeth   Sorry.

Cecily   You just made me eat your blood! Urgh!

Elizabeth   Well I did not mean to. It was supposed to be a . . . symbolic moment.

Cecily *wipes her tongue on her dress*

Elizabeth   Sorry. We can still shake on it.

Cecily   If I have to eat yours, then you have to eat mine.

Elizabeth   What?

Cecily   It is only fair.

Elizabeth   Well, that is not really how you are supposed to do it.

Cecily *shoves her bloody hand over her sister's mouth and holds her nose.* **Elizabeth** *has to open her mouth to breath and gets a mouthful of her sister's blood. She throws her hand off and coughs and spits.*

Elizabeth   Urgh. Pleurghh!

The two girls stare at each other with bloody faces

Cecily   You look like a witch, a child-eater!

Elizabeth   *You* look like a child-eater!

They crack a smile and laugh. The laughter trails away. They look at one another with sadness.

Elizabeth   I don't want to marry him.

Cecily   I don't want to marry him either.

They embrace tightly and urgently.

Elizabeth   He says I'm to leave my belongings. He'll buy me new clothes and a wardrobe in which to hang them.

She touches a hand to the wall of the wardrobe.

It belonged to our brothers; then 'twas mine; now 'tis yours.

Voice (*calling from off*)   Elizabeth!

The girls break apart.

Elizabeth   Oh God's death!

Cecily (*grabbing the axe, dagger and spoon*)   Go, go, I'll put them away. Go!

Elizabeth *wipes her face.*

Elizabeth   How do I look?

Cecily   Tired.

Elizabeth   You are supposed to say, 'Like a Queen.' And then we're supposed to have another 'symbolic moment'.

Cecily   How many 'symbolic moments' do you want to have, Elizabeth?

Elizabeth (*scoffing*)   Very well then.

She kisses her sister and exits.

Cecily *returns their stash of stolen goods to the secret compartment. She hesitates on the dagger, staring at it a moment, before burying the thought along with the dagger below.*

She exits the wardrobe.

Scene Two

The house of the Santamaria family, England, 12 May 1633, evening.

We can hear the sound of a church congregation singing Christian hymns or similar sounds of the time and place.

Since the late thirteenth century Jews have not been permitted legally to reside in England. During the Spanish Inquisition, the Ben-Moshe family (of Jewish descent) converts to Christianity under duress. They adopt the name of the church in which they were baptised, the Santa Maria, before being expelled from Spain and fleeing to England. Here they maintain the Jewish traditions of their ancestors in secret while publicly adhering to the Christian faith.

Two brothers – **Benjamin**, *seventeen years old, and* **Daniel**, *thirteen years old – sit opposite each other in the wardrobe, practising Hebrew. A candle or lantern glows between them filling the space with warm light. (Female performers could play the siblings as sisters:* **Ruth**, *the elder sister, and* **Abigail**, *the younger. If so, references to 'brother' should be changed to 'sister', and changes need to be made to the gender of the words spoken in Hebrew. Plus, the question in the opening section of dialogue, 'Are you a woman?', should be swapped with 'Are you a man?').*

Benjamin   'I.'

Daniel   *Ani.*

Benjamin   'I want.'

Daniel   *Ani . . . rotsa.*

Benjamin   Are you a woman?

Daniel   No.

Benjamin   Then you do not say, *Ani rotsa*, but *Ani rotse*.
Say it.

Daniel   *Ani rotse.*

Benjamin   Good. What is 'fish'?

Daniel   *Dag.*

Benjamin   So all together: 'I want one fish.'

Daniel   *Ani rotse dag a^at.*

Benjamin   No, 'fish' is masculine. So the 'one' has to
reflect the masculinity of the fish, and so you must say *e^ad*
not *a^at*, yes? Again.

Daniel   *Ani rotse dag e^ad.*

Benjamin   Good, very good. 'I want one fish and three
cakes.'

Daniel *groans.*

Benjamin   Daniel.

Daniel   *Ani rotse dag e^ad ve'shalosh ugat.*

Benjamin   I want one fish, three cakes and a bracelet.

Daniel   Do we have to?

Benjamin   Yes.

Daniel   It seems such a waste of time.

Beat.

Benjamin   Forgive me, brother. You are right: your time
could be so much better spent adventuring for treasures in
your nostrils and depositing them on the rims of cups.

Daniel   I don't do that. Any more. Besides, today I did in
fact unearth a treasure.

Benjamin   From your nose?

Daniel   From the market – such a thing as you have never seen!

He reaches into his pocket; **Benjamin** *stops him.*

Benjamin   No.

Daniel   But wait till you see it!

Benjamin   I said no. We came in here to study.

Daniel   But I'm never going to ask anybody for one fish, three cakes and a bracelet in Hebrew: this is 1633 and we live in England! So what is the point?

Benjamin   'Tis the language of our ancestors.

Daniel   Our ancestors are dead.

Beat.

Benjamin   What has taken hold of you?

Daniel   Nothing.

Benjamin   What happened?

Daniel   Nothing happened. I'm just sick of the hypocrisy. We go to church on Sunday and beg forgiveness for our sins from Jesus Christ, then run home, hide in our wardrobe, and whisper in a forbidden language. 'Tis no wonder they call us filthy, lying *merranos*!

He attempts to exit. **Benjamin** *stops him.*

Benjamin   Where did you hear that?

Daniel   Why do you not you teach me French?

Benjamin   Who said that to you?

Daniel   Or Dutch, or something actually useful? Do you not want to travel and see the world? Today I saw things that took my breath away.

He reaches into his pocket.

Benjamin   Who called you a *merrano*? Daniel, 'tis very important that you –

Daniel *pulls from his pocket a banana and holds it aloft.*
Benjamin *stops short and stares. Neither boy has ever seen one in their life before today.*

Benjamin   What is that?

Daniel   Is it not magnificent!

Benjamin *takes the banana from* **Daniel**.

Benjamin   How strange . . . (*Sniffing the banana.*) Most peculiar . . . Is it a lemon?

Daniel   No. No, it is absolutely not a lemon. But 'tis a fruit.

Benjamin   Is it poisonous?

Daniel   No, I saw a man eat three in a row and walk away unscathed.

Benjamin *sniffs the banana again*

Daniel   'Tis from Bermuda!

Benjamin   Bermuda . . . ?

Daniel *nods.*

Benjamin   Does it have a name?

Daniel   Indeed. They call it the (*mispronouncing*) banana.

Benjamin   The (*repeating the mispronunciation*) banana?

Daniel   Yes. Apparently it is sweet, and sticky.

Benjamin (*mispronouncing*)   Banana . . .

He sticks out his tongue and tentatively licks the banana skin. He grimaces.

Benjamin   Urgh.

Daniel   No, you grout-head, we have to peel it first.

Benjamin *searches the banana for an obvious way to peel it; it perplexes him.*

Benjamin   Well . . . how do I get in?

He attempts to snap the stalk (as we would normally do).

Daniel   No, that is the handle.

Benjamin   The handle?

Daniel   Of course. Hold it by the handle.

Benjamin *holds the banana by the stalk.*

Daniel   Now, I only saw him do this once . . .

He proceeds to peel the banana as a monkey would by pinching the dry, brown, blossom end between the forefinger and thumb of each hand and peeling the two sides apart to reveal the fruit inside. They both marvel at it.

Daniel   Go on.

Benjamin *takes a bite of the banana. He chews it slowly.* **Daniel** *takes a bite and chews slowly as well. After a moment they both nod in approval.*

Daniel   It is sweet.

Benjamin   And soft.

Daniel   Mushy.

Benjamin   Sticky.

Daniel   It is like sticky mashed potatoes.

Benjamin   With honey.

Daniel   Yes.

Benjamin   Most . . .

Daniel   Satisfying. (*Reaching into his pocket and retrieving a second banana.*) I have another.

Benjamin   If you were at the market, then you were not at school.

Daniel   Shall I open it or would you like to try?

Benjamin   Why were you not at school? Daniel?

Daniel *reaches into his pocket again, and instead of another banana he retrieves a quarto, a printed pamphlet, and tosses it towards* **Benjamin**, *who reads the front cover aloud.*

Benjamin   'The Famous Tragedy of the Rich Jew of Malta by Christopher Marlowe.'

Daniel   There is to be a revival by the Queen Henrietta's Men at the Cockpit theatre in London. I am going to see it with my class. Oliver Goodwyn said, in front of everybody, that I was surely looking forward to wallowing in the mud of my Jewish ancestry like the *merrano* pig I am. (*Beat.*) I do not see why I should be despised because of who my great, great grandparents were. I never met them. I can't even speak their boil-brained language!

Pause.

Benjamin   I know you wish to be like everybody else. But rather than thinking of yourself as different, why not think of yourself as having a secret instead?

Beat.

Daniel   A secret? (*Scoffing.*) I'm not a child: I'm thirteen.

Benjamin   I am eighteen and I think of it as a secret – a secret we share. The same secret our mother and father share. And their mother and father before them. And this – (*Gesturing to the confines of the wardrobe.*) This is a place for secrets.

Daniel   This is a wardrobe.

Benjamin   That's what a wardrobe is for – to guard your secrets. Warden, warder, wardrobe. And it is nearly one hundred and fifty years old. So imagine what secrets it has kept guard over in all that time. Father says it belonged to the aunt of King Henry the Eighth. Cecily something.

Daniel   Really . . .

Benjamin   But she fell out of favour and the King banished her to live in a nunnery, and sold all her belongings! When our grandfather fled Spain and came to this country he bought these pieces of English tradition. He wrapped them around himself like a disguise.

Daniel   Like a masked hero . . .

Benjamin   Yes, exactly. But on the inside, in here, we take off the mask and be ourselves. Our ancestors may be dead, but when we admit to who we truly are we keep their spirit alive.

Beat.

Daniel   What if I do not want a secret? I did not ask for it.

Benjamin   Nobody ever asks for a secret. A secret asks for you.

Daniel   How long do I have to keep it?

Benjamin   Not long. There will be synagogue in London in our lifetime.

Daniel   Do you really think so?

Benjamin   And when we go there, do you want to be the only one who cannot ask for a one fish, three cakes and a banana in Hebrew? Is banana masculine or feminine? What do you think?

They both look at the second, unpeeled banana.

Together   Masculine.

Benjamin   So then: one fish, three cakes and a banana.

Daniel   *Ani rotse dag e^ad ve'uga shalosha ve'banana.*

The brothers smile at one another.

Scene Three

A master bedroom of the Ainsley family home, Bolton, England, 28 May 1644, afternoon.

We hear the sounds of gunfire and explosions or similar sounds of the time and place – the first English Civil War between the Parliamentarians and the Royalists, now entering its third year.

The strongly Parliamentarian town of Bolton, near Manchester, is stormed and captured by the Royalists under Prince Rupert of the Rhine. Unlike a formal siege, usually preceded by a parley and ended by a negotiated surrender, the suddenness of the attack leaves the town without the protection of any laws or contemporary conventions of warfare, and the Royalist soldiers have been allowed to plunder the town and take whatever and whomever they want as reward.

Two of the Ainsley children, **Matilda**, *sixteen years old, and* **Henry**, *thirteen years old, seek shelter in the wardrobe. Dull afternoon light shines though the ornamental holes casting them in shadow. They shake with fear and hold each other close. Suddenly the door handle turns.* **Matilda** *screams.* **Henry** *struggles to jam the door handle shut but he's not strong enough – the door opens.* **Tobias**, *eighteen years old, the third of the Ainsley children, enters. He is wet from the rain.* **Henry** *stifles* **Matilda**'s *scream by clamping a hand over her mouth. Sounds of screaming and gunfire can be heard beyond the wardrobe through the window of the bedroom out on to the street.*

Henry   Toby! Matilda, it's only Toby!

He pulls **Tobias** *into the wardrobe.*

Matilda (*embracing* **Tobias**)   Oh Toby, thank heaven – you're alive!

Tobias   Matilda, Henry – are you hurt?

Matilda   No, we're well. (*Noticing blood on his clothes.*) You're bleeding.

Tobias   'Tis not mine.

Matilda *stares in horror at the blood*

Matilda   Where is Mother?

Tobias *doesn't answer*

Matilda   No . . . oh no . . .

Henry *makes to exit the wardrobe.*

Tobias   No, Henry!

He grabs his brother and bars his exit from the wardrobe.

Tobias   Henry, pray listen to me: you cannot go out there – it's bedlam! They're shooting people in the streets, there's blood and rain running in the gutters, you can hardly breathe for musket smoke.

Henry   But I must find her.

Tobias (*holding him back*)   I saw a boy insult a soldier and the soldier smashed his head with a rifle butt.

Matilda   Then, I'll go.

Tobias (*barring **Matilda**'s exit*)   Women are lying in the streets, dresses torn from their bodies. They are Royalist pigs and they'll show you no mercy – you cannot go outside. We have not choice but to hide in here.

Matilda   But Mother . . .

Tobias   'Tis too late.

Matilda *weeps.*

Tobias   All will be well. I promise you. How often have we played in here? No harm could come to us in here.

*The door of the wardrobe rattles. **Henry** and **Tobias** pull on the handle to keep the door shut. A serving girl, **Caryl**, sixteen years old, can be heard calling through the door.*

Caryl (*calling from off*)   Tis Caryl. Let me in!

Matilda   Toby, 'tis Caryl, she works in the kitchen.

Caryl (*calling from off*)   Please, Sir Tobias! Mistress Matilda, let me in!

Matilda   Toby, let her inside.

Tobias   There's no room. (*Calling through the door.*) You'll have to find somewhere else.

Caryl   Please, they're coming. They're coming!

Henry   Let her in, Toby.

Matilda   Toby, let her in!

Tobias *opens the door and pulls* **Caryl** *into the wardrobe. He slams the door shut behind her. She has blood on her face and in her hair.*

Caryl (*shaking with fear*)   They pulled Elsie into the street by her hair. Her hand got trapped in the door.

Tobias   Shush.

Caryl   'Tis still there on the mat.

Tobias   Be quiet!

Caryl *falls silent. The four of them organise themselves within the wardrobe. They are pressed up against the walls; possibly one is pushed into a sitting position while the others stand. Perhaps they pile on top of each other. There is hardly any room for any movement.*

Caryl   I can't, ouch –

Matilda   Henry, you're squashing me!

Caryl   Ow!

Tobias   Quiet! Nobody make a sound!

An unspecific noise is heard beyond the wardrobe. They freeze in terror.

Matilda   What was that?

Tobias *puts his fingers to his sister's lips.* **Caryl***'s breathing becomes laboured. Another unspecific sound is heard beyond the wardrobe.*

Caryl   I . . . Please, can you –

All   Shhh!

Caryl   I'm sorry, I can't . . . I can't breathe . . . in small spaces, please . . . .

Tobias   Be quiet, Caryl.

Caryl   I'm sorry, I can't –

Matilda   Caryl, there is somebody outside.

Caryl   No, you have to let me out. Help.

Tobias   Caryl, be quiet.

Caryl (*with rising hysteria*)   Help. Help me.

Tobias *clamps a hand over* **Caryl***'s mouth.* **Caryl** *fights to pull it off.*

Matilda   Please, Caryl.

Henry   Shh, Caryl.

Matilda   If they find us, they'll kill us.

Caryl *begins to struggle.* **Tobias** *applies increasing force to restrain her.*

Caryl (*pulling his hand free*)   Let me out, help! Help me!

The others attempt to restrain her. They push and pull her down on to the floor of the wardrobe; they pull a dress off a hanger and smother her mouth. **Caryl** *kicks and flails, but they apply pressure until the kicking and flailing subsides.* **Caryl** *suffocates and dies. Suddenly footsteps can be heard just beyond the wardrobe. They freeze. The door handle of the wardrobe turns. An explosion is heard beyond the house in the street. The door handle is released and the footsteps recede and disappear.*

They look at **Caryl***, who lies limp in their arms.*

Henry (*attempting to leave*)   I think I shall be sick.

Tobias (*holding* **Henry** *back*)   No, you can't go out there.

Henry   They've gone.

Tobias   How can you know? They might come back. We must stay in here.

Henry   I can't, not with . . .

Tobias   You must.

Henry   She's dead. We killed her.

Matilda (*gently rocking* **Caryl**)   There, there, Caryl . . .

Henry   We killed her.

Tobias   Listen very carefully: we came into the bedroom and we found her like this. A Royalist pig soldier had smothered her to death because she served a Parliamentarian family. We brought her into the wardrobe with us so that her body might not be defiled. She will never be a prisoner of Prince Rupert of the Rhine because now she is free.

Matilda   There now, Caryl . . .

Henry   How long shall we stay in here?

Tobias   All night if we must.

Henry *leans against the wall, exhausted;* **Tobias** *stands guard;* **Matilda** *gently rocks* **Caryl** *in her arms.*

Matilda   Hush now, Caryl . . . all will be well . . .

Scene Four

A bedroom of the Barwicke family home London, England, 18 September 1665, morning.

We hear baroque music or similar sounds of the time and place.

The Great Plague of London is at its height. The Barwicke family have evacuated to Oxfordshire leaving the house under the rule of the servants. Ladies' maids **Anne**, *seventeen years old,* **Mary**, *sixteen years old, and* **Sarah**, *sixteen years old, abscond from their duties to gossip in the wardrobe. Bright morning light shines through the ornamental holes.*

Sarah   I find it most amusing. (*Referring to the wardrobe.*) The mistress spends a royal fortune on the furniture only to flee to the country leaving it to stand empty.

Mary   I find it most convenient: since they left, there's been nothing to do.

Anne   I find it most inconvenient: the less there is to do, the more Red-Faced-Ramsey hounds us.

Sarah   Would he ever think to look in here?

Anne   Imagine if he did – three girls in one cupboard!

The girls laugh and imitate Red-Faced-Ramsay.

Anne   I'm so bored. I want to go for a walk, I want to eat hot rolls fresh from the bakery – I want to go to the theatre!

The others groan; they've heard this a thousand times before.

Sarah (*imitating* **Anne**)   'The King's Company has followed King Charles to Oxford!'

Mary (*imitating* **Anne**)   'They perform privately for him, don't you know!'

Sarah (*imitating* **Anne**)   'I am jealous beyond all measure!'

Anne   Mock me all you want, but as soon as the company returns I shall go straight to the theatre manager, Thomas Killigrew, and dazzle him with my audition piece.

Sarah *and* **Mary** (*imitating* **Anne**)   'Audition piece.'

Sarah   Yes, we know.

Mary   Why do you so desire to be an actress?

Sarah   Oh please don't encourage her.

Anne   I remember as though it were yesterday the first actress to ever grace the stage: Margaret Hughes playing Desdemona. Oh it caused such a stir! She was magnificent. I knew then there was nothing else I'd rather do.

Sarah   My father says that all actresses are . . . *ladies of the night.*

Anne   Well, performances are early evening actually, plus a Saturday matinee.

Mary   She means 'prostitute'.

Anne   Prostitute! Your father said that all actresses are prostitutes?

Sarah   Well, not exactly.

Anne   What exactly did he say?

Sarah   Pox-ridden, festering whores. He said they're to be shunned like the pla –

She stops short of uttering the word 'plague'. There follows a short pause.

Anne   Mark you, I am not the sort of girl to be selling anything other than my talent. Await the day, for it shall come, when all shall know my name.

She takes a small instrument out of her pocket and carves her initials into the wall of the wardrobe.

They will say it all over town. You will hear my name called from the taverns to the turrets of the tower.

Mary (*reading the inscription*)   A.R.

Anne   Anne Ransford! This wardrobe will be worth a fortune for the simple fact of my having trodden its boards. (*Beat.*) I just wish they would hurry home so I can perform my audition piece.

Mary   Show us then.

Sarah   Oh Lord above . . .

Mary   Ignore her. Go on.

Sarah   If you must.

Anne *stands and recites a speech from Shakespeare (a speech from*
Macbeth *is used as an example, but any other could be substituted).*

Anne
> The raven himself is hoarse,
> That croaks the fatal entrance of Duncan
> Under my battlements. Come, you spirits
> That tend on mortal thoughts, unsex me here,
> And fill me from the crown to the toe top-full
> Of direst cruelty! Make thick –

Sarah *coughs.*

Sarah *(clearing her throat)*   Sorry, carry on.

Anne
>   Make thick my blood;
> Stop up the access and passage to remorse,
> That no compunctious visitings of nature
> Shake my fell purpose, nor keep peace between –

Sarah *coughs a second time.* **Anne** *and* **Mary** *look at her with rising
alarm.*

Sarah   It's very good. Who wrote it? Play on.

Anne
> Come. Come to my woman's breasts.
> And take my milk for gall, you murdering ministers,
> Wherever in your sightless substances
> You wait on nature's mischief! Come thick night
> And pall thee in the dunnest smoke of hell – !

Sarah *coughs, and when she takes her hand away from her mouth there
is blood on her fingers.*

Sarah   It's not . . . it's just a cough.

*Suddenly the others pounce on her; they pull up her dress to look for signs
of plague – buboes – on her thighs.* **Sarah** *fights them.*

Sarah   It is just a cough. Coughing is not even a symptom!
Stop it!

The girls search her thighs but find no evidence of plague.

See? There's nothing.

The girls feel in her armpits; they find nothing.

I don't have it. I do not have the plague.

Mary and **Anne** *sigh with relief; they lean back and catch their breath.*

Mary Sorry, Sarah.

Anne Yes, sorry.

Sarah What would you have done? Thrown me out on to the street? I have nowhere else to go.

Mary Nor I.

Anne Nor I.

Sarah Go on, then. Finish your audition speech. It was quite good.

Anne (*wiping perspiration from her forehead and reciting once more*)
                              Come thick night
  And pall thee in the dunnest smoke of hell,
  That my keen knife . . .
  Not see the wound it makes
  Nor heaven peep . . . peep through the blanket of the dark
  To cry, h – hold!

She cries out in agony and sinks to the ground.

Mary Bravo!

Sarah Very realistic.

Mary Anne?

Anne *groans in agony.* **Sarah** *continues to applaud.*

Mary Sarah, stop. I think she is serious. Anne?

Sarah Anne?

Mary   Anne, what is it? Where does it hurt?

Mary *and* **Sarah** *pounce on her. They pull up her dress to reveal swollen lymph glands (buboes) across her thighs. They recoil in fear.* **Anne** *pulls down her dress in shame.*

Mary (*making to leave*)   We need to call a doctor.

Anne   There are no doctors left. Even so, who would care about me? Who would hurry to the bedside of a serving girl? (*Reaching out a hand.*) Please do not leave me.

Mary   We can't touch you. You know that. We can't even stand beside you.

Anne *withdraws her hand and lies down to weep.*

Mary (*making to leave*)   Sarah? Come.

Sarah   Wait.

Sarah *pulls a robe off a hanger and dresses in it backwards, as though it were a doctor's gown; she finds a pair of silk gloves hanging on the rail and pulls them on.*

Sarah (*to* **Mary**)   Help me.

Mary *fastens the robe at her back. She tends to* **Anne**.

Sarah   Await the day, for it shall come when all shall know thy name. They'll say it all over town. We'll hear thy name called from the taverns to the turrets of the tower, Anne Ransford.

Mary *ties a scarf around* **Sarah**'s *mouth to act as a face mask.* **Mary** *pulls on a pair of gloves. The two girls lift* **Anne** *off the floor and help her to exit the wardrobe.*

Scene Five

Any time between 1665 and 1770, night.

The wardrobe is no longer in England and has instead been sold to a family abroad. (The scene is to be translated into whichever language is relevant or interesting to the players.)

We hear sounds of the time and place.

One, *a seventeen-year-old, and* **Two**, *a fifteen-year-old, kneel opposite one another. (The sex of the characters can be assigned to suit availability.)* **One** *teaches* **Two** *how to defend against attack. They work by the light of a lantern of a style native to the time and place.* **One** *has* **Two** *in a chokehold.*

One   What do you do? What do you do?

Two *places her/his hands on* **One**'s *arms and attempts to remove them. She/he is unsuccessful.*

One   I am stronger than you. You have to get out of my grip. What do you do?

Two *doesn't respond*

One   Lift your right arm. Lift your right arm.

Two *reluctantly lifts her/his right arm.*

One   Swing it over my head and turn away from me. Do it.

Two *reluctantly swings her/his right arm in an anticlockwise motion over* **One**'s *head and turns around so that she/he is facing away from* **One**.

One   See, I've lost my hold on your neck. Yes? Now bend you left arm and raise your elbow. Aim for my head. (*Demonstrating.*) Bend your elbow like this, thrust it into the side of his head. One clean motion.

One *demonstrates the whole manoeuvre, swinging over the head with the right arm and punching with the left elbow.*

See? Yes? Your turn. Come on. Quickly.

Two *attempts the manoeuvre.*

One   Over with the right; up with the left. Faster.

Two *attempts to do the manoeuvre more quickly.*

One   Yes, good, run.

One *pushes* **Two** *away.*

One   But he will come after you. (*Catching* **Two**'s *wrists from behind.*) He will try to stop you.

One *now holds* **Two** *securely by the wrists from behind.*

One   What do you do?

Two *halfheartedly wriggles her/his wrists to try and get free.*

One   Pull your hands forward as though you were lifting a weight.

One *demonstrates the manoeuvre, lifting her/his hands as though lifting weights.*

He will lose his grip and then, as before, you turn to face him and punch with your elbow. Try it.

Two *reluctantly attempts the manoeuvre.*

One   Use your weight. Faster. Yes. But if he comes after you again . . .

One *presses* **Two** *up against the wall of the wardrobe.*

One   What do you do?

Two *struggles to break free of* **One**'s *grip.*

One   No, that's what he wants. He wants to exhaust you. He will keep going until there is no fight left in you. So what do you do?

Two (*pushing one away in frustration*)   I don't know.

Beat.

One   If a small bird flies into the room and I catch her in my hands what will she do? She will flap her wings and struggle, and I will tighten my grip around her until she is spent. But if instead she lies still and says, 'Please don't hurt me. Do want you want with me. I won't struggle', she convinces me she has nothing left, I open my hands and she takes off and flies away.

One *pushes* **Two** *up against the wall again.*

One   If he comes after you again, what do you do?

Two *struggles against* **One**.

Two   No, stop it. I don't want to do this any more. Get off me.

One   Don't fight, that's what he wants.

Two (*fighting*)   I said get off. Get off me!

Two *struggles, but* **One** *is too strong for her/him;* **Two** *remains pinned against the wall. Eventually she/he surrenders.*

Two   Please don't hurt me. Do want you want with me. I won't struggle.

One *relaxes her/his grip on* **Two**. *Immediately* **Two** *completes the self-defence manoeuvre: she/he swings an arm over* **One**'s *head, turns away and raises her/his elbow to affect a blow to the head. It is a proficient move.* **One** *is taken by surprise.*

One   Good. Good. Again.

Scene Six

A bedroom of Kenwood House, Hampstead, London, 5 May 1780, afternoon.

We hear music by Mozart or similar sounds of the time and place.

Dido Elizabeth Belle, *thirteen years old, is the illegitimate daughter of Sir John Lindsay, a British Navy captain, and an enslaved*

woman whom Sir John encountered while his ship was in the Caribbean.
Dido *is mixed race. She resides in the house of her childless great-uncle,*
William Murray, Lord Mansfield. A decade earlier, Lord Mansfield, a
leading judge, made a famous judgment in court freeing a slave from
imprisonment by his master on the basis that slavery was unsupported by
law in England and Wales (although this did not end slave-trafficking in
Britain altogether).

The door to the wardrobe opens, and **Dido** *quietly enters. She pushes*
aside the dresses hanging on the rail and clears a space for herself. The
afternoon sun filters through the ornamental holes, piercing her with
shards of light. She kneels on the floor and clasps her hands in prayer.
She hesitates, strains to listen, and when satisfied that nobody can hear
her begins to pray.

Dido   Dear God, my heavenly Father, thank you for today.
Thank you for the good weather we enjoyed and for the birds
outside my window. Thank you most especially for the fat
pigeon that comes to rest in the old oak. I have named him
Charlie. Fat Charlie. Thank you for coffee – powerful, rich
coffee. I'm grateful for the strong flavour that cuts through
my sluggish morning mouth. I'm grateful for the two hours'
work I did this morning. I'm grateful for the pages I edited,
and the progress I helped Uncle William to make with his
accounts. I'm grateful that you can't get lead poisoning from
stabbing yourself with a pencil. Thank you for that lovely
moment just now when I mouthed to Uncle William, 'I love
you', and he mouthed in return, 'I love you too, my dear.'
I am so grateful to have the love of this family. What else . . . ?
Oh yes, I'm so grateful that I am no longer scared of bees.
And thank you for this beautiful wardrobe, which my uncle
gave to me so I might hang my beautiful clothes in here.
Thank you for the smell of the wood, and the reassuring feel
of the panels under my knees holding me up. Thank you for a
place I can come to when I need to be alone. Thank you also
for the fact I could talk to Elizabeth for an hour about her
upcoming trip to the Derby race and I didn't feel hopelessly
dissatisfied that I will not attend. I am learning that the secret
to happiness is not how successful you are, or what people say

about you, or how you look, or whether your parents were married, but whether or not you can be thankful for what you have. And so, right now, in this moment, I am grateful to my uncle and his wife for all they have done for me and rescued me from. Today I am so grateful that I am not enslaved upon a ship, as my mother was. I am so grateful to my uncle that he struck down slavery in court. And because of him I live without fear of torture and oppression. I don't know why I've been dealt such a fortunate hand, but to whomever is responsible for my lucky, lucky fate I am truly, truly thankful. Even though my illegitimacy and the colour of my skin mean that I am not eligible to eat with the family at the table, or join their guests for dinner, or attend the Derby with Elizabeth, I am so thankful that the women do invite me to join them for coffee when supper is done. I am so grateful they afford me that kindness; they show me such unwavering generosity.

Suddenly she pulls a dress violently off a hanger and throws it down; she smacks the wall of the wardrobe in distress. She cradles her injured hand. She catches her breath. She clasps her hands in prayer once again.

Forgive me, Father, forgive my ungratefulness. Forgive my indulgence, my impatience, my selfishness. (*Short pause.*) I'm grateful to the concept of gratefulness for giving me a way to encourage happy thoughts and feelings. Thank you for giving me a way out of the dark and into the light.

Dido *kneels in silence for a moment. She kisses her hands and raises them to the heavens. She stands and smoothes her dress. She stares into space for a moment, all enthusiasm lost, before bracing herself and exiting the wardrobe.*

Scene Seven

A child's bedroom of the Hughes' family house, Liverpool, England, 2 August 1805, morning. We hear music by Beethoven or similar sounds of the time and place.

Britain has been a leader in the Atlantic slave trade for the past two centuries. While most of the slaves concerned are transported from Africa to the Americas, many arrive in England to work as household servants; some are paid while others are considered property. William Wilberforce's Slave Trade Act will not abolish the slave trade in the British Empire for another two years. Slavery itself will not be abolished in the British Empire for another twenty-eight years.

The door of the wardrobe opens and **William**, *sixteen years old, enters.* **William** *is an unpaid domestic servant to the Hughes family, brought to England from Africa as a slave at the age of three. He carries a freshly laundered coat belonging to his master's son,* **Jaffrey**, *also sixteen years old.* **William** *hangs the coat on the rail and smoothes the cloth. Suddenly he climbs into the wardrobe and closes the door behind him. He takes the coat off the hanger and dresses in it. He runs his hands over the fine embroidery. Suddenly the door to the wardrobe door opens and* **Jaffrey** *stands at the entrance staring at him; it is clear* **Jaffrey** *has been crying. Morning light filters through the ornamental holes. (Female players could perform this scene by simply changing the names.)*

Jaffrey   William!

William *(bowing his head in deference)*   Master Jaffrey.

Jaffrey   Why are you wearing my coat?

William   Forgive me.

Jaffrey   Take it off.

William *(removing the coat)*   Forgive me.

Jaffrey   Take it off at once.

William *(returning the coat to its hanger)*   I only meant to check the fit. I was hoping the process of steam-cleaning had not shrunk it.

Jaffrey   Wash it again. Return it to be washed again.

William   Of course, Master Jaffrey.

Jaffrey   Out. Get. Out.

William *bows to* **Jaffrey** *and exits.* **Jaffrey** *enters in his place and vents his frustrations on the clothes by shoving them aggressively aside and sinking on to the floor in a sulk. There is a knock on the door of the wardrobe; it startles* **Jaffrey**.

Jaffrey   Yes?

William   Master Jaffrey, it is I, William.

Jaffrey   Go away, William.

William   Please may I –

Jaffrey (*opening the door of the wardrobe*)   William, I said go away.

To his surprise **William** *climbs back inside the wardrobe.*

William   I am afraid I cannot do that, Master Jaffrey.

He closes the wardrobe door behind him, confining them both inside.

Jaffrey   What are you doing?

William   You see, if I return your coat to Miss Emily to clean, I shall have to explain why. And while I find it easy enough to lie to you, I should not like to lie to her.

Jaffrey   How dare you!

William   For she will be forced to report the misdemeanour to my master, your father, and I cannot have him know, so we shall have to come to some agreement, as gentlemen.

Jaffrey   How can you call yourself a gentleman?

William   You will not mention that I took the liberty of wearing your coat and you will not ask me to make mention of it either. And, in return, I will not mention what I saw pass between you and Master Arthur Scott, the night before last, in the passage leading from the library.

Jaffrey *stares at* **William** *in horror. Suddenly he lunges at him and they struggle.* **William**, *much the stronger, pins* **Jaffrey** *against the wall.*

Jaffrey   Let me go. Let me go at once!

William   Do we have an agreement?

Jaffrey *wriggles free of* **William**'s *grip and darts for the door.*

William   Do not doubt me, Master Jaffrey, I shall tell of what I saw!

Jaffrey (*stopping by the door*)   If you dare, I shall see you hang for it, do you understand me? It would be so easy for me.

He pulls the coat off the rack and scrunches it into a ball.

Father, my coat is missing . . . I last gave it to William to press . . . Father, do you think he might have stolen it? I remember I saw him admiring it the other day. He was touching it all over with his dirty fingers. We would watch you jerk and swing on the end of a rope within a week.

William   The master would not believe me a thief.

Jaffrey   Oh William . . . Poor deluded William . . . Do you really believe he would accept your word over mine? My father will never see you as a son. You are at best a pet, at worst nothing more than this wardrobe: to be bought and sold, one family to another.

William   You need not see me as your rival; I do not seek his love.

Jaffrey   His love! William, you embarrass yourself. You'd do well to remember your station.

He turns to leave

William   I have a friend who serves Arthur Scott's father.

Jaffrey *pauses by the door.*

William   My friend tells me he is a very cruel man, and that he is known to beat Arthur until his skin breaks. While you sit back and watch as I jerk and swing from a rope, you can be sure your good friend Arthur's bones will twist and break against his father's stick.

Jaffrey (*with sudden rage and alarm*)   If any harm comes to Arthur I swear will, I swear to God I will –

William   What? What will you do? I will already have been hanged. Master Jaffrey, there is no need for any one to hang, or for any bones to break, or for any masters to be told secrets and lies. I will never mention to a living soul what I saw, if you agree to do the same.

Jaffrey *stares at him in anger.*

William   You've never liked me; I know it. I've never liked you. There's no shame in that; we cannot all like each other. Your father has promised to endow me with my freedom upon his death. On that day, I swear to it, you shall never see me again. You shan't have to wait long: his health worsens by the day.

Jaffrey   As does his temper.

Beat.

William   So, then. Are we agreed?

He extends his hand to **Jaffrey** *to shake on the deal.* **Jaffrey** *stares at his hand.*

William   There is a first time for everything.

Jaffrey *shakes* **William**'*s hand.*

William   It's settled then. Good day to you, Master Jaffrey.

He makes to exit.

Jaffrey   William?

William   Yes, Master Jaffrey.

Jaffrey (*handing* **William** *the crumpled coat*)   This needs pressing.

Jaffrey *exits the wardrobe.* **William** *follows shortly after.*

Scene Eight

A child's bedroom of the Hughes' family house, Liverpool, England, 9 July 1827.

During the years of the Industrial Revolution, as manufacture in Britain transitions from hand-production methods to machines, children as young as four are employed in factories with dangerous and often fatal working conditions. By the early nineteenth century England has more than one million child workers who make up fifteen per cent of the labour force.

The doors to the wardrobe open and **Robert***, sixteen years old, drags* **Martin***, nine years old, inside, slamming the door shut.* **Martin** *carries a lit ship's lantern, which he uses to light the chimney for cleaning. (Female performers could play this scene by changing the names.)*

Martin   Get off me!

Robert   Get in there.

Martin   I weren't going to –

Robert   Keep yer voice down.

Martin (*more quietly*)   I weren't going to take it. I were just lookin' at it.

Robert   You were just lookin' at it?

Martin   It were really shiny.

Robert   It were really shiny. Ain't nobody taught you how to lie better 'n that?

Martin   I ain't lying. I just – I just wanted to touch one of 'em. What's a person need that many teaspoons for anyhow? All lined up on display like that.

Robert   For eating jelly. That's right, they all congregate en masse and eat jelly.

Martin (*scratching*)   What's 'en masse'?

Robert   It's French. For altogether.

Martin (*scratching*)   I ain't never spoke no French before.

Robert   Well, consider yourself . . . educated. Now your master'll come lookin' for yer any minute, so you best get . . . You haven't got fleas, have yer?

Martin (*showing him the bites*)   I got bites the size of pennies all the way up me leg. Look. You ain't seen nothing like it?

Robert (*looking*)   Call 'em bites? I'll show you a bite. (*Lifting his trouser leg.*) Rat bite. Afore I worked in the main house I worked up the mill. Slept thirteen boys to one room. Bottom bunk weren't so much a bunk as the floor. Floor's crawling with 'em at night.

Martin   How do I know that ain't just a scar?

Robert   Cos I'm telling you it's a bite. You want a scar, I'll show you a scar. (*Pulling open his shirt collar to reveal scars around his neck.*) One morning I was late for work and the master made me wear weights round me neck and walk the length of the mill up and down. Each time I fell he added more weight.

Martin (*pulling up his shirt to reveal welts on his back*)   Once I was late for work and the master beat me with his leather belt strap. See? That's where he caught me with the buckle.

Robert   That ain't worth a fart in a whirlwind. Look at this.

He shows **Martin** *patches of bald scalp.*

Robert   One night they left the doors unlocked. I made it
as far as a field of pigs. I gorged on pig-feed. The master
caught me, held me head on a bench and cut me hair off at
the scalp with a meat cleaver; he took great chunks of skin.
The hair ain't never grown back. And yer know what I says
to him? I said, 'May the fleas of a thousand stray cats find
your crotch, and may your arms be too short to scratch!' For
a week he dragged me naked from my bed and made me join
the assembly line holding me clothes.

Martin *rolls up the sleeve of his shirt to reveal suppurating skin
wounds on his elbows.* **Robert** *reels back in disgust.*

Martin   Comes from pressing your arms against the sides of
the chimney, that way I can hold my body suspended, knees
and elbows pressed against the walls, it peels the skin and
the soot gets in, all different kinds of soot and that causes the
festerin'. (*Rolling shirt higher.*) Look, takes weeks, sometimes
months to heal.

Robert   I lost two teeth when I passed out on the stone
floor from tiredness. We hardly got a wink of sleep, starting at
five in the morning.

Martin   I start at four.

Robert   Six days a week, one meal a day.

Martin   Once I were so hungry I ate acorns.

Robert   Once I were so hungry I ate a turnip frozen out of
the ground.

Martin   Once I were so hungry I ate cabbage.

Robert   What's wrong with cabbage?

Martin   I hate cabbage.

Robert   Once I were so hungry I was feeling faint while
cleaning the loom that I didn't hear the man shouting for me
to crawl out. He let go the brake and the carriage swung back

into place and crushed me arm. I managed to pull it free, but I paid the price with two of me fingers.

Robert *shows* **Martin** *his deformed arm and fingers.*

Robert   I were bleedin' all over the floor, and the blood were mixing with the cotton dust. It were like a field of red snow.

Martin   Once I were working too slowly up the chimney and Master Brindley lights a fire underneath me. Sure made me work quicker. I was dislodging so much soot that it was falling all over me and filling me pockets and getting me wedged. I was calling and begging Brindley to put the fire out, but he were asleep in the yard. The heat melted me three toes together afore a housemaid heard me screaming and fetched a bucket of water and threw it on the flames.

Martin *shows* **Robert** *his deformed toes.*

Martin   Now he doesn't light a fire but strips me naked and sends another boy up behind me with pins to prink the soles of me feet. (*Showing the soles of his feet.*) See? And me buttocks.

He attempts to remove his trousers to show **Robert** *his buttocks.*

Robert   'S all right, I believe you. I believe you.

Martin *smiles, thinking he's won the competition.*

Robert   A few pins, eh? You should consider yourself lucky. To punish me for losing me toes, the master put a nail through me ear.

He offers his ear for inspection. **Martin** *draws near.*

Robert   What happened to your eye?

Martin   Oh, I forgot. Once the master sent me up a chimney to get a stuck bird. It were a pigeon. Me mother says pigeons are just rats with wings. But this one were small, and delicate, and so frightened. She kept flying towards the light but her wings were so heavy with soot. I tried to take hold of her, gentle as I could, but she took fright and clawed at me forehead. She nearly took me eye. I couldn't see for a blood blister the size of a conker.

Robert   What happened to the bird?

Martin *stands and prepares to leave.*

Robert   Sorry, I weren't trying to upset yer –

Martin   I weren't trying to hurt 'er. And I weren't trying to steal 'em spoons. I earn my money. I been up them chimneys since I were six. That's four years. Every time me mother sees me come home with a coin in me hand she cries – big pearl-like tears hanging off 'er eyelashes. Every Sunday we eat meat, and I know I earned my share.

Robert   I weren't trying to –

Martin   Why do I need to explain meself? For all I know, you made the whole thing up. I bet yer just a serving boy who slept his whole life in a bed with feather pillows, serving jelly with silver teaspoons to rich folk in fine houses.

He makes to leave

Robert   When I were five me father sold me to the mill as a pauper apprentice. He told me I'd be transformed into a gentleman. He told me I'd eat roast beef and Yorkshire pudding. He told me I'd have money stuffed deep into me pockets. Me first meal was cold milk-porridge of a very green complexion and me first night I had me first beating 'cause I wouldn't stop crying. When I crushed me arm I was no use to the master no more. He would've turned me out, but as it happened the landowner passed away and his son, Sir Jaffrey, inherited the estate. There were a slave who worked here. He were released according to the landowner's wishes, so they were in need of an errand boy. So here I am. Upon me honour that's the truth.

Martin   I believe yer.

Robert   I believe yer weren't trying to steal a spoon.

They smile at one another.

Robert   You best get back.

Martin *turns to leave; he hesitates.*

Martin   I know thieving is a sin. But just one silver spoon and I need never climb another chimney again.

The boys look at one another. **Martin** *jumps from the wardrobe;* **Robert** *follows close after.*

Scene Nine

A boys' Catholic boarding school attached to an abbey and run by Benedictine monks, England, 11 November 1888. We hear singing choristers or similar sounds of the time and place.

The papers are awash with stories of a series of gruesome murders that have terrorised Whitechapel in London since the summer. **Tom***, fifteen years old,* **Archie***, sixteen years old,* **Hugo***, fifteen years old, and* **James***, sixteen years old, are students of the school. They huddle together in the wardrobe.* **Tom** *reads with flourish from a copy of the London* Times *dated 10 November 1888 by the light of a church candle or candle-lamp.* **Hugo** *scratches his initials into the wall with a knife.*

Tom (*reading*)   'During the early hours of yesterday morning another murder of a most revolting and fiendish character took place in Spitalfields. This is the seventh which has occurred in this immediate neighbourhood, and the character of the mutilations leaves very little doubt that the murderer in this instance is the same person who has committed the previous ones.'

Hugo   I thought there were only four.

James   Shhh!

Tom   'The scene of this last crime is at Number 26 Dorset Street, which is about two hundred yards distant from 35 Hanbury Street, where the unfortunate woman, Mary Ann Nicholls, was so foully murdered.'

Archie   Hugo, what are you doing?

Hugo   Writing my initials. Next to these ones. 'A.R.' Who do we know with the initials A.R.?

James (*to* **Tom**)   Get on with it, Tom.

Tom (*reading*)   'About one o'clock yesterday morning a person living in the court opposite to the room occupied by the woman heard her singing the song "Sweet Violets".'

Archie *sings the song 'Sweet Violets', chorus by Joseph Emmet, taken from his 1882 play* Fritz Among the Gypsies.

Archie (*singing the song*)
   'Sweet violets, sweeter than all the roses . . . '

James (*speaking over* **Archie**'s *singing*)   Shhh! Tom, finish reading it.

Archie (*continuing*)
   'Covered all over from head to toe.'

James   Tom?

Tom and Archie
   'Covered all over with sweet violets.'

Archie (*singing*)
   'There once was a farmer who took a young miss
   In the back of the barn where he gave her a . . . '

Tom
   'Lecture on horses and chickens and eggs
   And told her that she had such beautiful . . . '

Hugo
   'Manners that suited a girl of her charms
   A girl that he wanted to take in his . . . '

Tom
   'Washing and ironing and then if she did
   They would get married and raise lots of . . . '

Archie, Tom *and* **Hugo** (*deliberately taunting* **James**)
'Sweet violets, sweeter than all the roses,
Covered all over from head to toe,
Covered all over with sweet violets . . . !'

James (*snatching the paper from* **Tom**)   Well, if you won't read it, I will.

Hugo *snatches the paper from* **James**. **Archie** *snatches it from* **Hugo** *and returns it to* **Tom**. *They all laugh at* **James**.

James   Just read it, would you?

Archie   Somebody's hungry for all the gory details!

Tom   Maybe he's wondering what the papers are saying about him? If you can sneak out of the dormitory to come here, perhaps you can also sneak off to London.

James   Don't be ridiculous. Just get on with it.

Tom   All right. (*Smoothing the paper, deliberately taking his time. Reading:*) 'At a quarter to eleven yesterday morning, as the woman was thirty-five shillings in arrears with her rent, Mr M'Carthy sent an employee to No. 13 to get some rent. But knocking on the door, he was unable to obtain an answer. He then turned the handle of the door and found it was locked. A pane of glass in one of the windows was broken. He put his hand through the aperture and –

Archie (*shaking* **James** *suddenly*)   Boo!

James *lets out a little cry of shock. They laugh at him.*

James   You're such an infant, Archie.

Archie   You're the one screeching like a little girl.

Tom   Did you think it was the ghost?

The others make ghostly noises.

Tom   They say she was strangled to death.

Archie   In this very wardrobe.

Hugo   By a Royalist soldier during the Bolton Massacre of 1644.

Tom   They say she begged for life. (*Imitating the dying girl.*) Please, please don't kill me.

Hugo *and* **Archie** *re-enact the strangulation.* **Tom** *laughs.*

James (*standing to exit*)   Fine, if you're going to be like this about it.

Tom (*stopping* **James**)   Wait, wait. No more jokes.

James   Promise?

Tom (*crossing his heart with a finger*)   Cross my heart.

He winks at **Archie** *as* **James** *resumes his place.* **Tom** *continues reading (as he progresses through the article his tone sobers).*

Tom (*reading*)   'He put his hand inside the aperture and pulled aside the muslin curtain which covered it. On his looking into the room a shocking sight presented itself. He could see a woman lying on the bed entirely naked, covered with blood and apparently dead. Her throat was cut from ear to ear, right down to the spinal column. The ears and nose had been cut clean off. The breasts had also been cleanly cut off and placed on a table, which was by the side of the bed. The stomach and abdomen had been ripped open, while the face was slashed about, so that the features of the poor creature were beyond all recognition. The kidneys and heart had also been removed from the body and placed on the table by the side of the breasts. The liver had likewise been removed and lain on the right thigh. The lower portion of the body and uterus had been cut out and these appeared to be missing. The thighs had been cut. A more horrible or sickening sight could not be imagined.'

Pause.

James   It's him. It has to be.

Archie   But this is so much more . . .

Hugo   Gruesome.

James   He's evolving. He's developing new techniques.

Tom   Do I detect a hint of excitement, James?

James   No, of course not.

Tom   Do you like the idea of cutting a woman into little pieces?

James   Don't be disgusting. I'm just pointing out that he clearly has a fascination with dissection. Perhaps he's a medical student.

Hugo (*mocking* **James** *by imitating him*)   'Perhaps he's a medical student.'

Archie   Aren't you always reading medical journals?

Tom   James, isn't your father a doctor?

James   Very funny.

Tom   Perhaps they've got it wrong. We shouldn't be calling him Jack the Ripper, but *James* the Ripper!

Archie *cackles.* **James** *swipes at him and they play-fight. Suddenly the door handle of the wardrobe turns. They freeze. There is a heavy knock on the door.*

Tom (*a terrified whisper*)   Father Aloysius.

Archie   No, he's away from the Abbey until tomorrow.

The knocking on the door grows more aggressive.

Hugo   How did he find us?

James   You were laughing so loudly you gave us away!

Tom (*putting a finger to his lips to silence the others; whispering*)   I have the only key.

A key is heard in the lock. The handle of the door turns.

Tom (*imploring the other boys*)   Please don't leave me with him. Please. Please don't leave me with him.

The door of the wardrobe opens a crack; the room beyond is in darkness. One by one the boys exit the wardrobe: first **Archie***, then* **Hugo***, then* **James***.*

Tom (*to* **James** *as he exits*)   Promise me you won't leave me with him.

James *nods and crosses his heart with his finger. But as soon as he exits, the door is slammed shut behind him, sealing* **Tom** *inside.*

Tom   No. No!

The key turns in the lock. **Tom** *struggles to fit his key in the lock to open it, but in his terror he drops the key with trembling hands. He scrambles on the floor of the wardrobe to find the key before resigning himself to the inevitable, curling his knees up to his chest and hugging them close. He waits. He sings softly.*

Tom
   'Sweet violets, sweeter than all the roses . . . '

Scene Ten

An auction house, an industrial city in Great Britain, 19 June 1916.

We hear a recording of 'It's a Long Way to Tipperary' by John McCormack or similar.

The First World War has raged throughout Europe since 1914. In January 1916 a military service bill is introduced providing for the conscription of single men aged eighteen to forty-one. In May conscription was extended to married men.

Nell*, eighteen years old, opens the door the wardrobe. She carries a Sotheby's catalogue under her arm. Her fiancé,* **Anthony***, also eighteen years old, stands close behind. Beyond them can be heard the sounds of a busy English furniture sale.* **Nell** *inspects the wardrobe as* **Anthony** *reads from his own catalogue. The wardrobe is empty.*

Anthony (*reading*)   'A classic wardrobe of Tudor design with detailed carving including the classic Tudor arch and beautifully panelled doors. Handmade, solid mahogany. Believed to have originated in the late 1480s.' (*Looking up from the catalogue.*) That makes it . . . 1480 to 1917 . . . ? Four hundred and thirty years old. I'm surprised it's still standing.

This rouses no response from **Nell**. *She checks the wardrobe meticulously for flaws.*

Anthony   'It is believed that it first belonged to Elizabeth of York, daughter of King Edward the Fourth, and mother of King Henry the Eighth, to whom the wardrobe passed on her death.' Isn't that astonishing? We are touching what royalty once touched.

Nell   Why would Elizabeth of York ever have touched her wardrobe? With all the servants she had, I bet she never even saw the inside of a wardrobe?

Beat.

Anthony (*reading*)   'It was lately the property of Downside Abbey in Somerset. The monks used it to house the robes of choirboys. It was purchased from them privately before being professionally restored for resale. It is estimated to fetch a price at auction of – '

He breaks off.

Nell   How much?

Anthony   Didn't you want a painting?

Nell   How much do they say?

Anthony   Or what about that Victorian vanity table?

Nell *tries to snatch the catalogue from him, but he whisks it away. She opens her own catalogue and begins to search for the wardrobe,* **Anthony** *stops her.*

Anthony   Nell, if you want it, it's yours.

Nell   They've done an adequate job of restoring it I suppose, but there are still signs of wear.

Anthony   It's four hundred years old.

Nell   Look at that stain.

Anthony   It could be a *royal* stain.

Nell *is not amused.*

Anthony   Then what about a mirror?

He is about to turn away when **Nell** *climbs into the wardrobe.*

Anthony   Nell . . . ! Nell, I don't think you're allowed inside it.

Nell (*pulling him inside and shutting the doors*)   Shhh.

Anthony   If we're found in here –

Nell   Anthony, just be quiet.

Anthony *falls silent.* **Nell** *looks around the wardrobe.*

Nell   I always wanted a walk-in wardrobe.

Anthony   I don't think you're supposed to walk into this one.

Nell   I used to say, 'Ma, one day I'm going to have so many clothes they'll need to custom build a wardrobe big enough.' 'Fat chance,' she said. 'People like us have two outfits to their name: a set of flannel pajamas and a serving-apron. That's all you'll ever need.'

Anthony   Then why on earth are we hunting for antiques? I'll build you a wardrobe.

Nell   I don't want you to build me a wardrobe.

Anthony   Then . . . I don't understand. I'm bending over backwards to buy you the perfect wedding present. And if I didn't know you better I'd call you ungrateful.

Nell   I don't want a wedding present for a wedding I might never have.

Beat.

I know we said we wouldn't talk about it. I thought shopping would help. But it's not working. I think we should go home.

She stands to leave. **Anthony** *stops her.*

Nell   Anthony . . .

Anthony *rifles through the catalogue. Finding what he's looking for, he tears a corner from a page.*

Nell   I'm not just in the mood to buy anything.

Anthony (*reading*)   'Eighteen-carat rose-gold Georgian artisan-made wedding band.'

He folds the picture of the ring in half and tears a chunk out of the crease so that when he opens it again the ring has a hole in the middle.

Anthony   'Amazing condition for its age. You can still see the hallmarks. No visible wear.'

He presents her with the paper ring.

Nell   Anthony . . .

Anthony (*taking her hand*)   I, Anthony Edward Leveson-Gower, take you, Ellen Anne Rigby, to be my wedded wife, to have and to hold, for richer for poorer, in sickness and in health from this day forward until death us do part.

He slips the paper ring on to her ring finger.

Anthony   Do you, Ellen Anne Rigby, take me, Anthony Edward Leveson-Gower, to be your wedded husband?

Nell *nods.*

Anthony   You have to say it.

Nell   I, Ellen Anne Rigby, take you, Anthony Edward Leveson-Gower – why do you have to have such a long name? – to be my wedded husband.

Anthony   To have and to hold.

Nell   To have and to hold.

Anthony   For richer for poorer.

Nell   For richer for poorer.

Anthony   In sickness and in health from this day forward –

Nell   In sickness and in health from this day forward –

Anthony   Until death us do part.

Beat.

I'm coming back, Nell.

Nell   If you were just a year younger –

Anthony (*he's heard many times before*)   Nell . . .

Nell   If your birthday had been in January –

Anthony   Not December, I know

Nell   Then you wouldn't qualify for conscription.

Anthony   Maybe the moment I arrive they'll call a victory.
Maybe I'll never see the trenches. And if I do . . . well, I won't
take any risks or show off or anything like that. I'll be sensible.

Nell   No you won't.

Anthony   Yes I will.

Nell   No, you won't be sensible because you're too bloody
. . . *good.* There's nothing you wouldn't do for someone you
cared for. Like going back for a man fallen. Sometimes I wish
you were a bit more of a bastard and put yourself first.

They smile at one another

Until death us do part, then.

Anthony (*smiling with joy*)   A marriage isn't legal until you've
signed the register!

He grabs the catalogue and scribbles on the page. He offers it to her.

Sign your name, here.

Nell *signs her name.*

Anthony   Well. I now pronounce us husband and wife.

He tears the signed sheet out of the catalogue and feeds it through a gap in the wooden boards at the base of the wardrobe into the secret space underneath.

Anthony   I swear upon my honour that I will come back for you, and I will dig it out we'll take it to the town hall and have it signed officially by the mayor.

Nell   But how will you know where to find this wardrobe?

Anthony   Because we're going to buy it.

Nell   But it's so expensive.

Anthony   So what? I might die next week.

Nell (*slapping him on the shoulder*)   You can't make jokes like that.

Anthony   Sorry, from now on consider me silent as the dead.

Nell   Anthony!

Anthony   Come on. This wardrobe isn't going to buy itself!

He exits the wardrobe. **Nell** *follows close behind.*

Scene Eleven

Anywhere in the United Kingdom, anytime post the publication of The Lion, The Witch and The Wardrobe *by C.S. Lewis in 1950, but before the present day.*

We hear music or sounds relevant to the time and place.

A *leads* **B** *into the wardrobe.* **B** *shows some signs of being ill, perhaps (s)he wears a nightgown while* **A** *wears day-clothes, or perhaps (s)he has bandages on her arm, or perhaps (s)he wears a hospital gown.* **A** *carries a copy of* The Lion, The Witch and The Wardrobe *by C.S. Lewis.*

The object of this scene is for **A** *to read to* **B** *from the first chapter of the book while at the same time trying to re-create for* **B** *the experience as described by C.S. Lewis of Lucy's first adventure into the wardrobe.*

I suggest you begin at the moment in Chapter One, when Lucy first steps into the wardrobe. **A** *reads the relevant lines from the text while ushering* **B** *into the wardrobe.* **B** *is initially reluctant and resentful. (S)he interrupts occasionally with protests similar to 'This is so childish' or 'I can't believe you're making me do this'. However,* **A** *insists and they carry on.* **A** *encourages* **B** *to read aloud Lucy's lines of dialogue whenever they occur in order to give her the full 'Lucy experience'. As they continue, it becomes clear that* **A** *has planted props within the wardrobe.*

A *prises open a board in the base of the wardrobe and rummages around underneath for props — for example, a fur hat to represent the fur coats; scrunched newspaper or polystyrene peanuts underfoot to create the sound of crunching snow; a fir branch to brush against* **B**'s *hand; a sieve of icing sugar shaken overhead to re-create falling snow, etc.*

At one point **A** *retrieves the signed catalogue page hidden down there by Anthony in the previous scene.*

A *(reading from the catalogue page)*   Anthony Edward Leveson-Gower . . . Ellen Anne Rigby . . . Who are they?

B   Ellen Rigby is my — *(Insert approriate relation depending how long it's been since the previous scene.)*

A   Who's Anthony Edward Leveson-Gower?

B   No idea . . .

A *tosses the catalogue sheet aside and continues.*

I suggest that **A** *read through the text to the point at which Lucy steps out of the Wardrobe into Narnia and feels the snow falling from the sky. At this point* **A** *opens her/his satchel and attempts to set the scene of Narnia using household props. Please improvise the lines as necessary, but in a similar vein to the following:*

A   See . . . imagine this is the lamp post where she meets . . . and this is the White Witch and this is . . . *(Revealing a stuffed toy.)* Well, I expect you can imagine who this is. And me,

I'm . . . (*Throwing a scarf around his neck, collecting an umbrella.*)
I'm Mr Tumnus.

B *is lost for words*

A   It's okay . . . Don't cry.

A *reads the relevant line from the book about Lucy feeling frightened yet inquisitive.* **B** *nods in response to this.* **A** *has won her/him over. They smile at each other and continue to read.*

Scene Twelve

A museum, somewhere in Britain, 2014.

We hear music or sounds relevant to the time and/or place.

The doors to the wardrobe opens and **Friend One**, *any age between fifteen and seventeen, enters. (S)he sits on the floor, takes out her/his phone and begins playing a game. The light of the phone illuminates the wardrobe. The door opens and* **Friend Two**, *also between the ages of fifteen and seventeen, pokes his/her head inside.*

Friend Two   I knew it was you – what are you doing? You can't be in there, get out.

Friend One *ignores her/him.* **Friend Two** *climbs into the wardrobe and closes the door behind her.*

Friend Two   You know this is probably alarmed.

Friend One *ignores* **Friend Two**

Friend Two   Are we going to talk about this?

Friend One *ignores* **Friend Two**

Friend Two   Hello?

Friend One   Talk about what?

Friend Two   Er, we're in a wardrobe. In a museum.

Friend One *concentrates on her/his phone.*

Friend Two   We have to meet back at the gift shop in fifteen minutes. We're supposed to do the worksheet by then.

Friend One   I'm doing the worksheet

Friend Two   This is a wardrobe – it's not on the worksheet.

Friend One   Yes it is: Question 9.

Friend Two (*reading from the worksheet*)   'Identify an antique dating from the Tudor dynasty.'

Friend One   Identified.

Friend Two   Well we're not supposed to get inside it.

Friend One   We're investigating the primary source. A historian has to be thorough.

Friend Two   What about the other questions?

Friend One   Google 'em.

Friend Two   Look, I can't get another detention.

Friend One   Then go, no one's asking you to stay.

Friend Two *hesitates.* **Friend One** *resumes playing the game on her/his phone.*

Friend Two   Are you all right?

Friend One   Huh?

Friend Two   Are you okay?

Friend One   Am I okay?

Friend Two   Yes.

Friend One   Yeah, I'm fine. I thought you were going?

Friend Two   Nobody's talking about it any more.

Friend One   If you're gonna go, then go.

Friend Two   I'm just telling you that nobody's talking about it.

Friend One   Do I look like I care?

Friend Two   Well, you're hiding in a –

Friend One   I'm not hiding. You think I'm hiding? I don't care what (s)he's saying about me. I don't care what anyone's saying about me. They can say what they like; they can say I'm into horses for all I care. Horses, goats, sheep, whatever – it's boring. Haven't they got anything better to talk about? So don't even think about going out there and saying I'm hiding.

Friend Two   I'm not going to.

Friend One   I just can't be bothered with it, that's all. All that whispering and sniggering. It's so immature.

Friend Two   Yeah, I know.

Friend One   I can't deal with how fake it is; (s)he's so fake. Don't you think?

Friend Two   Well, I –

Friend One   I wish (s)he'd just be honest about it. Don't try telling me it was an accident. (S)he knew that picture was in there; (s)he knew what (s)he was doing when (s)he uploaded it. So just come out and say it. You want to make a point. You want to post pictures of me on Facebook. Just come out and say it. That'd be so much better. I'd have so much more respect for her/him if (s)he just came out and said it to my face.

Friend Two   I don't think that many people saw it.

Friend One   I don't care about the photo, whatever, it's just a photo – it's the dishonesty I don't like. I don't have time for that. That's why I'm in here.

Friend Two   Back in the closet?

Beat.

Sorry, I didn't mean –

Friend One   You know the thing that really pisses me off, yeah? Is that (s)he's trying to make out like (s)he's done me a favour. Like (s)he's helped me by telling everyone for me. As if I wouldn't rather tell them myself. So now (s)he comes out of it looking, like, decent, while I look like I've been lying. Because the fact is, yeah, the fact is I've never actually lied about it because nobody ever actually asked me. You all sit in the same class as me every day and nobody actually asked me, because if they did I would've said, yes, I am. And so is (s)he. And yes, we are. And so what? So. What.

Friend Two (S)he took it down; it's not up there any more.

Friend One   My cousin saw it. She told my aunt, and then my aunt told my mum and then my mum told my dad and then . . .

Friend Two   Oh . . .

Friend One   It's fine, it's not a problem, it's just . . .

Friend Two   I didn't know.

Friend One *can't help it, the emotion bubbles up and (s)he cries.*

Friend One   It's just . . . my dad . . . he just . . . he looked at me like . . . I was . . . some kind of dirty . . . like he was disgusted or something . . . I'm fine . . . I'm fine . . . I'm not upset, I'm just angry . . . it's just so annoying . . .

Friend Two   Hey . . . look, your dad will –

Friend One *(tracing her/his finger over the inscribed initials on the wall)*   It doesn't matter.

Friend Two   He can't be angry with you for ever.

Friend One   A.R. . . . H.T. . . . Who d'you think wrote that?

S(he) takes a key (or similar) out of her/his pocket and is about to add her/his initials.

Friend Two (*stopping her / him*)   No, don't. You can't: this is like a . . . famous antique.

Friend One   A.R. . . . Arthur Rex? H.T. . . . Henry Tudor?

Friend Two   Don't be ridiculous.

Friend One   It could be?

Friend Two   Stop touching it . . . It's bad enough that we're standing in here. Hey . . . I'm not saying we should leave. If you wanna stay, we can stay.

Friend One   I don't care.

Friend Two   Let's just sit in here and do the worksheet. Yeah?

Friend One *shrugs.*

Friend Two   Come on then. (*Taking out the worksheet and reading.*) 'Question 10. Identify the spinning mule from the exhibit "Children of the Revolution".' What's a spinning mule?

Friend One *searches the internet on her / his phone.*

Friend One   Spinning . . . mule . . . Here we go: 'The spinning mule is a machine used to spin cotton and other fibers. Mules were worked in pairs by a minder usually with the help of child labourers.'

Friend Two (*making a note on the worksheet*)   Identified.

Friend One   I don't get why everyone's making such a big thing about it.

Friend Two   The spinning mule?

Friend One   Shut up. About me.

Friend Two   'S just school. People need something to talk about.

Friend One   Yeah, but not . . . this.

Friend Two   Especially this.

Friend One   It shouldn't matter.

Friend Two   Well, maybe one day it won't.

Friend One   When?

Friend Two   I don't know. Soon. And when that time comes, d'you want to be the only one who can't (*Reading.*) 'Describe how the 1833 Factory Act finally changed working conditions for children'?

Friend One (*searching the net*)   1833 . . . Factory . . . Act . . .

The lights fade on the friends huddled together on the floor of the wardrobe.

Epilogue

A museum, Britain, 2014, a few moments later.

The wardrobe rotates so that we once more see it from the front. It is cordoned off by a red rope strung between two brass stands. Next to the wardrobe stands a placard with a detailed description of the exhibition piece.

A group of schoolchildren file past making lots of noise – chatting, telling jokes, pushing and shoving. A few of them stop opposite the wardrobe to read the placard and fill in a box on their worksheets. One among them calls the others away to see something much better offstage. They abandon the wardrobe and exit.

The Wardrobe
BY SAM HOLCROFT

*Notes on rehearsal and staging, drawn from two workshops
led by two directors and the writer held at the National Theatre,
November 2013*

*Workshops led by Caroline Steinbeis and Richard Twyman
with notes by Helen Edwards and Drew Mulligan*

How the writer came to write the play

Sam Holcroft said that she had always wanted to write
something in a confined space; to challenge herself to make it
interesting and surprising. She wanted to write a play with lots
of parts to give the actors an equal opportunity to explore
characters with conflict and comedy, and to write parts of equal
sizes. She also wanted to write characters from across a range
of time periods, to allow the actors to play a variety of roles.

These scenes exist on two layers. There is the conflict in each
scene, but also how the scene sits within a wider historical
context. This plays provides you an opportunity to delve into
history, to investigate issues from another time period. You
will find that some struggles for children are different and
some the same across the ages.

Approaching the play

Theatre is a visual art form; presenting pictures to an
audience. Think of the film version of the play in your head,
how would it look? What would it sound like?

Exercise

Draw the five most vivid images you find in the play. What
moments stand out? They could be images that are in the
scenes but also images that are relevant to the play, the
coronation of Henry VII for example. Take ten minutes to do
his. (Caroline Steinbeis played music while the group were
drawing; it was 'Caravan' by the Kronos Quartet.)

Here are some examples of the images and the discussions on *themes* and *staging practicalities* that came out of looking at the images.

- *Image of Caryl dead on the floor of the wardrobe in Scene Three:* Caryl is being held by Matilda; Tobias, the older brother, is looking at Henry, the younger brother – teaching him about life perhaps? This image could easily be translated into the staging of the scene. We had a few images of this scene, one of which was a wardrobe with no walls. This led to a discussion of how these images can inform the staging of the play as a whole and the question of what the wardrobe is in your production. How you form or create your wardrobe will be how you stage your play.

- One person spoke about an exercise in a movement class the previous day where eight people were in a confined space and were trying to escape. As people left it was interesting to see the shape and space that they had left behind. The image was of a body dissolving in time. This led to the question of how the wardrobe travels in history through the play and how the characters fit into that? Perhaps the transitions between the scenes would be good places to explore what happens to the bodies of the dead characters.

- *Image with the echoes of the other children in the play in the style of a Gustav Klimt painting.* What trace do their voices leave, how do we do that? Perhaps we could hear whispers as a sound effect throughout your production?

- *Row of soldiers destroying the town in Scene Three.* Here we see the wardrobe as a refuge with death and destruction outside.

- *An image from Scene Nine, in the Catholic boys' school, of a cross towering over the boy, almost reaching out for them.* This raised the question of religious symbols in the play and how they can be incorporated into the wardrobe and staging.

- *An image of blood.* Blood drips throughout this play – it is a repeated theme. How does it stay on stage from scene to scene? How does it change meaning? Technically, how does using stage blood affect the set and costumes in your production?

- *The idea of 'atmosphere'.* Caroline reminded us that, in the best possible sense, directors are manipulators and it is up to us to create an atmosphere in our production though music, sound, lighting and staging. It is up to us to decide the theme we want to draw out of the play and how we want the audience to feel.

- *An image from the end of the play where the wardrobe was ignored by the schoolchildren.* In this instance the wardrobe was very small. It was now empty of experiences. 'The wardrobe as a character' is a key point that Caroline emphasised. How does the wardrobe change throughout the play? Can it change size?

- *There were images of the bananas, the dagger and the coat worn by William.* Props and costume have huge significance through this play, choose them wisely. They tell us who the actors are and also the time period. An exercise for your actors could be to draw their own characters. The costumes and props they choose are significant and could be used in your design; they will help your actors inhabit their roles and the world of the scene.

Thoughts and discussions from the 'images' exercise

- How do we not overwhelm the audience with the weight of the history and horror that the children suffer in this play? The answer is to find the humour and lightness in the action. Each scene doesn't have to be about a child being fearful. Find the differences in each scene.

- Can we incorporate the whole company onstage the whole time? Could the actors form the walls of the wardrobe? Do they help each other to dress?

- Blackouts and transitions: how do you deal with the transitions between scenes? Caroline personally finds blackouts are dead space, and the transitions between scenes should be an opportunity for the director to impose their style on the play. Caroline's tip is to 'set up a rule and then break it'. You create an expectation in the audience which when broken creates an extra moment of significance that allows the director to show something particular.

This is a great exercise to do with the whole company. It gives them ownership of the play; they collaborate and share ideas and articulate what the play means to them. The images from this exercise were placed on the wall of the rehearsal room. It's a good idea to leave them up during the whole rehearsal process as they will help inspire the rehearsals and be a good reminder of what the company initially thought was important in the play. A next step from this exercise could be to make tableaux of the scenes and see what images and relationship come from that.

Note: when looking at a scene that you are having difficulty with, Caroline suggests closing your eyes and trying to visualise it. The image that comes to mind will give you a good place to start when working on that scene.

The key images exercise will also help you decide which of the nine scenes of this twelve-scene play you want to stage. For the NT Connections Festival the theatre companies were limited to a 45-minute playing time which roughly worked out at nine scenes. Fewer scenes could be performed, but not more. This meant that the choice of the scenes would go a long way to shaping your production.

Themes

Some of the themes Sam had identified in the play were solace, secrets, safety, suffering of children, friendship, allegiance and comradeship. She identified 'suffering' that is the one theme that is present throughout the play.

Getting to know your wardrobe

This is the biggest challenge and your decision will determine how you stage the whole play.

EXERCISE

- In small groups look at one of the twelve scenes, including the Prologue and the Epilogue.

- Read through the scene and mark down all references to the wardrobe. Take twenty minutes to draw the wardrobe in that scene and answer the following questions.

- What is it made from?

- How big is it?

- Can it move in the space?

- The big question – what does your wardrobe need to achieve for your show?

Here are some of the ideas, images and talking points that came from the workshop groups.

PROLOGUE

Wardrobe needs to be imposing, to radiate history at the same time warm and comforting. How does the wardrobe appear on stage? In this instance the stage space was made of wooden planks that rise up to form the walls of the wardrobe. These planks could be moved to change size of the playing space inside the wardrobe. We felt that the wood was a good texture, warm and denoting age.

SCENE ONE: ROYAL COURT, 1485

The wardrobe is regal and imposing as it belongs to a lady from a noble house who is soon to marry the King of England. The girls need to fit inside it, robes need to be hung in it and there are ornamental holes which let the light in. There needs to be a compartment to hide the objects they find. The compartment needs to contain props. Questions that arose: What is the status of the wardrobe in the context of each scene? Is it in the master's bedroom or hidden away in some corner of the house? How is the wardrobe treated by the characters within it? Do they treat it well or deface it?

SCENE TWO: SANTA MARIA FAMILY HOUSE, 1633
A scene lit by candles. How practical is this? What is the
lighting source?

SCENE THREE: BOLTON, CIVIL WAR ENGLAND 1644
The wardrobe is in a room next to an open window from
which we hear noise in the street. This is the first scene we
experience the wardrobe where the playing space extends
beyond the confines of its walls. How could the wardrobe be
smaller in this scene, to make the hiding place more cramped?
Could the wardrobe shake with the explosions outside?

SCENE FOUR: LONDON IN THE GREAT PLAGUE, 1665
In this scene one character carves her initials on the wall of the
wardrobe. How can you do this practically? Is it a fresh piece
of wardrobe every time and what material do you use? How
can you make a small action read for a large audience – filmed
and projected on to a large screen possibly?

The wardrobe is meant to be empty as the family of the house
have fled town taking their clothes with them. However, the
characters find a robe, dresses and silk gloves. Is the wardrobe
bigger in this scene, making it seems empty even with some
clothes hanging in there?

How many access points does the wardrobe have? Front, back,
sides? A chance to be inventive and surprise the audience.

SCENE FIVE: NOT ENGLAND, BETWEEN 1665–1770
How do we indicate the location of the wardrobe? Make a
decision as to where it is and when. The language and accent
of the actors would give an indication but so might the contents
of the wardrobe. Could you use the Brechtian method and
'title' the scenes?

SCENE SIX: KENWOOD HOUSE, 1780
Dido is praying to God. Do you have a Christian cross? Could
the walls of the wardrobe disappear and form into a cross
perhaps?

SCENE SEVEN: LIVERPOOL, 1805
The coat is the symbol of power in the scene. Could the inside
of the wardrobe be like the inside of the coat? William pins
Jaffrey to the wall. The walls of the wardrobe need to be
braced or fixed. If you don't have solid walls how are you
going to do this moment? It was suggested that the wardrobe
might have levels in it. This would help with a scene that is a
power game between the two characters and a battle to see
who has the higher status.

SCENE EIGHT: LIVERPOOL, 1827
In this scene the wardrobe is a place of comfort and security
for the two boys to share their stories. How can the wardrobe
reflect this?

SCENE NINE: BOYS' BOARDING SCHOOL, 1888
Here the wardrobe is not a place of safety and refuge but a
trap for the boys. The key is a very strong element, so think
about the lock and the handle – do they need to be realistic?

SCENE TEN: INDUSTRIAL CITY IN ENGLAND, 1916
The wardrobe has been refurbished for sale at auction – how
are you going to show that?

SCENE ELEVEN: AFTER THE NARNIA BOOKS, 1950
In this scene it was felt that the context of the scene and why
A was reading to B would inform the characteristics of the
wardrobe. So, find out what this scene is?

SCENE TWELVE: A MUSEUM, 2014
If the wardrobe was moved around then it needs to be on
castors, so find some that are strong enough.

EPILOGUE
Wardrobe is seen from the front. How has it changed in
features and in size? What do you want it to look like and say
for the final image of the play?

CONCLUSIONS

The repetitive nature of the scenes means that you have to keep being inventive with your wardrobe. Surprise the audience with the wardrobe and how it changes.

Caroline's key images for the wardrobe were 'The Exploded Shed' (sculptural installation) by Cornelia Parker and an illustration of Lucy entering the Wardrobe in *The Lion, the Witch and the Wardrobe* by C.S.Lewis.

Structure of the play

THE TIMELINE
This play travels through time from the fifteenth century to the present day. Create a timeline of the action in the play and put it up on the wall. This can then be added to throughout the rehearsal process. Mark the important moments, pin up pictures, bits of research, songs, colours, or anything that is connected to a particular moment in the play or is significant to the scene or the characters.

You can set research task into the specific historical moments mentioned in the play: these really help the actors understand who these people were and what was important to them.

IDENTIFYING THE 'EVENTS' IN A SCENE
An event is 'a moment in the play that changes the action of every single character'.

By identifying the 'events' in each scene we can determine the important pieces of action. There can be many 'events' in a scene. They can be important point of action, changes in the dynamic and direction of the scene, a revelation of an important bit of information, a moment of theatrical surprise – the entry of a character for example.

They can also happen before, after or during the scene but in another location. They can be huge or they can be everyday but they need significance.

As an example, what is the most important event of Scene One? Perhaps the moment when Cecily hears from her sister that if Elizabeth dies she will marry the king. This is the *Dramatic Event*.

In the broader historical context, there are three pieces of information we hear before the scene starts: Richard III is dead; the new king is to be Henry Tudor; the coronation is soon. We have to decide which one of these is the prime *Historical Event*.

EXERCISE

Create a timeline for the play and add the *Dramatic Event* (DE) and *Historical Event* (HE) for each scene. Here is an example:

Prologue
HE   The wardrobe is built.
DE   The wardrobe rotates so we can see in it.

Scene One
HE   Richard III is killed by Henry Tudor.
DE   Elizabeth tells her sister that if she dies Cecily will become queen.

Scene Two
HE   The boys are living in a country and pretending to be of another religion to hide their Judaism.
DE   Daniel reveals to his brother that he has been called a '*merrano* pig' and that their real faith might not be secret.

Scene Three
HE   Surge of Royalist forces into the Parliamentarian area of Bolton.
DE   The suffocating of Caryl.

Scene Four
HE   London has been hit by the plague
DE   Anne has the first signs of being infected.

Identifying the key events (and there can be many 'sub-events' in each scene) is really important. It allows you to tell the story clearly.

TITLES EXERCISE

Get your groups to title each scene. There are five different titles you could try.

• Title to describe the action of the scene.

• One-word description of the scene. e.g. 'Knife' for Scene Five.

• Title to reflect the emotional state of the scene – anger, fear, survival.

• Weather state of the scene – this influences the atmosphere.

• Physical state – slash, stab, punch.

All these titles help you understand the individuality of each scene and help you differentiate them from each other.

Rehearsal exercises

FACTS AND QUESTIONS

Work through the play as a group, compiling a list of the facts and questions in each scene. You could group the facts together, with a group for the world of the play and a group for each of the characters. You could put the facts into chronological order and create a timeline for the action within and outside the scenes, and a biography for each of the characters.

Here is an example of facts and questions that came up for Scene Three.

FACTS	QUESTIONS
Set in a master bedroom.	What kind of bedroom?
Belongs to the Ainsley family.	How wealthy are they?
Belongs to the parents.	How many rooms are there?
Bolton, England.	What kind of family?

May 1644, afternoon.

We hear the sound of gunfire.

Children: Matilda, sixteen, and
    Henry, thirteen.

Children in a wardrobe.

Wardrobe has a design feature.

Children are afraid – close
    relationship.

The wardrobe has a handle
    (inside the door).

Weather?

Time?

What does gunfire sound like?

How far away is the gunfire?

Why is there gunfire?

Why are they here?

What happened?

Where have they just come from?

Is the wardrobe where the
    children always seek shelter?

Does the wardrobe have a handle
    inside?

How does the internal doorhandle
    appear to the audience?

What is in the wardrobe?

How big is it?

Are Tobias and Matilda twins?

Henry's physicality.

Tobias, sixteen, enters.

Matilda and Henry are so
    frightened they try and lock their
    own brother out of the wardrobe.

It's been raining.

Tobias has been outside
    recently.

Sounds of gunfire outside on the
    street.

These children know each other.

Tobias knows the children are in
    the wardrobe.

Henry is comforting Matilda.

Where has Tobias been? Why has he
    been outside but not the others?

Do Matilda and Henry know Tobias
    has been outside? Where did they
    think he was? Did they believe he
    was dead/missing?

Tobias has blood on his clothes.

Is it his blood? Whose blood is it?
    Is it his mother's? Does he know
    whose blood it is? If it is his, is he
    hiding it from Matilda and Henry?

They are shooting people in the
   streets.

There is smoke.

Tobias has seen people be killed.

Where is their mother?

Why don't the children ask about
   their father?

MONOLOGUE EXERCISE

- Select an appropriate monologue. Get into pairs (A and B). Person A reads the scene to person B. Then switch, B reading the scene while A listens with their eyes closed. Ask B to read the monologue one thought at a time while A is asked to nod once they've created a clear visual image of that thought in their mind.

- Person A, who has been creating the visual movie in their head, then describes the scenes back to B, explaining what they had seen when they had heard each line. After explaining their movie, ask Person A to read the monologue again to Person B. Ask Person B to note any changes in delivery style.

The group noticed that when reading the monologue for the second time, after they had created the visual images in their mind, the performers became much more subtle and considered in their delivery of the speech. The lines seemed to become their own thoughts and the speech came alive for performer and listener.

This isn't just a monologue exercise, it can easily be applied to a duologue or group scene, and is an excellent way of making your cast place themselves in the scene they are performing. Somehow visualising each image for themselves helps actors to deliver the lines as if they are their own thoughts.

It is also worth doing this exercise with stage directions and descriptions in the text to create clear visual images of the setting of each scene.

GESTURE EXERCISE

- Ask the group to stick their copies of the Dido speech to the wall, scattered around the room, then to perform the speech including a gesture with each word. Encourage the group to become extravagant with this exercise and not to feel scared about looking silly.

- Then ask the group to get into pairs and read the speech back normally to each other, this time putting an emphasis on the small words in the text. There is often a lot of meaning in the small words, but actors and particularly young actors can throw these small words away and consequently lose the key meaning of the line. By taking time to focus on performing every word in a speech an actor will tease out the subtext within the speech and make it more interesting for an audience to watch.

A variation on this exercise is to choose one member of the group who is less confident at reading aloud and ask them to read a speech to the group, being supported while they are reading by the rest of the group huddling close to them and physicalising the speech using gestures and actions for each word. This will help the actor who is reading to develop confidence as they don't focus solely on what they are doing; instead their attention is also drawn to the rest of the company acting out the speech alongside them.

A second variation is to read a speech in pairs – one actor reading the speech while their partner listens with their eyes closed and feeds back words from the speech that have particularly resonated with them. It's a good way for an actor to indentify which lines and phrases are landing with an audience and which are still being thrown away with not enough consideration for their meaning.

RHYTHM AND PACE EXERCISE

- Two actors read a scene. Next they read it again, inserting a pause after every line. The pause should bring out the thought process of each character as well as the subtext of the scene.

- You want the actors to think on the line so repeat the reading but asking the actors to take the pauses out again. Now the thought processes are not lost but the rhythm returns to the piece. It brings out the 'engine of the scene' and what drives it forward.

Actioning – 'DRAMA ONLY COMES FROM CONFLICT'

Every actor must be trying to do something to the other actors onstage. So you assign an 'action' to each line of text. An 'action' requires a transitive verb (a doing verb): 'I —— you.'

Take a piece of text and try to *action* it.

- 'I always wanted a walk-in-wardrobe' – *entice, persuade?*
- 'I don't think you're supposed to walk into this one' – *reprimand, amuse?*

Try to say these lines with these actions and see how they change the meaning of the line and the relationship between the characters. Note: don't do this with a large group as it takes time.

Stanislavsky objectives

Find the Stanislavsky objectives in each scene for each character. The objective is what they want in the scene. The super-objective is what they want in life. The super-objective is usually 'to find happiness'. The objective can change scene by scene.

In Scene Eleven Nell's objective could be to stop Anthony going. Anthony's objective could be to make Nell happy.

Ask each character their objective and super-objective, no matter the size of the character's part.

Managing the rehearsal room

As a director you need to manage the room. This is not just telling everyone what to do; it is how you manage the room and the atmosphere. Caroline varied the activities during the workshop so that no one got bored. She played music to inspire us. It is your responsibility to keep those in the room attentive. It is in your control: be prepared to follow your instincts and throw out any plan you might have if something better appears.

What to do with the other actors that aren't in the scene you are rehearsing? Perhaps you could get them to do some research and then feedback to the group. They could split into pairs of scenes and direct each other before you look at them. You could stage it so that the actors are on stage all the time.

References

The BBC *History Magazine* website – www.historyextra.com – is a good place to start examining the time periods in the play.

Heritage

by Dafydd James

To the young people of Mess Up
The Mess Theatre Company
and the pupils of Ysgol Gyfun Cwm Rhymni

Dafydd James is an award-winning writer, composer and performer, working in both English and Welsh. He trained in the Lecoq pedagogy and holds a PhD in Theatre Studies from Warwick University. His work includes *The Village Social* (National Theatre Wales); *Llwyth* (Theatr Genedlaethol/Sherman Cymru; Theatre Critics of Wales Award); and *My Name is Sue* (Dafydd James & Company; Total Theatre Award). He also writes for *Gwaith/Cartref*, winner of a Celtic Media award for Best Drama Series. He performed *My Name is Sue* last summer at Edinburgh, and its sequel – *Sue: The Second Coming* – toured the UK at Christmas 2013. He currently has commissions with BBC Radio 3, National Theatre Wales, Sherman Cymru and Fiction Factory.

Characters

Tubbsy
Jackson
Cari-Ann Chubb
Bradley, *known as Dickhead*
Lisa, *though she insists on being called 'Liza'*
Douglas
Jamie, *a musician*
Genevieve, *voice only*
Guinevere, *voice only*
Deirdre-May
Jinx
Melony, *'Smelony'*
Mark, *'Jurassic' Mark*

Setting

The play takes place in an open enclosure – a paddock – surrounded by a high electric fence. There is a gate leading into the paddock, stage left, though we do not necessarily see it. CCTV cameras and a PA system are attached to the electric fence.

All the characters wear a 'traditional' uniform, apart from 'Jurassic' Mark and Tubbsy. This uniform might suggest a 'folk' tradition or may even remind us of the von Trapp family singers. Tubbsy is dressed in jeans and a hoodie. 'Jurassic' Mark is dressed as a stegosaurus.

Over the PA system we hear a young person singing the 'Northbridge Anthem', a cappella. It is haunting and beautiful.

Voice

 We serve you, dear Fatherland,
 Home of the free;
 For ever your children,
 We bow unto thee.
 We kneel at your altar,
 We fall on your sword,
 We may lose our blood
 But we'll reap your rewards.
 Our love asks no questions,
 Our love feels no shame,
 Your traditions we'll honour:
 United we sing in your name.

During the above, we hear the sound of a buzzer – industrial, loud, foreboding – as the gate unlocks and swings open.

Tubbsy *runs in from stage left; he struggles with a heavy rucksack in his arms. The gate shuts behind him. He doesn't notice* **Jackson** *sitting upstage right, watching him.*

He runs across the paddock. Suddenly we hear the sound of an electric shock as **Tubbsy** *touches the fence. He screams as he's thrown backwards. He just about manages to save the contents of the bag as it falls to the ground.*

Tubbsy That's so not fair!

Jackson What's in the bag, Tubbsy?

Tubbsy *(suddenly terrified)* Nothing.

Jackson What's in the bag?

Tubbsy Nothing.

Jackson It doesn't look like nothing.

Tubbsy Doesn't it?

Jackson No. It looks heavy.

Tubbsy   Leave me alone, Jackson. It's got nothing to do with you.

Jackson   So there is something in it. What's in the bag?

Tubbsy   I've got to go. Let me . . . (go).

Jackson   Show me.

Tubbsy   I can't.

Jackson   You can. Show me. Now.

Beat.

Tubbsy   Alright. But you've got to promise not to tell . . .

Jackson   You know I can't promise that. Though I'll definitely tell if you don't.

He slowly opens the zip of the bag.

Tubbsy   It wasn't my fault. They made me do it. I . . .

Jackson *looks in and reels with shock.*

Jackson   God, Tubbsy!

Tubbsy   It wasn't my fault.

Jackson   There's a cat in there.

Tubbsy   I know.

Jackson   It's dead.

Tubbsy   It's not dead.

Jackson   You've got a dead cat in your bag.

Tubbsy   I haven't. It's hibernating.

Jackson   Cats don't hibernate.

Tubbsy   This one does.

Jackson   But it's summer.

Tubbsy   It's confused.

Jackson   It's not confused. It's dead. Why have you got a dead cat in your bag, Tubbsy?

Tubbsy   It wasn't my fault.

Jackson   What did you do?

Beat.

Tubbsy   *They* told me to do it.

Jackson   Who?

Tubbsy   The twins.

Jackson   Do what?

Tubbsy   I got him stoned.

Cari-Ann Chubb *appears from the shadows holding a book:* The Diary of Anne Frank.

Cari-Ann   OMG, I'm so telling.

Tubbsy (*desperate*)   You didn't tell me she was here!

Jackson   You didn't ask.

Cari-Ann   You're so twisted, Tubbsy.

Tubbsy   You shouldn't spy on people.

Cari-Ann   I wasn't spying. I was reading *The Diary of Anne Frank*.

Jackson   What you reading that for?

Cari-Ann   We're related.

Jackson *rolls his eyes.*

Cari-Ann   You're so dead, Tubbsy. Rehearsal starts in five minutes.

Tubbsy   It wasn't me. It was the twins.

Cari-Ann   No one's gonna believe you over them, though. It's not worth it.

Tubbsy I didn't do anything!

Cari-Ann You're gonna be in so much trouble!

Tubbsy Shut your cake-hole, Cari-Ann!

Cari-Ann I'm not shutting up! You stoned a cat.

Tubbsy I didn't stone a cat. I gave it a blow-back.

Cari-Ann Tubbsy, that's totally disgusting!

Tubbsy Blow-*back*.

Cari-Ann Oh. (*Beat.*) Well that's still awful! You forced that poor little kitty to smoke. It'll get lung cancer.

Tubbsy It's already dead!

Cari-Ann You gave a cigarette to a dying cat?! That's practically electrocution.

Jackson Execution.

Cari-Ann That's what I said. Execution. I'm so going to report you to the Provost. That poor, innocent, beautiful, little kitty.

Jackson OK, that's enough. Stop being so dramatic, Cari-Ann.

Cari-Ann I am not dramatic. I'm depressed. They are very different things.

Tubbsy Look I'll give you a fiver if you don't say anything.

Cari-Ann (*quickly*) Tenner.

Tubbsy It's a deal.

Cari-Ann And let me see it . . .

Tubbsy Quick then. Before the others come.

Cari-Ann *looks into the bag.*

Cari-Ann Ooh, it looks a bit like Hitler.

Jackson *and* **Tubbsy** *share a look.*

Cari-Ann   Have you put gel in your hair, Jackson?

Jackson   So?

Cari-Ann   Who are you trying to impress?

Jackson (*to* **Tubbsy**)   You should go. Hide it.

Tubbsy *runs back towards the gate.*

Jackson   Whose cat is it anyway, Tubbsy?

The buzzer. **Bradley** *enters through the gate.*

Cari-Ann   Oh. Hi-ya, Dickhead.

Bradley   Hi-ya.

Cari-Ann   You OK, Dickhead?

Bradley   Not really.

Beat.

I've lost my cat.

Silence. **Bradley** *looks at* **Tubbsy**.

Bradley   What's in the bag?

Cari-Ann (*improvising suddenly*)   A dinosaur.

Jackson *rolls his eyes.*

Bradley (*incredulously*)   A dinosaur?

Tubbsy (*through gritted teeth*)   Don't be silly, Cari-Ann. How could I possibly have a dinosaur inside here?

Cari-Ann   I mean a bone.

Bradley   You found a dinosaur bone?

Tubbsy   Um . . . Yes.

Cari-Ann   Isn't that amazing? Can you believe that
Tubbsy somehow managed to find the remains of a dinosaur
miraculously preserved for millions of years down by the river.

Bradley   That's quite hard to believe.

Jackson   Well, you better believe it.

Cari-Ann   Yeah. You better believe it.

Bradley   Which part?

Cari-Ann   Its elbow.

Beat.

Bradley   I meant of the river.

Cari-Ann   Oh.

Beat.

Bradley   Do dinosaurs even have elbows?

Cari-Ann   Well we don't know, do we, Tubbsy? We're not
sure what part it is.

Bradley   How do you even know it belongs to a dinosaur?

Jackson   Well, Mark told him, didn't he?

Bradley   Jurassic Mark?

Jackson (*sarcastic*)   No. Mark Antony. Or Mark who was
friends with Jesus. Or Mark from Marks & Spencer, 'cause
he's pretty hot on dinosaurs apparently. Of course he means
Jurassic Mark. You're such a dickhead, Dickhead.

Beat.

Bradley   May I see it?

Tubbsy   I haven't got time, sorry I've got to . . . got to go
and . . .

Jackson   You've got to go back and change, don't you?

Tubbsy   Yes. That's right. I've got to back and change.

Cari-Ann   Why didn't you come in uniform, Tubbsy?

The buzzer. **Lisa**, **Douglas** *and* **Jamie** *enter.* **Douglas** *carries a basket with a tea towel over it and* **Jamie** *carries his musical instrument.*

Tubbsy   I should go.

Lisa   Sorry, Tubbsy. You can't go anywhere. I need you for the rehearsal. Happy birthday, by the way.

Jackson   I didn't know it was your birthday, Tubbsy.

Tubbsy   I didn't want anyone to know.

Lisa   Have you got gel in your hair, Jackson?

Jackson (*angrily*)   So what if I have?

Lisa   Ooh, touchy! Right, singing formation, everybody!

Douglas   Not everyone's here, Lisa.

Lisa   Well, we'll just have to start without them. We've only got forty minutes.

Tubbsy   I have to get my costume . . .

Lisa   Well you should have thought about that before you came. We need to rehearse.

Jackson   Who made you boss?

Tubbsy   Yeah. You can't tell me what to do.

Lisa   Yes I can. In forty minutes, May Day festivities will come to an end and we'll be on that stage singing our anthem in front of the whole village. The *whole* of Northbridge. And I consider that an honour. No one else has been chosen. It's a great privilege. So we need to get it right! We need to sing beautifully. Sing as if our lives depended on it.

Tubbsy   Who cares?

He heads towards the gate.

The voice of **Genevieve** *explodes over the loudspeaker.*

Genevieve   I wouldn't touch that gate if I were you!

Tubbsy *jumps.*

Tubbsy   Was that Genevieve Saunders?!

Lisa   Yes.

Tubbsy   Where the hell did that come from?

Bradley   Up there! Look!

Cari-Ann   You've got to be kidding me!

Tubbsy   What?

Douglas   Look. There's cameras. And a speaker.

Tubbsy   They can't do that.

Jackson   Looks like they already have.

Tubbsy   What is this? Big Brother?

Lisa   It's for our own protection, I'm sure.

Tubbsy   Well, I've got to go . . .

He goes to go again. The voice of **Guinevere** *explodes over the PA.*

Guinevere   Perhaps my sister wasn't clear enough.

Tubbsy   Oh . . . not Guinevere as well! They're blinking everywhere!

Guinevere   You touch that gate and I'll tell my father precisely what you did with his whiteboard pen last week before you put it back on his desk.

Tubbsy *is agog.*

Genevieve   What did he do with the whiteboard pen?

Guinevere   I'll tell you later. But it needs a good wash.

Tubbsy   Well, tell him then!

Lisa   They can't hear you, can they? They can only see us.

Tubbsy   Well then they can see this then!

He sticks his middle finger up at the camera then walks to the gate.

I'm going.

But as he touches it he gets another electric shock. He's thrown backwards.

Genevieve   We tried to warn you.

Guinevere   Yes. We tried to warn you.

Cari-Ann   They can't do that!

Jackson   They already have.

Douglas   That's barbaric!

Lisa   No it's not. It's just what they used to keep the cows in.

Cari-Ann   In case you hadn't noticed, we are not cows!

Lisa (*under her breath*)   I'm not so sure.

Cari-Ann   What did you say?

Douglas   She said 'it's a bit 1984'.

Cari-Ann   You what?

Douglas   Never mind.

Lisa   Come on. Let's rehearse.

Tubbsy   Hang on a minute, will you! Doesn't anybody else think it's a little bit weird that we're all being kept? Like . . . like livestock!

Lisa   Don't be ridiculous. We're not being kept here like livestock . . .

Tubbsy   Yes we are. We're allowed in but we're not allowed out. They're treating us like animals.

Douglas   Or Oompa-Loompas. They never got to leave the factory did they? That Wonka if you ask me was a wa –

Lisa   Douglas!

Douglas Well, he was.

Lisa No he wasn't. He was saving them, wasn't he? From the Vermicious Knid.

Douglas They were all slaves!

Lisa He was doing them a favour. They were better off in the long run.

Douglas I think that's debatable.

Lisa They had all the chocolate in the world.

Douglas Not much good if you're lactose intolerant.

Lisa Douglas. Why on earth do you think they were lactose intolerant?

Douglas They were orange. Something definitely wasn't right.

Tubbsy Just like here. We're trapped!

Lisa Don't be so dramatic. We're not trapped. We're safe. It's a beautiful day and the Provost said we can make as much noise out here as we want without disturbing the celebrations.

Douglas As long as we're watched by the fruit of his loins . . .

Cari-Ann Are you talking about his schlong?

Douglas No, Cari-Ann. I'm talking about his offspring. The twins.

Cari-Ann Oh right. Yeah. It's not fair. That's favouritsm.

Lisa It's got nothing to do with favouritism.

Cari-Ann But they're the Provost's spring-offs!

Douglas Offspring.

Cari-Ann That's what I said. Offspring.

Lisa   And that's why they're probably the most competent people to do the job.

Jackson   I wouldn't say that . . . They're girls.

Cari-Ann   You can't say that, Jackson. It's sexist. You should treat girls equally to boys.

Lisa   And anyway, Jackson, there's nothing you can do about it. It's just for thirty-five minutes until . . . Oh my goodness. We've only got thirty-five minutes! Singing formation everyone!

Douglas   Well, I don't think it's on either. First of all, we can look after ourselves and . . .

Cari-Ann   And B . . . ! They're the same age as us! Why should we take orders off people the same age as us?

Lisa   Mum and Dad take orders off the Provost and he's the same age as them.

Cari-Ann   That's way different.

Lisa   No it's not! *That's* democracy!

Genevieve   Is Cari-Ann causing trouble down there?

Cari-Ann   Seriously. They're like totally gonna get my fists in their mouths . . .

Lisa   Oh yeah? You and whose army?

Cari-Ann   My army! (*Raising her fists at the camera.*) Both my arm-ies! I'm gonna shove my fists so far down their brown-nosing mouths they'll be . . . they'll be . . .

Douglas   Brown-nosing *mouths* . . . I think you rather mixed your metaphors there, Cari-Ann.

Lisa   And I'm not sure if you should really call them brown-noses . . .

Douglas   Yes. Because actually brown-nosing your father could be classified as an act of incest.

Cari-Ann (*raising her fists at* **Douglas**)   Do you want a piece of me as well?

Genevieve   Threatening behaviour will be punished.

Guinevere   You know the Youth League rules, Cari-Ann.

Lisa   So for your own good, maybe you should keep quiet from now on.

Cari-Ann   Why? They can't hear me, can they?

Lisa   No, but they can see that you're talking absolute rubbish.

Cari-Ann (*raising her fists*)   And you, Lisa Maloney!

Lisa   My name's Liza. Li-za.

Cari-Ann   Your name's Lisa.

Lisa   Well I've changed it: to Liza. After Minnelli. Not that I expect you'll be able to comprehend such a subtle shift, you dyslexic cretin.

Douglas   You shouldn't make fun of dyslexia, Lisa . . . Liza. Liza.

Lisa   Are you dyslexic too, Douglas?

Cari-Ann   I am not dyslexic! I'm just a little bit thin.

She sits down in a huff.

Lisa   OK. So we're all a little bit excitable. It's understandable. (*Looking at her watch with a hint of anxiety.*) Because in thirty-four minutes we're going to be singing in front of the whole village; so perhaps we should rehearse.

Cari-Ann   Well, I don't want to rehearse without any adults.

Lisa   Don't be so weird.

Cari-Ann   I'm not being weird. This is weird!

Tubbsy   See.

Lisa Look. You both know as well as I do that there are no adults available because they're all participating in the 'Dance of the Horned Ram'. It's tradition.

Tubbsy It's a stupid tradition.

Lisa No it's not! It's wonderful!

Jackson How do you know? We've never seen it.

Lisa I can imagine: all those bells and clogs! It's probably quite a spectacle.

Jackson It's sheep-rape.

Lisa It is not sheep-rape, Jackson! It's an age-old tradition based on the mating ritual of the ram told through the power of dance –

Jackson It's sheep-rape.

Lisa – to usher in the fruitfulness of the summer harvest.

Jackson Sheep-rape.

Tubbsy Isn't bestiality illegal?

Lisa I can assure you: no ewes are harmed during the dance.

Jackson How do you know?

Tubbsy Yes. How do you know?

Lisa Because the Provost loves animals, doesn't he?

Douglas He didn't love these cows though, did he?

Cari-Ann Ha ha! Yes! Poor cow-wows. Imagine. You spend your last hours on earth getting electrocuted and then you get your throat slit.

Lisa For the feast! It's tradition.

Cari-Ann Well, you can hardly call that kindness to animals, can you?

Beat.

Bradley   God. Do you think my cat's OK?

Beat.

Lisa   We're wasting precious time here. Let's rehearse.

Jackson   Seriously. Who put you in charge, Lisa?

Lisa   Someone needs to take control.

Jackson   But why should that be you?

Lisa   You don't even like singing, Jackson.

Jackson   No. But I like being in charge.

Lisa   Well, you can't be in charge. They're in charge – (*Referring to* **Genevieve** *and* **Guinevere**.)

Jackson   And that's OK with you, is it?

Lisa   Well, it's just safer this way, isn't it? And I'd rather that than . . .

She tails off, noticing **Tubbsy** *staring at them.*

Jackson   What?

Lisa (*whispers*)   You know? . . . We all know what happened to . . .

Tubbsy   What are you two whispering about?

Lisa *and* **Jackson**   Nothing.

Beat.

Lisa   How are your parents coping, Tubbsy? Since . . . you know . . .

Tubbsy   Mind your own business.

Beat.

Cari-Ann (*to* **Douglas**)   What's in your basket, gay-boy?

Douglas   I am not a gay-boy, Cari-Ann. By gay-boy, I assume you are referring to a homosexual, or a male whose sexual preference is for men. As I am not interested in men, I am not a gay-boy.

Beat.

I'm not actually that interested in women either, but that's by the by.

Cari-Ann   Whatever, gay-boy.

Douglas   You shouldn't use the word 'gay' as a derogatory insult, Cari-Ann.

Cari-Ann   I'm not.

Douglas   Yes you are.

Cari-Ann   No I'm not. 'Cause I don't know what derogatory means.

Douglas   You wouldn't say 'nigger', would you?

Cari-Ann   No.

Douglas   Or call a Jewish person Yid.

Cari-Ann   Duh! Of course I wouldn't. I'm related to Anne Frank, aren't I?

Lisa   No you're not.

Cari-Ann   I am! Shut it, Lisa.

Lisa   Liza!

Cari-Ann   Whatever.

Jackson (*to* **Douglas**)   Hypocrite. I've heard you shouting 'Southbridge Bastards' along with everyone else.

Lisa   But that's just a bit of fun, isn't it?

Jackson   What's the difference, Lisa?

Lisa   Liza!

Cari-Ann   Sorry, Lisa, but you can't change your name, just because you feel like it.

Lisa   Why not?

Cari-Ann   'Cause you can't. Stick with what you're given.

Lisa   But Liza suits me better.

Cari-Ann   You're such a fake. You can't just make it up as you go along.

Lisa   Why not? You've just invented your whole blinking ancestry for dramatic effect. You're the fake.

Tubbsy   You're all fakes.

Lisa   No we're not!

Tubbsy   So why are you all dressed in ridiculous costumes then?

They contemplate this. **Tubbsy** *feels victorious for a moment.*

Tubbsy (*to* **Douglas**)   What *have* you got in your basket?

Douglas   Home-made strawberry preserve if you really must know. It's my contribution to the feast.

Cari-Ann   Yes, because jam goes wonderfully with dead cow.

Douglas   Well, there's also a few chutneys.

Tubbsy   Oh my God, that *is* gay.

Lisa   Tubbsy! Please don't say that.

Cari-Ann (*proud of herself*)   Yeah. It's gay-ist . . .

Douglas   I think you mean homophobic.

Cari-Ann   Yes. That. Don't be phobic.

Lisa   The gays have brought us many wonderful things, haven't they?

Douglas   Yes.

Jackson   Like what?

Cari-Ann   Velcro.

Douglas   The gays didn't bring us Velcro.

Cari-Ann   Didn't they?

Douglas   No.

Beat.

Cari-Ann   Jamie's awfully quiet.

Lisa   You leave Jamie alone.

Cari-Ann   Just saying.

Lisa (*quickly*)   We really need to rehearse the anthem now.

Bradley   Everyone's still not here.

Lisa   Well, tough. We can't wait for them. We need to get on. Right. If we could all gather together and . . .

Bradley   But we don't have any altos at the moment: Jinx, Melony . . .

Cari-Ann   Smelony . . . .

Bradley   Don't be mean, Cari-Ann.

Douglas   And . . . who else?

Jackson (*almost too quickly*)   Lydia.

Cari-Ann   Ooh . . . Waiting for her to arrive are you? *Gel-boy?*

Jackson   I swear I'm gonna . . .

Douglas   Actually, I wouldn't count on her turning up if I were you, Jackson.

Jackson   Why?

Douglas   She was crying earlier.

Jackson   Where?

Douglas   In the girls' toilets.

Cari-Ann   What were you doing in the girls' toilets, pervert-features?

Douglas   I don't like the smell of urea in the boys'. It makes defecating a far more unpleasant experience.

Jackson   Why was she crying?

Douglas   I don't know. I didn't ask.

Jackson   Why not?

Douglas   Because I was doing a poo. And she'd gone by the time I came out.

Jackson   So how do you know it was her?

Douglas   I asked her to pass me some more toilet paper. She very kindly obliged . . .

Cari-Ann (*under her breath*)   Freak.

Douglas   I can see why you like her, Jackson.

Jackson   I don't like her.

Tubbsy   Yeah. Right, gel-boy. That's why you carved her initials into your left arm with a compass.

Jackson *grabs* **Tubbsy** *by the scruff of the neck.*

Guinevere   JACKSON MCDONALD! DON'T EVEN THINK ABOUT IT! LET HIM GO.

Jackson (*whispered to* **Tubbsy**)   One more word like that from you and I might just let the cat out of the bag.

Tubbsy   You wouldn't . . .

Jackson   Wouldn't I?

Genevieve   ARE YOU DEAF AS WELL AS HANDSOME? I SAID DON'T EVEN THINK ABOUT IT!

Jackson *lets* **Tubbsy** *go.*

Guinevere Did you mean to say 'handsome'?

Genevieve What?

Guinevere You said 'handsome'.

Genevieve No I didn't.

Guinevere Yes you did.

Genevieve No I didn't.

Guinevere You did!

Silence.

Tubbsy (*mumbles*) Someone's got poor taste . . .

Jackson *grabs him again.*

Genevieve Jackson McDonald, raise that fist again and I'll be forced to sound this klaxon in my hand, and if that klaxon sounds then the Mayday celebrations will be interrupted and Daddy –

Guinevere The Provost . . .

Genevieve – the Provost, followed by a hundred angry adults, will come a-running and a-weeping in your direction. Do you want that on your conscience? Do you?

Jackson They don't have a klaxon!

The buzzer sounds. They all jump.

Deirdre-May *wanders in as if in a daze.*

They all breathe a sigh of relief.

Oblivious to everyone, she walks downstage and sits next to **Bradley**. *The mood shifts.*

Lisa I wasn't sure if you'd come, Deirdre-May.

Deirdre-May (*staring straight in front of her*) I'm not sure if I had much choice.

Lisa Are you alright?

Deirdre-May   Not really. But who is these days?

Everyone looks at **Lisa**, *confused.* **Lisa** *quietly mouths 'her gran' and mimes holding a pistol to her head and shooting herself. She also mimes her brains splattering out the other side. She enjoys it a little bit too much.*

Everyone nods, understanding, except for **Bradley** *who stares out front, like* **Deirdre**.

Bradley   I've lost my cat, Deirdre-May.

Deirdre   I've lost my nanna.

Hearing this, **Tubbsy** *zips up his rucksack tightly.*

Lisa   Right! Come on, everyone! Let's rehearse.

Douglas   But we need the whole group.

Lisa   Well, we don't have the whole group so we've no choice: the show must go on. Just ask Liza Minnelli.

Douglas   She's not here.

Lisa   No need for sarcasm, Douglas. The point I'm making is that when she contracted viral encephalitis, the doctors predicted that she would never speak again and that she'd spend her whole life in a wheelchair. But she didn't accept, did she? No! She wouldn't accept. Instead, she turned to what she knew best, better than anything. She turned to rehearsal. She rehearsed herself to life again.

Douglas   We haven't got viral encephalitis. We're just down on a few altos.

Jackson   Who *is* Liza Minnelli anyway?

Lisa   You know? She was in that film we watched at Youth League to warn us against the dangers of excess.

Buzzer. It frightens them for a moment. They are pleased to see **Jinx** *and* **Melony** *enter.*

Melony (*to* **Lisa**)   Sorry we're so late, babes. I was getting a tattoo, wasn't I, Jinx?

Jinx Yes.

Jackson You weren't getting a tattoo, Melony.

Melony Yer I was. I was getting a tattoo, wasn't I, Jinx?

Jinx Yes.

Jackson No you weren't. You're not brave enough.

Melony I was.

Jackson Who gave it to you then?

Melony The tattoo man.

Jackson Bull. What tattoo man? There's no tattoo man in Northbridge and even if there were he'd be kind of busy right now, wouldn't he?

Melony Well, we crossed the bridge, didn't we?

Everyone's surprised. **Lisa** *gasps.*

Jackson You're lying.

Melony We're not.

Lisa You went to Southbridge?

Melony Yes.

Lisa But you've broken the rules!

Melony They're there to be broken.

Jackson She's full of it.

Deirdre-May That *is* brave, Melony.

Jackson It's not brave because she didn't do it!

Bradley I'd never have the guts to do that.

Jackson What? Be a traitor?

Melony We snuck past the guards, didn't we, Jinx?

Jackson No you didn't.

Melony   We did. We were very cunning, weren't we, Jinx?

Jinx   Yes.

Jackson   Show us then.

Melony (*begrudgingly*)   OK. Well first of all it was like . . .

She falls on the floor and mimes doing a belly crawl. **Jinx** *joins in.*

Melony   And then it was like . . .

She does a rather ridiculous acrobatic stunt.

And then it was like . . .

Jackson   No. Show us the tattoo.

Beat.

Melony   I can't.

Jackson   'Cause you haven't got one. That's why.

Melony   No . . .

Jackson   Yes.

Melony   I can't show you, can I? 'Cause it's somewhere private. Isn't it, Jinx?

Jinx   Yes.

Jackson   That's convenient.

Melony   It wasn't actually. It wasn't, was it, Jinx? It was very inconvenient. Inconvenient and very painful.

Deirdre-May   What did you get tattooed, Melony?

Douglas   'I went to Southbridge and all I got was this lousy tattoo'?

Melony   I can't say I'm afraid. It's a secret.

Jackson   It's a secret 'cause you haven't got one.

Melony   I have so. Haven't I, Jinx?

Jinx Yes.

Jackson Seen it have you, Jinx?

Jinx Yes.

Jackson Where exactly is it, Jinx?

Jinx *looks away.*

Jackson You're such a liar, Smelony.

Melony (*really hurt*) Don't call me Smelony!

Jackson Why not? You stink of fish. And you're a stinkin' liar.

Lisa That's quite enough, Jackson.

Jackson Shut it, Lisa.

Lisa It's Liza!

Douglas Don't you think you'll come to regret it in the future, Melony? It's highly unlikely that you'll still want it in years to come?

Melony I will.

Douglas How do you know?

Melony I just know.

Douglas How do you know?

Melony I'm not going to change.

Douglas Everyone changes. We all have to evolve.

Buzzer. They jump. **Mark** *enters, dressed as a stegosaurus.*

Mark Sorry I'm late. The tail slowed me right . . . .

Silence as everyone stares at him. The truth gradually dawns on **Mark**.

Mark Oh no . . .

Cari-Ann Why are you dressed like a tyrannosaurus, Mark?

Mark   I'm not dressed like a tyrannosaurus!

Cari-Ann   Um . . . You are!

Mark   I'm a stegosaurus!

Tubbsy   You idiot!

Mark   But Tubbsy, you said . . .

Tubbsy   You stupid idiot!

Mark   But you said fancy dress!

Tubbsy   I said *traditional* dress; you must have misheard me.

Mark   I didn't! You said things were different this year and we could wear whatever we wanted to express who we are.

Cari-Ann   So are you actually a dinosaur then, Mark?

Mark   But he said that!

Tubbsy   I didn't, Mark. It's really not my fault you decided to come as a tyrannosaurus . . .

Mark   I'm a stegosaurus!

Beat.

Jackson   You're seriously the stupidest boy I've ever met.

Mark   But Tubbsy doesn't have a costume!

Tubbsy   I do. I just don't feel like wearing it right now.

Cari-Ann   I thought you said you'd left it at home.

Tubbsy   I lied.

Mark   Did you want to get me into trouble, Tubbsy?

Silence.

Why would you do that?

Deirdre-May   It's a very good costume, Mark.

Mark   Well I'll just have to go home and change now, won't I?

He goes for the gate.

Tubbsy   You can't.

Mark   Why not?

Tubbsy   The gate'll electrocute you.

Mark   Ha ha. Very funny. You expect me to believe that, do you?

Tubbsy   It's the truth.

Cari-Ann   Seriously, Mark. He's telling the truth.

Jackson   Don't listen to her, she keeps telling everyone she's related to Anne Frank!

Cari-Ann   I am!

Jackson   See. You can't believe a word she says.

Lisa   Jackson!

Jackson   What?

Lisa   Why you saying that?

Jackson   Because she's not related to Anne Frank!

Douglas   But the gate *will* electrocute him.

Melony   Don't be ridiculous. They're being ridiculous, aren't they, Jinx?

Jinx   Yes.

Jackson   Finally! Someone speaks sense.

Melony   Exactly.

Tubbsy   You called her liar a minute ago.

Deirdre-May   Why would the gate electrocute you? The Provost's very strict on health and safety.

Bradley   It electrocuted Tubbsy.

Melony   No it didn't.

Tubbsy, **Cari-Ann**, **Bradley**, **Lisa** *and* **Douglas**   It did!

Mark (*getting upset*)   I don't believe you! I don't believe any of you. You're just being mean. You're just making fun of me. Like usual.

He puts his hand on the gate. He flies back with an electric shock.

Mark   Aw!

Tubbsy   Told you.

Jackson *laughs.*

Genevieve   For goodness sake, will people stop trying to leave? It's getting terribly tedious.

Guinevere   I don't know . . . I'm rather enjoying it, actually.

Melony   What's going on?

Those in the know point at the CCTV cameras and PA.

Melony   We're being watched!

Lisa   It's for our own protection.

Melony   And electrocuted!

Deirdre-May   It's not right.

Lisa   Don't be ridiculous. It's only there because it stopped the cattle escaping.

Melony   And they're all dead now!

Lisa   OK. Things have gone far enough. We're winding each other up now for no good reason. We need to come together. Because in case any of you've forgotten, in twenty-five minutes we'll all be singing . . .

Mark (*to* **Melony**)   Why did you lie to me?

Melony   We didn't know, Mark. Honestly.

Mark   You did. You all did.

Jackson   No they didn't.

Beat.

But I did. And I did it anyway.

Mark   Why would you do that?

Jackson   Because I wanted to know if my theory was right about why the dinosaurs got extinct.

Mark   What theory?

Jackson   That they all died because they were really, really stupid.

Mark   It hurt, Jackson. It really, really hurt.

He sits, exasperated, next to **Cari-Ann**. *She looks up from her book.*

Cari-Ann (*sympathetically*)   You're just like Anne Frank.

Mark   What?

Cari-Ann   A bit of a girl.

Beat.

Did I tell you we're related?

Douglas   You're not related to Anne Frank, Cari-Ann Chubb.

Cari-Ann   I am!

Douglas   But she's Jewish!

Cari-Ann   From afar.

Douglas   And Dutch.

Cari-Ann   How do you know I'm not Dutch?

Douglas   Your surname's 'Chubb'.

Cari-Ann   So?

Douglas   I looked it up once.

Cari-Ann   See?! You are a pervert.

Douglas   You can call me what you like. You're named after a short, fat fish with a voracious appetite.

Cari-Ann   I am not.

Douglas   That's what it said. Short, fat and sluggish. What was it you said, Cari-Ann? 'Stick with what you're given'?

Cari-Ann   I hate you.

Lisa   Please, please. Let's not fight. Can't we just be nice to each other for once? We're a team aren't we? A union? Unity is . . . ?

No one answers.

Lisa   Come on guys. Unity is . . . ?

No one answers.

Jackson (*aggressively*)   She asked a simple question. Unity is . . . ?

Everyone (*except* **Tubbsy**)   Power.

Jackson   Tubbsy?

Tubbsy (*reluctantly*)   Power.

Lisa   Thank you, Jackson. Now for the last time, can we please rehearse?

Jackson (*powerfully*)   No. I think we should wait for Lydia.

Melony   Well, in that case, you'll be waiting until the cows come home.

Jackson   What do you mean?

Lisa   I hope you don't mean these cows, because they're not *ever* coming home are they?!

Jackson   What do you mean, Melony?

Melony   It was a metaphor, Lisa.

Lisa   Li-za. And I know it was a metaphor. I was making a joke. Smelony.

Melony   Melony.

Jackson   Melony?

Melony   That's right.

Jackson   No. What do you mean about Lydia?

Melony   Oh right. Well, we saw her on our way here with the Provost, didn't we? She was crying and he was waving his arms about wildly. Wasn't he, Jinx?

Jinx   Yes.

Jackson   Oh, another lie!

Melony   It's not. I promise.

Jackson   What was he shouting about then?

Melony   I don't know. Something about lewd, filthy and disgusting behaviour . . . Not that I was listening or anything.

Jackson   You're lying.

Melony   I'm not. I mean I couldn't really hear him 'cause I was in a rush to get here, but I think I heard him say something about how she'd let herself down, but more importantly, she'd let the league down by frater . . . frater . . .

Douglas   Fraternising?

Melony   Fraternising with the enemy . . .

Jackson   What enemy?

Cari-Ann   Maybe she went to the tattoo artist as well?

Jackson   There is no tattoo artist!

Melony   Well, whoever it is, apparently she's a traitor for having such obscene photographs or something, and if the Provost ever gets his hands on the scum from Southbridge who sent them then he'll be lucky to even retain his manhood, let alone display it in such graphic, shocking definition and high-pixel density.

Everyone's surprised by her specificity.

Melony   Or something like that. As I said, I wasn't really listening.

Cari-Ann   Ooh, sounds like Lydia's been a naughty girl. Bet you wish you hadn't used so much gel now, Jackson!

Jackson (*screams*)   Shut up!

Everyone stares at him agog.

Melony   I might have got it wrong . . .

Beat.

Jackson   Where is she now?

Melony   I don't know.

Jackson (*threatening*)   Tell me! What happened to her?

Melony   Stop it. You're scaring me, Jackson.

Jackson   Then tell me.

Melony   I don't know.

Jackson   Tell me, Smelony!

Melony   Don't call me Smelony!

Genevieve   Is everything alright down there?

Guinevere   There's an awful lot of gesticulating going on.

Lisa   Everything's fine. Everything's fine.

She does a big thumbs-up to the camera.

I'm going to lead a warm-up now. Anyone want to join me?

Lisa   Jackson?

Jackson   No.

Lisa   But we really should . . .

Jackson   I said NO!

Lisa   Dickhead?

Bradley   I'd rather not, if that's OK? I'm still worried about my cat.

Lisa   Tubbsy?

He shakes his head.

Deirdre-May?

She shakes her head.

Lisa   *Anyone?*

Beat.

Lisa   Cari-Ann?

Cari-Ann (*nodding to her book*)   No. I want to know if she escapes.

Beat.

Douglas   She doesn't.

Cari-Ann   I hate you!

Lisa   Mark?

He shakes his head.

Lisa   Melony? Jinx?

Melony *nods her head.* **Jinx** *copies her.*

Lisa   But we'll embarrass ourselves. We're not ready.

Douglas *edges towards* **Lisa**. *He lowers his voice right down.*

Douglas   Look, Liza . . .

Lisa (*without thinking*)   Liza.

Douglas   I said 'Liza'.

Lisa   Oh yes.

Douglas   Something smells a bit fishy if you ask me.

Lisa   Melony?

Douglas   I'm being serious.

Lisa   So am I.

Douglas   Something's not quite right.

Lisa   Why?

Douglas   Because . . . well, for starters: this paddock, the fence . . .

Lisa   You're paranoid, Douglas!

Douglas   The CCTV, the twins . . . I mean, the Provost's turning into a bit of a megalomaniac.

Lisa   Oh Douglas, you don't half use funny words. The Provost's right: you need to stop reading.

Douglas   But don't you see? This sense of pride we're meant to feel for Northbridge . . .

Lisa   I do feel it!

Douglas   Nobody else here seems to.

Lisa   Well, more fool them.

Douglas   And these silly costumes . . .

Lisa   I happen to like these silly costumes. They're wonderful to dance in.

Douglas   But why do we have to wear them?

Lisa   They're *traditional*. It means we belong to something.

Douglas   By making us all the same.

Lisa   Don't be stupid. We're all beautiful in our unique way. I mean, look at Mark . . .

Douglas   Yes. Mark is special I must admit.

Lisa   There you go.

Douglas   But the anthem! What's that all about . . . 'Fall on your sword . . . Our love asks no questions.' It's telling us to commit mass suicide . . .

Lisa   Oh, don't be ridiculous! That's a metaphor!

Douglas   Is it?

Lisa   Yes!

Douglas   What about Deirdre-May's nanna then?

Lisa   What? You think she's dead because she took the anthem a little too seriously?

Douglas   No.

Lisa   What then?

He pauses for a moment.

Douglas   Maybe she didn't take it seriously enough?

Lisa (*in hushed tones*)   Now, stop it, Douglas! I must insist you stop it! You're over-reacting.

Douglas   Am I?

Lisa   Yes. Deirdre-May's nanna was bonkers. That's why she killed herself. She was doolally! End of story. Doo-la-lly. Just like her granddaughter.

Douglas   Deirdre-May's not doolally. She's just *different*.

Lisa   She talks to the dead!

Douglas   Well, yes . . . they probably don't ignore her like we do.

Lisa   Please, Douglas. Can we just talk about something else?

Douglas   Hear me out.

Lisa   No, Douglas. I've heard you out! And I must insist you stop it with these weird conspiracy theories.

Douglas   But what about Tubbsy's brother? No one really knows what happened to him either, do they?

Lisa   Andrew left.

Douglas   He was made to leave.

Lisa   Well yes, but . . .

Douglas   But none of us actually saw him go, did we?

Lisa   Stop it, Douglas! Stop it! You've gone nuts over a tiny bit of patriotism . . .

Douglas   There's a really big difference between feeling passionate and feeling superior . . .

Lisa   You think way too much.

Douglas   Maybe you don't think enough.

Lisa (*hysteria rising*)   Well, we can't all be as clever as you, Douglas. And actually, sometimes it's nice not to have to think. I mean: I for one was quite pleased not to have to make a wardrobe decision today. Because – often – I find it impossible deciding what to wear. Yes! I do! I find myself staring into the wardrobe. For hours! I can be there for hours! My mother thinks I'm lazy and that I take ages to get out of bed, but I've been standing there since six deciding between a tie-front and a denim. We have way too much choice! It's terrifying. I panic when I have to make any decision. Sometimes I panic so much I throw up. Isn't it lovely, just for once, Douglas . . . Isn't it lovely, just to be told what to do?

Everyone's looking at **Lisa**.

Genevieve   Is everything OK, Lisa?

Lisa (*barks*)   Liza!

She collects herself and smiles through gritted teeth at the camera with her thumbs up.

Everything's fine! Everything's fine! Come on, everyone. Chop, chop! Let's rehearse. Tubbsy, you really ought to be thinking about getting into your costume. Let's remind ourselves of who we are!

Melony   Who we're told we are. I'm more of a hoodie and thong kind of girl.

Everyone recoils at the thought, except for **Lisa**, *who's too het up to notice.*

Lisa (*manic*)   I'm going to warm up now, and I really think it would be a good idea if other people joined in with me because if they don't I'm going to get very, very angry! Jamie! Accompany us. Something soothing.

Jamie *immediately begins to play the theme tune from* Schindler's List.

Lisa (*barks*)   NOT THAT!

Jamie *plays the melody of the Northbridge anthem.*

Cari-Ann *continues to read.* **Jackson** *stares out into space.* **Tubbsy** *sits moodily next to his bag.*

Melony, **Jinx**, **Douglas** *and* **Mark** *join* **Lisa** *as she leads a physical warm-up.*

Deirdre-May *turns to* **Bradley**.

Deirdre-May   Dickhead?

Bradley   Yes.

Deirdre-May   Why do they call you Dickhead?

Bradley   Because that's my name.

Deirdre-May   Your mum and dad actually called you Dickhead?

Bradley No. Jackson did once and it caught hold.

Deirdre-May Don't you mind?

Bradley I did. But I don't mind so much now. I just got used to it.

Deirdre-May And were you?

Bradley What?

Deirdre-May A dickhead.

Bradley I don't think so. I did use to cry a lot though.

Deirdre-May Why didn't he just call you cry-baby?

Bradley I don't know. But I prefer Dickhead. It has more . . . gravitas. Don't you think?

Deirdre-May Do you think you'll always be called Dickhead?

Bradley Yeah. Probably. I thought it might stop once Mark moved here and they started to pick on him but it's just . . . well . . . it's just my name now.

Beat.

Deirdre-May Well, I don't think you are.

Bradley What?

Deirdre-May A dickhead.

Beat.

Bradley Thank you.

I'm sorry to hear about your nanna.

Deirdre-May I'm sorry to hear about your cat.

Bradley Thanks, but hopefully he's not dead like your nanna.

Deirdre-May *withdraws slightly.*

Deirdre-May   You need to think before you speak, Dickhead.

Bradley   Sorry.

Bradley   Is it true she shot herself?

Deirdre-May   Yes. I found her. She had a very big brain.

Bradley   Poor you, Deirdre-May. That's awful. You must be in terrible shock?

Deirdre-May   No. I'm not sure if anything shocks me. Not any more.

Bradley   Why did she shoot herself?

Deirdre-May   To be honest, Bradley. I'm not so sure that she did.

Lisa *suddenly stops the warm-up.*

Lisa   OK. That's enough warming up.

Douglas   We haven't done a vocal warm-up.

Lisa   Oh yes, we should do a vocal warm-up. Why don't we all sing 'Happy Birthday' to Tubbsy? (*Sings.*) Happy Birthday to you . . .

Tubbsy (*explodes*)   SHUT UP!

Silence.

Melony   Maybe we don't need to do a vocal warm-up.

Lisa   Fine, if you want to get nodules . . .

Melony   Why would I want to get a Chinese now?

Lisa   Not noodles. NOD-ULES. Like Julie Andrews or Connie Fisher.

Melony   Who?

Lisa   Connie Fisher?

Mark   You know. The one who's in *Star Wars*?

Melony   I haven't watched *Star Wars*!

Lisa   She wasn't in *Star Wars*! God, Melony. You really are stupid sometimes.

Melony   Mark said it . . .

Lisa   Yes, well, we expect Mark to be a pleb don't we?

Melony   You little . . . (bitch).

She grabs **Lisa** *by the hair: a catfight is about to ensue . . .*

Genevieve   Smelony Cooke! Stop that at once!

Guinevere   Or I'll sound the klaxon!

Melony   Oh screw you and your klaxon!

She lifts her skirt and moons towards the camera. **Cari-Ann** *happens to get caught in the crossfire.*

Genevieve   Just you wait until Daddy finds out.

Guinevere   You'll get suspended from the Youth League for that.

Melony   Oh yeah. Well . . . I'll suspend you too! I'll dangle you both by your bra straps off the village tower and play you like a game of swing ball!

Everyone gasps.

(*Exceptionally pleased with herself.*)   Now who's in charge?!

Pause.

Cari-Ann   Melony . . . Why have you got Jackson's name written on your bottom?

Melony *gasps.* **Lisa** *beams with relish.*

Melony   What you talking about, Chubbster?

Cari-Ann   Jackson. You have his name in capital letters spelt across your bum.

Melony   No I don't.

Cari-Ann   You do. In big, black, capital letters.

Melony   She's lying.

Cari-Ann   I'm not.

Lisa   Oh my God! Is that your tattoo? Did you get Jackson's name tattooed across your arse?

Melony   No!

Lisa   You did, didn't you?

Melony   I didn't! Tell them, Jinx . . .

Douglas   Oh my God! You so did!

Melony   You can't believe a word Cari-Ann says! She's a liar.

Cari-Ann   You're mental!

Melony   I'm not mental!

Douglas   You've got Jackson's name tattooed across your arse! I hardly think that vouches for your sanity.

Cari-Ann   You've actually gone and got Jackson's name tattooed across your arse!

Melony   Shut up!

Cari-Ann   Is that because you know that's the only way you'll get Jackson anywhere near your –

Jackson   Everyone be quiet.

Cari-Ann   Don't you care, Jackson? Don't you care that she's got your –

Jackson (*with real menace*)   SHUT UP, I SAID!

Everyone looks at him, a little frightened.

Jackson   If we really want to know the truth, then we should make her show us, shouldn't we?

Silence.

Jackson   Pull your knickers down, Smelony.

Silence.

Jackson   I SAID: PULL YOUR KNICKERS DOWN!

Melony *looks terrified.*

Lisa   Jackson . . .

Cari-Ann   You're going too far . . .

Jackson   You were the ones who wanted to know . . .

Douglas   I don't want to know any more.

Jackson   PULL YOUR KNICKERS DOWN!

Pause.

NOW!

Terrible pause.

He bursts out laughing.

I'm only joking, aren't I! Look at your faces!

Beat.

I'm joking!

Cari-Ann   You didn't sound like you were joking . . .

Jackson   Of course I was joking!

Melony *laughs, but it's obviously an act.*

Melony   I knew you were joking, Jackson. Seriously. You're hilarious you are.

Silence.

Cari-Ann   No wonder Lydia's not interested in you. You're a nut-case.

Jackson *grabs* **Cari-Ann** *by the neck and raises his fist.*

Jackson   What did you say?

Genevieve   Jackson McDonald! One more stunt like that and you'll be punished.

Guinevere   Severely!

Jackson *backs off. Everyone stares at him.*

Cari-Ann   You were going to hit me. You were actually going to hit me. You can't do that.

Jackson   Why not?

Cari-Ann   You can't hit a girl.

Jackson *(quietly)*   Why not? I should treat girls equally to boys, shouldn't I? *(Beat.)* I'm joking, guys! I'm joking. God. You're so gullible!

Lisa *(quickly)*   Guys! Guys! What's happening to us? Seriously? What about some team spirit? In twenty minutes we'll be singing our little hearts out, proving what outstanding citizens of Northbridge we are. But look at us! None of us are being outstanding. We're tearing shreds out of each other. What we need is a group activity. Might I suggest that we have a little rehear –

Everyone   No!

Jackson   No one wants to rehearse, Lisa.

Lisa   Well it was just a suggestion.

Beat.

And my name's . . .

*Something in **Jackson**'s look stops her.*

Deirdre-May   We could always do a Ouija board!

Cari-Ann   Oh please! Seriously! You and your blinkin' Ouija boards. I hardly think now's the time to summon the dead.

Deirdre-May   I think now's the perfect time. All this negative energy will attract the spirits and they might help heal us.

Lisa   I'm sorry. But surely a little collective singing is better for us than meddling with the occult. Though it's understandable, Deirdre-May . . .

Deirdre-May   It's not for me. It's for Bradley.

Tubbsy   Who's Bradley?

Bradley   I'm Bradley.

Tubbsy   Oh. Dickhead.

Deirdre-May   His name's Bradley. And he's lost his cat. And Nanna could help us find it.

She gets a Ouija board from her bag.

Cari-Ann   You carry a Ouija board with you in your bag?

Deirdre-May   Just in case.

Cari-Ann *mouths 'Just in case?' sarcastically, behind her back, and then points to her head: 'She's completely bonkers.'*

Deirdre-May   Come on, everyone, we haven't got long. Listen . . .

They listen. The distant strains of music are heard: the accompaniment to the Dance of the Horned Ram.

Jackson   The Dance of the Horned Ram.

Bradley (*shudders*)   That poor ewe.

Lisa   No ewe is harmed. I can assure you!

Still no one moves.

Deirdre-May   It's just a bit of fun, that's all. It'll help take our mind off things.

Everyone except for **Tubbsy** *and* **Melony** *heads towards* **Deirdre-May**.

Deirdre-May   How about you, Tubbsy?

Tubbsy   I don't want to.

Deirdre-May   It would be good for the group.

Tubbsy   I don't care about the group.

Jackson (*loaded*)   What you scared of, Tubbsy?

Tubbsy   Nothing.

Deirdre-May   Melony?

Melony *shakes her head, still desperately upset.*

Jackson   Come on, Melony. Please.

Melony *shakes her head again suspiciously.*

Jackson   It's just a bit of fun.

She shakes her head again.

Jackson   I'd really like it if you did.

It's all she needs. Everyone else is slightly suspicious.

Deirdre-May *sets up a glass on a Ouija board.*

Genevieve (*threateningly*)   Um . . . What is that?

Cari-Ann   Oh God, here we go . . .

Guinevere   Is that a Ouija board?

Everyone looks up and nods.

Genevieve   The Youth League is a Christian organisation and we simply cannot allow you to engage in such dark matters.

Guinevere   Yes. We must insist that you pack that up at once and . . . .

Jackson *quickly whips out a gun and shoots it towards the camera. The bang makes everyone scream.*

Lisa   What the hell do you think you're doing, Jackson?

Jackson   Chill your knickers, Lisa. It's just a pellet gun.

Cari-Ann   OMG, you're mental you are! You're blinking mental!

Melony   That was awesome! That was awesome, wasn't it, Jinx?

Jinx   Yes.

Genevieve (*real panic*)   What just happened? We can't see you! Is everything alright down there?

Bradley   You hit the camera!

Douglas   They've got no idea what's going on!

Guinevere   Is everything alright?

Mark   Why have you got a pellet gun, Jackson?

Jackson   Well, you never know when it's going to come in handy, do you?

Mark   But . . .

Melony   Oh be quiet, Mark. At least we don't have those two sticking their noses in any more . . .

Genevieve   What should we do?

Guinevere   I don't know. Do you think they're in any . . . danger?

Genevieve   It's probably just a . . . you know . . .

Guinevere   Yeah . . . a technical difficulty . . .

Lisa   But it was for our own protection . . .

Melony   Well, Jackson can protect us now, can't he?

Genevieve   It's probably just a technical difficulty but maybe we should . . . Do you think they can still hear us? Um . . . can you still hear us? Um . . . just sit tight and we'll . . . we'll . . .

Guinevere   What if they're in trouble?

Genevieve   What kind of trouble?

Guinevere   I don't know. *Trouble.*

Beat.

Genevieve   We're going to the hall to get help!

We hear them leaving their watch tower. A mini-celebration amidst the young people.

Melony   Jackson, that was sick. You were so quick they didn't even see it!

Jackson   I've been practising.

Mark   For what?

Lisa   Yes. For what?

Jackson   Are we going to do this Ouija board?

Beat.

Deirdre-May?

Deirdre-May   Um . . . OK. If everyone wants to put a finger on the glass.

Everyone does so.

Melony   Quit pushing, Cari-Ann!

Cari-Ann   I'm trying to get away from Mark: he stinks!

Mark   It's not my fault my body's changing.

Cari-Ann   You're telling me, Tyrannosaurus.

Mark   I'm a stega –

Cari-Ann   Oh they're all the same.

Mark   No they're not. That's racist.

Deirdre-May   We've got be quiet or the spirits won't come.

Mark   But she's standing on my tail.

Cari-Ann   It's not *your* tail, Mark.

Deirdre-May   We need to try and keep calm.

Lisa   Maybe Jamie could help? Why don't you try and play some music to help us focus? We're all a bit nervous, aren't we? About singing in front of everyone. That's all. Would you mind, Jamie? Playing something suitable?

Jackson   You're the boss now, are you, Lisa?

Lisa   Um . . . no . . . I just thought . . . I'm not the boss. I'm a . . . *facilitator*. Would you like Jamie to play some music, Jackson?

Jackson   Yes.

Jamie *leaves the group and goes to his instrument. He starts playing the theme tune from* Jaws.

Lisa   Not that.

Deirdre-May   Could you play something else, Jamie? It's affecting my chakras.

Jamie *plays some eerie music.*

Cari-Ann   Oh gross! Has someone just farted?

Beat.

Jinx   Yes.

Everyone   Oh, Jinx!

Deirdre-May   Shhh, everyone. Come on. Concentrate . . .

Beat.

Nanna are you there?

Silence.

Nanna are you there?

Douglas   Was your Nanna shy, Deirdre-May?

Deirdre-May   Shh, Douglas. I think I can feel something.

Cari-Ann   So can I. Mark's got a stiffy!

Mark   I have not! That's my dorsal plate.

Cari-Ann   You should get that looked at.

Deirdre-May   Shhh! Look! The glass is moving.

The glass begins to move.

Douglas   You're pushing it, Deirdre-May.

Deirdre-May   I'm not pushing it.

Bradley   I'm not sure if I like this . . .

Deirdre-May   It's OK. She won't hurt you.

Lisa   Someone's definitely pushing it!

Melony   I'm not pushing it.

Lisa   Who's pushing it then?

Deirdre-May   No one's pushing it. It's the spirits. Is that you, Nanna?

The glass suddenly moves to 'No'. They all let out a little gasp/scream.

Bradley   I definitely don't like this.

Deirdre-May   You don't have to be scared. They don't come to harm us. They come because they've got something they want to say.

Bradley   Yeah. And I'm scared of *what* they might say.

Mark   Ask it who's there?

Douglas   As a man of science, Mark, I thought you wouldn't have much care for such things.

Lisa   He's dressed as a dinosaur. I think he's lost all sense of credibility, don't you?

Melony   Go on, Deirdre-May. Ask who's there . . .

Bradley   I don't want to, I'm scared. We don't know what we're letting ourselves in for. It's all going to go wrong.

Douglas   This is silly.

Melony   Is anyone going to ask?

Douglas   This is absolutely ridiculous.

Melony   Is anyone going to ask it who's there?

Douglas   It's group hysteria!

Jackson   Knock, knock?

Everyone   Who's there?

They all gasp as they realise what they've just done. **Jackson** *smiles.*

They wait in silence. At first nothing happens. Then slowly the glass begins to move. No one seems to breathe.

Deirdre-May   J . . . C . . . No! It's still going . . . A.

Melony   A. Does anyone know anyone beginning with A?

Silence.

Tubbsy   You're all stupid!

Jackson   Shut it, Tubbsy. Just because you decided not to join.

Deirdre-May   It's moving again . . . P . . . No . . . no . . . wait! N! . . . N! A . . . N . . .

Cari-Ann   O.M.G.

Deirdre-May   No. It was definitely A, N.

Cari-Ann   No! O.M.G . . . *A, N*!

Lisa   Are you speaking in code, Cari-Ann?

Cari-Ann   No! A . . . N! It's Anne Frank!

Lisa   Don't be so stupid.

Melony   Yeah. Shut it, Cari-Ann.

Cari-Ann   No seriously. I think it's Anne Frank. I think I might be channelling her. It's because I'm prone to depression.

Douglas   It's not Anne Frank!

Cari-Ann   How do you know?

Douglas   Because I hardly think she'd choose to come to Northbridge.

Cari-Ann   Why not? She might have done. Deirdre-May's nanna might have told her how nice it was . . .

Douglas   I doubt that somehow.

Mark   I suppose it could be her . . . Can ghosts swim?

Douglas   Don't be so stupid, Mark.

Mark   Or maybe she came on the Eurostar.

Douglas   Seriously? Are you seriously saying that Anne Frank, after everything she's been through, decided that what she'd like to do, more than anything in the world, is to get on the Eurostar and come to Northbridge . . .

Cari-Ann   Ask her. Just ask her!

Beat.

Deirdre-May   OK, OK! Are you Anne Frank?

After a short pause, the glass begins to move again.

Cari-Ann   Yes . . . Yes . . .

The glass continues towards the 'No'.

Cari-Ann   Oh.

Bradley   Don't worry, Cari-Ann. You could have been right. It could have been her.

Melony   Oh yeah? And how do you work that one out, dufus?

Bradley   Because maybe she became an angel and flew?

Deirdre-May   That's really beautiful, Bradley.

Melony   That's not beautiful. That's moronic. Isn't it, Jinx?

Beat.

Jinx   No. Wouldn't it be nice if we could all fly away from here?

Pause.

Melony   What is wrong with you? Don't speak. It doesn't suit you.

Jackson   Let's just get on with it.

Deirdre-May   Yes, of course. Now, where were we?

Douglas   Sorry, Deirdre-May. I like you and everything, but really – I have to say – this is absolute rubbish.

Lisa   Douglas! That's hardly in the spirit of things. We're doing this to bond the group.

Douglas   That doesn't mean I shouldn't question it though, does it?

Lisa   Well actually, Douglas, I think in this instance it does. Sometimes, just for the sake of getting along, it's good not to question.

Deirdre-May   Why do you think it's rubbish, Douglas?

Douglas   Because I don't think ghosts would stop for dramatic pauses.

Deirdre-May   What do you mean?

Douglas   Well, if it really were a spirit controlling the glass, don't you think he, she or malevolent 'it' would have *continued* to spell their name, rather than wait politely for us to finish our argument?

They consider this for a moment.

Cari-Ann   Anne Frank was exceptionally polite.

Everyone   It's not Anne Frank!

Cari-Ann   I was just saying.

Deirdre-May   The spirits use the energy of the group to communicate, Douglas. It only works when we're all focused.

Jackson   He's just interfering because he's scared. You're scared, aren't you?

Douglas   I am a bit scared actually.

Beat.

Lisa   Come on, Douglas. Everything's fine. Let's just get on with it, shall we?

Jackson   Yes. For the good of the group. Right, Lisa?

Lisa   Um . . . right. Yes. Exactly. For the good of the group.

Beat.

Bradley (*tentatively*)   What about Tubbsy?

Jackson   What about Tubbsy?

Bradley   Well, he's part of our group too.

Jackson   I'm not so sure. He's not wearing our uniform, is he?

Tubbsy (*quietly*)   I am.

Slowly, he pulls off his hoodie to reveal the uniform underneath.

Jackson   Then join us.

Tubbsy *shakes his head.*

Jackson (*turns back to the group*)   Come on. We haven't got long.

Lisa (*unsure*)   It *is* just a bit of fun, isn't it? Right, Jackson?

Jackson   Sure. It's just a bit of fun. Shall we carry on? Unless anyone else is desperate to say something?

Jamie *puts his hand up. They all stare at him with a huge sense of anticipation.*

The buzzer goes off. They all scream.

Genevieve *and* **Guinevere** *enter the paddock. They are dazed. They speak functionally.*

Lisa   It must be time!

Genevieve   Can Mark come to the hall, please?

Cari-Ann   Mark? Why Mark?

Guinevere   He's won a prize.

Lisa   Are you OK, Genevieve?

Genevieve   For best costume.

Mark (*excited*)   A prize! I've never won a prize before! I've won a prize!

Douglas   What prize?

Lisa   Ooh. No one told me there was a prize? I've got loads of costumes! I could have come as a Geisha!

Guinevere   Now, Mark.

Douglas   I'm not sure if you should go, Mark.

Deirdre-May   No. I'm not sure if you should go either. Guinevere, is everything alright?

Mark   Of course I should go. There you go again. Well you're just jealous. You're just jealous because I've won a prize and you haven't!

Genevieve   Mark, can you make your way now then, please.

Lisa   Shouldn't we all come?

Guinevere   Just Mark.

Genevieve   Just Mark.

Mark *follows* **Guinevere** *and* **Genevieve** *out of the gate.*

Mark (*beaming*)   I never win anything!

The gate shuts.

Lisa   Well, good for him, don't you think? Good for him.

Silence.

Deirdre-May   I'm not sure if I feel like doing this any more.

Jackson (*wanting to feel in control*)   You'll do as I say. Fingers on the glass.

No one moves.

Fingers on the glass, I said!

They put their fingers on the glass.

Thank you. I'll lead, shall I?

Nobody answers.

I'll lead. Yes. I'll lead. Is there anybody there?

Nothing.

I said. Is there anybody there?

The glass moves to a 'Yes'.

Who are you?

The glass begins to move again, confidently.

Jackson   A ... N ...

The glass continues to move ...

D ... A, N, D ...

Bradley   Let's stop. Please. Let's stop ...

Jackson   Tell us who you are?

The glass moves again

R. A, N, D, R . . . .

Lisa   We *should* stop. It's gone too far.

Jackson   We can't, it's too strong.

Douglas   Jackson. You're pushing it.

Jackson   I'm not pushing it!

Douglas   Then we're all pushing it!

The glass continues to move . . .

Deirdre-May   A, N, D, R . . . is that an S? That doesn't make sense.

Melony   I think it is. I think it's an S. That's definitely an 'S', isn't it, Jinx?

Jinx   'S'.

Jackson   No, wait, look! It's moving. To an E. That's definitely an E.

Melony   He's right. It's an E.

Jackson   A, N, D, R, E . . . it's moving again, it's moving again . . . W.

Beat.

Lisa   Andrew.

They all slowly take their fingers of the glass. They cannot look at each other.

Jackson   Maybe we should ask him what he has to say?

Tubbsy (*quietly*)   Do you think Andrew's dead?

Silence.

I said, do you think Andrew's dead?

Lisa   No one said he was. It's probably a different Andrew.

Tubbsy   But that's what you're all thinking?

Deirdre-May   We're not thinking anything of the sort.

Tubbsy   Aren't you?

Bradley   No, Tubbsy . . .

Tubbsy   But you did that. You all did that!

Jackson   It wasn't us.

Tubbsy   It was! You pushed the glass . . .

Jackson   It wasn't us!

Tubbsy   Who was it then?

Deirdre-May   It's OK, Stephen. I understand why you're upset . . .

Tubbsy   No you don't. You're just horrible. You're all just horrible, vile human beings. Every one of you.

Melony   Don't talk to us like that, Tubbsy.

Tubbsy   Why not? It's the truth.

Lisa   Please, Tubbsy, don't . . . .Please. Can't we just be nice to each other. Can't we just for once be nice to each other!

Tubbsy   Nice to each other! There's no point us being nice to each other! We're finished. We're all finished!

Douglas   Just calm down now, Tubbsy. Let's just calm down. You're right. We shouldn't have done the Ouija board. It was stupid. And Andrew's not dead . . .

Tubbsy (*screams suddenly*)   Of course he's dead! Of course he is. We all know that! We all know that deep down, but we're too terrified to admit it . . .

Lisa   Don't be silly, Tubbsy, everything's fine!

Tubbsy   EVERYTHING'S NOT FINE! Open your eyes!
Let's all be honest with each other for once. He's dead. He's
dead, isn't he?

Lisa   No . . .

Tubbsy   Yes! He was killed, just like Deirdre-May's nan,
just like . . .

Jackson   Don't listen to him! He's lying.

Tubbsy   Oh, Jackson, you think you're in charge, but
you're not. You think you're really powerful, but you're not.
Because you don't know anything. You just pretend you do.
But that's not power. That's fear. You're scared, Jackson. Just
like Andrew was. But he spoke out. Despite that. He spoke
out. And that's why he's dead . . . He's dead and he's not
coming back. (*Repeating, with realisation: he hasn't said it before.*)
He's dead. And he's not coming back. And I'm a coward and
I'm still here. It's my birthday and I'm still here. But none of
us deserve to be, do we?

Lisa   Stop it, Tubbsy! Stop it!

Tubbsy   Because look at us! Look at us all! We're useless.
We're as bad as them. We *can't* be nice to each other. We
don't even like each other . . .

Bradley   I like you, Tubbsy . . .

Deirdre-May   So do I . . . .

Tubbsy   You're lying.

Cari-Ann   I like you too, Tubbsy. Really I do.

Tubbsy   We're all liars. Because we've turned into them.
We've actually turned into them. It's too late. There's nothing
we can do! Because soon . . . soon . . .

Lisa   Soon everything will be fine because we'll all be
singing! It's going to be beautiful. We're going to sing
beautifully.

Tubbsy   Soon we'll be dead.

Pause.

Just like Mark.

Jackson   He's lost it! He's completely lost it!

Beat.

Lisa (*quietly*)   Has he?

Jackson   Don't say you believe him do you?

You actually believe him?

Beat.

You think Tubbsy's speaking the truth?

No one answers.

You think Tubbsy's right in the head, do you?

Silence.

Well, do you?

Silence.

Ask him what's in the bag then!

Silence.

Ask him.

Silence.

Ask him what's in the bag!

Best.

Alright. I'll ask him.

Beat.

What's in the bag, Tubbsy?

What's in the bag?

Bradley   It's a dinosaur bone, right?

Jackson   Ask him.

Bradley   That's what you said. You and Cari-Ann said . . .

*He looks at **Cari-Ann**. She looks away.*

Bradley   Cari-Ann?

*He looks back at **Tubbsy**.*

Bradley   What's in the bag, Tubbsy?

Silence.

What's in the bag?

Jackson   Why don't you open it, Bradley?

Beat.

Go on. Open it.

Bradley *walks towards the bag.*

Cari-Ann   Don't, Bradley. Don't.

He pauses next to the bag.

Bradley   Why not?

Cari-Ann   Don't.

Bradley *crouches next to the bag. He slowly opens the zip . . . The sound is excruciating.*

*He's interrupted by **Genevieve** and **Guinevere** on the P.A.*

Genevieve   We hope you can still hear us.

Guinevere   Because we just wanted to say . . .

Genevieve   We're really sorry.

Guinevere   We're really, really sorry.

Everyone listens, terrified.

Genevieve   We wanted to warn you.

Guinevere   Yes. We wanted to warn you.

Genevieve   But they saw us watching.

Guinevere   They saw us.

Genevieve   Watching the ewe . . .

Guinevere   Watching the ewe . . .

Genevieve   Watching the ewe get slaughtered.

Beat.

Guinevere   Poor Lydia.

Beat.

A gunshot. Another gunshot.

An eerie silence.

They are all frozen for a moment.

Lisa   Well, I really think we should sing now.

Bradley   What?

Lisa   Well it's time, isn't it? For us to sing? I've been trying to get us to sing for ages.

Bradley   But . . .

Deirdre-May   She's right. We need to stay focused. We . . . We . . .

Douglas   We should all stand together, shouldn't we? To help us concentrate.

Lisa   Yes, Douglas. That's an excellent idea. You really do have a brilliant mind, don't you?

Douglas   Do you think so?

Lisa   Oh yes. Melony, you'll join us won't you?

Melony *stares at her.*

Lisa   We need to rehearse.

Jinx *walks nervously towards them.* **Melony** *sees her go and she follows.*

Lisa   Cari-Ann, will you join us?

Cari-Ann *stares at her.*

Lisa   I really want you to join us.

Cari-Ann *walks towards her.*

Lisa   Jamie? Would you take it from the introduction?

Jamie *slowly walks towards his instrument.*

Lisa   Thank you, Jamie?

Jamie *begins to play the introduction to the song.*

They begin to sing (twice):

> We serve you, dear Fatherland,
> Home of the free;
> For ever your children,
> We bow unto thee.
> We kneel at your altar,
> We fall on your sword,
> We may lose our blood
> But we'll reap your rewards.
> Our love asks no questions,
> Our love feels no shame,
> Your traditions we'll honour:
> United we sing in your name.

Lisa   Jackson, please come and sing with us.

Jackson   Lydia.

Beat.

Lisa   Please. Sing with us, Jackson.

Jackson *walks over and joins in the singing. The singing increases.*

Lisa   Bradley?

Bradley *slowly walks towards them, but rather than stopping, he continues and walks over towards* **Tubbsy**. *He reaches out his hand.* **Tubbsy** *looks at it for a moment.*

Tubbsy *takes off the rest of his clothes to reveal the full uniform underneath. He takes* **Bradley**'s *hand.* **Bradley** *leads him to the group.*

They join in the song. We hear the buzzer go and the gate open. They all look towards the gate, terrified, as their singing grows in intensity.

Just as the song ends, in the half-light we can see **Tubbsy**'s *rucksack. For a moment, there is stillness. Then, quite suddenly, a cat crawls out of the bag and runs towards the gate.*

Blackout.

Northbridge Anthem

Dafydd James

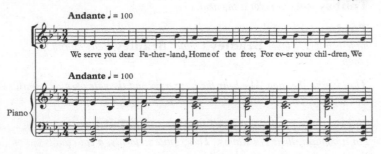

We serve you dear Fa-ther-land, Home of the free; For ev-er your chil-dren, We

bow un-to thee. We kneel at your al-tar, We fall on your sword, We

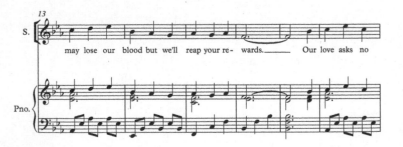

may lose our blood but we'll reap your re- wards._____ Our love asks no

2

ques-tions our love feels no shame,___ Your tra - di-tions we'll ho-nour: U - ni-ted we'll

sing_____ in your name   Fa-ther-land, Home of the free; For

We serve you dear Fa-ther-land, Home of the free; For

Heritage
BY DAFYDD JAMES

*Notes on rehearsal and staging, drawn from two workshops
led by two directors and the writer held at the National Theatre,
November 2013*

*Workshops led by Mike Longhurst and Adam Penford,
with notes taken by Rachel Bagshaw and Kate Budgen*

How the writer came to write the play

Dafydd James wanted to write a play that explored cultural
heritage and, growing up as a Welsh-language speaker, he
participated in all kinds of traditions and rituals that he thought
to an outsider might seem bonkers! He was particularly
inspired by a yearly cultural and artistic festival for young
people called the Urdd National Eisteddfod of Wales, an event
in which thousands of young people take part in music, theatre,
poetry, dance and literature competitions. The traditions kept
alive by this festival are an extremely important part of
sustaining and celebrating what is a marginalised culture, but
it got him thinking: what happens when 'traditions' are
prioritised over the needs and desires of young people? He
wanted to write a play that explored the darker side of culture
and the line between patriotism, traditionalism and fascism.

Dafydd was particularly excited about the chance to write for
a large cast – to write for so many actors is quite a rare
opportunity. He was also really interested in having so many
productions of the play. This is also a little scary for him, as
usually he gets to work on the play right up until the first
production, whereas with this he has to hand it over to all the
directors now! He believes that a play is never finished: it
continues to evolve in front of an audience, and for him this
process is only part-way through. He is really excited to see
what all the different directors come up with and how they
might all imagine the world he has created.

Dafydd talked about his writing process as being in three
parts. The first stage is Dream – he doesn't write anything, but

just lets the ideas percolate and work around in his head. The second stage is Vomit – he starts writing and just lets the characters start to speak and explore the world. Then in the final stage – Sculpt – he shapes the play and the story, turning the ideas and thoughts into the play. As part of the process, he led two workshops with young people and asked them to share what culture means to them. It felt similar to what he remembers from when he was a teenager – the struggle with power and trying to fit in.

While the play offers many clues to what is actually going on, Dafydd has deliberately left things ambivalent and open to interpretation. He doesn't have all the answers, and urges directors to really embrace the creativity and individuality of the young people and bring the world of the play to life in a way that is meaningful to them.

Approaching the play

Northbridge is a mythical, fictional place. There are many clues in the text as to what kind of world it is, but it is up to you to use these clues to decide for yourselves how you want to present Northbridge and the people who live there. It is important that everyone feels a sense of ownership and connection to the world.

Below are some exercises that may help determine what the play is about for you, both individually as a director and collaboratively as a group.

FACTS AND QUESTIONS

This can be done by the director as preparation work before rehearsals begin, or if time allows and you think it would benefit the group, you could do it altogether.

Go through the text and make two lists. The first should be a list of every single fact that is presented in the script. These should be non-contestable, non-negotiable facts about the world of the play, not about the action of the play. The second should be a list of questions large and small that arise as a result of identifying the facts. As you go through the play, you will find that some of your questions will be answered in the text and you can cross them off. The questions that remain unanswered by the text can then be researched to find the answer, or, based on what you know from the text, you can make a decision yourself or with your group. You will find that the first third of the play will be extremely dense in facts and questions, and will become less so as the play goes on.

See below for an example list of facts and questions for the first section of the play, from the stage direction on the first page '*The play takes place in an open enclosure . . .*' to Jackson's line, 'What did you do?'

Example list of facts
- There is an open enclosure, a paddock.
- The paddock is surrounded by a high electric fence.
- There is a gate leading into the paddock.
- There are CCTV cameras and a PA system attached to the electric fence.
- All characters except Tubbsy and Mark wear a 'traditional' uniform.
- Tubbsy is dressed in jeans and a hoodie.
- Mark is dressed as a stegosaurus.
- There's something called the 'Northbridge Anthem', sung by a single young voice.
- There is a buzzer.
- There is a character called Tubbsy.
- Tubbsy has a rucksack in his arms. It is heavy.

Example list of questions
- What is this open enclosure like?
- Where is it?
- Why is there an electric fence surrounding it?
- How tall is the fence?

- Who put it up and why?
- Why is there CCTV and a PA system?
- What is the quality of the PA?
- What is the uniform?
- Are the uniforms new or old?
- Is it normal for these children to wear uniforms?
- How long have they been wearing them?
- Who has told them to wear them?
- Why are they wearing them?
- Why is Tubbsy not wearing the uniform?
- Why is Mark dressed as a stegosaurus?

You can then divide and collate these facts and questions into useful lists. For example:

- All the facts/questions about Northbridge.
- All the facts/questions about the Youth League.
- All the facts/questions related to individual characters.
- All the facts/questions related to events that have happened before the action of the play begins.

These lists can then form the beginning of your understanding of location, world, character and back story. For example, you can use facts about specific characters to begin to build a biography for them. Set out your character facts in order, then see what decisions you need to make to create a full back story.

There are lots of events that occur before the play starts. It might be useful to try and put these events in order to create a timeline, so that everyone is clear what has happened and when. You could choose some of these events and improvise them, to give the company a shared memory of what happened.

Structure

Dafydd set out to write the play in real time, with events unfolding for both characters and audience at the same time. There is a time pressure on these young people and it is useful to pay attention to all the references in the text that are to do with time. The play is structured around the rehearsal, building towards the moment when the anthem is sung. They are running out of time for rehearsals and for their lives.

Music forms an important part of Dafydd's work. He has written the anthem in four-part harmony, but is open to this being adapted or simplified. He is also happy for companies to compose their own music to fit the words.

The play is written as one long act, with no scenes denoted. It would be useful to try and divide the play up into sections that you can use to rehearse. Try and find where the shifts in the play are – the important events – and use these as a way of breaking it down into chapters.

Events within the play

The play can be split into events. An event can be described as 'something that happens in the action of the play that affects everybody and that changes what everyone onstage wants'. Identifying events is a personal process and opinions can differ, there is no right or wrong. Go through the play marking an 'E' next to each moment you identify as an event. Identifying an event is vital for the ensemble dynamic as it means that everyone onstage can have a clear reaction and attitude to something happening. A good example of an event is someone entering or leaving a space.

The trigger event and the main event

It is helpful to decide on the 'trigger event', which occurs before the action begins and sets the play in motion. Then determine what the 'main event' of the play is – what the play is building towards. Having discussions and deciding on these two things can help give the process and the production focus and clarity.

THE TRIGGER EVENT

- Is it the May Day festivities?
- Is it the disappearance of Tubbsy's brother Andrew?
- Is it the selection of the children to sing on May Day?

It is useful to find a trigger event that affects as many of the characters as possible, and so perhaps a useful trigger event is the disappearance of Andrew? It becomes increasingly clear that those who speak out are punished or got rid of and much of the play is about the children choosing not to confront what happened (perhaps due to fear of what will happen if they do?). The fact that Andrew's name appears on the Ouija board suggests the impact his disappearance has had on everyone.

THE MAIN EVENT

- Is it the spelling out of Andrew's name on the Ouija board?
- Is it the twins' death?
- Is it the realisation that Lydia is not coming?
- Is it the singing of the Northbridge Anthem?

The singing of the song is possibly the main event of the play. The whole play has seen them avoid rehearsing the song and refusing to sing, but at the end they are left with no choice but to do so. It is an incredibly powerful moment for each character. There is a paradox in the act of singing. Are they singing the song as an act of defiance? Or an act of submission? Or have they all been brainwashed? What have they won or lost through singing it?

The play is set in a mythical, fictional world and Dafydd invites directors to interpret this in their own way. Northbridge is a fictional place and while the play has been inspired by Welsh culture, it does not have to be set in Wales. In fact, Dafydd specifically chose Northbridge as it doesn't sound particularly Welsh and is keen that this could be any place. It may be useful to draw on your own local area and reference points to create a shared world for the play.

The play is a journey for these characters as the truth about
their society unfolds and they realise that they are not safe. At
the beginning, the world of the play is a happy one – there is a
festival and singing, sunshine and birdsong. Dafydd feels it is
key to build this world in order for the characters to go on
their journey over the next forty-five minutes.

Themes

It could be useful to brainstorm a full list of all the themes in
the play, and then refine your list until you have three or four
themes that you think most of the characters have a relationship
with. Themes would include: fear, power, control, denial,
delusion, pride, authority, cultural heritage, nationalism,
patriotism, fascism, identity.

Language

Our culture is reflected and produced by the language we use.
Language can be used to include or exclude. It can be a
powerful means of oppression or empowerment. How
individual characters use language is important. The actor
should consider whether their character is using language
flippantly, without thought or consideration, or in ignorance,
without thinking of the consequences. Do they use language
they have been taught, without really examining what it is
they are saying?

There are racial references in the text that Dafydd says can be
adapted or replaced if the ethnicity/cultural diversity of the
group requires it.

Music is essential to Dafydd's writing and he writes plays as
though he is writing a piece of music. Therefore, the rhythm is
a vital part of his writing and should not be changed. The beats,
silences and punctuation are all there to help reveal the rhythm
of the play and should be closely observed by the actors.

The play will work best when the young actors own the world
as theirs and so it needs to sound authentic. The content of the

play needs to remain as Dafydd has written, but he is open to you making small tweaks here and there to suit your group if needed.

Characters and characterisation

The characters in the play have all evolved from people Dafydd knew from school (for example, the inspiration for 'Jurassic' Mark was a boy in his class who was obsessed with dinosaurs – and is now a palaeontologist!) with a little bit of himself in every one. It is very much an ensemble piece, but the group is made up of some strong identities and individual personalities.

A vital question to ask is why this particular group of young people have been selected. Is it because they don't fit into the Provost's society? Because they are misfits? Or purely because they can all sing? Explore this with your cast and use it to make clear choices about the world you are building. It would also be useful to spend some time exploring what the Youth League is. What do the group do? Are all young people in their society members or are they the chosen few?

It is also useful to determine what is the normal 'nine-to-five' life for these characters? Do they go to school? What are they used to in this world? What is strange/new to them?

Even when not speaking, characters have to remain alive and connected to what is happening. A way of achieving a layer of activity that supports the text is to ask each actor what their character is trying to achieve in each section of the play (e.g. do they want to find out the truth/embarrass another character/ gain the attention of another character?) and how they feel about each event that occurs during the play. These objectives/ attitudes can be played non-verbally underneath the text. If you find that this non-verbal activity gets too distracting, you can introduce an obstacle which makes it harder for them to achieve what they want (for example: someone might have the objective of wanting another character to notice them, but you can temper how they do this by giving the obstacle that they don't want to embarrass themselves in the process).

Spend some time exploring the characters in real detail through looking at the text and writing down all of the following:

• Character description and stage directions.
• What does my character say about myself?
• What do other characters say about me?
• What do I say about other characters?

You might want to use this exercise as homework, or set it up as something to do in rehearsals through hot-seating or interviews.

In Adam's workshop, the group also spent time exploring the characters physically. Explore how they might move. Think of a colour that the character might relate to, an animal, and what body part they might lead with. Use these starting points to create a specific physical language for each character.

Below are notes on some of the characters as they came up in the workshop:

TUBBSY appears not to care about the situation when in fact he is perhaps one of the only members of the group who knows what is really going on. He appears not to be the smartest and gets electric shocks from the fence several times over. He comes across as a victim but is also trying to hide – just as his uniform is hidden under his clothes at the start.

JACKSON is the most similar to Lisa, but they are also at loggerheads for much of the play. He is also aware that something isn't quite right with the situation, especially when it emerges that Lydia has disappeared. His fear makes him rely on his bullying tactics as the play unfolds.

LISA is a perfectionist and would like everything to be normal. She tries to lead the group in the rehearsal and is desperate to ensure that they get the performance right.

GUINEVERE AND GENEVIEVE have been with Tubbsy just before the start of the play, and were encouraging him to

smoke dope. They are the Provost's daughters and have been
asked to watch over the group. They seem to know what is
going to happen to the others and do say sorry at the end. It
would be useful to think about whether the twins are identical
or if they have different character traits.

DOUGLAS is a miniature adult. He was inspired by a young
Welsh boy who was an antiques dealer on TV in the late 1980s.

CARI-ANN is the only character who is referred to by her full
name on a regular basis. Dafydd felt that she was so dramatic
that she earned the right to have a surname.

DIERDRE-MAY is another character who knows that something
is not quite right with the situation. She is still coming to terms
with her grandmother's death and hopes that she makes things
right by using the Ouija board.

BRADLEY AND MARK are both outsiders – even from this group.

There are two characters who say very little in the play. Dafydd
was interested in writing parts for young people who wanted
to take part but didn't want to speak on stage. Both Jinx and
Jamie have very little to say. JINX operates almost as a shadow
to MELONY – in fact she almost only says 'Yes' in the whole play.

JAMIE doesn't speak at all. Mike talked about the importance
of Jamie still having a character arc – the actor still needs to
make active choices about how to play him. Why doesn't he
speak? Does he choose not to? How much does he know?
Although he doesn't speak, he is key to the rehearsal as he is
the musician. They group can't sing without him. All the
characters need to be there in order for the action to happen.
Jamie's silence also reflects the story – the young people are
living in a community which is silencing individualism and
creativity.

There are several crucial characters we hear about but never
see, such as the Provost, Andrew, Lydia, the children's parents.
It is important that everyone in the company has a shared idea

of what these characters look like (it might be useful to bring in images of how you imagine each one to appear and put them up on the wall of your rehearsal room), what they sound like, what their personalities are like, etc.

Tubbsy's brother Andrew is a key character. We are led to understand that he spoke out about something and subsequently disappeared. Why he disappeared and where he has gone are on the minds of all the young people but, for whatever reason, it is too dangerous to speak out about it. What actually happened? What did he say? How did he say it? Dafydd suggested his disappearance might have happened about a year ago, but that this is open to interpretation.

The character of the Provost has been left deliberately ambiguous. The word itself is meant to sound mythical and a bit strange, but it suggests an authority figure. It is vital that the group comes to a collective decision about who this person is and what they stand for. The ideology of the Provost underpins the whole play. What are the Provost's objectives? What is his/her value system? How long have they been a figure of authority? How were they brought to power? Dafydd compared the Provost to Miranda Richardson's character Queenie in *Blackadder 2*. She would shout 'off with his head' on a whim. Dafydd felt that this crazy, skewed sense of power was interesting to explore with the Provost.

Casting

Dafydd deliberately wrote a play lots of people could take part in, with a diverse range of characters to choose from. The play could work with a range of ages. It is possible to change the gender of characters as long as this works within the context of the action.

Production, staging and design

The play is wide open to interpretation in terms of staging and can work to fit any space or budget. Several directors felt that it would work in-the-round, so that the group is surrounded, while others are working in an end-on configuration that allows for the audience to watch as though on the other side of the fence. Think about the space you are working in and make it a strength of your production.

Consider both artistic and practical choices. Are you making decisions based on the needs of the group or for the story? Are there areas where you may have to compromise? What will give the most dramatic potential to your actors? It might be useful when thinking about the design to imagine what it would look like if you could only use lights? Or if you could only use sound? Or if you could only use props? Then you can determine what you really need to tell the story.

SOME OTHER QUESTIONS TO CONSIDER

- How much of the modern recognisable world is visible in the design?
- Do you need to physically represent the barrier/fence/gate? Are there other ways of suggesting the paddock?
- What is important to represent?
- How do you create the watchtower where the twins sit?
- How can you make them as powerful as possible?

Dafydd would encourage directors to consider the power of them remaining an invisible presence until they appear in the script. He referenced *The Wizard of Oz*, with the assumption that the voice belongs to someone incredibly powerful and evil, but in real life he is just a small and timid human. Similarly, the twins sound all-powerful and terrifying, but they are eventually revealed as small and vulnerable and just trying to do something good. It might be an interesting idea to explore with the performers, that having an important presence is more than just being visible onstage. If you do decide they are visible, how can you still find a sense of another world beyond the paddock? Can they be represented using shadows and silhouettes/gauze and lights/a live video feed, etc.?

The fence is a key element of the design. You might want to keep it imaginary or mark it out in some way. Think about what the fence represents and create something that works for your actors and is within your budget and time. For example, the fence and the electric shocks could be marked with lighting and sound, or perhaps your actors would work better with something physical that they can interact with.

The space needs to evolve emotionally in order to tell the story. At the start it should feel summery and positive – the festival is taking place. By the end, the paddock has become a prison for the young people. Play with how you can tell that story through the set, sound and lighting.

The costumes feel like traditional folk costumes and will seem at odds with Tubbsy's hoody and jeans. Mike suggested thinking about how each character might wear their costume. For example, Lisa probably wears hers exactly as it should be worn, whereas Jackson might alter his in some way.

A big question in terms of staging is the final moment of the cat emerging out of the bag. The cat represents the truth emerging – literally the cat being let out of the bag. Think about what else the cat is a metaphor for: Dafydd suggested that the cat might also be a symbol of hope. The cat is able to be released at the point in the play when the young people are imprisoned. In terms of staging, work within the theatrical language of the aesthetic you have created. Perhaps there is a blackout and then we see an empty bag. Or you might wish to use a sound cue so we hear the cat. Dafydd did say that ideally there would be a real cat onstage which the audience will see escape, but he realises the difficulty of this!

Style and technique

Dafydd sees writing for live performance as a visceral process and writes as if the play were a piece of music. Therefore, the rhythm and musicality of the text is very important and should be carefully considered during rehearsals. There are specific beats and silences which should be played where they are given in the text. These will shape the rhythm and pace of the dialogue. Dafydd stated that the play should rattle along.

The theme of denial/avoidance could be used to help prevent too many pauses; everyone in the play needs to distract themselves from confronting the truth by talking, and letting in silence makes distraction more difficult.

Encourage performers to think 'on the line' instead of reacting before they speak.

The characters' intentions can be used to accelerate the action of the play. For example, Liza urging everyone to start rehearsals can grow more and more urgent as the time pressure grows. The play should run at fifty minutes, and her frequent time checks could be a useful marker as to whether the pace is fast enough.

Much of the play's humour emerges because of the high stakes of the situation, but it is also present in lots of throwaway moments where the characters shrug things off. Adam talked about using the stakes to create situations which allow the humour in the play to sing. For example, the moment where Melony mimes scaling the fence is high stakes and results in highly physical comedy, whereas underplaying other moments creates the humour. Adam also talked about the make-up of the group of young people, and how the status of each person is vital to the comedy in the play.

Play the banter and humour with a lightness of touch so that the darkness of the story can do its own work. As the truth of the situation unfolds, the stakes get higher. The comedy will come alive when the stakes and the status games within the group are highlighted. Explore these fully in rehearsals to bring the dialogue to life.

Exercises for use in rehearsals

- Ask the young people to brainstorm their thoughts on heritage, tradition, culture, and if they have any personal experiences growing up of these things.
- With the group, make a map of Northbridge, so everyone collectively can decide on the geography and where the paddock exists in relation to the main festivities/the river/ the bridge/Southbridge.

Bringing visual images into the rehearsal room can help to suggest the world of the play and allow a shared imaginative connection.

WAITING

Waiting is a really key part of the story. Spend some time exploring how the characters wait. Set up the space as the paddock. Allow the characters just to be in the space. How do they interact with each other in silence?

BOMB AND SHIELD

Each actor should choose one person as their shield (their ally) and another as the bomb (their enemy). Now move around the space keeping the shield in between you and your bomb. Don't get too close to your bomb or you will explode!

This game reveals much about the nature of the relationships in the play. It reveals physical patterns about how the characters look to others for protection.

POST-IT NOTES

Give each actor some Post-It notes. Ask them to play a scene in the space and really think about playing objectives. Each time an actor succeeds at their objective she sticks a Post-It note on the other character. The aim is to 'win' as many points as possible within the scene.

Status and stakes improvisations

MOVING THE CHAIR EXERCISE

- Two actors. One chair. One actor is the boss and has to get the other actor to move the chair. The chair weighs a ton. The boss has to use any tactics possible to get the employee to move the chair.

- Up the stakes – the employee is on a final warning/has a large family to feed/bills to pay.

- Up the stakes – the boss will get a large bonus from the customer if the chair is moved in the next minute.

- Introduce a new character – the customer. They want the chair moved into the house in one minute otherwise their partner will be really upset.
- Introduce a new character: the partner – the Prime Minister is going to visit the house in one minute and they return home to this scene.
- New character: the Prime Minister arrives to visit the house.

This is a really clear exercise to explore objectives, obstacles, status and stakes. Each character will need to engage a range of tactics in order to achieve their objective.

Finding ways of playing the comedy in the play – upping the stakes – makes things more and more ridiculous.

GROUP STATUS EXERCISE: LOST ITEM

- Split the group in half. One half is the audience. The other half have all lost an item – ranging from one (a dirty tissue) to ten (a winning lottery ticket for a million pounds).
- The actors stand in a line and one by one each does a ten-second improvisation of realising they've lost the item. The audience then decide on the order they should be standing as each improvisation is revealed.

This is a brilliant exercise to get your actors to explore playing the stakes truthfully. Often actors are playing lower stakes than the circumstances actually require. This is also a really useful exercise for young actors as it shows those who under- or over-perform.

STAY OR LEAVE IMPROVISATION

- Set up two chairs side by side. Ask two actors to sit down and give them the situation. They are watching TV. One wants to leave to turn the kitchen light off, the other doesn't want them to leave as they are enjoying the programme. The starting point is two/three (out of a possible ten). Try to get the actors to match each other's level.
- Next stage – one person has just returned home to discover the other has killed the pet dog. She wants to leave. The

other wants her to stay as she is all she has. The two have to employ a range of tactics to achieve their objectives.

The comedy in the play is about playing seemingly low stakes to begin with. But as the situation unfolds the stakes become higher and higher. Use improvisations such as this to get your actors to engage with the levels of stakes in the play.

Suggested references, reading and viewing

Dafydd has written a blog about the play on the National Theatre of Wales website: http://community.nationaltheatre wales.org/profiles/blog/list?tag=Welsh+writer+Dafydd+James

Books such as Philip Pullman's *His Dark Materials* trilogy and J.K. Rowling's Harry Potter series might be useful references for fictional worlds that are recognisable but 'other'.

It might be useful for the group to watch the film *Cabaret*, as this is what the Youth League were asked to watch in order to learn about the dangers of excess.

It also might be useful for the company to research traditions and festivals within their own community, or in general to research May Day festivities.

Other film references include: *The Wicker Man*, *The Village*, *Jesus Camp*, *The Wave*, *The Master*, *Hunger Games*, *Never Let Me Go*, *Martha Macy May Marlene*, *Lord of the Flies*, *The Beach*, *If . . .*

A Letter to Lacey

by Catherine Johnson

Catherine Johnson is the award-winning writer of *Mamma Mia!* (stage and screen) and the audio-guide for ABBA The Museum (Stockholm). Her stage plays include: *Through the Wire* (NT Connections); *Shang-a-Lang* (Bush Theatre and tours); *Little Baby Nothing*, *Dead Sheep*, *Boys Mean Business* (Bush Theatre); and *Rag Doll*, *Too Much Too Young* (Bristol Old Vic). Her TV scripts include *Casualty*, *Love Hurts*, *Sin Bin*, *Linda Green* and *Love in the 21st Century*. She lives in Bristol.

Characters

Kara One, *age nineteen*
Kara Two, *ages from fifteen to sixteen*
Kara Three, *ages from sixteen to seventeen*
Lisa, *ages from fifteen to seventeen*
Reece, *ages from eighteen to twenty*
Jake, *ages from eighteen to twenty*
Liam, *ages from seventeen to nineteen*
Julie, *Reece's mum, age thirty-six*
Terry, *Reece's stepdad, age thirty*
Auntie Rhiannon, *age forty-two*
Charley, *age sixteen*
Kym, *Kara's mum, age forty-four*
Nurse, *male or female, age twenty-four*

Kara is played by three actors, illustrating the progression of her relationship with Reece. We watch her grow up through the play.

NON-SPEAKING ROLES

Chris; the people in the pub; young offenders, prison officers and other visitors; friends and family at Reece's homecoming party; sales assistant; Hannah; mums on maternity ward, visitors.

Some roles can be doubled up, e.g. Julie with Hannah, Rhiannon with Charley. The non-speaking parts can be played by anyone who isn't named in the scene, except for the Karas and Reece.

Settings

Kara's space; the park; Reece's car; Kara's bedroom; the pub; prison visitors' hall; Julie's garden; Topshop; Reece and Kara's flat; maternity ward.

Scene changes should be fast and fluid: we're seeing these scenes as Kara remembers them, so they should feel like they snap into each other.

Prologue

Spotlight on three girls: the **Karas**. **Kara One** *is casually fashionable;* **Kara Two** *is in school uniform;* **Kara Three** *wears baggy tracksuit bottoms and top. They're wearing beehive wigs and cats-eye sunglasses.*

Music intro: melodramatic full-blown sixties girl-band style, e.g. Shangri-Las/Shirelles. NB: the last line is a direct steal from 'Leader of the Pack' so do lay on the melodrama!

The Karas
My baby tells me lies
My baby makes me cry
My baby blacks my eyes
And I wonder why I love him so
The words I long to hear
He whispers in my ear
I see his pain and fear
I dry my tears – no one will know

The **Karas** *remove their sunglasses to reveal their black eyes.*

The music continues under:

Kara One
Hey Kara?

Kara Two
Uh huh?

Kara Three
Say Kara?

Kara Two
Uh huh?

Kara One
Is that a love-bite you're wearing –

Kara Three
– or a bruise?

Kara Two
  Maybe . . .

Kara One *and* **Kara Two**
  Uh huh?

Kara Two
  It's crazy . . .

Kara One *and* **Kara Three**
  Uh huh?

Kara Two (*sings*)
  I just don't know any more.

They put their sunglasses back on and sing:

The Karas
  My baby says we're through
  My baby makes me blue
  My baby's so untrue
  And I'm stuck like glue, I love him so
  He needs me in his life
  One day I'll be his wife

  There'll be no more trouble and strife –
  Just put down that knife, oh – baby –

Kara One (*screams*) NO!

Kara Two and Kara Three
  Look out – look out – look out!

Blackout as song ends abruptly. The **Karas** *remove their wigs, sunglasses and black eyes.* **Kara One** *goes into her space.*

Scene One

Kara One *is sitting with her open laptop, trying to think what to write.* **Kara Two** *and* **Kara Three** *stay in the shadows. She types. Stops. Looks at what she's written and reads it back to herself:*

Kara One   Dear Lacey. (*She deletes this, types.*) To Lacey. (*She deletes this, types.*) Hi Lacey . . . (*Typing fast.*) You don't know me but you've heard all about me. I'm Kara. Or 'that ugly ass skank – Kara' or 'Kara Stink-Minge' or 'The Bitch' – yes, you've heard about me. I did try and friend you on Facebook but you never replied. Did you see my profile pic? I suppose you guessed it's Keeli on her second birthday – doesn't she look like her daddy? Reece, I mean. She's the spitting image of him, isn't she? Even wearing fairy wings and cake all over her gob. That same cheeky grin . . .

Scene Two

Lights up on the park.

Four years earlier. **Kara Two** *puts on a school blazer and joins her best friend* **Lisa** *on the children's roundabout, which they trundle round with their feet.* **Lisa** *is wearing the same blazer. As* **Kara Two** *is getting into position,* **Kara One** *continues:*

Kara One   . . . and she don't know the meaning of fear – he'd love that about her.

She stops writing. She's remembering . . .

Back to the letter.

Did he tell you how we met? I bet he won't remember, but I do. He scared me shitless!

Kara Two (*to us*) . . . I'm seeing this boy, Chris? He's in my year at school.

Things are – OK, but . . . (*To* **Lisa**.) Chris is such a dick. He said he was stopping in tonight.

Lisa   Doing his homework? Looks like it.

Lights on Chris and his mates, also in the park.

Chris is mucking about on his skateboard and acting like **Kara Two** *doesn't exist.*

Kara Two *rings Chris. We hear his ring-tone. He takes out his mobile, looks at the caller ID then turns his phone off and puts it away, not looking over at* **Kara Two**.

She's crushed, but trying not to show it.

Lisa   Kara! Did you see what he did? (*Shouts.*) Chris! Oi – Chris, ya tosser –

Kara Two   Shut up, Lisa.

Lisa   What – you think that's OK?

Kara Two (*defensive*)   No. But he isn't like that when it's just me and him.

Lisa   You're too soft, Kara. He's taking the piss.

Kara Two (*to audience*)   Why am I going to take relationship advice off someone who's never had a boyfriend?

Kara One   And then this car showed up.

Car stereo playing dance music announces **Reece**'s *arrival in his souped-up Nova.*

Chris *and his mates cluster around the car and* **Reece**. *He's a local legend.*

Lisa   Ooh, look who it isn't? – Reece Lee.

Kara Two   Who?

Lisa (*gets up*)   You don't want to know.

She goes over to **Reece**.

Kara Two (*to audience*)   I do.

She joins **Lisa** *and Chris and the others hovering around* **Reece**. *He checks her out as she approaches.*

Kara Two (*still to audience*)   Ooh – hello. *He*'s fit. And he's got a car, he's not an immature little schoolboy on a skateboard. (*To* **Reece**.) Well, if it isn't Reece Lee.

Reece (*to* **Kara Two**)   Do I know you?

Kara Two   Do I know *you*?

Reece   No, but you want to.

Kara Two   Oh – yeah? What makes you so special then?

They look at each other.

Kara One   And Reece goes –

Reece   Get in.

Kara Two (*to audience – fist-pumping*)   Get. In!

Scene Three

Reece's *car.*

Reece *is at the wheel.* **Kara Two** *is in the passenger seat, straightening her skirt in a promising way.* **Reece** *leans over.*

Kara Two (*to audience*)   He's gonna kiss me! Right in front of all of them – Suck it up, Chris!

She lifts her face up to him.

Oh.

Because **Reece** *doesn't kiss her. He is doing up her seat belt.* **Kara** *looks away, embarrassed.*

Kara   Going red! But I don't think he noticed . . .

Reece's *grin tells us – yes, he did.*

Kara Two (*still to audience*)   This is mad. Getting in a car with a strange boy I don't know. I don't care! This is me – I'm up for anything!

She turns back to face **Reece**.

Reece   You ever done a doughnut?

Kara Two   Done a do-what?

Reece *performs a series of 'doughnuts' in his car, complete with squealing-tyres effects. He raps over the music in his car.*

Reece
Yeeh, I'm a maximum rev head,
Leave those cruisers for dead
Your car's a shed, I ride a thoroughbred,
And when I really hit it, bitch gonna shit it
Begging me 'quit it', crying, got my wheels flying
Got my I.C.E. amplifying, it's 'electrifying'
She squeal 'don't crash it', for real I'll thrash it
She goes for the door, put my foot to the floor
Ignore the whore make her heart-sore – heart soar
Girl gonna implore she want more of my Big Bore.

Kara Two (*through this*)   I'm not scared, I'm not scared, I'm not gonna let him see I'm scared –

Reece (*to* **Kara Two**)   Scream if you want to go faster!

Kara Two   Whatever.

Reece *glances across, approvingly.*

The car slows and stops. Beat.

Reece   Who's your boyfriend?

Kara Two   Chris.

They freeze.

Kara One (*writing to Lacey*)   Believe, I know I shouldn't have said that. You'll know what Reece is like about telling the truth, but that's one little white lie I could have got away with, I could have said 'no one' and saved myself years of grief. But no, mouth-almighty wasn't thinking . . .

Kara Two (*to* **Reece**)   Chris. I mean, he *was*. He's not any more, not really.

Reece   Yeah? Well, when you've made your mind up, let me know.

He stares ahead, ignoring **Kara**. *She gets out of the car.*

Kara Two   Cheers then. (*Beat.*) Reece?

Reece *revs the car, ignoring her.*

Blackout – screeching = tyres effects.

Mixing into – the sounds of a fight:

Shouting, breaking glass – silence.

Scene Four

Kara*'s bedroom.*

Light on **Kara Two***, getting ready to go out. She's dressing up and doing her hair and make-up, looking good.*

Kara Two (*to audience*)   Chris is such a dick. I just text him it's over and he text me back *he* is dumping *me.* Yeah, so immature.

She picks up her phone and calls.

Light on **Lisa***, answering her phone.*

Kara Two (*to* **Lisa**)   Yeah, mate, I need Reece's number?

Lisa   Reece Lee?

Kara Two   No, Reece Witherspoon, you moronatard, I'm her biggest fan. Of course Reece Lee.

Lisa   Oh my God. You don't know then?

Kara Two   Know what?

Lisa   Know about Reece?

Kara Two   Know *what*?

Lisa   Oh my God. You're not gonna like it.

Kara Two (*to audience – sing-song*)   'I know something you don't know'. She loves it. (*To* **Lisa**.) If you're gonna tell me he's got a girlfriend, so what?

Lisa   No, it's not that . . .

The Karas
   Hallelujah! Hallelujah! Hallelujah!

Lisa   . . . he's gone and got himself arrested.

Kara Two   No! What for – speeding?

Lisa   Fighting? I heard he beat shit out of the kiddy.

Kara Two (*taking this in*)   Oh.

Lisa   And it's not like it's the first time he's been done for assault. He's gonna go down, they reckon.

Kara Two   Oh.

Lisa   I mean, I heard it was self-defence, the kiddy had a pop at Reece.

Kara Two (*visibly brightening*)   Oh, right – self-defence, so it wasn't his fault?

Lisa   Oh no. It never is.

Kara Two (*to audience*)   She's just jealous.

Lights down on **Kara Two** *and* **Lisa** *as:*

Kara One (*writing to Lacey*)   I hope you got mates looking out for you, like Lisa was trying to look out for me. But who takes any notice when they're falling in love? I was all 'misters before sisters' . . . 'dicks before chicks' . . .

Effects – noisy pub.

Scene Five

The pub.

Reece, **Liam** *and* **Jake** *are having a few beers.* **Jake** *is reading out a joke from his iPhone. during this section.*

Lisa *and* **Kara Two** *come into the pub and get into a corner table where they can see the boys.* **Reece** *is aware of* **Kara Two** *from the moment she comes in, but doesn't acknowledge her.*

Jake   'What do you do when your dishwasher stops working?'

Reece *and* **Liam** *(together)*   Punch her in the face.

Jake *is disappointed his joke's fallen flat.*

Reece   Haven't heard that one since Year Seven.

Jake *(rallying)*   The old uns are the best.

Reece   Yeah, that's what your mum keeps telling me.

Liam *and* **Reece** *laugh at* **Jake** *as* **Lisa** *comes over to their table.*

Liam *(spots her first)*   Go away, you're under age.

Lisa   Like I'm gonna get ID'd in here? All right, Reece?

Reece   All right, Liam's sister?

Lisa   It's Lisa, actually.

Liam   No one cares. Go home.

Lisa   Am I even talking to you? *(To* **Reece***.)* You know my mate Kara? She wants to speak to you.

Liam *(in a girly voice)*   'My mate fancies you.'

Jake *and* **Liam** *laugh.* **Reece** *gives them a look before replying to* **Lisa***.*

Reece   Well, here I am.

Kara Two *looks over, quickly looks away.*

Lisa   She's a bit shy.

Jake   Is she a virgin?

Reece   Shut up, you cock – *(To* **Lisa***.)* Is she?

Lisa   I'm not telling.

Reece *sees* **Kara Two** *keeps looking over. He pats the seat beside him.*

Reece I'll get it out of you.

Lisa You won't!

Reece You try me.

Lisa, *with a smirk at* **Liam**, *sits down next to* **Reece**.

Kara Two (*to audience*) What the – ?

She heads over to the table, affecting nonchalance.

Jake Handbags!

Lisa Oh – Kara – I was just telling Reece you wanted a word with him?

Reece Don't lie, you were all over me.

The boys laugh. **Kara Two** *picks up* **Jake**'s *glass from the table and pours the dregs into* **Lisa**'s *lap.*

Jake Oi!

Lisa Kara!

Kara Two Oops!

Reece (*to* **Lisa**) You asked for that.

Lisa I'm covered in cider!

Reece Yeah, but your o-beast thigh's like a kitchen roll, innit?

More laughter. **Liam** *high-fives* **Reece**.

Lisa, *close to tears, gets up and pushes past* **Kara Two** *to get out.*

Kara Two (*to audience*) I shouldn't have done that, I don't know what came over me. I should go after / her.

Jake Here – you owe me a pint.

Reece There was nothing in there, you clown. (*To* **Kara Two**.) You showed her, babe. Funny as.

He pats the seat beside him.

Kara Two (*to audience*)   He called me 'babe'! (*To* **Reece**.) Isn't that seat wet?

Reece   No – it all went up her camel-toe.

Kara Two *joins in the laughter against* **Lisa** *and sits down next to* **Reece**.

Reece   So where's your boyfriend tonight?

Kara Two   I broke up with him.

Reece   Did you do that for me? That's sweet, babe.

Kara Two (*to audience*)   Is he taking the piss? I can't work him out. But it makes me want to make him like me.

Reece   You're not going to be just another little prick-teaser, are you?

Lights down on the pub.

Music – guitar riff intro in the style of eighties hair metal: Poison, Def Leppard, Bon Jovi, etc.

Lights up on the **Karas**. *They are wearing massive mullet wigs with an eye-patch over one eye. they rock out with air guitars:*

The Karas   Aye aye me hearty! Let's party!

C'mon my pirate of pleasure
Give me measure by measure
I'm your frigate and you're coming aboard
I'll take a taste of the cat
Uh-huh, I like it like that
Shoot your pistol and stick me your sword

You're a blaggard, I know
And you're all hands below
You'll pillage and plunder away.
Don't leave me a-flounder
Won't you run me a-grounder?
I'll welcome you into my bay.

You're my pirate of pleasure
Dive down to my treasure
With your yo-ho and a bottle of rum
And boy, if you ask it
I'll unlock my casket
We'll yo-ho and ho-ho till we're numb

Shiver me timbers! Me bucko is limber! Arrggh!

Song ends. Lights down on the **Karas** *as* **Kara Two** *joins* **Reece** *in the next scene, casting off her props as she goes. NB: snap straight into the scene; the sex is implicit, not shown.*

Scene Six

The park.

Night-time. **Reece** *stands over* **Kara Two***, doing up his flies.*

Reece   You're not going to like what I'm going to tell you, but it's for your own good. It's not that I think you're a slag, but you carry on getting off with anyone who wants it and no one's going to want it. Don't get upset. You're lucky I'm looking out for you. You ought to have a bit of self-respect.

They exit. **Kara One** *is back at the computer, writing her letter:*

Kara One   Yeah, Reece was soooo romantic. One minute I'm a prick-teaser if I don't do what he wants, the next I'm a slag because I do what he wants. But he totally pushed the right buttons. I did feel he was looking out for me because, really, my mum should have been the one teaching me about self-respect, but *she* didn't know the meaning of the word. I remember when my dad had a go at her, she'd just sit there, taking it. Smiling, even, like she agreed with all the names he was calling her – and I'd be getting more and more wound up, wanting her to stick up for herself. And then I'd think, 'Well, I can't blame him for getting mad at her – look at her, she's *pathetic*.' And when he finally left, I just ignored her for weeks.

Don't get me wrong – I love my mum. But she's a pushover. She's all 'anything for a quiet life'. I was sneaking out and seeing Reece and she couldn't stop me.

I'm not going to be like that! Keeli is going to tell Mummy *everything* or she doesn't get to go out, simple as!

Scene Seven

The park.

Daytime. **Reece** *and* **Kara Two** *are hanging out on the roundabout.* **Jake**, **Lisa** *and other friends are in another part of the rec, messing around, practising dance-steps.*

Kara One   After that night in The Swan, me and Lisa didn't speak for a couple of days, but then I said I was sorry and she said she was sorry and we made up. But we didn't really hang out like we used to.

Reece   You keep looking over there – do you want to go over?

Kara Two   I don't mind.

Reece   Go on then. If you want Jake and that lot perving over your arse. Cos that's why you're wearing those jeans, innit?

Kara Two   No.

Reece   It don't bother me. It should bother you, mind, shit they say about you.

Kara Two   What do they say?

Reece   'What do they say?' That's all you can think about, 'Who's looking at me? Who's talking about / me?'

Kara Two   It isn't!

Reece (*tweaks her nose*)   Pinocchio! (*He grins at her.*) That's what I like about you, Kara. You're a terrible liar, I can see right through you.

Kara Two   You like me?

Reece   'I shags you, don't I?'

They both laugh.

Yeah, but maybe we should call it a day?

Kara Two   Why? What have I done?

Reece   I got my court case coming up. No one believes me what really happened. I'm going dahhhn.

Kara Two   But you know I'll wait for you.

Reece   Yeah. You say that now.

He looks down and away – a tried and tested move.

Kara Two (*to audience*)   I wish he could trust me. But actions speak louder than words. I'll prove I'll always be there for him.

Lights down.

Kara One   I bet you're thinking, 'Get to the point!' Sorry. It's now I've started, I can't stop remembering . . . I don't care what you've heard – I did love him, I'd have done anything for him. When I left school I had this place lined up at a hairdressing salon, but Reece had just got slapped with a six-month sentence and I was devastated. I knew I wouldn't get time off for visits so I didn't show up for work. I thought, 'I can always find another job, Reece needs me now.'

Effect of a prison door slamming.

Scene Eight

Prison visiting hall.

Prison officers watch the visitors and the young offenders, who are sitting at tables. A buzz of chatter, including very young children.

The young offenders, including **Reece***, are identified by coloured prison bibs.* **Kara Two** *sits with* **Reece** *and* **Jake***.*

Kara Two *(to audience)*   I hate this place. I can't go in by myself cos you have to be eighteen and obviously I can't ask Mum to take me so I have to go in with Jake or Liam or one of that lot and I never know what sort of mood Reece is going to be in.

She reaches over to touch **Reece***'s hand. He pulls away from her.*

Reece   Don't paw me in front of the screws, stupid – they'll stick me on shit watch.

He rolls his eyes at **Jake***.*

Reece   She hasn't got a clue, has she? So what's been happening?

Jake   Not a lot. Liam pulled this right dirty minger down The Swan Saturday – it was gagging for it, so he had to put it out of its misery.

Reece   You don't look at the mantelpiece when you're poking the fire. Ask your mum. *(To* **Kara Two***.)* Oi – face. Don't go earwigging if you don't like what we're saying.

Kara Two   I'm not . . . I was just watching that little girl over there? She shouldn't have to see her daddy in a place like this.

Reece   What's it got to do with you? You think you're better than everyone else, is it? Your shit don't smell and you fart rainbows?

Jake *laughs.* **Kara Two** *thinks it's best to say nothing.*

Reece   Look, if you don't want to come here, you only got to say. Or would you miss your little 'rides' with Jakey-boy here? Is that it? You haven't got no friends of your own so you're getting in with mine?

A prison officer is heading over. **Reece** *looks up.*

Reece   No drama, boss.

As the prison officer walks away, **Reece** *leans in – to* **Kara**.

Reece   He just wanted to look at your tits. Good top for a prison visit, Kara, you got everyone staring at 'em.

He turns back to **Jake**. *Their conversation continues silently through:.*

Kara Two (*to audience*)   I could go. I could just get up and walk out of here – what's he going to do? He can't come after me. I'm sick of being told what to think and what to wear and never getting it right. Mum will come and pick me up and that's it. That's all it takes – so long, Reece – yeah, you look at me like I'm something nasty you found on your shoe, but I'm gone, gone, gone. I'm out of here.

Reece   Who are you smiling at?

Kara Two   No one.

Kara Two (*to audience*)   If I go, I'll never see him again. He'll never forgive me. I could go. (*Beat.*) I'm not gonna. But it's my choice to be with him. I'm not being weak. I can take whatever he throws at me. Water off a duck's back.

Kara Two, **Jake** *and the visitors exit the scene.*

The young offenders line up to use the payphone, with the prison officer supervising.

Kara One   I thought I could handle it. I thought I was in control.

Scene Nine

The prison phone.

Reece *is making a call:*

Reece   Happy birthday. Did you get my card? . . . No, of course I didn't send you one, work it out, is there a Paperchase in here? Wait till I get back, I've been thinking how we can celebrate . . . Oi – you're not going out, are you? You know it does my head in, thinking about you down the pub. You can't take care of yourself . . . Yeah, you keep saying you wouldn't get up to nothing, but – couple of drinks, it's your birthday . . . I'm not saying I don't trust you, but don't you care what it's like for me? This kiddy on my wing tried to hang himself last night cos his girlfriend missed a visit. If they hadn't found him and cut him down . . . It's like that in here. All you do is think about what's happening on the out – it makes you paranoid. I promise we'll do something together when I get home. I promise I'll make it up to you.

He replaces the phone.

Beat. He takes off his bib, hands it to the guard, then walks into the next scene.

Scene Ten

Julie*'s garden.*

A family barbecue to welcome **Reece** *home: music playing, sausages sizzling.* **Reece** *is greeted by friends and relatives, including* **Jake**, **Liam**, **Julie**, **Terry** *and* **Auntie Rhiannon***. Everyone is drinking wine or beer or cider.* **Reece** *is given a can. He knocks it back in one and starts on another.*

Kara One   I was too excited to sleep the night before his release. I couldn't wait to get Reece on his own. But then he told me his mum was doing this big family barbecue so I had to go to that.

Kara Two *comes on. She has made a big effort to look nice for the homecoming, with a new dress and hair, bag over her shoulder. She makes her way through the party to* **Reece**.

Reece   Here she is, then. (*Looks her up and down.*) Well, you might have made an effort.

Julie   Oh Reece – that's not a very nice thing to say.

Reece   'Oh, Reeeece!' (*To* **Kara Two**.) This is my mum. She'd be lethal if she had half a brain.

Julie   You must be Kara. We've heard nothing about you, as usual.

Kara Two (*to audience*)   Awkward!

Kara Two (*to* **Julie**)   Hiya.

She puts out her hand for a handshake.

Julie   Oh, come here –

She hugs and kisses **Kara Two** *on the cheek.*

Julie   Would you like a drink?(*Calls.*) Terry!

Reece   Don't drag the old waster over here – she'll have a cider and same again for me.

Julie   Please don't call your stepdad an old waster.

Reece   Sorry. I should've said 'the old wanker'.

Julie *tuts and hurries off to get the drinks.*

Reece *turns to* **Kara Two**.

Reece   At last –

He goes to embrace her, her bag is in the way.

Just get rid of this . . .

He puts **Kara**'s *bag down on the ground. He kisses her.*

Reece   Been a good girl?

Kara Two   Oh, Reece – you know I have! I've missed you so much.

Reece   Well, you got me for good now, babe – think you can handle it?

Kara One   I was on cloud nine. This was the new start I'd been dreaming of.

Julie *is coming back, with two cans and* **Terry***.*

Julie   Here's your drinks and Terry wants to say hello to Kara.

Terry   Hello, Kara. What a pretty dress.

Reece   Paws off, you perv, she's spoken for.

Terry *laughs genially as he moves forward to shake* **Kara Two***'s hand. She, meanwhile, thinks it's going to be another hug and kiss.*

The move is fumbled and ends up with **Terry** *kissing her on the lips.*

Terry   Oops! Well, there's an unexpected pleasure. You can come again!

Reece (*coughing into his hand*)   Paedo.

Julie   Reece!

Auntie Rhiannon *is muscling in.*

Auntie Rhiannon   Just thought I'd introduce myself – I'm Rhiannon, I'm Reece's dad's sister – luckily, they don't hold that against me.

Julie   Oh, Rhiannon, you're more like family than he ever was.

Reece   Here we go. What's that supposed to mean?

Julie   Nothing, Reece – don't start.

Reece   I'm starting? (*To* **Kara Two**.) It's always me.

Terry   Come on, it's a nice afternoon.

Auntie Rhiannon   Yes, your mum's done you proud, Reece. Now it's your turn to return the favour and stay out of trouble from now on.

Reece *wafts his hand in front of his nose.*

Reece   Pwaugh – did something crawl in there to die?

He goes to move away.

Auntie Rhiannon *grabs his arm.*

Auntie Rhiannon   No, you can listen for once. You carry on the way you have been and you'll end up right back where you just came from.

Reece (*wrenching his arm away*)   Get off me, you nasty old drunk!

Julie   I'm sorry, Rhiannon, he doesn't mean it.

Auntie Rhiannon   I'm sorry, Julie, but he's an even bigger waste of space than you-know-who.

Reece   'You-know-who'? 'You-know-who?' You're on about my dad, so just say it to my face!

Kara Two   Reece –

Reece   No wonder he left, dumb-ass bitches like you pair in his face / 24/7 –

Auntie Rhiannon   Well, we all know *that's* not the reason he left, don't we? He couldn't keep it in his trousers. / I'm sorry, Julie, *but* –

Reece (*losing it*)   Get out! – go on, get out – it's *my* party, I never asked you!

Terry   All right, son, calm down. / She didn't mean –

Reece   'Son'? 'Son'? You stupid twat!

Terry   Now put a flaming sock in it, Reece, I'm warning you!

Reece *squares up to* **Terry**.

Everyone at the barbecue is either coming over to intervene or watching.

Reece   Come on then. Come on!

Julie   Reece! Stop it!

Reece (*in* **Terry**'s *face*)   D'you want some? Hard man? Do ya?

Kara Two   No! Don't!

Terry   I'm not going to hit you. You can't make me.

Beat, then **Reece** *whips round and kicks over a table. As everything goes flying, he grabs* **Kara Two**'s *arm.*

Reece   We're going.

He drags **Kara Two** *away from the party, as* **Julie** *and* **Terry** *pick up the table.*

Kara Two *tries to stop* **Reece**.

Kara Two   I haven't got my bag.

Reece *continues to drag her away from the house.*

Kara Two   Reece, please. Let me go!

They are away from the barbecue – out of sight from everyone there.

Kara *pulls free.*

She starts to head back to the house.

Reece *pulls her arm again and as she turns towards him he hits her across the head.*

Kara Two *staggers, but* **Reece**'s *grabs both her arms to keep her upright.*

As he strikes, **Kara One** *puts her hand to her head and continues:.*

Kara One   It's weird – I wasn't even surprised he hit me. I mean, he wanted to hit someone and I was there. He thought I was choosing them over him. I just screamed at him:

Kara Two   I haven't got my bag!

Julie *appears.*

Julie   Reece?

Kara One   His mum had come after us. He let go of me.

Julie   Oh, don't go, son. Don't let her spoil everything.

Kara One   And for a second, I thought she meant me. But she didn't even look at me.

I don't know if she saw him hit me – she's never said.

Julie   Come and get another drink. It's your party. Won't be the same without the guest of honour.

Reece *allows his mother to take him back to the barbecue. They exit.*

Kara One   What could I do? I had to get my bag.

Kara Two *exits.*

Kara One   Some girls, if you ask them what they'd do if their boyfriend hit them, would say, 'I'd be out of there, no messing. No second chances.' Some girls would say, 'It depends what I'd done to deserve it.' I was in the middle. I didn't think I deserved it, but I had to give Reece his chance to explain.

Music intro: in the style of a country ballad (Dolly Parton / Tammy Wynette / Kenny Rogers style). Spotlight on: **Reece**. *He is sitting on a bar stool, cradling a glass of JD, as he tells his story. The* **Karas** *are grouped around him, wearing sparkly stetsons, huge blingy sunglasses and crooning the chorus.*

Reece
  My old man was a legend. Made me what I am today.
  Yeah, they can run him down and bad-mouth
      him, but they can't take that away.
  I was a little sissy. Head full of baby curls.
  Wasted on a boy, they said. Curly hair's for girls.
  Dad took me to the barber's, his little lamb to the slaughter.
  I cried through my crop, begged them to stop.
  That's when he called me his daughter.

The Karas
> Daddy's little girl is a man now
> He learned to dish it out, just like the rest
> Daddy's little girl grew up strong and hard and mean

Kara One
> Daddy, stick a medal on your chest.

Reece
> 'You're no son of mine,' he said. 'I've never in my whole
>   life cried.'
> I knew that wasn't bullshit, cos plenty big men tried.
> I used to quite like drawing. But my father took the piss.
> 'Why don't you take up knitting too, you wussy little miss?'
> I didn't want to play outside, boys were fighting in the street.
> So he chucked me out and shut the door –
> 'Time to stand on your own two feet.'

The Karas
> Daddy's little girl is a man now
> He put the old man's teachings to the test
> Daddy's little girl grew up strong and hard and mean

Kara One
> Daddy, stick a medal on your chest.

Reece
> The door was locked, I rang the bell.
> 'They're coming to get me,' I shouted.
> All I could hear was his laughter,
> Mum scared she was going to get clouted.
> 'Who's the bitch?' the boys said.
> Feeling their breath on my neck.
> I turned right round and I banged a few heads.
> That day I earned some respect.

The Karas
> Daddy's little girl is a man now
> Daddy knew that tough love was the best
> Daddy's little girl grew up strong and hard and mean.

Kara One *and* **Reece**
  Daddy, stick a medal on your chest.

Reece *stands and* **Kara Three** *removes her stetson. He takes her hand and they walk away from the other two.*

End of song.

Reece   He never said he was taking off. I saw him putting his case in the back of the car and I asked him, 'Where are you going?' He ignored me. So I said, 'Can I come with you, Dad?' But he just drove away. He should have took me with him.

Kara Three   You think everyone you love is going to leave you. So you hurt them before they can hurt you. But I'm never going to leave you.

Reece   Is that what you said to Chris?

Kara One   When you fall in love with someone who's insecure and got issues, they don't just learn to trust you overnight. I thought I'll just be strong and keep reassuring him and it will all work out OK.

Reece *and* **Kara Three** *exit.*

Scene Eleven

Topshop.

Background music plays through the scene.

Lisa *is looking through a rack of clothes. a sales assistant is standing by the changing rooms.* **Kara Three** *comes out, holding a top she's just tried on. She is wearing tracksuit trousers and a baggy top. She gives the Topshop top back to the sales assistant and goes over to* **Lisa**.

Lisa   Getting it?

Kara Three   Nah . . . I'm too fat.

Lisa   Shut up! You're not fat! Who says?

Kara Three's *mobile beeps – a text message.*

Lisa   Let me guess – Reece again?

Kara Three   Hang on, I got to text him back.

Lisa   Why? What happens if you don't reply in thirty seconds? Does your phone explode?

Kara Three *stops writing, distracted by* **Lisa**.

Lisa   Or is it Reece that explodes?

Kara Three   What are you saying?

Lisa   Nothing – just we hardly see each other any more and when we do go out, you got your head in your phone all the time!

Kara Three   He's my boyfriend, Lisa, he's allowed to text me.

Her phone rings. she answers immediately.

Hiya – yeah, I did, I was just texting you . . . Still in Topshop with Lisa . . . what? . . .

Holding her phone out to **Lisa**.

Kara Three   Reece wants to say hello.

Lisa *looks at* **Kara Three**. *Then takes the phone.*

Lisa   All right, Reece? . . . In Topshop . . . Yeah, they play music in here, that's right . . . OK . . .

She passes the phone to **Kara Three**.

Lisa   He wants to speak to you again.

Kara Three   Hiya . . . Did she? I don't know . . . Yeah, something like that! . . . OK, I won't be long then . . . Love you, hun . . . Yeah., Bye. (*Turns off the phone – to* **Lisa**.) He thought you sounded pissed off with him.

Lisa   Aren't *you* pissed off with him, breathing down your neck all the time?

Kara   He's not.

Lisa   Yeah, right – you didn't text him back so 'ring, ring'. It would do my head in.

Kara Three   It isn't like that. I don't expect you to understand.

Lisa   Why don't you turn your phone off?

Kara Three   Why should I?

Lisa   He's done it to you. When he went away on the lads' weekend?

Kara Three   He ran out of credit.

Lisa   I seen him down the pub, Kara. When you're not there, he makes a joke of turning off his / mobile

Kara Three   A joke, yeah! He's messing around – you know what he's like. What's your problem?

Lisa   It's not my problem.

Kara Three   Because if you want to say I shouldn't trust my boyfriend, come out and say it.

Lisa *hesitates a fraction.*

Lisa   Look, I don't like to see him taking the piss. That's all. I'm your mate, I'm gonna stick up for you.

Kara Three   Yeah, but – I'm fine? I love Reece, he loves me and we're happy.

Her phone beeps again.

Anyway. I ought to be heading back.

Lisa   You out later?

Kara Three   I'll text you?

She is reading her phone as she exits.

See ya.

Lisa   Yeah. Right.

Lisa *stares after* **Kara Three**.

Kara One   At the end of the day, it was easier to stop seeing her.

Reece said she would never understand that what we had was stronger than other couples, because we went through so many emotions together. He said he couldn't be in a boring, safe relationship where no one ever said a cross word and I wanted what he wanted.

Lights down on Topshop.

I'll never know what really happened when Terry kicked Reece out   I only ever heard his side of events. He turned up with his stuff in a black bin bag and it made me feel – I don't know – so protective of him, really. I'd never let him down like everyone else did.

Mum said he could stay a couple of nights – ended up nearly a year.

I thought it was going to be great, being together all the time, but two's company, three's a crowd. Mum got on my nerves. Whenever me and Reece had a bit of a row she'd be: 'Is everything all right, Kara?' I'd pretend it was fine, then Reece would have to get her on his side, by making out it was my fault. I know it would have turned nasty if she'd got in his face and stuck up for me, but she had to play the peacemaker, had to see both sides. I'd make it up with Reece and still feel sour with *her*.

We were all relieved when me and Reece got our place together. I was like, a new start, I'm really gonna make this work.

Scene Twelve

Reece *and* **Kara***'s flat.*

Reece *is drawing and listening to music on headphones, so he doesn't hear* **Kara Three** *coming in. She's wearing a cleaner's overall on top of her baggy clothes – her hair is tied back, no make-up. She's carrying a supermarket bag with a few things in it. She's tired, but excited about something:*

Kara Three   Reece – ?

She stops as she sees **Reece** *is engrossed. She tiptoes up behind him. Right at the last moment he grabs her and gets her in a headlock. She drops the bag.*

Reece   Sniper skills!

Kara Three   Get off – if you've broke that bottle, you'll be sorry.

Reece   You will, you mean. Pisshead.

He lets go and picks up the bag. As he inspects the unbroken bottle of wine, **Kara Three** *inspects the drawing.*

Kara Three   Here – did you do this? It's awesome!

Reece   Don't sound so surprised.

He is pleased, but he holds his hand out to take the drawing back. **Kara Three** *still wants to look at it.*

Kara Three   It's really really good. Is it supposed to be – me?

Reece   Supposed to be, yeah. Give it here.

Kara Three   You have noticed my tits are like half that size?

Reece   When I come up on the Lottery, I'll treat you to the tits you always wanted.

Kara Three *gives the drawing back. The moment has soured.* **Reece** *starts to put his drawing stuff away.* **Kara Three** *picks up the shopping.*

Kara Three   So guess what I heard? There's a trainee job going at Toni & Guy?

Reece   I don't know, babe. It's shit money. What's wrong with the job you got?

Kara Three *doesn't say anything. She takes the bag off to the kitchen.*

Meanwhile, **Reece** *looks at his picture, decides it is crap and screws it up. He feels hurt, so he is going to be hurtful.*

Kara One   He didn't want me hairdressing because he didn't want me touching other men's heads. He liked me doing cleaning because I worked with women and it was always early morning and evenings. Now I understand how controlling he was. But then it seemed only natural that we would discuss things and I shouldn't go against what he wanted because we were a couple. Besides, I got tired of all the fights. Anything for a quiet life.

Kara Three *returns with two glasses of wine.*

Reece   Saw your boyfriend down the pub.

Kara Three   Who?

Kara Three (*to audience*)   I know who.

Reece   Chrissy-boy. 'All right, Reece?' he goes to me. 'How's Kara?'

Kara Three (*to audience*)   Shit.

Reece   Did you squeak?

Kara Three   No.

Kara One   He had a thing about Chris. He couldn't bear it that, as he put it, 'Chris had been there first.' And he'd convinced himself that I only went with him to make Chris jealous. I used to get really upset and beg him to see Chris meant nothing to me, but he was obsessed.

Kara Three   Want a packet of crisps, babe?

Reece   'Chris'-ps? Bet you like eating 'Chris-ps', don't you? What else do you like?

Kara Three   I don't know.

Reece   KRIS-py Kremes. Chris's KRISPY KREMEY cock, I mean cake.

Kara Three *stands up.*

Reece   Where are you going?

Kara Three   I don't have to listen to this. You know I've never done anything to make you jealous.

Reece   Who says I'm jealous? Don't go projecting your paranoia on me, babe. Remember when you beat up your best mate just cos she was sitting next to me?

Kara Three   I only sloshed a bit of cider /on her

Reece   You made her cry: I should have seen what I was letting myself in for. Going through my phone all the time.

Kara Three   I don't do that.

Reece   Not since I set my little trap. 'Who's Amber, Reece? Why's she texting you?' Gotcha!

Kara Three   I said I was sorry.

Reece   How do you expect me to trust you when you can't trust me back? You let me down, believing I was seeing someone else.

Kara Three   I believed you when you said it was just Jake messing around.

Reece   Cos it was! Or – was it?

Kara Three *looks at him.* **Reece** *gets up.*

Reece   Ah, what's up, babe? Lost your sense of humour? I'm going out while you look for it.

He heads for the door. **Kara Three** *grabs his arm.*

Kara Three   Where are you going?

Reece   Get out my way.

Kara Three   It's not fair, Reece – you can't just wind me up and walk out!

Reece   'It's not *fair*' – 'It's not *fair*' – can you hear yourself? You're pathetic. This is why I *have* to go out.

He tries to wrench himself away., **Kara Three** *hangs on.*

Kara Three   You're not going to walk out on me – I won't let you.

Reece   I'm warning you to let me go, Kara. I'm warning you – don't make me . . .

Kara Three (*screams in his face*)   I don't care! Do what you like, Reece, I don't care!

Reece *head-butts her – it is a swift, instinctive movement.* **Kara Three** *cries out in pain and turns away.*

At the moment of impact, **Kara One** *jumps to her feet.*

Reece *looks at* **Kara Three**. *He is tense and defensive.*

Reece   I warned you!

Kara Three *doesn't say anything. She's moving towards the chair, covering her face with her hand.*

Kara One *is watching.*

Reece   *You* did this! You couldn't leave it, could you? You had to keep pushing the button . . .

He stands over the chair, looking down at **Kara Three**.

Reece   Are you happy now you made me hurt you?

Kara One *turns away*

Lights down on **Reece** *and* **Kara Three**.

Kara One *is now speaking to the audience, not Lacey – these memories are too painful to share:*

Kara One   He could make everything seem like my fault. The way he messed with my head was worse than him hitting me.

Music – maybe a soulful, sexy mix of 'Pirate of Pleasure'.

Lights up on **Kara Three** *and* **Reece** *slow-dancing together.*

Kara One   But it had got to the stage I just couldn't imagine my life without him – and I didn't know what he'd do without me. What no one else could see was he needed me. He used to say, 'You're everything to me.' One minute he'd be kicking me around the room, the next he'd be crying, going, 'I'll kill myself if you ever leave me.' It was me and Reece against the world and I wore the battle scars.

Music fades as **Reece** *tries to kiss* **Kara Three***.*

She turns her head.

Reece   What's the matter, babe?

Kara Three   I haven't brushed my teeth since tea, I got onion breath.

Reece   I don't mind.

He tries to kiss her again, but she pulls away.

Kara Three   I was just going to get in the shower.

Reece   Good idea.

Kara Three   By myself? I've got to scrub this tan off.

Reece   No. We'll get in the shower together.

He starts to propel her towards the bathroom, she tries to move away.

Kara Three   Reece – please – I'm not in the mood.

Reece   You never are, are you? Don't worry. You don't have to do anything.

Kara One *moves forward as if to stop him, but of course, she can't.*

Reece *marches* **Kara Three** *off. As they exit he kisses her hair.*

Moment.

*Then the **Karas** cover their heads with their arms. They all speak softly (with **Kara Three** off).*

The Karas   I'm not here. I'm not here. I'm not here.

Reece *comes back in and sits down.*

Beat.

Kara One *and **Kara Two** uncover their heads*

Kara Two *looks at **Kara One**.*

Kara One   I'm sorry.

Kara Two *shrugs and turns away.*

Kara One *looks over to the bathroom door.*

Kara Three *hasn't reappeared.*

Reece   I'm sorry.

Kara One *goes back to the letter:*

Kara One   It was something he just couldn't control and just wouldn't talk about. At the end of the day, he was ashamed of himself and the worse he behaved, the more he lashed out next time. I didn't know how to stop him – we were locked into this life together.

Lights down.

Music – dance mix. Sounds of house party. everyone having a great time.

Scene Thirteen

Reece *and **Kara**'s flat.*

*Night. **Kara Three** is lying on the sofa, in her dressing gown. She's fallen asleep in front of the TV.*

*Sounds from off of **Reece**, **Liam** and **Jake** coming in with **Hannah** and **Charley**. They're all high and happy after the party.*

Hannah *falls over in the hallway – there is laughter and 'shushing' as they pick her up again.*

It wakes **Kara Three**. *She sits up, awkwardly. We can see she's about seven months pregnant.*

Reece, **Liam**, **Jake**, **Hannah** *and* **Charley** *come into the room.*

Reece *is supporting* **Hannah**: *she leans against him.* **Hannah** *and* **Charley** *are dressed for partying.* **Liam** *is holding a bag of bottles.* **Reece** *turns on the light, saying:*

Reece   Keep it quiet.

Kara Three (*gets up*)   Reece?

Reece *quickly lets go of* **Hannah**. *Luckily* **Jake** *and* **Charley** *catch her.*

Reece   All right, babe? Why aren't you in bed?

Kara Three   I nodded off – what time is it?

Reece   What have I told you about sleeping on the sofa? And you moan your back hurts – come on, let's get you into beddy-byes. I'll tuck you in.

Liam *and* **Charley** *put* **Hannah** *down on the sofa.* **Kara Three** *looks daggers at* **Hannah**, *who is beyond coherent conversation.*

She turns to **Charley**.

Kara Three   Do I know you?

Reece   They're mates of Jake's.

Charley (*to* **Reece**)   We should go.

Reece   No, stay.

Putting his arm round **Kara Three**.

Reece   Kara doesn't want to break up the party, do you, babe? Stick some music on, I'll be out in a minute.

Kara Three *shakes off his arm and exits to her bedroom.*

Reece *shrugs and grins apologetically. Starts going after* **Kara Three**.

Reece   Hormones.

He exits.

Liam (*calls*)   Night, Kara.

He starts to hand out the beers.

Charley   Is that his missis?

Jake   Yep.

Charley   Is she . . . pregnant?

Jake   Yep. Or it's a nasty case of wind.

Charley   Ohhh . . . I feel bad now. She should have a drink with us. (*Calls.*) Hey – um – I don't know your name? Come back here! Come and be friendly!

Liam   Oi, shut up. Don't stir it.

Charley   What? What did I say?

Reece *comes back out. He takes a beer off* **Liam** *and sits down next to* **Hannah**.

Charley   Is she all right?

Reece   Who – Kara? Why wouldn't she be all right?

Jake   He's got her trained.

Charley   Trained! (*She laughs.*) Dance, little monkey! Oh, but is she really all right with us being here?

Reece   Just shut up and drink.

Music blasts on. **Jake** *and* **Charley** *cheer and dance.* **Liam** *drinks his beer and watches them.* **Reece** *leans over* **Hannah** *and she looks up and grins at him.*

Lights down.

Kara One   The thing about losing your self-respect is you don't really notice when someone is just chipping away at it, a little bit at a time. Especially if you don't have a lot to start with. I was like I'd been brainwashed. It was only me. I deserved it. Only me. How low could I go? Oh – lower than that. Who fucking cared? It was only me.

Sound of a new-born baby crying.

And then . . . it wasn't. I woke up feeling like shit (as usual). Feeling like I been kicked around town (as usual) . . . but I start smiling like it's Christmas morning cos lying in her little hospital cot right next to me is my baby girl. My Keeli.

Scene Fourteen

Hospital visiting time. The new mums chat with their visitors. **Kara Three** *is in bed. There's a hospital cot beside it.* **Kym** *and* **Reece** *are sitting on the bed,* **Kym** *is holding baby Keeli.*

Kym   She's perfect. Absolutely perfect. Isn't she, Kara?

Kara Three   Yes, Mum.

Kym   I'm so proud of you, love.

Reece   I had something to do with it too.

Kym (*in a jokey tone*)   You hope!

As she continues to murmur, **Reece** *gives* **Kara** *a look.*

Kym   Ah . . . look at those little fingers. / You forget . . .

Kara Three (*to audience*)   Thanks, Mum. Thanks a lot.

Kym   Oh, she's so like you, Kara. But all that lovely blonde hair! (*To the baby.*) Where's she get that from? Not Mummy and Daddy . . .

Reece *gets up, abruptly.*

Reece   I'm going outside for a smoke.

Reece *exits.*

Kym Well . . .

Kara One I wanted her to say something. To stick her neck out for a change and tell me Reece was being a dick. Stop making excuses.

Kym I expect he's tired, isn't he?

Kara Three Yes.

Kym You'll be exhausted too. (*Getting up.*) I'll leave you to get some rest, you're going to need it for the next twenty years.

She puts Keeli back in the cot, kisses **Kara Three** *goodbye and leaves, during:*

Kara One I thought – 'twenty years', yes, this is it. I'm a mum. It's never going to be only me now.

Kara Three *leans over to look into the cot.*

She strokes Keeli's head.

Kara Three I will always look after you. I will always keep you happy and safe.

She doesn't see **Reece** *coming back in.*

He leans over her to stare into the cot with her, pressing her down with his weight.

Reece Ahh. 'Look at all that lovely blonde hair.'

Kara Three Ow, that hurts.

Reece *picks up the baby, getting an elbow into* **Kara Three** *as he does.*

She stifles a yelp and tries to take the baby from him, during:.

Reece Where did she get the blonde hair, Kara?

Kara Three Shh. Be careful /with her

Reece   I asked you a question? Who do we know who's got 'lovely blond hair'?

Kara One   I knew exactly what he was thinking but I wasn't going to say.

Kara Three   Get off me, Chris!

Reece *looks startled. Then triumphant.*

Reece   Ohh – Chris, is it?

Kara Three   No! I don't know why I said that!

Reece   It's the truth at last.

Kara Three   It's not – I only said it because I knew it's what you were getting at, you're always using him against me, even though it's absolute crap! Lots of babies are born with blonde hair and it goes darker later.

Reece   Nice try. Slag.

Kara Three   Reece, I swear to you – on my life – on our baby's life, I've never been with Chris or anyone.

Reece   You're lying. I can always tell when you lie. Your lips move.

Kara Three   Please don't do this! She's your baby and she's only a day old and already you're spoiling *everything*!

The ward has fallen quiet as everyone is listening in to the row.

The **Nurse** *is coming over.*

Reece   You are such a little whore. I always knew it. You wait – I'm going to kill the / prick . . .

Kara Three   Reece, stop – this is stupid, this is so so stupid.

Nurse   Is everything OK?

Reece *gets up.*

Reece   Hunky dory, Nursie. I'm off to ring Jeremy Kyle – get me a paternity test.

Reece *exits as:*

Kara One   Everyone was looking at me and I wasn't just ashamed for myself. I was ashamed for my little girl. It was all very well me putting up with Reece's behaviour but I didn't want Keeli growing up in that sort of home. I didn't want her to see him hit me. And I knew he wouldn't stop and I was tired of it all. All the dreams I'd had about 'our little family' was just that, silly dreams.

Nurse (*to Keeli*)   Your daddy's a funny 'un, isn't he?

Kara Three   He doesn't mean it. He loves her to bits.

*The **Nurse** looks at **Kara Three**.*

Kara One   And I could see myself, telling lies and making excuses for the rest of my life and knowing deep down, no one believed me. When I showed up with a split lip or bruises on my arm, we all just pretended I was clumsy or unlucky. 'My battle scars' I'd called them, like it was something to be proud of, getting hit. I just felt so sorry for myself. For all the life I'd wasted. For getting everything so wrong. But then I saw my Keeli, all brand new and ready to be loved and looked after. And I knew I could do it right for her.

Lights down.

Kara One*'s phone rings. She picks it up.*

Kara One   Hiya, mate – sorry, I lost track of time, d'you want me to pick Keeli up now? . . . Ooh, a sleepover, she'll love that . . . (*Starting to grin.*) . . . That's a plan. You dig out a DVD and I'll pop in the offie on my way over, have a girls' night in . . . Did I what? . . . Oh, yeah – I've nearly finished it . . . Lisa, I don't care, she's got to *know* . . . Yeah, well, maybe I am. (*Laughs.*) Laters.

She ends the call, goes back to her letter.

Kara One   Lisa's just told me I'm on a crusade. She didn't want me to write this because she says you'll tell Reece and it'll wind him up.

During the next bit, **Kara Two** *and* **Kara Three** *join her.*

Kara One   She says I should leave it alone, now he's finally stopped threatening to 'tear my fucking head off'.

And I want to. It's been unbearable all the shit he's said about me and the pictures he posted online for everyone to see when he *promised* he'd deleted them –

Kara Three   – and then when he decided to 'forgive' me, I've had people I hardly know come up to me in the street saying why won't I let Reece see his baby? And I want to say to them, do you know what Reece did to Chris just out of his temper and spite and do you know what it's like having Chris and his mum and dad thinking it's all my fault? But everyone thinks there's no smoke without fire, unless it's happened to them.

Kara Two   Even Mum says: 'Oh it would be lovely for Keeli to get to know her dad' and 'Maybe you can't forget, Kara, but you could try and forgive.'

Sometimes I think I'm the only person who doesn't count in all this and what Reece put me through didn't mean very much. So when I heard he had a new girlfriend, I was like, thank God, he's got someone else to pick on.

Kara One   And then I started thinking about you. And I wondered – do you ever feel like everything you and Reece argue about it's all your fault? Has he ever hit you and told you he'll never do it again?

Are you ashamed of what happens between you and do you think no one can understand?

That's why I had to write this . . .

Music: intro 'Message to You, Rudy' by the Specials, Dandy Livingstone, etc.

*As the **Karas** sing, they're joined onstage by the rest of the cast. By the end of the song, everyone is singing and dancing together:*

The Karas
Stop him messing around
(Ah, ah, ah)
Better think of your future
(Ah, ah, ah)
Time to straighten him out
(Ah, ah)
Cos he's bringing you down
(Ah, ah, ah)

Lacey – a letter to you, Lacey
A letter to you

Good lovin' ain't about pain
(Ah, ah, ah)
Unless you've chosen a safe word
(Ah, ah, ah)
Time to make yourself heard
(Ah, ah)
This can't happen again
(Ah, ah, ah)

Lacey – a letter to you, Lacey
A letter to you

You know what you gotta do
(Ah, ah, ah)
You know that you're not alone now
(Ah, ah, ah)
Time to walk through the door
(Ah, ah)
I'll be waiting for you

Lacey – a letter to you, Lacey
A letter to you
Lacey – this is my letter to you
Lacey
Oh, a message to you, Lacey

About the Play

A Letter to Lacey was originally written as a monologue for Myrtle Theatre and Meriton School in Bristol to explore issues around partner abuse. It was then developed into this play for NT Connections.

Kara's relationship with Reece traces the nature of abuse in a series of short, sharp scenes. She doesn't attempt to analyse this, but it would be a useful exercise to look at each scene and examine how the abuse escalates. If you want to do some research, there is an interesting document called 'Partner Exploitation and Violence in Teenage Intimate Relationships' on the NSPCC website (skip the academic stuff and read the interviews) – but any information you can find or personal experiences you can talk about will help to contextualise what's going on.

It's important to avoid 'victim blaming'. Help the audience understand why Kara doesn't just walk away by exploring her back story: what her parents' marriage was like, what she wants in a relationship. Reece gives us a lot of background too – the character is conflicted and angry. Where does that anger come from? Try and avoid playing him as a stereotypical thug and dig out the truth of being Reece.

The friends and family are affected by this relationship. No one involved remains completely uninvolved, so try and show what the others are feeling when they are around Kara and Reece – without laying it on too thick! For example, do Jake and Liam ever discuss the way Reece treats Kara? Would they treat their own girlfriends the same way? What is it like being Lisa, knowing your best friend is being treated badly and unable to get through to her?

The songs show how intense, destructive relationships are celebrated in music – not to mention movies and literature: the greatest love stories are usually tragedies. From The Crystals' 'He Hit Me (It Felt Like a Kiss') to Eminem and Rihanna on 'Love the Way You Lie', the message is: the more you love, the more it's gonna hurt. Love should make your heart race, give you butterflies, make your spirits soar, give you sleepless nights. Love should never feel shameful, disempowering, bruising and sour. And it's never too late to learn this.

Catherine Johnson
June 2013

A Letter to Lacey

BY CATHERINE JOHNSON

*Notes on rehearsal and staging, drawn from a workshop
with the writer held at the National Theatre, November 2013*

Workshop led by James Brining, with notes by Lucy Foster

Themes

A key reason why so many teachers and youth theatre directors chose this Connections play was the subject matter and themes. It was felt that exploring with students a play about partner abuse, as opposed to one about domestic violence, was important as it made it clear that this wasn't something that just happened to 'mums and dads'. Many who had read the play through with their students had found that it had surprisingly made the students laugh, but also that they had become very angry, particularly towards Kara, questioning how she could act like that. The students had felt that it captured their voices without being patronising.

Many young people are growing up in a sexist culture that is finding new pernicious manifestations through the internet. 'Slut-shaming' was referenced as an example where, usually, a girl is egged on to send a naked photo to her boyfriend, who then posts it online once they break up. Once on the internet it is the girl who is blamed for being the slut. The themes of the play very much tap into this current climate.

In developing the play Catherine Johnson found she wanted to bring in the songs in order to explore the cultural influences on the characters. She feels the play is very much from Kara's point of view, and is not meant to fully explore Reece's experience. In developing the play she did, however, feel it was important to show that what happens in their relationship affects everyone around them.

The idea behind splitting the role of Kara into three was to show how she changes, and also to suggest that this doesn't just happen to one girl but could happen to anyone.

Structure, scene by scene

The action we see in the play happens over the four years prior to the letter being written. During this time things have calmed down for Kara. She has found herself a place to live with her daughter Keeley and got a job. You will need to explore with the actors what that is, as well as exactly what happened with Reece following the break-up and why Lisa urges her not to stir it up by writing the letter.

During the workshop the director, James Brining, worked with Catherine and the workshop participants to look at what the key narrative, character, thematic and stylistic developments are within each scene.

PROLOGUE   There is a dynamic set-up in the first exchange between the three Karas of a cross-examining of Kara Two, the least experienced, by Kara Three and Kara One. This exchange is also important in establishing the connection between the three Karas and the theatrical convention of the same character split between three actors. After this initial exchange they do not then continue to address each other, only the other characters within the scenes and the audience, and this decision feels important in creating a sense of Kara's isolation.

SCENE ONE: Kara's motivation in writing the letter is to inform Lacey about Reece, but in the process she also reflects on her own experiences. In writing the letter Kara starts off as more functional, wanting to get the job done, but then becomes increasingly reflective and emotional.

SCENE TWO   This scene shows both Kara and Reece as confident. As the play goes on Kara's confidence will drop away and Reece's will stay the same. The fact that Kara and Lisa are hanging out on a children's roundabout quickly suggests they are bored and killing time, but also there's still a connection to childhood and innocence. We see from this scene that Kara forgives quickly. Reece arriving in his car pulls status when set against Chris's skateboard. Kara getting into the car with Reece is very much motivated by being hurt by Chris, and so we see a tendency to not really deal with the treatment she receives as an issue for her. The seeds of much of what happens to Kara can be found in this scene. One example is that she *has* gone after Reece largely because of Chris's rejection. So when Reece later accuses her of still being into Chris, there is a sense that she has indeed not been honest. This is key as it blurs her thinking about which of Reece's other accusations are true.

SCENE THREE   In this scene we see Reece testing Kara as to how much she will let him get away with. The tone of their later relationship is very much set here.

SCENE FOUR   Here we see how quick Kara is to justify Reece's violence when she hears about the assault charge against him. Her reaction to what she learns about him is the key thing we learn from this scene. This scene takes place a couple of days after the ride in Reece's car.

SCENE FIVE   This is the next encounter between Kara and Reece at the pub. It is the same evening as Lisa and Kara's phone call. Reece cleverly separates and divides the two girls, setting them against each other. Narrative-wise it is a key moment as it is where Kara and Reece get together.

SCENE SIX   In contrast to the previous two scenes there is more reflection than action here, and it provides a different kind of energy to the previous scenes. Kara Two has no lines and it will be interesting to consider how she reacts during this scene.

SCENES SEVEN, EIGHT AND NINE   Through these scenes the tone is consistently uncomfortable. This is where we see Reece deploying the full set of skills and tactics that he uses against Kara. We see how he pulls his friends into the treatment of Kara and there are signs that they are not quite sure how to react, although for the most part they go along with him.

SCENE TEN   This is a meaty scene, where we get a direct insight into Reece's family. We can now understand what he is allowed to get away with by his mum; he talks to her like dirt and she more or less allows him to call her names. This is key, as she is the other main woman in his life and we see here the nature of that relationship. We see that Terry, his stepdad, is making an effort to have a relationship with Reece, and he won't hit Reece despite provocation. Reece is wholly set against Terry, which may be as much because he's another man as because of who he is. We see Julie not helping the development of a relationship between her son and partner by failing to really stand up to Reece when he insults Terry.

SCENE ELEVEN   We have shifted forward in time and have moved to Kara Three. We see a new phase where Kara Three has lost all her confidence.

SCENE TWELVE   Kara and Reece's relationship has deteriorated to a far worse place. At the end of the scene we see the Karas coming together. Kara One apologises to the other two. From this point the structure begins to become more hazy dramaturgically, with a less clear sense of time passing than before. This suggests the disorder Kara Three's life has slipped into. There is little ambiguity by this stage about the nature of her relationship with Reece; by now she acknowledges her own inability to escape it. She understands it is an awful thing but does not yet have power to act.

SCENE THIRTEEN   There is now a sense that Reece's friends know exactly what is going on but do not do anything. They seem quieter than before, and are perhaps unhappy about things but do not feel able to say anything. When Liam urges 'Shut up. Don't stir it', we get a sense of this. We see how the relationship is corrosive for all the relationships around them.

SCENE FOURTEEN   The narrative in this scene changes direction. The change is precipitated by new life – the birth of Kara's daughter. The moment that something clicks for her is not, however, the fact of Keeley's birth itself but rather when Reece abuses her in front of the baby. In this scene we also meet the Nurse, who is objective about the relationship and we see how it appears through her eyes.

Language

The language in the play is carefully chosen and reflects the aggressiveness of the language that can be used between some young people, and specifically as a form of abuse. There was discussion at the workshop about the blocks that many run up against, especially within schools, to using any swearing within public performances. It was felt generally that the particular issue with losing any of the swearing or sexual language from this play was that it is a play as much about verbal as physical abuse. Other particular word choices were discussed:

Kiddy   Kiddy is a Bristolian term meaning 'bloke' or 'geezer'. Many at the workshop felt that it was not something that would ever be said in their region. Catherine was happy for an alternative regionally appropriate word to be found.

Reference to Keeley as blonde   If working with non-white students then these references to character appearance could be changed or taken out. Please check any of these changes with Catherine first.

Reference to Kara washing off fake tan   Again if working with non-white students this part of the line could be removed.

Characters and characterisation

KARA   Catherine on Kara:

Kara One is now in a place where she feels confident. She understands why certain things have happened to her, and that she is making a choice to put her head above the parapet in writing to Lacey. She wants to convey to Lacey that she is her friend and she is trying to make it clear what Reece is like. She has grown up and is now letting her experiences inform who she is. She is now a strong, healthy girl in many ways.

Kara One's decision to leave Reece and not go back comes from the shift in her thinking brought about by the birth of Keeley. With the birth of her daughter there is a new sense that she needs to protect someone else, and that she will now not only be covering up for herself but for her child. She recognises that her own mum did not protect her.

There is also a progression through the play for Kara One, which make her feel like more than just an effective narrator for her own story. As she becomes more involved in telling the story she gets more upset and apologises to her past selves. In her understanding of others' actions there is also a progression through her view of her mum. In Scene Six she condemns her mum for not teaching her any self-respect, but by the end we see signs of more understanding and forgiveness for her.

REECE   He needs to be charming and someone who the young people in the play would clearly navigate towards. He is the kind of young man who will get trapped at that age. Nevertheless, at seventeen he is the most charismatic boy around. James said that 'Reece's position is as much about the status which is assigned to him as much as what is claimed by him.'

For Kara he brings a new circle of friends and a new world, which is clearly very exciting for her. We know from early on in the play that Reece is known to be aggressive; he goes to prison for GBH. Reece's use of violence clearly stems very much from what he has learnt from this dad, who we hear encouraged him to fight. He seems to be fairly in control of the violence he uses against Kara, and we get the sense that he believes this is just what you do.

LISA   On one level Lisa is a strong and feisty character, particularly next to Kara. We see her making her own choices and standing up for herself. Having a boyfriend is not essential to her identity. She is not, however, a one-dimensional character. We do not see someone who is a hundred per cent sorted. There are several moments where she enjoys the power she has over Kara in having information that she wants about Reece. In the scene in the pub she begins trying to help Kara but is clearly enjoying the power this gives her and the chance to chat to the older boys.

KYM   We hear Kara's belief that her mother never taught her self-respect. At the end of the play Kym seems to have no awareness of the reaction her comments about the baby being blonde might trigger in Recce; we see here the extent to which she has been in denial about his behaviour as much as Kara has.

The songs

Catherine felt that the songs serve a number of purposes. They are there to bring light relief. When the play was workshopped early on at Winstanley College it was evident that the songs had the potential to be hilarious. They also draw on the long tradition in pop history of connecting love with pain and suffering. That we listen to and absorb these songs then has an influence on how we feel about relationships.

The songs also come at moments when the action of the play needs to move on, and sometimes they are used to suggest the passing of time. They are also key in allowing the final song to feel earned. If everything was the same style throughout the play the upbeat quality of the final song would seem to come out of nowhere.

In giving the genre of each song Catherine wanted to create really clear divides between the era and musical style, ranging from 1960s girl band to country to rap. She feels that it is important that the musical genres named in the play are kept to, as they reference the range of cultural contexts from which attitudes to, and acceptance of, partner abuse has emerged.

The genres suggested, however, are reference points rather than allusions to particular songs, apart from the final one, which has specifically been written to be sung to the tune of 'A Message to You, Rudy'. The lyrics were not written with the intention of being sung to the music of an existing track. Aside from the possible legal bars to performing an existing track in this way, the idea is that they suggest the musical genre rather than quote a specific song.

'A Message to You, Rudy', while performed most famously by The Specials, was a song from 1967, which has been extensively covered. By resisting over-pastiching, through not singing to recognisable songs before the final number, will make the final recognisable 'A Message to You, Rudy' more satisfying.

James said that: 'The song at the end is really celebratory. There is a sense that change is possible. This is the important message that could come out of the play. In approaching the songs, be playful.'

Catherine has chosen the Karas to sing because it empowers them. It was discussed as to whether you could add in additional ensemble to sing with the Karas and it was felt by Catherine that this would be fine as long as the Karas still had a visible presence.

James felt that the play is in many ways unrelenting in terms of its theme and that the music gives it a dramaturgical energy, providing important shifts of gear. They explore different textures to the dialogue and direct address to the audience. They also add an important aspect of cultural comment, making the play about a wider culture rather than just the individual characters within it. This makes a clear link that the ideas that the play explores are pedalled and reflected by popular culture. The songs are a brilliant way of making the play shift from being about individual characters to a broader social comment.

DEVELOPING MUSIC FOR THE SONGS

James suggested working with students to explore the music of each specified genre, and using inspiration from that to write new songs in the style of existing tracks. You might want to explore working with the music department at your school, music students from a local college, or to set your own students the challenge of writing something on Garage Band or a similar application. The music is an opportunity to have fun and offer different creative opportunities to your group.

During a workshop on the music with music director David Shrubsole, it was discussed how once you have immersed yourself in the musical genres suggested, you may be able to borrow chord sequences that give your songs a similar sound.

The choice of instruments and the production done on a track are also key to giving it a certain sound. If you were able to have a live band on stage this would be great, but recorded backing tracks to sing over will also work well.

Hand-held microphones, on stands or otherwise, are a good idea to amplify the singing, but try to avoid radio microphones, particularly when time is limited for the Partner Theatre Festival. If you are using a live band it would be wise to use your own amps for the Partner Festival, as this will guarantee the equipment you need and take up less tech time.

A LOOK AT A SELECTION OF THE SONGS

First song, 1960s girl-band style   The play arrives somewhere dark very quickly, so by making this first song glamorous and fun the bigger the arc will be when it gets dark. Living outside the chronology of the play, much like a prologue, it announces in a tongue-in-cheek way to the audience that things are not going to go well for this girl, and lays the seeds of the themes that will unfold.

Reece's rap   Using rap here is clearly referencing another example of popular music that often condones misogyny and violence against women. The specific period of rap doesn't matter.

Reece's song   The choice of a country-music ballad reflects the music that Reece's dad might have listened to. It is also traditionally a self-pitying form. In this song we hear Reece's explanation of why he is the way he is. The song exists outside of the scenes, and uses a heightened style to justify the introduction of the narrative of this life. Reece's story of why he is damaged is key as it becomes Reece and Kara's justification for why he treats her as he does. Catherine said: 'The song is not intended to ask for a particular reaction from the audience. Reece believes this version of events – that this is what happened to him.'

'He Hit Me (It Felt Like a Kiss)'   This song by The Crystals was a major starting point for thinking about the songs' role.

Casting

A number of questions were asked during the workshop by directors about the casting challenges they face:

Question   Do the Karas need to look the same?
Catherine   No, they don't. In fact if they looked different it would suggest the universality of their situation.

Question   Would you want to use something like costume to link them?
Catherine   Yes. I think the clues to them being linked are also in the text, but you could also have a shared piece of costume.

Question   I will be working with mainly black students. What shall I do about the references to blonde hair and washing off fake-tan?
Catherine   Make those changes you need to make to make it work practically.

Question   I am working with a girls' school. Do I need a framework, such as setting it in a women's prison?
Catherine and *James*'s feelings were that this wasn't necessary and that you could just do it with the girls. It seems also that Reece needs to be male, whether played by a boy or girl. There is no reason why female actors can't play the intention and energy of the male characters chillingly accurately.

Production, staging and design

Black eyes and make-up
Catherine imagines that the black eyes would be lost after the initial image, where the sunglasses are removed to reveal them. The idea is that each time they present as a new band they would have a new look. James suggested looking for ways to incorporate taking the make-up off into the world of the play and its action.

Staging the violence within the play
How this is done is a question of stylistic choice – whether a naturalistic or more stylised approach is taken. Whichever

choice is made, what is key is that these moments strongly register. The scripted moments of violence that need to be staged are: Reece headbutting Kara; Reece hitting Kara on the head; Reece leaning on and elbowing Kara; and various arm-grabs.

In rehearsing this stage combat work, some key things to remember are:

* Feedback from a partner is key on what feels safe and comfortable.

* The victim is always leading where there is any dragging.

* Sell the pain through the victim's reaction. This is a large part of what makes any stage combat look believable to the audience.

* If hitting the head let the hand brush along the side of the head to avoid impact, and make sure contact is made with the side of the head so that the neck is not affected.

* With the headbutt the safety is in keeping the distance.

* It will take fifty practices before any of it looks real!

Staging the scene in the car
However you choose to do this, capturing the sense of movement, speed and, crucially, jeopardy are the important things. The belief and intention of the actors are key. Some ideas that came out of the workshop were:

* Using wheely chairs.

* Sound effects on microphones done live.

* Using a remote-control car.

* Using a skateboard to create the car.

* Supermarket trolleys.

* Projection of a car and the view out the back of it, old movie style.

* Sitting on blocks, steering a wheel.

Exercises for use in rehearsals

NAME GAME

Standing in a circle, the beginner (Number 1) starts by making eye contact with another person across the circle (Number 2) and saying their name. Number 2 responds by saying Number 1's name back to them. Only then is Number 1 released and can begin to walk towards Number 2. As they cross the circle Number 2 must repeat the process, making eye contact with another (Number 3) and saying their name. Number 3 must say Number 2's name back to them to release them, before Number 1 reaches them. The process is repeated until everyone has been chosen. The game can then evolve so only pointing is used to indicate who you are choosing (Number 1 would point at Number 2 who points back and then chooses another to point at), and the game is played in silence.

THE QUICK BROWN FOX JUMPS OVER THE LAZY DOG

Standing in a circle everyone labels themselves with a letter going through the alphabet, A to Z. If you have fewer than twenty-six, some people take more than one letter. You can also have people take 'space' or 'full stop'. As a group you then spell the sentence 'The Quick Brown Fox Jumps Over the Lazy Dog', which includes all the letters in the alphabet. You can play the game so that people are 'out' if they make a mistake, and each time this happens the group reassigns the alphabet.

In the early stages of rehearsal take time to read through the play scene by scene with the whole cast, to give a chance for specific questions to be asked after each scene. You may want to ask, what do these characters each want? What do they want at the start of the play and what do they want at the start of each scene?

Suggested reference

There is a lot of research on the NSPCC's website, as recommended. The suggested document is called 'Partner Exploitation and Violence in Teenage Intimate Relationships'. Catherine felt the interviews within this document were particularly useful.

A Shop
Selling Speech

by Sabrina Mahfouz

Sabrina Mahfouz is a British-Egyptian poet and playwright. She is currently an Associate Artist at the Bush Theatre, a Global Shaper at the World Economic Forum and the recipient of a 2013 Sky Arts Futures Fund Award for her poetry work. Her first short play, *That Boy*, won a Westminster Prize for New Playwrights at Soho Theatre in 2010. Her debut solo show, *Dry Ice*, received a nomination at *The Stage* Awards for Best Solo Show in 2011. In 2012, her play *One Hour Only* won an Old Vic New Voices Edinburgh Award. The Traverse Theatre presented her latest play, *Clean*, at Edinburgh Festival 2013.

Characters

Sara
Sherif
Mahmoud

Fatima
Ahmed
Noura
Mo
Sahmia

All are aged between sixteen and nineteen.

Setting

The setting is a shop.

The time is the present day, whenever that may be, in Cairo, Egypt.

Events that are referred to throughout the play are not necessarily events of a particular date. History does have a tendency to repeat itself.

A dash (−) at the end of a sentence indicates that what follows should be overlapping, quick-paced.

One

Sara *stands strong, with a gun and a balaclava.* **Mahmoud** *and* **Sherif** *stand behind her looking tough, all in black; maybe both with a baseball bat or similar, but not a gun or knife.*

Kneeling on the floor below her are some of the shop workers – **Fatima**, **Ahmed**, **Sahmia**, **Noura** *and* **Mo**.

There is silence and stillness.

One of the workers shuffles and **Sara** *quickly aims the gun at them.*

Mahmoud   Don't move!

Sherif   Don't speak please!

Mahmoud   Look at the floor!

Sherif   Look at your feet please!

Mahmoud   Don't breathe!

Sara *inclines her head to* **Mahmoud***; he's gone a bit far. He looks apologetically at her.*

Mahmoud   Er, well, breathe of course. Just quietly!

Moments of tense silence.

Sara *raises the balaclava from her face.*

Sara   I don't want to harm you. I just want you to be scared enough to do as I say.

Mahmoud   Will you do as she says?

Sherif   Please, do as she says.

None of the staff say anything.

Mahmoud   Why don't you say anything?

Sherif   Why won't you say anything?

Sahmia *(under her breath)*   You told us not to speak.

Sherif   Louder.

Sahmia   You, you told us not to speak. Not to move.

Sara   We have a smart one, a live one.

Fatima   What do you want?

Sara   Two now!

She steps closer to the group, menacing with the gun. **Mo** *is whimpering.* **Noura** *gently comforts him.*

Mo   Please don't shoot, I'm going to –

Sara   Silence!

Mahmoud   Silence!

Sherif   Silence, please.

Sara   I won't shoot if you do as I say. I am here for the speech tokens and the quicker I get them, the quicker I leave. The doors are locked, you are surrounded. Who's found themselves in charge of this sorry shop?

Fatima   I am.

Sara   Take me to the tokens.

Fatima *tries to get her mobile phone out.*

Sara   No, no phones. Mahmoud, Sherif, collect all of their phones now.

Mahmoud *and* **Sherif** *collect all the phones from the workers, who are very nervous.*

Sara   Take me to the tokens, *yalla.*

Fatima   I, I don't know where they are. Only my father knows. He owns the shop. I need to phone him.

Sara   I don't believe you. Your eyes are hard. Where are they, Hard-Eyes?

Fatima   Only my father knows –

Sara   I don't believe you –

Mahmoud   Neither do I –

Sherif   Or I –

Sara   Hard-Eyes is a liar –

Mahmoud   Liar –

Sherif   Liar –

Fatima *puffs up her chest, becoming angry.*

Fatima   I am not. And my name is Fatima. And . . . and you don't scare me. We've all seen enough people with guns to know that you're all full of empty words and no action so –

Sara *puts the gun to* **Fatima**'s *head. The workers gasp.* **Noura** *covers her eyes.* **Mo** *puts his arms around her.*

Sara   I am a woman of impeccable actions, my dear, do not test me.

Mahmoud   I have seen her slice the head from a chicken with her fingernails –

Sara *smiles and moves the gun away from* **Fatima**'s *head and sits down on the desk/counter.* **Fatima** *remains standing.* **Sherif** *and* **Mahmoud** *flank* **Sara**.

Sara   So, Fatima. If your father owns this shop, you must know where he keeps the speech tokens. This is a shop selling speech; I did come to the right place?

Fatima   Yes, it is. But no, I can't help you. All I know is that there is a safe, somewhere. My father is the only one who knows the code and the location.

Sara   Dubious and dubiouser my dear. But whatever the truth, it seems that *you* are the best way to access what I want.

Now, for all of you. I just want to make it clear what we're doing here. We are not your regular, selfish robbers, we're not animals –

Sherif   We are not animals. We are doing righteous work –

Mahmoud   We are fighting for freedom –

Sara   For the right to speak –

Sherif   To speak loudly –

Mahmoud   To speak freely –

Sara   About freedom –

Sherif (*looks up*)   About heaven –

Mahmoud (*looks towards* **Sara**)   About love –

Sara   For too long, the right to speak has been given to the few and we are here to change that, to take it to the masses, to dance with words in the streets –

She twirls around and **Mahmoud** *and* **Sherif** *act as her 'dance' partners.*

The workers start to look at them differently – they're not really as scared any more. They begin to get restless. **Sahmia** *stands up, followed by the others.*

Sahmia   You speak quite a lot already, don't you, so what's the problem?

Sara stops 'dancing' and twirls the gun to point at **Sahmia**.

Sara   You are very mouthy for one who has a gun pointed at her head.

Sahmia   I've been in the front line too many times at too many protests to be scared of a little gun like that.

Sara   Ahh, a protestor, people. We have a protestor in the house –

Sahmia   An activist, actually and I have seen more deaths than all of you have had hot dinners –

Mahmoud   I don't think you know how much I like to eat –

Sara   A fighter, I like her. OK, OK. I feel I must win you all over with more than a gun, because you are also the workers, the masses. I want you to *want speech to be free.* You must want it, otherwise there's no point to anything, is there? Hard-Eyes, when does your father return?

Fatima   My name is Fatima. He probably won't come back for at least an hour, the traffic is a never-ending centipede in this city.

Sara   So, we wait.

Sherif
Excuse me, sister.
May I say that
we Egyptians have waited for too long,
always for someone
to come back from somewhere
to sort something out.
Let's find and open the safe ourselves!

Sara   No. We wait. We do it as we planned.

Sherif   I am ready for the plan to change. I don't want to wait.

Sara   I said, we wait.

Sherif   Forgive me, sister, but I say you're wrong.

Sara *stares at him. Considers his rebellion. She aims her gun at him and snatches whatever weapon he has and hands it to* **Mahmoud**.

As she says the following, she ties **Sherif***'s hands with cable ties from her pocket.*

Sara   Sherif, I am not your sister. I am your boss. I have been kind to you because you're always polite and quiet and your father knew my father. But I will not tolerate this sort of behaviour.

Hard-Eyes, pass me some masking tape.

Sherif   Think about what you're doing here, sister –

Sara   Hard-Eyes?

Sherif   I am on your side –

Fatima   I don't think we have –

Sara   Stop lying, Hard-Eyes.

Fatima *passes* **Sara** *masking tape or similar.* **Sara** *starts taping up* **Sherif***'s mouth as he struggles, but not too much to slow her down.*

Fatima   Are you sure he can breathe?

Sara   Would you like to swap places with him, Hard-Eyes? He wanted to destroy your shop. But I will swap him for you, if you wish. Do you?

Fatima   No, no, I –

Sara
Right then. He'll remain here as a reminder to you all
of how crazy I am,
how much I believe in my plan,
how very determined I am.

Thank you for your assistance, Hard-Eyes. It would have been impossible without you.

She throws the tape back to **Fatima***.* **Sherif** *is now tied up in some way / place.*

Sara
Everyone listen.
I will tell you all how I plan
to give speech new homes in the mouths
of those held down on the ground for so long.
I will hope that you join my fight.
First, we must all remind ourselves what we are fighting
     against.
Peasants of the Shop Selling Speech, let me present –

The following is a quick-paced interruption, the first time the workers start to relax slightly as a group, maybe ironically emboldened by the fact that the group of robbers has lost cohesion. **Sara** *is surprised by the interruption, but interested to see where it goes.*

Sahmia   We are not peasants, we're working here to make money to do things with our lives, to make our country great –

Noura   I'm making money to get out of this country –

Mo   Me too, I hate it here –

Ahmed   Ah man, don't say that –

Mo   I do –

Noura   Mo, why do you hate it here?

Mo
   I hate it here because . . . I'm scared all the time. I'm bored.
   Everybody just smokes and gossips
   and thinks that because they went out on the streets a few
      times
   and it went on the news that they've lived a life,
   but this isn't a life, this is just the same as before,
   boring boring

Sahmia   So you think we shouldn't have went on the streets? Left things as they were? Dictatorships and darkness and damning existences for the non-elites –

Ahmed   Sahmia, I don't think he's saying that, you know, he's just frustrated, like most of us –

Mo   No, I am saying that: it was a waste of time and now things are worse –

Sahmia   Both of you bring shame to this country, *wallahi.*

Ahmed   Come on, Sahmia, I was there, I fought –

Sahmia   From your open-plan living room with your iPod in your ears! Not there, where it mattered –

Ahmed   It mattered where I was too, I made things possible, don't try to make out like you're the only one who knows what they –

Noura   What were you trying to do? I still don't know –

Mo   I don't know –

Noura   I just want to be in America –

Mo   Me too! We could –

Sara   Enough! We won't be saying that again today. You are not in America. And *allahamdullah*, because if you were, you would probably all have your own guns and I wouldn't be standing here right now.

> Back to my plan.
> While we wait for the patriarch to return
> with the keys to the castle,
> we remind ourselves of the mess freedom is in,
> you awaken your senses and believe in me and my gun.
> Let's begin! Let's show what is being shown to the people
>   of Egypt.

She presses play or makes actions indicating a show/screening is about to begin and a pre-recorded infomercial begins on a screen – or this could be acted out in a very over-the-top, cheesy way:

Man (*voice recording*)   Hello, people of Egypt. We, your democratically elected, well-connected, never knowingly rejected Government, would like to inform you of a new system being introduced to ensure everyone in this country gets their voice heard –

Woman (*voice recording*)   Yes, because we've heard that you weren't being heard and we heard how absurd this was from those who are better at words than us and so we bring you –

Both/Crowd (*voice recording*)   Speech tokens!

Man (*voice recording*)   Machines have been installed on the corners of all major streets!

The workers begin to briefly talk over the infomercial, overlapping each other:

Sahmia   The streets that we fought for –

Mo   The streets I don't want to walk down –

Noura   The streets that whistle at me and grab my sleeves –

Mo   I won't let anyone do that to –

Ahmed   The streets that don't see me –

Sara   The streets that *we* plan to make free –

They turn their attention back to the screen.

Woman (*voice recording*)   Oh my, they are so new and shiny! And look, the loudspeakers are the most modern in the Middle East! How do they work, I hear you say –

Man (*voice recording*)   Easy-peasy! Buy a speech token, stick it in the machine and there you have it, one two three – your voice will be heard for a maximum of sixty seconds per day. Free to say what you want to say!

Woman (*voice recording*)   I say the best thing is, nobody will be arrested or tortured or exiled or killed for their loudspeaker words, which is quite revolutionary.

Man (*voice recording*)   Quite revolutionary, indeed.

Both/Crowd (*voice recording*)   Buy your free speech now from recommended retailers!

The show ends. **Fatima** *claps. Nobody else joins in. They look a bit nonplussed.*

Sara   Thoughts, workers?

Fatima   I think this solution –

Sahmia   I do not see that this government has created any solutions of any consequence –

Ahmed   But you had no solutions either, did you? Do you? If you'd have worked with us more, we could have helped you, the international community was waiting, was there –

Sahmia   The international community made the mess in the first place –

Ahmed They made Facebook too though, man, you got to
work together –

Sahmia *huffs and turns away from* **Ahmed**. **Sara** *stops their
conversation, stands in front of the workers, gun by her side.*

Sara How do you get the tokens to put into the machine,
Fatima?

Fatima You have to buy them.

Sara From shops like this?

Fatima Yes.

Ahmed Also, there's an app that rewards you with them
the less you go online, which is kind of a contradiction, I
suppose, but –

Noura Yeahm and I got one for baking cakes for this
charity thing once but then when I put it in the machine it
didn't work and I was shouting and shouting but nobody
could hear me –

Sahmia Like you'd have anything to say anyway –

Mo Hey –

Sara
So, Fatima. The only people in this country –
this revolutionised, game-changing country –
who have access to 'free' speech are . . .
those who can pay for it
or those who are rewarded it by someone who the
    government approves of
for doing something the government approves of?

Fatima Yeah, I suppose.

Sara And still you don't see?

Fatima See what?

Sahmia   Oh for God's sake, Fatima, she's right, it's ridiculous. This isn't what I was fighting for, I wanted us all to be equal. Bread, justice, freedom. That's what we chanted!

Fatima   And we have all those things –

Sara   *You* have all those things, princess –

Sahmia   I won't join you because I don't agree with your gun, but I do agree that things should be equal, we shouldn't just be allowing those who are able to afford speech tokens or get them through some dubious reward system to be the ones who speak –

Fatima   But don't you guys get it? If people are hard-working enough, they can buy the tokens. They're not ridiculously expensive, they're fairly priced.

Mahmoud   Fairly priced to you. Where is your accent from? Where did you study?

Fatima   In England.

Noura   Oh my God, so lucky! I begged to go abroad –

Sara   None of you know about begging, especially not our daughter of an empire, Fatima here.

Fatima   I had like, a really hard time at school, actually. I hated it there. I love Egypt. This is my home.

Sara   But in your home, that you love, you believe that everyone who is too poor to buy speech tokens is in this position through either choice or laziness?

Fatima   Maybe not in every case, but yes, I believe there are opportunities out there for everyone –

Ahmed   That isn't really true, you know, if you look at what people our age are saying on Facebook –

Sahmia   Oh, shut up about Facebook! If people can get on to Facebook then they're not really suffering are they?

When we were lying with our bones broken, we weren't on
Facebook –

Noura   Well, you were, actually, that's how the whole
world knew –

Sahmia   I'm just sick of this, nobody realises the sacrifices
that were made in *real* life. People *died*. Hundreds of people
died. Revolutions happened throughout history without
Facebook and Twitter. It takes action and people on the
streets –

*The workers gather together and become raging protesters, shouting 'One
hand, one people!' and 'Bread, justice, freedom!'*

Ahmed *steps out from the group, who become silent. He addresses this
to* **Sahmia**.

Ahmed
    My brother did what you do, many moons ago.
    He was my hero.
    He taught me everything I know, from coding to hacking to,
    well, things I won't share here.
    He went out on protests.
    Out on to the streets.
    Your precious streets.
    A real person, in action.
    Hands in the air, feet to the ground.
    Immoveable, incorruptible, a real person
    with a real heart and real hands
    and real flesh that bleeds when it is whipped
    and cut and carved and stamped and unstuck.
    He got arrested, we couldn't see him.
    Disappeared behind the sun,
    wara al shams, as we say.
    He was tortured in prison and
    he died. He was twenty-one.
    So, Sahmia,
    I do realise the sacrifices that have been made.

I just choose a different way than you
to make sure they weren't in vain.

Silence.

Eventually and slowly:

Sahmia   I'm sorry to hear that, Ahmed. Many of my friends suffered the same fate. I . . . I do respect what you do.

Sara *jumps amidst them and starts swinging her gun around.*

Sara   It is a cruel, cruel world people. Most of us won't live to see the changes we are trying to make.

Sahmia   Especially when some of us are trying to make changes using weapons.

Sara   Sometimes you must speak in the language of those you fight –

Sahmia   And sometimes you should find a new vocabulary.

Sara   If you're not allowed to speak, then how will you do that?

Sherif *makes some sort of noise or struggle here.* **Sara** *notices, but does not pay attention.*

Sara
No answer, motor mouth, as I thought.
Now, Hard-Eyes, how long until Daddy returns?

Fatima   Half an hour?

Sara
I haven't had to use my gun yet,
but my fingers are getting restless.
It is best
we continue with my plan
to convince you of the integrity of my actions.
To do this, I must know a little more about you,
the workers, the masses,
know where to pitch my rhetoric.

Each of you tell me why you're here, ready to work in this shop,
this shop that will sell a basic human right to those who can afford it.
Why, I repeat, are you here?

The workers could line up? Present this as a 'chorus line'; an audition etc.; or just a chat.

Noura *steps out.*

Noura   That's easy for me.

Me, Noura El Gammal.
My surname means 'camel rider'.
I have never ridden a camel.
I have never travelled outside of Alexandria,
outside of Egypt,
missriya.
I have seen the sea but I have never been on a boat.
I can peek the tops of pyramids from my bedroom window,
but I have only watched tourists try and climb them,
I don't like heights.
But that's why I'm here.
To climb heights.
To go up into the Egyptian sky
in a plane that takes me far away from the dust that gets everywhere
and the neon lights that shine through my mind when I try to sleep,
a plane that takes me to Europe, to America,
the places I was meant to be
but unfortunately, my parents don't agree.
So they told me if I want to see these places in the world,
I must work and make my own money to do it.
So, that's what I'm doing here.

Sara   And what will you do when you get to these faraway places?

Noura   Work, study, whatever. Stay for as long as I can, get married – what does anyone do anywhere?

Mo   Get married?

Noura   I mean, maybe, eventually, you never know, right?

Mo   Right.

Sara   And why can't you do all those things here?

Noura
   Have you tried walking down the street here?
   With a *hijab* or without,
   with an *abaya* or without,
   it is constant and relentless harassment
   and shopkeepers talk to me as if I can't be trusted to know
      what I want to buy,
   let alone managers wanting to employ me in any sort of
      good job –

Sara   But I am a woman and

Noura   And you have a gun. That's not really my style. I just want to walk down the street and feel unaware of the fact that I'm a woman and that as a woman I am considered not as good a part of the human race –

Mo   You are the best part –

Sara   You will find that wherever you go, my dear, it is impossible to be unaware that you're a woman.

Noura   Nowhere can be as bad as here.

Fatima   It can, trust me.

Noura   Well then, I want to know for myself.

Mo
   Me too. I mean,
   I want to know what's out there.
   I've always wanted to blow the world apart with my mind,
   some kind of . . . big thinker, you know?
   But I didn't finish school,

I spent too much time looking out of the window
and so now here I am.
With a half-baked plan to save up enough to go travelling
to somewhere where they value ideas and creativity
more than a percentage on a piece of paper.
I have the flight booked, but no money for when I arrive.
I want to touch the sky and find it filled with answers.
I don't know.
All I know is that I'm too old to be told no
and too young to know what to say yes to
and I feel very confused,
because I work in this shop selling speech
but I wouldn't even buy any
because I don't even know what I want
or what I want to say.

Noura *reaches out to touch* **Mo***'s arm tenderly.*

Noura   That's beautiful, Mo.

Sara   You need a purpose and we need people with big ideas, so perhaps you and I –

Fatima   Please don't also try to steal my staff –

Sahmia   We won't be your staff when they've stolen all the speech tokens, there'll be nothing left to sell!

Sara   Nothing left to sell! My utopian dream. And why are you are here, activista?

Sahmia   My name is Sahmia, actually, and I'm here for my own reasons. I don't need to tell you.

Sara   No. But if you don't, then you will give Sherif over there some company. I can't imagine you'd like the feel of tape over your mouth, so use it when you're asked to.

Sherif *struggles again.*

Noura   Oh go on, Sahmia!

Pause. **Ahmed** *smiles and nods at her. She shrugs and begins.*

Sahmia
My whole life has been laid out for everyone to comment on
and give their say
their opinion
their advice,
they know best
they want what's best
they they they
and they never asked me.
I didn't agree with their opinion, their advice, what they
    thought was best.
I always knew what I wanted to do
and it had nothing to do with medicine or marriage.
It was to do with right over wrong,
with letting those who weren't able to fight themselves
know that they had a friend.
That I would be their friend.
I would listen to them and I would fight for them.
I'll never stop doing that.
But this, I needed to do this to live.
My family won't support me
because of my actions since that January.
I stay with some friends.
I don't speak any other languages so charities won't
    employ me.
I thought that here, maybe,
I could make enough money to eat
whilst developing strategies to free our country from
    oppressive regimes
and I thought, I suppose I thought that maybe,
being behind the scenes of the speech industry,
I would learn how to speak for those whose voices are
    unheard.
That's why I'm here.
To make a positive change.
Without guns.

Sara   But you would use rocks and stones?

Sahmia   Only to protect myself.

Sara   Hmm. So, Ahmed, is it? You're the only one left.

Ahmed   What about Fatima?

Sara   It's obvious, isn't it? She works here because Daddy dear asked her to?

Fatima   I wish you would stop speaking for me –

Sara   Millions could say the same to you –

Fatima
     Actually, I want to be a social enterprise entrepreneur.
     To make money whilst doing good things, you know,
     this is the way of the future, it has to be.
     Wallahi I don't want to be rich,
     but my business must be profitable for me to survive.
     I think clean water pipes worldwide would be my ultimate
          ambition.
     But for now, I believe that for humans to reach their true
          evolution
     they must be able to speak freely
     and there is nowhere I would rather be than here in this city,
     helping people to speak.
     Yes, they might have to pay a small fee,
     but what is that compared to the silent alternative?
     You pay for medicine and education and transportation –
     all necessities for life that leave us lighter in the pocket
     but we understand we are paying
     to make our lives liveable.
     Nothing comes for free.
     Selling speech is to me a social enterprise.
     My father is an entrepreneur.
     We are –
     we will be –
     making money from doing something good.

Sara   Your level of delusionment is inspirational, Fatima. Thank you.

Ahmed, over to you.

Fatima *is angry at the way* **Sara** *dismisses her speech. She crosses her arms.*

Ahmed
>My reason is kinda simple, man.
>I work all night online trying to fight the good fight.
>I share and spread videos and messages and meetings
>and even though I'm not the best hacker, I do what
>   positive damage I can.
>Nobody pays me for this.
>My brother died, as you know.
>He used to make money for us.
>My mum, she, well she can't work,
>so you know, things are tight.
>The light from my bedroom window
>is blocked by dust and dark concrete
>as taller buildings rise around us
>and I want my mum to know that she can trust me
>even as everything changes
>and even as she hates what I do,
>I have to show I can bring money home,
>to make our lives liveable,
>I suppose.

Sara   What about your dad?

Sahmia   Leave him be. He's said why he's here, to make money for his family.

Sara   Until you have a gun replacing your tongue, I won't take orders from you. But luckily, now I have heard your – I must say less than satisfactory – reasons for being here, I am ready to share with you my plans. Mahmoud, help me.

Mahmoud *comes over to help* **Sara** *climb on to the table/counter she was sitting on before. She stands on the table and* **Mahmoud** *stands guard beside her. The workers crowd round to watch.* **Sara** *coughs and puffs her chest out, opens her arms wide as if she is addressing a huge crowd of people.*

Sara   My father wasn't much of a believer in religion –

Sherif *starts mumbling something at this point. Some look over but most ignore him.*

Sara
Or monarchy,
or the thin line between dictatorship and democracy.
He was a believer in the people and equality.
He saw how our freedom
was being sold to lands
who cannot excavate their own history.
He saw how those who felt free
paid such high prices
for this false feeling.
He wanted people to wake up,
wake up and extricate themselves
from the legacy of self-laceration and oppression.
When I was old enough to stand at his shoulder,
he was cruelly, unjustly killed fighting for these things.
I, too, understand the sacrifice
that has gone into trying to create a better country.
And so I stand here,
before you, the people,
to continue his noble legacy.

Fatima – we plan to force your father –
through moral urging at first of course,
but by gunpoint if necessary,
to hand over the speech tokens to us.
I will then distribute them,
I will throw them to the hands of the masses,
I will be an enabler,
I will enable the people of Egypt to speak –
for free!

Mahmoud *applauds.*

Noura (*whispering to* **Sahmia**)   I really need to pee!

Sara
   I declare
   that speech should be equally accessible and available
   no matter what wage you have or savings you've made,
   because we are all capable of saying something that
      matters
   and these words should be heard
   inside and outside of the palaces and the cameras and the
      papers.
   A merchant, independent or not,
   should not be able to monopolise
   the very thing that should be free.
   Speech!

Mahmoud *applauds with love in his eyes. The workers clap hesitantly, except* **Fatima**. **Sara** *bows. She now sits on the table.*

Sara   When is your father going to be here, Fatima? We need to speed this day up.

Fatima   Soon, I suppose.

Sara   Equality is waiting.

Ahmed   Forgive me for making such a basic point, but if we're all looking for equality, aren't we all on the same side? Don't we all want the same thing? Just a better, fairer life for everyone?

Fatima   Yes! That's why we all came to work here, isn't it?

Sara   Why are there so many of you actually?

Fatima   What do you mean?

Sara   So many workers, for a shop that sells things you can't see and only one person – the owner – has access to the very things people come in to buy. Why do you need four staff members, plus you and your father?

Fatima   Daddy expects it to be busy. We don't open properly until tomorrow. This is training day.

Sara   Ha, training?

Fatima   Yes. For registration, sales pitch, customer service –

Sara (*laughs*)   And do you do refunds?

Fatima   No.

Sara   So what kind of service can a customer expect?

Things begin to get even more heightened with very fast-paced, overlapping speech and expressionistic style. The characters are very lively and excited, engaged in a role-play in which they are not necessarily always playing their usual character – a show within a show.

There is freedom to use music here if it feels helpful; it could be part done like a song? The speech can be played with for musicality, volume, repetition, etc.

Fatima
Hello. Hello. Great to see you. How are you and your family on this fine day?

Noura
Who me?

Fatima
Yes, yes, you madam.

Noura
I, er, I –

She is unsure of what is going on, but is being pulled into the role-play of the situation. **Mo** *is encouraging and she suddenly gets into it.*

Mo
Noura, pretend it's an audition or something –

Noura
My family and I are doing fantastically well, thank you.

Fatima
Allhamdulillah. And can I help you in any way today?

Noura

Er, yes. Yes, you can. I would like to buy speech.
Speech for me and my family
so I can stand on the corner of the streets
and shout out to all the men who won't let me live my life
    freely,
that I can see them, I see them all and one day,
one day they will be, they'll be so very –

Fatima

Sorry to interrupt, madam, but you look like a discerning
type of buyer.

Noura

I am, I am, in fact I came here because

Fatima

You heard we're the very best –

Mo

Very, very best yes

Ahmed

Best! Yes, be the best you can be, people!

Noura

I heard you were the only ones in the area who sell –

Sahmia

Oh what the hell –

Mo

We love to sell –

Fatima

We do indeed sell –

Sara

You bunch of sell-outs –

Ahmed

I am here today to sell –

All
Speeeeech! Speeeech, speech!

Fatima
Yes, we sell it –

Mo
We yell it –

Ahmed
We roll it –

Mo
Control it –

Fatima
No we don't control!

Mo
We do.

Fatima
We don't –

Mo
We won't tell you to get the cheap stuff we will try and
flog the speech that costs the most so yes we control it –

Fatima
It mostly all costs the same, actually –

Mo
Mostly, but 'mostly' still leaves quite a discrepancy between
the cheapest and the priciest, doesn't it?

Fatima
Oh, for God's sake, we don't control it!

Sahmia
There's an element of control let's just say, when we sell
this speech –

Ahmed
We roll it –

Fatima
We really really know it –

Mo
We throw it around like it's free –

Noura
But it's not, free –

Fatima
We treat it carefully –

Noura
We need it –

Ahmed
We feed it –

Fatima
We keep it safe –

Noura
I don't know what to say –

Mo
Say yes, you want the best speech we have –

Fatima
The speech that makes you –

Mo
You!

Ahmed
You and only you –

Fatima
It's true, it's you –

Mo
And due to this fortunate event, you being you, once you have purchased the speech that tells everyone who you are, I would just like to offer advice –

Fatima
Mo, be nice –

Mo
As a sales advisor at the shop selling speech –

Ahmed
Speech is sellable –

Fatima
Yellable –

Noura
You guys are terrible! *Yalla!*

Mo
Enviable, you mean. We get to be at the forefront of
speech sales, tales being told because of us –

Sahmia
Enough about us now, back to you –

Mo
Yes, you. You, being a lady, a female, a woman.

Noura
I don't understand –

Mo
In this world of wicked words and deeds, madam, we see
that your speech should be one which is less harsh than
a man's, bring less harm if shouted out loud, you know –

Noura *and* **Sahmia**
No!

Ahmed
Uh-oh, bro.

Noura
You have different speech for different genders?

Mo
Yes, *habibti*!

Fatima
No, we do not. The speech is the same –

Mo
Tell her the truth of the game, Fatima –

Fatima
The speech *is* the same it's just –

Noura
Just? Just?

Ahmed
I wouldn't trust any of this –

Fatima
It's just that the . . . well, the price is different.

Pause.

Noura
Why?

Fatima
Our words are worth more, sister.

Noura
But why should a man get his words cheaper if mine are
worth more, if mine are worth more, more people need
to hear them so surely it should be the other way round?

Sahmia
I agree, madam, but –

Mo
Shhh, don't make a sound, you're lucky to be in here at all –

Fatima
Another small thing, madam –

Noura
I am not happy with this service –

Ahmed

It's not the service it's the system, miss, the rules, what can we do?

Fatima

The thing is, madam . . . we can also choose to not serve you the speech if we feel you're –

Ahmed

You know, not right –

Noura

But I can pay –

Mo

We can't just let the speech go to anyone, madam –

Ahmed

Imagine the violence –

Sara

Violence –

Sahmia

The influence –

Mo

The riots –

Fatima

Many people can't read, how can we let them speak –

Noura

But I –

Fatima

I know, I know, it's frustrating –

Mo

Nauseating –

Noura

Degrading –

Sahmia
Why don't we just give it all away for free?

Fatima
That wouldn't be wise –

Mo
Or fair –

Ahmed
Rare to give things away for free, really –

Fatima
The business would make no money –

Mo
We would make no money –

Fatima
Free speech would equal –

Mo, Ahmed, Fatima, Noura and **Sahmia**
NO MONEY!

The group are perhaps in a circle as they say this line.

As they part, spotlight on **Noura** *and* **Mo***, who begin to dance together.*

Everything is in slow motion.

The others quietly disperse with their own heightened physical movements.

Noura *and* **Mo** *are finally together, falling in love.*

Meanwhile, on the other side of the stage, **Sara** *is staring at* **Ahmed** *intently.*

Sara   Ahmed, come here.

Ahmed *approaches* **Sara** *who is still sitting on the table/counter. She stands up on the table/counter. The focus is split-stage between her and* **Noura** *and* **Mo** *dancing in slow motion.*

Ahmed   Yes?

Sara   The more I look at you, the more familiar you appear.

Ahmed   Oh. I dunno, my face is around online quite a bit.

Sara   That's not it.

Ahmed   Maybe we've met –

Sara (*in extreme shock*)
No, no, that's it, is it really?
Am I going finally completely
doolally
crazy
off the wall
have you shamed me?
Off my rocker
what a shocker
no, it can't be!
But the awful truth is
Yes,
it is, it's true!

Ahmed   What, what?

Sara   Your father was in the army, wasn't he? An army man, an angry man, definitely not much of a family man.

Ahmed   Er, I –

Sara   I know who you are. Yes.

I had a picture of you ripped from the paper. I carried it around with me for years. You were only a child but you have the same face as you do now, a bit fatter maybe. You, your brother, your mother, your father – the wounded soldier reunited with his family. A hero.

Ahmed   He left, I don't know –

Sara   Do you know how he was injured, Ahmed? How he got his heroic discharge from our heroic hero-tastic army? Is that what motivates you to try and right all his wrongs?

Ahmed   I don't know –

Sara   He killed my father. My father was fighting for people like us, like me, like you, like him, like them – to have a better life. His own comrade in arms. Shot him down like a dog that scurries for chicken bones.

Ahmed   I . . . I . . .

Sara   Don't pretend that he didn't boast and brag over it, telling people how he discovered a traitor –

Ahmed   He said it was the right thing to do –

Sara   My father was no traitor, they have no idea of loyalty, of sacrifice –

Ahmed   I – I'm sorry but –

Sara *is pacing on the table and muttering increasingly crazily to herself:*

Sara
  What should I . . .
  what should I do,
  An army man
  An angry man
  Definitely not much of a family man
  Not a family man
  family
  take revenge now,
  kill him,
  but it will ruin the plan,
  the plan,
  the army man
  the family man
  the hero
  no
  the speech,
  what should I . . .

While she is saying this, **Sahmia** *and* **Fatima** *are arguing about something and haven't noticed* **Ahmed***, who is trying to think of a way* *to escape.* **Sherif** *is watching everything and* **Mahmoud** *is on guard, not fully aware of what is going on but, recognising* **Sara** *is acting erratically, preparing himself for action, waiting for instructions.* **Noura** *and* **Mo** *are still dancing.*

As **Sara***'s pace quickens in the speech above and in her physical movement, so does* **Noura** *and* **Mo***'s dancing.*

They dance closer and closer to the table and to coincide with **Sara***'s muttering, they crash into the table in slow motion, when* **Sara** *gets to the climax of the following:*

Sara
    The speech is
    The speech is
    The speech must be
    Must be
    Must be
    The speech must be
    Free
    For Daddy
    Daddy the speech will be
    FREE!

She falls from the table in slow motion as **Noura** *and* **Mo** *bang into it.*

The till or anything that represents the taking of money (credit card machine/change box, etc.) from the table/counter flies up in the air from the desk and falls on to **Sara***'s head.*

Sara *is on the floor with the 'till' covering her head or part of her body. It is the fall that has knocked her out, not the till/money, etc.*

Noura *and* **Mo** *snap out of their bubble and everyone rushes round* **Sara***.*

In the confusion, **Fatima** *steals the gun from* **Sara***'s limp hand and hides it somewhere on her person.*

Mahmoud   Everyone get back! Now!

Silence, as **Mahmoud** *checks* **Sara***'s pulse on her wrist.*

Mahmoud   Her pulse is weak, but it's there, it's there,
I can feel it!

Ahmed   What shall we do?

Noura   How did that –

Mo   It wasn't our fault, we didn't know –

Mahmoud   Release Sherif, he's trained in first aid, he'll
know how to help, take the tape off his mouth, untie him!

Sahmia   I'll do it –

Mahmoud   Hurry!

Fatima *brandishes the gun.*

Fatima   Leave him where he is.

Ahmed   Fatima –

Sahmia   No, he knows –

Mahmoud   What are you doing, this is no time for –

Fatima
Everyone just stay where you are.
Now, you came into my shop
with your gun and your angry words
and your threats and your theories.
You wanted to kill us if we moved.
She tied him up because he disagreed
with her
and he wanted to ransack my shop
and now you want us to work together?
Make things right?

Mahmoud   I want you to save a life!

Sahmia   Fatima, what are you –

Fatima   Sherif will be staying there until my father gets
back. He will explain what you have all done, what you have

planned. He will tell us where you live and how many more there are like you.

Mahmoud   For now just let him tell us what to do for −

Fatima   I will tell you what to do. Give me my phone.

Mahmoud *gives over her phone.*

Fatima *dials a number.*

Fatima   Hello. Emergency ambulance please. Yes, charge it to the account. Thank you.

They are on their way. Business comes in useful for you now, I suppose.

Mahmoud   It will take them for ever in this traffic! Just let Sherif help until they get here −

Mo   She doesn't look good −

Fatima   Dishonesty never does −

Ahmed   We should really do something −

Fatima   We will wait. Like she said so many times.

Sahmia   But how will that help you, Fatima?

Ahmed   Think about what you're doing −

Fatima   I am always thinking about what I'm doing.

Right now, I'm putting things right. Sara will go to hospital, we can deal with her later. Sherif will be the informant for my father. Mahmoud, you will stay and join our side.

Mahmoud   I will not leave Sara!

Fatima   Then take her now and suffer the consequences later.

Mahmoud   What do you mean?

Fatima   If you don't wish to change sides then get out. Take her outside, wait outside for the ambulance.

Mahmoud   I shouldn't move her –

Noura   He shouldn't move her –

Fatima   Now. Unlock the doors you locked and get out.

Mahmoud *picks* **Sara** *up under her arms and drags her offstage. The other workers are nervous, not sure what to do about this new* **Fatima** *with a weapon.*

Sahmia   Fatima, I really think you should put the gun down –

Fatima   I really think you should all listen –
  listen good. I'm about to give you all the chance to do
    something so good.
  Good, good, so good it might be great, I'm sure it will be
    great.
  When Daddy gets back, after we sort all this mess out,
  I'm going to tell him that with a percentage of the profits
  from the sales of speech, speech, glorious speech –
  we are going to set up a development agency –
  a development agency
  for the positive development of this country.
  We can be the biggest force for good in this brave new
    world –
  selling speech to those who can afford it and
  distributing development opportunities to those that can't –
  and anyone who doesn't agree with my policies,
  well. I might shoot them, threaten them
  send them to hell and back
  and all of you
  you will all be part of it
  at the heart of it –
  good business,
  doing good!

The following happens very quickly (or in slow motion). As **Fatima** *reaches the crescendo of her speech, she is looking up and has got lost in what she's saying.* **Noura** *takes advantage of her lapse of focus and rushes over, struggles with her for the gun.* **Mo** *rushes to help* **Noura**.

Sherif gets the attention of **Ahmed***, who rushes to untie him, slightly unsure of what is best.* **Sahmia** *is frozen. As* **Sherif** *is untied the gun goes up in the air. It lands closest to* **Sherif***, he picks it up. Ambulance sirens are heard.*

Everyone is still. **Sherif** *points the gun at* **Fatima***. Waves it at the others as he says:*

Sherif   Everybody else, leave now. Go!

The workers all look at each other, hold hands and leave offstage.

Sherif   Now it is just me and you.

Fatima   So it seems.

Sherif   This is a very big mess.

Fatima   Not too big for my father.

Sherif   I'm glad, sister.

He moves the gun closer to **Fatima***.*

Fatima   What do you want?

Sherif   Your plan, I like it. Very much. I want you to tell your father you plan to set up this development agency with me, Sherif. I am your chosen partner because I know the country well – urban, rural, intellectual, illiterate.

Fatima   What is the advantage for me?

Sherif   I don't shoot you or take you hostage and make your father give me the speech tokens by force or by bribery. You get my expertise, my wisdom, my experience, my never-to-be-doubted, undying loyalty. I also tell you everything about Sara and Mahmoud, you become your father's hero. I am an old friend from school.

Fatima   What is the advantage for you?

Sherif
   Power, legally obtained.
   Contacts, friends, acquaintances in high places.

The ability to reward myself
      with as many speech tokens as deemed necessary
by the official development agency guidelines.

Fatima   Do I have a choice?

Sherif   In this life, don't we always have a choice, sister?

Fatima *hesitates momentarily. Looks towards the door, towards the gun. Goes towards* **Sherif** *and they appear to look as if they would shake hands — but will they?*

Glossary

Allahamdullilah (all-ham-du-llah) – Praise be to God/Thank God

Habibti (ha-bib-tee) – Term of endearment: dear, darling, etc.

Missriya (miss-ria) – Egypt (in Arabic)

Wallahi (wah-laa-hee) – I swear to God

Wara al-shams (wa-ra al-shams) – Disappearance of political prisoners; literally 'behind the sun'

Yalla (ya-la) – Come on/Hurry up

A Shop Selling Speech

BY SABRINA MAHFOUZ

*Notes on rehearsal and staging, drawn from a workshop
with the writer held at the National Theatre, November 2013*

Workshop led by Hettie Macdonald, with notes by Jack Low

How the writer came to the play

For Sabrina Mahfouz, the play began when she was in Cairo
researching the significant and pivotal role women played in
the 2011 uprisings and their subsequent incongruous omission
from public life following the initial post-uprising euphoria.

While in Cairo, her focus gradually shifted and the play
became more about free speech. The excitement that many
people in Egypt had initially felt at finally having what they
thought would be the opportunity to speak and write publicly
without heavy censorship had been replaced mainly by
disappointment and a realisation that censorship would still
exist for years to come, if only under a different guise.

Sabrina wanted to write a play with young Egyptian
characters, as she felt that they were not often represented in
the UK – whereas in Egypt young people are constantly
bombarded with the stories of Western youth, mainly via
music, television and film.

Sabrina wanted to explore the definition of democracy and
felt sceptical about the use of the word 'democratic' to
describe the post-uprising elections in Egypt.

She felt sceptical about the low turnout at poling stations and
the high number of illiterate vote counts (lots of people voting
using pictures who might have been bribed for their vote, in
Sabrina's opinion). She is unsure of how democratic the
process was: were there different ways of pushing votes? Did
richer areas have more influence? Were polling stations closed
and opened at strategic times? Why did people queue but not
end up voting? Was there a strategy to get Morsi into power
and what was that strategy?

Approaching the text

We opened the workshop day by reading the play from beginning to end. This is an excellent first task. It's one thing to read a play through in your head; it's another to hear it out loud with the group you're going to be working with for the duration of the project.

Give out roles but don't worry about casting. It can be useful to have the director read the stage directions so that the rhythm of the reading is led according to what you as the director want to do and the temperature and atmosphere you want to set.

The workshop then broke out into a series of open conversations, exercises, tasks and debates. The headings below outline thoughts which emerged throughout the day.

Hettie Macdonald asked the group of directors to write down what they think the play is about. Here are some of the responses from the group:

- Standing up for what you believe in.
- Freedom of speech, equality and corruption in Egypt and the whole world.
- Struggles and turmoil.
- Past, present and future governments making the same mistakes.
- Young people attempting to understand their lives.
- Love – of home, country and history.
- Shifts of power and uncertainty about life, ambition and the future.
- An equation: power + might = freedom of speech.
- The attempt to keep free speech.

Sabrina Mahfouz responded: 'Different factions or sections of society can hold the gun but in the end it is business that always holds the power. If this is how things are being run on all levels then what value does free speech truly have?'

Hettie Macdonald then asked why people chose the play. Here are some of the responses from the group:

- It felt like a challenge.
- The play taps into something honest and truthful.
- There is a mix of comedic moments and darker moments.
- The large universal themes can be a challenge for the students as it introduces them to alien ideas; this is a positive reason for doing the play as I'm always looking for a learning process.
- It has awareness for a wider world beyond the UK.
- The characters are passionate and opinionated.
- There are parallels to south-east London youth feeling disempowered.
- It's not a stereotypical teenage 'issue' play.
- It explores young people attempting to take control.
- Simple situation and circumstance.
- Single time, single space.
- Scope to be creative with the monologues.
- The language is adult – which is helpful when working with young adults.
- Using it to open up wider discussions about the referendum in Scotland.
- It matters to now. It's not irrelevant.

Hettie then asked: what are your anxieties about putting the play on?

- Making it relevant to south-east London and for the young people I'm working with.
- Finding the right way of pitching the production of the play – stylised and naturalistic together in the same world.
- Characterisation and the number of different opinions that characters have in the play.
- Having an all-female cast.
- Dealing with the sexual politics.

- Making sure we have a deep enough understanding of the context of the Arab Spring, getting the details right and not oversimplifying.
- Working with a large cast.
- Staging moments such as the cash register falling on the head or the gun sequence.
- Creating a set.
- Deciding on costumes.
- Language and form of the play.

Hettie Macdonald assured the directors that there are no 'right' answers, but noticed that everyone was grappling with the big political questions in the play. Hettie urged the directors to find the clues in the play and to be rigorous with the text. It's important to be as true to the text as possible.

Sabrina Mahfouz emphasised that the play is not a literal piece of work. She wants to give the directors freedom to own their production and make the play connect with their groups. Apart from the opening, which needs to be still and tense, she would encourage the directors to be as inventive as they like.

Research exercises

Divide the group into twos and threes and set them tasks that you want them to go and research. Write a list of questions that you would like them to answer in order to research the political situation. Be specific and think about questions which will build up a picture of what it's like now, what happened after 2011 and what happened just before the revolution.

Sabrina suggested that the following questions might be a good place to start:

- What is the Egyptian version of the BBC?
- How many journalists have been arrested in Egypt since 2011?
- How much foreign aid has been received since 2011?
- Can you find one piece of visual art, comedy, theatre and poetry which relates to the uprisings?

- Who are the political parties active in Egypt?
- What does the constitution of 2012 say?
- What are the largest ten companies in Egypt?
- What is the literacy rate in Egypt?
- Find ten Facebook groups with Egypt in the title

Hettie added:

- Where is Mubarak now?
- Where is Morsi now?
- What controls do the army have?

It was suggested that as a group you come up with a fundamental timeline of the revolution and the protests. This research will form an important part of the rehearsals. Can your group come up with inventive ways of presenting the research? Acting it out, playing a song they've found, etc.

Textual analysis: facts and questions

This is a useful technique for starting to explore the characters. The notes that follow focus on three characters to demonstrate how to run this exercise.

AHMED

Initial observations

- He's involved with his family and talks about them a great deal.
- He takes a lot of responsibility. He has to take charge and earn the money for the family.
- He's a people-pleaser, diplomatic. He always finds the reasons for other people's actions.
- Is he the hero of the play?

Facts about him (taken directly from the play)

- He had a brother aged nineteen.
- His brother died at twenty-one.
- His father was in the army.

- His mum can't work.
- He is an internet whizz.
- His dad left.

Things he says about himself (*taken directly from the play*)

'I work all night online trying to fight the good fight.'

'Even though I'm not the best hacker,'

Things he says about other people (*taken directly from the play*)

- His brother was a hero to him.
- His brother taught him coding and hacking.
- 'My mum can't work.'
- 'My father abandoned us.'
- 'He left' (Dad).
- 'He's just frustrated' (Mo).

SHERIF

Initial observations

- His language changes from 'We' to 'I'.

Facts about him

- He trained in first aid.
- He has tape across his mouth.

Things he says about himself

- 'We are not animals, we are doing righteous work.'
- 'We Egyptians have waited too long.'
- 'I am ready for the plan to change.'
- 'I don't want to wait.'
- 'I know the country well.'

Things he says about other people

- 'Liar!' (to Fatima).
- 'I say you're wrong' (to Sara).

FATIMA

Initial observations

- She's quite reactive.
- She's watching, waiting, being canny, and when her moment comes she seizes control.
- Keep an eye on her. The ones that say a lot tend to dominate, but with characters like Fatima and Sherif there's a lot going on.

Facts about her

- This is her home.
- She got her accent in England.
- She doesn't know where the tokens are.

Things she says about herself

- 'I am (in charge).'
- 'I hated it' (speaking about her time as a student in England).
- 'I love Egypt.'
- 'I am Fatima.'

Things she says about other people

- 'I believe there are opportunities out there for everyone.'
- 'You don't scare me' (to all of them in the group).
- 'You're full of empty words' (to all of them in the group)

Structure

The play is structured in a single space and single time, which creates a sense of tension.

Language

The language of the play is very specific and rhythmic. Sabrina emphasised the importance of paying attention to the overlapping of the words. She intends the play to be performed at quite a speed and suggests that the directors do exercises to keep the pace up.

It might be useful to look into poets and spoken-word artists during rehearsals to give an alternative way into performing the play. This might not suit every performer, it is a different rhythm which doesn't feel natural to everyone, but some actors will just be able to hear it. It might be useful to see the speech as musical. You could try elongating certain words and snapping into and over lines. Each actor should find their own style of performing.

The play needs a sound design that will support the performative elements of the show, for example using drums or an instrument or recorded sounds.

Sabrina notes that the Egyptian words are written phonetically and she doesn't mind how you pronounce the names.

See the Glossary of commonly used Egyptian words on page 400.

Casting

If you have a large cast you could consider using movement. Perhaps using a large silent ensemble might be effective for a play about freedom of speech.

Some suggestions for casting profiles/attributes

SARA

- Strength
- Physical presence
- High status
- A bit of bite
- Got energy, drives the show – huge responsibility for this actor
- Confidence to do this act
- A bit older
- Volatile
- Unpredictable
- Manipulative
- Approaches things from different angles
- This actor will set the tone for everybody

FATIMA
- Sabrina notes that she's given the opportunity to make decisions more than anyone else
- Composure
- Control
- Cerebral, more calculated
- Subtle
- Tough, ateely
- Educated
- Ambitious
- Maturity
- Earn the comment 'hard eyes'

AHMED
- Sympathetic
- Genuine
- Access to emotions
- Laid back
- Not afraid to ignore the fast-paced conversation
- Takes his time
- Consistent
- Create a slower pace

MO
- Comfortable physically
- Drives the 'selling' aspect of the role-play
- Shy and eager
- Versatile

NOURA
- Strong, assured but quiet
- A bit younger
- Dreamer

SAHMIA

- Confident
- Politically motivated
- Middle of the age group
- Has a lot to say

SHERIF

- An actor who can see the bigger picture of the play so that the end is believable

MAHMOUD

- Strong stage presence as he doesn't say much
- Has a crush – he's a puppy dog around Sara
- He's reactive
- Stroppy
- Caution at over-simplifying him
- He's the only person who shows true loyalty

Dancing

Sabrina and Hettie strongly felt there should be dancing in the play and this should be worked in from the start of rehearsals. Sabrina said there is a flexibility to the way you follow the stage directions: she wants you to find your way though the play. The punctuation of the dance does feel really important, however.

Set

They have all sorts of shops in Cairo, from modern minimalist designs to traditional (souk-style) shops. It is competely up to you whether you choose something like this or something far more abstract.

Pauline McLynn has written ten successful novels, including two for young readers in the *Jenny Q* series. She is also an award-winning actress known for her television roles in the recent *Father Figure* (BBC1), *Bremner, Bird and Fortune, Father Ted, Shameless* (Channel 4) and *Jam and Jerusalem* (BBC). She has also appeared as Winnie in *Happy Days* at the Crucible Studio in Sheffield. Films include *Gypo* and *Angela's Ashes*.

Characters

Angel 1 (Em)
Angel 2 (Frankie)
Angel 3 (Arri)
Gabby
Dan
Sue
Lola
Liz
Tim
Joe
Shawn

Setting

The setting is an overgrown old graveyard. There are ancient gravestones and crosses at a tilt, a mausoleum/tomb and three 'stone' Angels. Two Angels are standing statues with large wings and these should be solid shapes within which are placed actors in flowing angelic robes, so that even when the Angels move their shape appears to remain static. The third Angel is stretched weeping across the slab of a grave beside the statue of a lamb.

Scene One

It is late on a summer evening and in the distance we hear the sound of a hedge party in another part of the graveyard.

*The **Angels** sing part of the classic 'Someone to Watch Over Me' (not the intro but the first two stanzas of the song).*

They give a lovely whispery angelic sigh. Followed by enough silence to register the hedge party happening in the cemetery.

Angel 1 (Em)   The party has started early this evening.

Angel 2 (Frankie)   It's the weather, Angel Em, it's too good so they can't believe it's happened and that makes them a bit mad, I think.

Angel Em   Let's just be thankful they've opted for the other side of the yard and not here – the mess they made last time was epic, even for them.

Angel Frankie   The Living are a mystery to me, always will be, I fear.

Angel 3 (Arri)   Well, it's evening so it's time for the other wildlife to appear too. I swear if that fox sprays me one more time I won't be answerable for my actions.

*The other two **Angels** roll their eyes.*

Angel Arri   And that's before we get to the birdshit we're all covered in. Sometimes I think they're deliberately aiming at us. Living things are disgusting, truly and utterly disgusting.

Angel Em   In fairness, Angel Arri, there's not really much you can do about it. We're sort of *hindered* by the fact that we're made of stone and therefore can't move or shout –

Angel Arri   – much . . .

Angel Em   Erm, *at all* . . . strictly speaking . . .

Angel Arri   As if I wasn't unhappy enough, stuck here, silently wailing and weeping for all eternity.

Angel Frankie   Oh cheer up, misery guts. You should be thankful you have a job –

Angel Em   – for life!

Angel Frankie   For ever!

Angels Em *and* **Frankie**   *Hallelujiah!*

Angel Arri   You two make me want to puke, truly and verily you do. *Puke.* Amen.

Angel Em   At least we'll be getting a good wash this week when the clear-up starts, that's something to look forward to. I'll be all beautiful and sparkling again.

Angel Arri   Coarse youths with bad attitudes, no doubt. You'll forgive me if I don't jump up and down with joy – oh hang on, of course not, because . . . I *can't*, I am made of stone – HALLELUJIAH!

Angel Frankie   Mocking is below you, dear, or it should be.

Angel Arri   Oh zip it, Frankie.

Angel Em   Hush, we have incoming . . . .

The light has faded to near darkness now. An owl screeches and the atmosphere is a little spooky. A shadowy, hooded figure steals into the **Angels**'*patch, checks no one is looking, then enters the mausoleum.*

Angel Em   Home sweet home.

Angel Arri   Okay, you two seem to be 'liberal' in a crazy way so I don't mind being the one to point out that *that* has no place here. It is certainly *not* home sweet home! We must rid ourselves of this imposter.

Angel Em   Our job is to watch over this place, to stand sentinel.

Angel Arri   Yes, and our people are named – those whom we guard are named, here on the graves. His is not the name on that tomb and therefore he has no right to shelter here.

Angel Frankie   Oh I hate it when we get into rules. I can never remember half of them. Surely we can have the charity to bend a bit, from time to time?

Angel Arri   Frankie, you are an airhead. We have a few simple guidelines, that's all, and you can't even get to grips with those.

Angel Frankie   I just think we can be nice. It won't make all that much difference to us. And I don't feel like he's going to stay for all eternity?

Angel Em   There is nothing we can do. We protect only, we should not take action or interfere.

Angel Arri   I don't like it and I can't accept it and he has got to go.

There is a brief silence, then:

Angel Frankie (*clearly smarting*)   And for your information, Arri, I'd prefer to be an airhead than angry all the time.

Scene Two

Morning. Birdsong and bees buzzing. **Angel 1** *and* **Angel 2** *sing the opening of 'There Must be an Angel' by the Eurythmics. (The whole company could sing from the wings for a joyous, great sound.)*

Angel Arri (*interrupting*)   Bloody, bloody fox! I'm destroyed. How can any creature defile such beauty as I am.

Angel Em   Vanity, Arri, beware vanity.

Angel Arri   You, Em, are a sanctimonious bore. What you should *beware* is that false modesty thing you do, as if you are really humble.

Angel Frankie   Good morning, Angels, ding ding and TIME OUT!

Gabby (*fifteen*) *and* **Dan** (*thirteen to fourteen*) *arrive.*

Gabby   Remember what I said.

Dan   Yeah, yeah – you don't know me, I don't know you, I am not to approach you or look you in the eye or agree with you or laugh at your pathetic jokes.

Gabby   You made some of those up. Never mind, as long as you have the general gist of what you can and can't do, we should be fine.

Dan   But Mum said . . .

Gabby   I don't care what Mum said, *plus* she was slurring so it was hard to understand, *plus* she probably doesn't even remember what she said any more either, so can it. Now, back off before anyone else arrives and my credibility is shredded.

Dan   Ooh, *credibility*, been reading novels again?

Gabby   You should try it sometime, shrimp brain.

Dan   Nah, if it makes me as up myself as you I'll pass, thanks.

Gabby   Suit yourself.

Dan *sniggers because this is a lame retort.*

Gabby   Oh shut UP!

They sit away from one another, looking around, wondering where any others may come from.

Gabby   Whose stupid idea was this anyhow?

Dan   Mum's . . .

He fools about in front of the tomb door, using his own arm as if it's someone else's from behind the door attacking and choking him.

No, no! Let me go. Help! Please help! Someone help me! (*Deep growly voice.*) Resistance is futile.

*The **Angels** speak over his action.*

Angel Em   This good weather is definitely overheating people's brains and making them mad.

Angel Frankie (*quietly*)   Oh not just people . . . (*Indicates* **Angel Arri**.)

Angel Arri   I'm not deaf, you know, even if I'm facing the other way.

There is chattering and **Sue** *and* **Lola** *arrive.*

Sue   Oh. My. Actual. GOD. We just met at the gate and can you guess? We have the same shoes!

Lola   I know, isn't that *the* most incredible thing!

Gabby (*drily*)   J'amaze.

Lola (*misses the mockery*)   I KNOW! Look.

They show the shoes, which are identical plimsolls.

Sue   We gotta tweet this.

They arrange a photo of their feet, each take a pic and start tweeting. During this **Joe** *arrives. He is wearing an anorak that doesn't really suit the good weather and looks like a bit of a nerd. He carries a big bag that appears to be full of heavy stuff.*

Joe   Is this the place for the community project?

Gabby   Hope so, or we're in for a long day doing nothing.

Sue   I'm Sue, how do you do.

Lola   I'm Lola, pleased to know ya.

Sue   We are *so* in sync!

They high-five each other, then go to the others and do air kisses. **Joe** *is particularly horrified by this and backs off.* **Dan** *notices this.*

Dan (*to* **Joe**)   They just met but they've got the same shoes and that's, erm, stupendous? . . . I guess it's a girl thing?

Joe (*puzzled, but matter-of-fact*)   They don't have the same shoes.

Lola *and* **Sue**   We so do! Look.

They display the plimsolls.

Joe   Those are not the same.

Sue   Do you have trouble with your eyesight?

Joe   No. I'm just stating the obvious. They're similar shoes but they're not the same. Otherwise you'd both be sharing one pair of shoes.

Sue *and* **Lola** *look at him like he's got several heads.*

Lola   Eh, riiiight . . .

Joe (*shrugs*)   It's just logic, a fact actually.

Dan *looks well impressed and moves a bit closer to* **Joe**, *an ally and a bloke.*

Gabby   He's not wrong.

Lola   But he's not, like, totally right either, is he?

She looks puzzled, trying to figure out the right and wrong of it all.

Gabby   I'm Gabby, by the way.

Sue   Sue.

Lola   Lola.

Dan   Dan.

Joe   Joe.

There is a silence, no one has much else to say.

Sue   It's not very spooky in daylight, is it? The graveyard.

Lola   Bet it is at night, though. When the ghosts and ghouls walk –

Sue   – the Undead . . .

Lola   – the flesh-eating zombies . . .

Lola *and* **Sue** *do a few 'ooohs'.*

Liz *arrives. She is pregnant and looks tougher than the others already here.*

Liz   Is this the place for the clean-up arse?

Gabby   Yes. We think so anyhow.

Liz *grunts acknowledgement and sits, arms folded, on a tomb. She sees* **Lola** *and* **Sue**, *thinks they're staring at her.*

Liz   What you starin' at, rude girls? Never seen a chav before? Never seen someone up the duff?

She turns her back on them before they can answer.

Angel Arri   These are going to be a noisy bunch.

Angel Frankie   I do hope they won't wake the dead with their bickering.

Angel Arri   That's hardly likely now, is it?

Angel Frankie   I was actually joking, Arri.

Angel Em   Well, even if they did manage to wake them, the dead aren't much for complaining, usually . . .

Tim *arrives with armfuls of jumpsuits.*

Tim   Hi, I'm Tim. We're to wear these to protect against the dirt. Apparently, we need to start over by the chapel wall and work our way back to here for today. Watch out for anything sharp, particularly needles and glass.

Sue   I did a first aid course so I'll know what to do if there's an injury. Not that I hope that happens, but I'd, like, love some practice with, like, bandages and so on, that would be *so* cool.

Lola   OMG. These are like prison-issue onesies.

Sue   Chic?

Lola *and* **Sue**   NOT!

They high-five each other again. Everyone gets into a jumpsuit and they're all quite identical as a result.

Lola (*to* **Sue**)   Are you you still, or are you me now?

Sue   Hard to say, what with the shoes and now the onesies!

Lola   These are like giant Babygros, aren't they!

They both realise what they've said.

Sue and Lola   Oops, sorry.

Liz   You know what?

Sue *and* **Lola**   What?

Liz   Try thinking before you speak, then maybe you won't have to be sorry all the time, yeah?

The girls give this some actual consideration.

Sue   That is, like, true.

Lola   Yeah, we'll try.

Liz (*groans*)   If they keep this up for the day I'm gonna kill one or both of them.

Gabby (*to* **Liz**)   Sue has medical experience so she'll be able to cure anyone who dies, including herself.

Tim   Plenty of opportunity for killing and curing – we're here all week.

Dan *sees that* **Tim** *is wearing an ankle tag and almost points at it.* **Tim** *meets his eye and shakes his head slightly to warn him off mentioning it.* **Liz** *cops it too but says nothing.*

Sue (*to* **Liz**)   I could deliver your baby if that happens while we're here.

Lola   That would be, like, awesome. I could be an assistant trainee midwife. When are you due?

Liz   Never.

She distances herself from the others.

Lola   She's in denial, right?

Sue (*nodding*)   Hormones too, I'd say. She'll be full of them now because of the baby . . . or something like that anyhow, I think. I've been concentrating more on my first aid skills up till now, so I'm not all that expert on pregnancy.

Liz (*calls over to them*)   I'm not deaf too, you know.

Tim (*defusing the situation as much as anything else*)   Right, line up for inspection, you horrible lot.

They do. They are a motley collection in their ill-fitting jumpsuits. He dispenses rubber gloves and everyone looks even nuttier now. He also has face-masks, the ones that go over your nose for smells/fumes, which they all take.

Tim   Dear, oh dear. Well, you mightn't be much but you're all we have. Go forth and clean for your community, living and dead.

Liz   For our sins more like.

Tim   Those too, I guess, if you have any.

Liz   Don't you start.

Dan   We should take a picture of the group before we start.

Joe   It's a good idea to record the moment.

Dan   Everyone up on the tomb.

The group climbs up with the **Angels** *and poses.* **Joe** *arranges a camera to take the picture on a timer, then joins at the foot of the arrangement, not actually making bodily contact with anyone.*

Angel Arri   Dear Lord, is there no end to their insufferability?

Angel Em   Cheer up, Arri, smile!

Angel Frankie   Oh do, no one has taken our photo for ages. *Smile!*

All three **Angels** *do smile and pose.* **Dan** *checks the photo, shows it to the others.*

Dan   TA-DAH! It's mad but even the angels look like they're smiling!

Tim   Off to work then!

They start to exit on their mission.

Lola (*to the tune of Macklemore's 'Thrift Shop'*)
    I'm gonna c'lect some trash,
    I got a facemask and some marigolds

Sue (*joining in*)
    We got instructions,
    Welcome destruction,
    Look out dirty graveyard

Dan (to *the* **Angels**)   Later, dudes.

Angel Arri   Dudes? I am an angel, not a mere dude!

When the group has gone, **Shawn** *pops up from behind the tomb, looking wary.* **Tim** *returns to get a roll of bin-bags.*

Tim   Oh, hi. We've just started. Here's the gear. I'm Tim.

Shawn   Shawn.

Shawn *looks perplexed but takes the jumpsuit and follows* **Tim** *off.*

Angel Em   I don't think Mr Shawn was expecting that. Maybe it'll do him some good.

Angel Frankie   It makes a change having live people to watch over.

Angel Arri   We've been through this before. That's not our job, we're here to keep watch over the dead.

Angel Frankie   The excitement is nice though. Some life in the old place.

Angel Arri   Speak for yourself, I'm worried they'll wreck more than they fix. Things can be 'improved' to the point of ruin, you know.

Angel Em   Why can you never see things in a good light?

Angel Arri I have been here for over a hundred and fifty years being shat on by nature's creatures, that's why. And no one ever visits my people any more.

Angel Em Yes, that is a pity.

Angel Arri I don't like them being ignored. Their story should continue to be told. They mattered then and they matter now.

Angel Em We do look after the living from time to time, when they join us for a while.

Angel Arri Never lasts long.

Angel Em No, well, it's not that comfortable a place to live, unless you're dead or made of stone like we are. Mind you, the nightly revellers don't seem to mind that – the party people who gather by the gate.

Angel Arri Ne'er-do-wells and delinquents, that lot. I want nothing to do with them.

Angel Frankie Perhaps this youth group will take an interest in our history? The stories that our graves tell?

Angel Arri Don't get your hopes up. People are selfish, especially the young ones. They think only of themselves.

Angel Frankie Oh, I hope that's not true.

Scene Three

Angel Arri *sings the first eight lines of 'I Am Stretched on Your Grave' (Kate Rusby's version of this is what it should sound like).*

Gabby *returns, followed by* **Tim** *a moment later.*

Tim Heard you singing just then. Very nice.

Gabby *(looking surprised)* Wasn't me.

Tim *(shrugs)* Suit yourself.

Gabby   No, really, it wasn't me.

Tim   Must have been one of these guys so. (*Referring to the* **Angels**.)

Gabby   I didn't hear anything.

Tim *sits and puts an arm over* **Angel Arri**.

Tim   It's beautiful here, isn't it? Just the trees whispering and the birds singing.

Gabby   I guess. It's quiet anyhow. Peaceful.

Chattering getting closer, clearly **Sue** *and* **Lola**.

Gabby   *Was* peaceful. Past tense now.

Tim   You gotta envy how happy those two are.

Gabby   If they had any brains, they wouldn't be.

Tim   Maybe. I think they're fun.

The rest of the gang arrives carrying the black sacks of rubbish. **Sue** *and* **Lola** *are rapping again in the style of the 'Thrift Shop' song.*

>We collected some trash
>We got bin-bags full of rubbish
>It's disgustin',
>This stink-filled bustin'
>People're mostly awful

Sue   I found three condoms . . . *used*! Eeuw.

Lola   Better safe than sorry!

They laugh, then catch **Liz**'*s eye.*

Lola   Oh, sorry.

Liz   Don't be. It's true. Always use a condom, kids. (*She says this without any real feeling.*)

Dan   I got lots of empty cider bottles, alcopops, cigarette butts, two scarves, a pair of green frilly pants – *oh*, and a twenty-pound note!

He gets everyone's attention with this news.

Gabby   What?! Money?

Dan   Joking. I do have the knickers if you want them?

Gabby *shoots him a look, but he has to be careful how he reacts – after all, they don't know each other!*

Joe *rummages in his bag and finds medicated wipes with which he is meticulous about cleaning his hands.* **Tim** *has a bottle of hand sanitiser that the others use. Then everyone settles down to their packed lunches.* **Joe** *produces his from his big bag.*

Dan   Looks like you brought your whole house, Joe. What else is in there?

Joe   Stuff. Notebooks, pens. I like to record things. Information.

Sue   You could probably fit a small dog and a few kittens in there too.

Joe   Yes, I might be able to, but I haven't.

Lola   Fact!

Dan   What will you write about us being here?

Joe   I am going to record the gravestones and what they say.

Sue   Why?

Joe   It's history. I like history. It's interesting.

Liz   I think it's useless. What good is it to us?

Joe   We might learn something from it.

Liz   Like what? Same shit, different day kind-of-stuff.

Joe   Yes, that, sometimes, for instance. Anyhow, it's why I volunteered for this project.

Liz   What? You're doing this willingly?

Joe   Yes, isn't everyone?

Liz   I'm not. It's supposed to be like community service twatology for me, because I'm a menace to society or something.

Tim   What did you do?

Liz   Smacked a woman who told me to put my litter in a bin. No biggy. I was eating my chips, she wrecked my buzz.

Gabby   What good did that do?

Liz   Made me feel better.

Sue   Isn't that assault, though?

Lola   And, like, awful?

Liz   People should mind their own business.

Dan   I'm sort of not here willingly. My mum made me come along.

Gabby   Mine too.

Dan   I like it though.

Gabby *notices* **Shawn** *is not eating, has no lunch.*

Gabby   Would you like one of these? Not much, just ham and cheese.

Shawn   Sure, if you have some to spare. Forgot mine. (*He's lying.*)

Dan   Gabby is a good cook.

Gabby *shoots him a look – has he forgotten he's not supposed to know her?*

Dan   Erm, obviously, good at sandwiches anyhow. Like, they *look* yummy. So, if that's anything to go by . . .

Shawn   They're delish. Thanks, Gabby.

Tim   Maybe you can start your collection of gravestones here, Joe. This angel has an inscription underneath.

He scrapes off some leaves and dirt. **Joe** *rummages in his bag for a notebook and pen.*

Joe I wrote down a popular verse from other graveyards of this era.

'As you are now so once was I
As I am now so shall you be
Prepare yourself to follow me'

Lola Oh, is that one of those brainy riddle things?

Joe It is actually very clever.

Sue Like you.

Joe I am not *very* clever. I am moderately clever, I think.

Gabby So what does that sodding grave say?

Tim Relax. It's been here over a hundred years, it's not suddenly going anywhere in a hurry.

Joe A weeping angel usually symbolises grief for an untimely death.

Liz Which is what, in English?

Shawn Someone who died young?

Joe Most likely.

Sue Ooh, is this going to be sad? I don't do sad. I don't like sad.

Lola Me neither.

Joe (*reads*) 'Here lies Annabel Smith, beloved wife of Alfred, who died in childbirth June 1, 1853.'

Gabby Oh.

Sue See? Sad.

Joe 'Aged 17 years. R.I.P.'

They look at one another in silence and sadness.

And here beside the angel, as you can all see, there's a statue of a lamb. They're often used to mark a child's grave. (*He clears the inscription and reads:*) 'Baby Smith. Died June 1, 1853.'

Lola   *No!* They both died!

Sue   That's not just sad, it's too sad.

Liz   I'm seventeen years old, same age as her when she died. Having a baby.

She gets up and starts to pace, agitated.

Lola   You've upset her.

Sue   You're an idiot, Mr Know-it-all.

Joe   What did I do? I merely read what's here, what is literally written in stone. Infant mortality was high, then, and death in childbirth was common. That's what I mean about learning from history – times have changed, improved. That was then, this is now.

Gabby   Say you're sorry for upsetting her.

Joe   I didn't mean to, I was just stating the facts.

Shawn (*softly*)   Do it, mate.

Joe (*reluctantly, this is hard for him*)   I'm sorry, Liz. I'm . . . not very good at dealing with, erm, emotional situations . . . with people . . .

Tim   Who is, Joe? Relax. This place takes getting used to. We're surrounded by death so I guess it's an odd place to be if you're going to be bringing new life into the world . . . and all that jazz.

Gabby (*laughs a little*)   Jazz? Nice one, Tim. Covers it all.

Liz   Right, you lot, I've had enough of this pissing around.

Gabby   He said he was sorry, Liz.

Liz   Oh not just that, all of it.

Dan   Are you okay?

Liz   I can't continue with this. With *this*.

She indicates her belly

Lola   Oh no, Liz, don't say that. You have to have your baby!

Sue   You're giving the gift of life.

Shawn   Yeah, Liz, you've got to go ahead with that. You *have* to.

Liz   No I don't. I can't.

She reaches inside her top and removes a cushion. She is suddenly no longer pregnant.

No more baby. Never was one in the first place.

Everyone is stunned.

Tim   What was that all about then?

Liz   Dunno. It just kind of took off as an idea. I did it first to make my bloke give me some respect, but that didn't work, he just split. I got lots of attention, though, and after a while it was too late to tell anyone that it was all a lie. And I kind of liked that people were looking out for me but they were leaving me alone too, not annoying me with shit stuff to do, or expecting me to get a job or even stay at school. But all this, here, that baby's grave, and the baby's mum, and you lot pissing me off, well I've just had enough, really.

Joe   Plus, you can't have an imaginary baby when the time comes.

Liz   No shit, Einstein.

Joe (*shrugs, stating a fact*)   It's just biology.

Lola   I *so* wouldn't like to be you.

Liz   Don't get on your high horse. You don't live my life.

Lola   No, I don't even mean that – you are *so* going to be in *such* trouble when you get home.

Liz   Whatever. I've been in trouble before. I probably deserve it this time.

Sue   I think you should probably be ashamed of yourself.

Liz   I am. Rub it in, why don't you?

Sue   Just saying. Everyone thinks it's okay to just say sorry and that's it, you're automatically forgiven. Maybe there should be more to do than that, than just words.

Tim   If the words are heartfelt, that's a good thing. It's a start.

Liz   Look, I'm sorry, okay? It just got out of hand. I was wrong and I'll deal with it. Okay? Jeez, I can't believe I'm getting such a hard time from a bunch of losers I've only just met.

Shawn (*quietly*)   In a graveyard.

*As the group sits in an awkward silence the **Angels** converse.*

Angel Frankie   The Living make a lot of problems for themselves, don't they.

Angel Em   I'm guessing it's hard to be human, not that I would know, of course.

Angel Arri   What I can't get over is that they never tire of that ugly, chattery noise they make, especially when they're arguing. Why can't they sing instead, like us?

Angel Em   We bicker too, all the time.

Angel Arri   We *discuss* important things.

Angel Frankie   Like pigeon poo?

Angel Arri   I know you're trying to bait me into an argument so I shall rise above that.

Angel Frankie (*to* **Angel Em,** *softly*)   For once.

Shawn   Do you have any more sandwiches to spare? I'm still starving.

Gabby   Sure. Wouldn't do to have you expire on us, even if you're in the right place to do it.

Joe (*matter of fact, as usual*)   We couldn't bury him here if he died now. The last burial here was in the mid-twentieth century. There's no room, the place is full up.

He looks at their frowning faces.

Tim   Joe says no?

He has gallantly made a joke for **Joe**. *The others smile at his effort.*

Dan *hops up on the tomb, using the moment to distract and entertain the group. He pretends his fist is an imaginary microphone and launches into his mini-version of a stand-up routine.*

Dan   Hello graveyard! How you all doing? Hello there, Miss, what's your name?

Sue   Sue.

Dan   Sue? How do you do. Where are you from, Sue?

Sue   Waterside.

Dan   Aah. *Waterside*. Problem area. I think it's all that water, you see. I don't trust the stuff. What's water up to, eh? What does water *do*, really? We have to have it to live, isn't that right, Joe?

Joe *nods and gives a 'yes'.*

Dan   But why? It's not tasty. It hasn't got any vitamins or medicine in it. So what good is that? And it's everywhere. How much water is on the earth, Joe?

Joe *is clearly confused but he knows the answer and therefore goes along with* **Dan**.

Joe   At least 70 per cent of the earth's surface is covered in water, but . . .

Dan   But? There's a 'but', Joe?

Joe   Well . . . less than one per cent of the water is fresh water, the rest is salt water and glacier ice.

Dan   What?! And it's the fresh stuff we need to live, right? See what I mean? That's just plain sneaky. I say *no* to water!

Everyone is smiling or laughing now.

Joe (*puzzled*)   Most of that is correct.

Sue   He's funny, Joe.

Joe   Oh. I have no sense of humour. That's what my parents say. I don't think that's a bad thing, though. I wouldn't like to mock people by finding them funny.

Dan   I wouldn't be insulted if you laughed at me, Joe.

Joe (*trying to process this in his hyper-logical brain*)   Oh, okay.

Gabby   Don't worry Joe, I don't think he's all that funny either.

Dan   Thumbs up if you enjoyed the show, folks!

*The **Angels** and all the group except **Joe** and **Gabby** give thumbs up, with a few cheers too.*

Dan   Let's hear it for thumbs – they're weird things, but they're handy.

Joe   He did a pun just there, with thumbs and hands, that's clever, and it's amusing too . . . isn't it?

Gabby   Oh, get off, you're rubbish!

Lola   HEY, where do you get off being so mean to Dan?

Sue   Yeah, lay off Dan. Pick on someone your own size.

Lola   What did he ever do to you?

Gabby   Oh butt out, airheads.

Sue   Better to be an *airhead* than a total bee-atch.

Dan *doesn't know what to do – he's not supposed to know* **Gabby** . . . *but he has to explain somehow*

Dan   No, no, it's okay . . . she's . . . my sister. (*He shrugs.*) I annoy her.

Sue   Still no excuse for being rude.

Lola   And hurtful.

Dan   Well, it kind of is . . . like, it's family and all that.

Tim   Anything goes?

Dan   More or less.

Tim   Tough love, eh, mate?

Liz   She's wrong, anyhow, you are funny.

Gabby   Yeah, well, you don't have to live with it all the time.

Liz   Bet you're a very annoying person to live with too.

Sue   Yeah! *So* negative, like.

Lola   And bad-tempered

Shawn   Okay, ladies, we'll leave it at that.

Liz   I'm calling it a day. I've had enough of this.

Joe (*to* **Tim**)   Is she allowed do that?

Tim   Don't ask me, I'm not in charge. We're supposed to decide all that between us.

Joe   Like a co-operative.

Tim   Well, yeah, like that but with co-operation.

Gabby   I think we did good enough today, so I vote we go home. (*To* **Liz**.) I'm pretty fed up too.

Lola   You know what would be really cool?

Gabby   Somehow, I think you're going to tell us.

Lola   We should come back in the 'dead' of night to see if the *Dead* are awake, moving about . . .

Sue   Ooh, that would be so scary and so cool.

The others mull it over, while **Sue** *and* **Lola** *give 'spooky' oooh noises as encouragement.*

Liz   Why not? I'm up for it. I might actually be dead then anyhow when my family find out about the baby.

Joe   You mean the cushion.

Liz   Whatever.

Tim   All in favour say 'aye'

There is a general raising of hands and saying of 'aye's.

Joe   I have to point out that there is no science to back up a walking dead or even a haunting.

He gets a general 'Oh shut up'.

Tim   Let's say midnight, then? We'll all meet back here. Bring a midnight feast if you like.

Liz   Or vodka.

Dan   We can bring wine, there's lots of that in our house.

Liz (*wrinkling her nose*)   Whatever.

Gabby   I guess it doesn't matter what your vocabulary is now, 'whatever', or if you drink. You don't have any responsibility to a baby.

Liz (*shoots her a venomous look*)   Like you have no responsibility to your brother here?

Gabby   I'm not his mother! Our mum is. *She's* responsible for him if she'd take her face out of *her* drink for five minutes. *She* should be looking after him, not *me!*

She storms off.

Dan   She's fine. She's got a lot to put up with. See you all later.

He goes and the others gather their stuff and start to take their leave.

Liz (*aside to* **Tim**)   Don't you have a curfew if you have an ankle-tag?

Tim   Why don't you let me worry about that, Liz. I won't be far from home so it shouldn't be a problem.

Liz   As long as you're not a danger to society . . .

Tim   Not any more than you are, Liz.

Liz (*smiling sarcastically*)   Oh suddenly the world feels so much safer.

They all go except for **Shawn** *who hangs back, pretending to sort his stuff. He doesn't look at the* **Angels** *and when he speaks it should be as if he is answering voices in his head.*

Angel Em   They'll find out who you are eventually, you know, Shawn.

Angel Frankie   Sooner rather than later in my view, if life is anything to go by.

Shawn   I'm not that bothered any more, to be honest. I don't care what happens to me now. It just doesn't matter. I'm so tired, I want to sleep and never wake up.

He takes the cushion and cradles it under his head as he lies on the tomb. **Angel Arri** *sings the chorus of 'Angel' by Sarah McLachlan (with a slight change in the words − 'cold graveyard home' rather than hotel room). As* **Arri** *sings, the* **Angels** *all embrace* **Shawn**, *creating a protective cocoon over him with their robes.*

After, as the light fades, **Liz** *appears behind the tomb. Darkness.*

Scene Four

Midnight in the graveyard. Wind is rustling through the trees. Animals and owls call out, some of them as if they're crying. Sounds of unseen creatures moving through the undergrowth. We see torchlight beams coming through the dark as **Gabby** *and* **Dan** *arrive, with some bottles of wine.*

Gabby   You can't have any of this, by the way, you're too young and I won't allow it.

Dan   Erm, what was that about you not being my mum earlier?

Gabby   She'd agree with me if she knew, and/or if she was here.

Dan   She would also kill us for stealing her wine.

Gabby   Actually it's probably the one thing she might notice. Still, she's asleep now so we should get away with our new life of thieving . . . and vagrancy. Oh God, I can't believe my first big night out in for ever is in a graveyard!

Dan   Cool.

They leave their torches so it's as if the beams are 'lighting up' a main central space.

Gabby   Dan, you *were* funny earlier, I was just in a foul mood and not up for laughing.

Dan   That's okay. I probably shouldn't make fun of *every*thing in the world.

Gabby   Especially water.

Dan   Yeah. What was I thinking? Water is serious shit.

They're both smiling now, having fun.

Gabby   It's how you deal with things. You're the joker. So just keep on doing what you've gotta do.

Dan   Mum's always better when Dad is around. This time, when he gets back, maybe I should have a word with him and tell him how things are when he's not here.

Gabby (*gently teasing*)   Man to man, like?

Dan   Pretty much. And I won't feel like I'm squealing or anything because if she guesses someone has had a word with him, she'll automatically think it was you. So! All in all, it's a win–win for me.

Gabby (*laughing*)   You crafty little shit. (*More serious.*) It's worth a try. We can't keep going with the way things are right now.

There is the sound of people approaching, going 'whoooo' in a mock-spooky way.

The Terrible Twins arrive . . .

Two figures whoosh in covered in white bedsheets, bumping into graves, etc. because they can't really see where they're going. **Sue** *reveals herself.*

Sue   Bet you were spooked!

Gabby (*deadpan*)   Oh yes, terrified.

Lola   We couldn't cut eye-holes in the sheets because we'd be, like, murdered by our mums, so it was actually quite dangerous coming over here.

Sue   Have we missed any ghostly encounters or sinister sightings?

Gabby   No. You might have frightened off any paranormal guests with your arrival though.

Lola   Bummer! Say that's not true.

Gabby   We'll never know now, will we?

Dan   She's teasing, Lola. Besides, no self-respecting ghost would appear to anything less than a full house and we're a few short of that yet.

Gabby   Not to mention a few sandwiches short of the midnight feast too, if you ask me . . . metaphorically speaking.

Lola   You read a lot, don't you? I can tell by all those big words.

Gabby   Yes, thank you, I do.

Lola   Oh, I didn't mean it in as a compliment.

Dan   Ladies, would you care for a glass of wine?

Lola *and* **Sue** *accept a cardboard cup each, taste it and grimace.*

Sue   Yeuch.

Gabby   It's nasty stuff alright.

Lola   Might save it for later.

Both **Lola** *and* **Sue** *discreetly abandon their drinks on a tombstone.* **Tim** *and* **Joe** *arrive.*

Sue   You know what? No one knows we're here – if we disappeared right now, no one would ever know where to even start trying to find us.

Liz *has arrived unseen by the others, so when she speaks everyone gives a start.*

Liz   BOO! Tim's wearing an ankle-tag so he'll be traceable. If they find him, they'll find us. No one hides for long in this world.

Gabby   Ooh, you're a bad boy, Tim. Who would have thought? You look so square.

Tim (*drily*)   Gee, thanks.

Lola (*almost in awe*)   Are you dangerous?

Tim   The *man* thinks so.

Dan   Cool.

Joe   What are you tagged for?

Tim   Information and protest.

Liz   Quit bigging it up, what did you do?

Tim   Graffiti.

Liz   That's it?

Tim   Yup. It's vandalism, apparently. According to the authorities anyhow. Though I try to make things beautiful. And helpful too. Art, you know?

Joe   What did you write?

Tim   The one I got tagged for was a supermarket wall. I just wrote ENTRANCE and did a big arrow pointing towards the door. In very pretty colours. Very tasteful, I thought.

Lola   I know that sign – it's still there!

Tim   Exactly. They left it because it's so useful and I got charged and tagged. I should have been paid for it, not tagged like a criminal.

Joe   Didn't that entrance sign also say 'IF YOU MUST' underneath it? And 'BOYCOTT BIG BUSINESS' on the other side of the main door?

Tim   Well, yes. They painted over those bits. You see the *information* was the arrow to the entrance, and the *protest* was against multinational chains.

Dan   Bad-ass.

Tim   Thanks. All illegal activity, though. Of course, there had been a few other pieces around and about the town so the cops knew my tag and then they caught me in the act at that supermarket so I now have a record.

Gabby (*deadpan*)   Art is a dangerous business.

Tim   Exactly!

Joe   You were spoiling someone else's property. It's like when people desecrate this place. Same difference.

Tim   I would never ruin somewhere like this.

Sue   You can't choose your own bits of the rules.

Tim   No, I guess that's why we just have to change the rules.

Liz   Now that is a scary idea, whereas this place is not. Not one single ghost in sight.

During the next bit, everything should slow a little and get darker to build up a scary atmosphere. The girls, in particular, earnestly relish telling their ghostly tales even though we may find them funny because they are ridiculous. Each person who speaks could hold their torch under their face to creep it up.

Joe *takes out a sound recorder and sets it on a gravestone.*

Joe   For a scientific record of tonight's vigil, I am going to tape proceedings.

Lola   Maybe we're in the wrong bit. Maybe we need to be in the most unhappy section of the graveyard, where the dead are not at rest?

Joe   In some church graveyards the north side was used for the burial of murderers and suicides. It was considered less holy than the rest because it was unblessed.

Sue   So there might be dead murderers stalking the grounds, looking for still-living victims to sacrifice.

Lola   I heard when they were closing down the church here they found lots of bones and skeletons in a tunnel underneath it and that maybe those were the bodies of parishioners that were deliberately walled up and left to die there.

Sue   Yes. And a banshee screams in the night every Friday because that's when she was burnt at a stake here many centuries ago.

Lola   And once during a burial the mourners heard knocking coming from a coffin that was already in the grave and when they opened it they saw that the corpse had scraped the inside of the lid so he must have been buried alive.

*The door to the tomb creaks open and all shine their torches to see a hooded figure appear. Everyone screams and backs off, running around in pandemonium and in the melee **Dan** falls and stays down, stock still.*

Shawn   Take it easy, guys, it's only me.

Liz   Shawn! What the hell are you doing? You scared the shit out of us.

She beats him a bit.

Shawn   Easy, Liz! I was just joining the group!

Liz   From a friggin' TOMB!

Gabby *nudges **Dan** with her foot.*

Gabby   Get up, Dan, stop being such a noticebox.

She pulls at him

Very funny, ha ha, I'm laughing, so you can get up now. DAN! Will one of you talk to him, he won't listen to me. Come on, anyhow, I thought we were having a feast and all that.

*The group starts settling into more comfortable positions, chatting away, and **Gabby** gives one last kick at **Dan**. He still doesn't move. She kneels beside him and tugs at him a bit, then gets very concerned, eventually a bit hysterical.*

Gabby   DAN! (*Shakes him again.*) He's not moving. Oh God, he's hurt . . . He's, he's dead! *Is* he dead? Oh God, I think Dan is dead.

She shakes him but he remains limp and lifeless. The others gather round.

Sue   No, don't do that, Gabby, you might hurt him even more. Is he breathing?

Gabby   NO! No, I don't think so!

Tim   Should we put him in the recovery position?

Sue   No. We might do even more damage if he's broken anything.

Gabby   That won't matter if he's bloody well dead!

Shawn   Calm down, Gabby.

Gabby (*to* **Shawn**)   Calm down? CALM DOWN? You just killed my little brother with your stunt. Don't you dare tell me to calm down!

Shawn   You didn't care that much about him earlier when you couldn't even crack a smile at his jokes. Don't go all protective over him now when it's too late

Gabby   So you admit it! You killed my brother. You murdered my little brother.

Tim   Stop it, you two!

Lola (*to* **Sue**)   What can we do?

Sue   If he's not breathing maybe I should do mouth-to-mouth resuscitation?

Lola   Just save him, Sue. Bring him back to life. Otherwise he won't have peace and he'll haunt this place for ever. He'll walk and howl with all of the other unhappy spirits.

Joe   There really aren't any, Lola. Science says there cannot be, so there aren't. They're myths.

Tim   Could someone please help Dan? Especially if he's dead!

Liz   There's no way *she'll* be able to do anything. (*Referring to* **Sue**.)

Lola   You shut up! At least she's not someone who gave birth to a *cushion*!

Gabby (*crying now*)   I loved that little guy.

Lola   Tell him that, Gabby, it might bring him back.

Sue *holds* **Dan***'s wrist.*

Sue   I can't feel a pulse.

Gabby   Is he . . . is he . . . dead?

Sue   I'm afraid so.

Lola   You've got to try *something*, Sue.

Sue *pinches* **Dan***'s nose shut and opens his mouth as she prepares to give him mouth-to-mouth.*

Sue   I doubt this will do any good, seeing as he's dead, but . . .

Gabby   I love you, Dan, please come back to us.

Suddenly **Dan** *stirs.*

Dan *(groggy)*   I love you too, sis. Sue, are you trying to kiss me?

Above them all, the **Angels** *start laughing among themselves.*

Angel Em   The Living really are pretty ridiculous, aren't they?

Angel Frankie   Unbelievable.

Angel Arri   They're impossible to take seriously.

Angel Em   It's almost endearing.

Angel Arri   *Almost.* Scary when you think they'll be running the world one day, though.

Angel Frankie   They're learning, Arri, let's give them a chance.

The group fusses over **Dan***, making him comfortable.*

Dan   I'm fine, honestly, I just fell and bashed my head a bit.

Lola   Was it fright from the hooded figure?

Dan   Not really, I just tripped. I'm just clumsy, in general.

Gabby   He's a total goofbag.

Dan   But you love me all the same.

Gabby   Doesn't mean I won't kill you when you're well enough to feel the pain of it.

Tim   I'm thinking maybe a life of human nursing isn't for you, Sue. Maybe you could think about veterinary medicine.

Sue   Are you kidding me? You need to be twice as brainy for that! Vets have to look after all kinds of creatures, but a doctor or a nurse has just one kind of animal to look after.

Joe   What were you doing in that tomb, Shawn?

Liz   He lives there.

Gabby   Yeah, right.

Liz   He does.

Gabby   And how would you know?

Liz   I saw him. When you were all gone for your tea. I stuck around. I couldn't face going home and all the shit that's gonna hit the fan over the baby.

Lola   The *cushion*.

Shawn   It's hard as a rock, that thing. I had a snooze on it earlier and woke up with a terrible crick in my neck.

Liz   Er, *yeah*, have you ever felt a baby bump – it's *solid*. I did my researches, you know. (*To* **Joe**.) *Scientifically.* You'd have been proud of me.

Tim   Man, do you really live in the tomb?

Shawn   Right now, yes.

Lola   Wow. What's it like in there? Are there bones?

Shawn   Have a look yourself. There are shelves but no coffins or anything. They must have been removed at some stage.

Sue   And you live in there?

Shawn   Yeah.

Dan   Why?

Shawn   Haven't got anywhere else right now. Did anyone bring food? I'm ravenous.

He drinks the wine **Sue** *and* **Lola** *abandoned earlier. Then pours himself some more.*

Sue   He's, like, actually serious, isn't he?

Lola   I feel so ordinary. I have nothing to confess to. I live in a house, I don't hate my brother or have a boyfriend or some big secret that's going to get me into deep doodoo.

Sue   Me neither. I'm normal and it's boring being normal, isn't it? I don't think I mind, though. I don't think I'd be able to keep up with being *not* normal, it seems to be a lot to take on.

Joe   I'm kind of not *normal* normal. I'm *nearly*, you know? But not quite. But it's not so bad. I get by. And I *can* be boring . . . and not normal.

He gets a small laugh from the group for this and that seems to please him.

Gabby   Don't you have family you could be with?

Shawn   I used to, not any more.

Gabby   Did you fall out with them?

Shawn   No.

Gabby   What then?

Shawn   They died.

That has shut everyone up.

Dan   When did that happen?

Shawn   Week before last.

Tim   All of them? All of them died?

Shawn   There was just my mum and my kid brother. But, yeah, they both died.

Liz   Of what?

Shawn (*shrugs, still trying to figure it out himself*)   Lots of things. Poverty for one And me, I let them down. Me, most of all.

Tim   You don't have to say anything, talk about this, if you don't want.

Shawn   No, no, I think I want to.

We lived in this shitty little council house. My dad's been gone years, anyone else just came and went without staying long. Mum was so exhausted all the time from working all these different shifts to make ends meet. On . . . *that* . . . day . . . I went out to get some milk and Mum fell asleep while she was cooking the dinner . . . the chip pan went on fire . . . and Mum and my little brother, Patrick, died in the blaze. He was two years old.

But I should have been there. If I had been there I could have saved them. If I had been there, it never would have happened.

Gabby   You can't blame yourself, Shawn. It was an accident.

Shawn   A litre of milk. They died from overwork and . . .

Tim   Gabby's right, you can't blame yourself for what happened.

Shawn   Oh, I can. I wouldn't have had to go for the milk if I hadn't had cereal in the middle of the afternoon . . . all because I was too lazy to make myself a sandwich.

Angel Em   Well, now they know . . . his grief . . . his guilt . . .

Angel Frankie   It's why we must give him any shelter we can. You know that, Arri.

Angel Arri   Yes, yes I do. I lost sight of basic kindness. It's easy to forget. I'm sorry, Angels.

Angel Frankie You sang to him earlier and gave him some rest. That was kind.

Angel Arri It was all I had. It is all I have.

Angel Em And it's enough. For now.

Tim I know where that house is . . . was . . .

Shawn I just wanted to get away from everything when it happened so I dropped out and came here.

Tim You were never here for the Community Course.

Shawn No. I ran into you by accident yesterday. I was just going out to find food and somewhere to wash.

Dan And you got us instead.

Joe How do you live in a graveyard?

Shawn I like it. I wanted to be with the dead. I feel like I'm closer to Mum and Patrick here.

Gabby Does it not make you feel even sadder to be here alone?

Shawn The dead don't mind if you cry. And the angels are looking after me . . . I think. Sometimes I think they're talking to me. Which makes me nuts as well as sad, I suppose.

Gabby We really can't leave you here. You should come home with us, with me and Dan.

Shawn No. I really am fine. I even have a cushion for my new bed now, thanks to Liz.

Liz (*smiling wanly*) Don't mention it.

Shawn I will go back, you know. Just not yet.

Tim You're sure? You could come to mine?

Shawn Really, no. I have some stuff to sort in my head before I go back.

They gather up their things.

Lola   Okay, so me and Sue have put together all the food and drink you'll need to get you through the night. And we have sheets, too, if you want them?

Shawn   Are you kidding me? Your mothers would go nuts on your asses if they went missing. Get out of here you lot. I'll see you all in the morning.

Gabby   Later, you mean. It's already tomorrow.

Joe   Well, it's tomorrow in Australia now.

Gabby   Joe.

Joe   Yes?

Gabby   Not now.

Joe   Right. Not now. No.

Gabby   I really am sorry about your mum and brother, Shawn.

Dan   Me too.

Sue   Us too, Shawn, me and Lola.

Tim   What was your mum's name, Shawn?

Shawn   Maria.

Tim   Maria and Patrick. (*Does a knuckle-bump with* **Shawn**.) Bro.

Liz   Sorry, Shawn. So sorry.

Shawn   Good luck out there. I'd say you're going to need it.

They leave **Shawn** *with the* **Angels** *who sing the third verse of 'Underneath the Stars' by Kate Rusby) as he readies himself for bed. (I suggest changing 'I' to 'you' in the verse to make it clear he is not attending to his life in the lyric too, as this makes more sense for this moment in the play.)* **Shawn** *sees that* **Joe** *has left the recorder and though he shouts after him, there's no reply from* **Joe**, *so he leaves it be.*

Scene Five

Morning in the graveyard. Birdsong. **Shawn** *sits on the gravestone beside* **Angel Arri**, *his face towards the sun.* **Joe** *arrives and goes immediately to his sound recorder.*

Shawn   I left it on, for scientific purposes.

Joe   Good. And thanks. Not that I expect to find anything out of the ordinary on it.

Shawn   Still got to run the experiment, though, just in case.

Joe   Exactly. You have to be rigorous in scientific matters, do proper research and all. Otherwise the results can't be backed up.

He starts to listen to the recording.

Sue *and* **Lola** *arrive, quieter than usual.*

Shawn (*teasing*)   You're late.

Sue   It was *so* hard getting out of bed today.

Lola   Ditto, *so* hard. Brought you breakfast, though. One bacon sarnie.

Shawn   You are a princess, Lola. Miss Susan, do you have an offering?

Sue   Yes, Mr Shawn, I do. A flask of instant coffee, milk and sugar already in.

Shawn   You guessed my sweet tooth.

Sue   I just thought it might give you a nice sugar rush after spending another night in a tomb.

Shawn   You may make a nurse, after all.

Gabby *and* **Dan** *arrive.*

Gabby   You made the local paper, Shawn. See? A photograph and a piece saying you're missing.

Dan   The police want to trace you.

Gabby   You're not in any trouble. They're just worried something has happened to you.

Shawn   That maybe I've hurt myself?

Gabby   Maybe.

Dan   You're not going to, are you Shawn?

Shawn   No. Me topping myself wouldn't do anyone any good, not even me. If I did that I'd probably end up a ghost haunting this place, unable to rest. And I'd make sure even you had a hard time disproving that scientifically, Joe.

Liz *arrives.*

Sue   How did your baby news go down?

Lola   She means 'lack of baby' news, obviously.

Liz   No one's noticed yet. Un-be-fucking-lievable! Everyone was asleep when I got home and no one was up when I left. It's all still ahead of me. I'm in bits! Not being pregnant is worse than pretending to be pregnant used to be.

Joe (*still listening to the recording*)   This is strange. There's a lot of stuff I just can't figure out.

Shawn   Well, it's hardly a state of the art system you were using.

Joe   It's not that, it's more that I'm hearing a conversation I don't remember from last night, about people being ridiculous, and then something about kindness, and singing . . .

Gabby   Maybe it's a play?

Lola   Ooh, high brow.

Sue (*nodding*)   Maybe you were picking up Radio 4. My mum loves that.

Liz   I passed by your old house on my way here, just to pay my respects and all. I took a picture. There are lots of flowers and teddies. There are cards pinned to the big hoarding they've put up around the place. And right there in the middle there's this new thing. Look. The paint is still wet it's so fresh.

Shawn (*looks at her phone and reads*)   'RIP Maria and Patrick. Poverty kills.'

Liz   It's beautiful and it's a protest.

Tim *arrives.*

Tim   Sorry to be late. I had something to do first.

Shawn   We know . . . *I* know . . . Thanks.

Tim   Least I could do. They can't exactly double tag me. I'll just get more community service like this, which isn't so bad.

Sue   I *so* can't believe I volunteered.

Lola   Me neither. And look where we ended up – on a chain gang.

Tim   Everyone into uniform then. We have work to do.

They get back into the jumpsuits and gloves, grab masks and plastic sacks. **Joe** *is still listening to the tape.*

Lola   Hey everyone, how about a group hug? That'll set us up for the day.

They begin to huddle together.

Sue   Joe?

Joe   Oh, no. No. I can't do that . . . I can't do the . . . hug . . . thing. Way too big, way too soon . . . maybe ever.

Gabby   Tell you what, why don't you stand as close by as you can bear and hold your arms open like you're doing a virtual hug.

Joe *stands beside* **Angel Em**, *the two of them are holding their arms wide. The group hugs then* **Sue** *and* **Lola** *lead some Thriftshop-*

style rapping as they all leave for another part of the graveyard, fading in sound as they go.

> We've got some shizz to shovel
> Cos Shawn can't live in a hovel
> We'll fix this graveyard up
> To look incredible
> He'll be so goddam proud
> It be frickin' awesome

Joe *gets into his jumpsuit. The tape recorder plays the song the* **Angels** *sang as* **Shawn** *prepared for bed last night.* **Joe** *is clearly puzzled, looks around but all he sees are stone statues.*

Angel Arri   I've never heard myself sing before. I'm really rather good.

Joe (*talking to himself*)   The machine must have picked up someone's stereo nearby. That's the only logical explanation.

He turns off the recorder, collects his big bag and goes after the others.

Angel Em   Well, Angels, you heard it here first. That could never have happened. And why?

All Angels Because Joe says 'no'.

They laugh and sing the thirteen opening notes of 'There Must Be an Angel' (the vocal gymnastics, no words).

Blackout.

Angels
BY PAULINE MCLYNN

*Notes on rehearsal and staging, drawn from a workshop
with the writer held at the National Theatre, November 2013*

Workshop led by Jonathan Humphreys with notes by Will Wrightson

Approaching the play

Angels is an unashamedly theatrical play. Although it seems to
be realistic, it has a surreal quality, and the sense that a bit of
magic is happening is crucial. The magic should feel like it is
conjured up rather than being tricksy or a 'sleight of hand'.

Although the play is set in a graveyard, because this is a very
potent setting, it does not intend to comment on religion.
The juxtaposition of the youthful characters and the death
surrounding them is a key dynamic in the play. It explores
what happens when a young person comes into contact with
death for the first time. This must never feel mawkish or
sentimental. Jennifer Yane defined art as 'spirituality in drag'
and Jonathan Humphreys suggests this play could be thought
of in these terms as well, in the sense that it is about something
profound but it treats the profundity with irreverence.

Organising initial impressions of the play

Read through the play in a group or on your own and write
down what you think the play is about. If the play were an
object, what would it be?

Some of the responses from the group included:

- Death and young people dealing with it.
- Developing awareness.
- Identity.
- Stereotyping.

Pauline McLynn added that the play is also about responsibility.

Exercises to explore character journeys

Character journeys are useful because they take facts from the play and root them in a specific journey of a character.

DAN'S JOURNEY
From *flippant* to *serious*. From *innocence* to *experience*.

GABBY'S JOURNEY
From *mother* to *sister*. From *closed* to *open*.

SUE'S JOURNEY
From *naivety* to *awareness*. From *actress* to *self*.

LOLA'S JOURNEY
From *naivety* to *opening her eyes*. (Echoes Sue's journey: in minor key to Sue's major key.)

JOE'S JOURNEY
From *outsider* to *insider*. (Does he know that he has been accepted into the group?)

TIM'S JOURNEY   From *confusion* to *clarity*. From *self* to *selfless*. (Pretender to leader.)

LIZ'S JOURNEY
From *invisible* to *visible*. From *falsehood* to *honesty*. (No one pays any attention to her at home; the pregnancy is designed to counteract that. The bump must look authentic to the audience so the reveal is most effective.)

SHAWN'S JOURNEY
From *dead* to *living*. From *darkness* to *light*. (The relationship between Shawn and the Angels is important, particularly on the basis that the angels represent death and the group represents the living. Where does Shawn sit on that spectrum? Good to keep whether or not he is alive ambiguous in the early scenes.)

THE THREE ANGELS' JOURNEY
Their lifespan is practically geological and we are seeing such a small part of that journey. How do you present the fact that they have 'seen it all before'? Is there a way you can demonstrate their experience, wisdom and age, perhaps using voice? As a company you must decide: who are the angels?

Are they people who have died? Stone from the earth that has been shaped into angels? Are they a chorus? Can you find a human equivalent of these characters, e.g. the person who is always put upon, the self-righteous one, the leader? Other questions to consider are: how can Em and Frankie be distinct even though they are similar, and does the fact that Arri has to lie down explain his bad temper?

ANGEL EM: From *purposeless* to *purposeful*. Em is called 'sanctimonious'. Em is a mediator.

ANGEL FRANKIE: aggressor.

ANGEL ARRI: miserable.

Extra information about some of the characters

The character of Joe is on the autistic spectrum. Pauline references the female detective from *The Bridge* as a key inspiration for writing Joe because of her lack of emotions. He is hyper-logical. The production should not send him up and none of the characters makes fun of him. He is no stranger than anyone else; he's just different. His hyper-logical take on the world performs a key function in the play, because it forces him to come face to face with the evidence for magic. It is important that he is the one who makes this discovery at the end.

The angels can come from any culture, any background, either gender, but it is certain that they require a big choice from you, and lie at the centre of the decisions you will have to make when staging the play. However you choose to solve them, do it with boldness. Don't shy away from the theatricality of the characters. The world of the play is heightened, so embrace it. When considering how you will portray the angels in your production, think about what symbolic purpose you want them to have – what do you want them to represent?

FURTHER CHARACTER EXERCISES

- Performers could set up a Facebook page or Twitter account to flesh out their characters' lives.

- Performers could create their characters' biographies. The more detail the better (these needn't be written).

- Hot-seating (perhaps put characters together, for instance Dan and Gabby)

- Split room up between a 'yes side' and 'no side' (on a sliding scale from zero to one hundred per cent), then ask performers questions and see where people put themselves in response to these questions, for instance: 'Does Dan like comedy films?'

Design

In the workshop, Jonathan quoted Bob Crowley, a regular National Theatre designer, who says that the key to designing a show is to find the central metaphor. In order to explore what this might be, the group shared the objects they thought of when they read the play. Recurring ones include: masks, a snow globe, blankets and a whiteboard with pens and an eraser or Etch-a-Sketch.

This object game helps to order your initial impressions of the look and feel of the play. The fact that *Angels* is set in one location gives you something concrete to begin with when designing your production. The production's challenges lie in the depiction of the Angels and the tomb.

DESIGN EXERCISE 1

Split the group up into three sub-groups and ask them to come up with three design ideas, each ordered by:

- *No budget*   Only using recycled and found goods, such as leaves (snow globe and graveyards); chalking outlines on a black wall; using graffiti to denote shapes and back projection; using performers as set.

- *Budget of £50*   Papier-mâché; putting the angels in bins so the bottom half cannot move and creating wings that are separate from the body but fixed behind, like an illusion; over-starching material for rigidity.

- *Unlimited budget*   Site-specific performance in Highgate
  Cemetery; building a vast snow globe and creating
  'reactive' seats (for instance, ones that shake); in a theatre
  but using real grass and graves and having tombstones
  rising from the ground.

The angels need to be able to move but must have a distinct
permanence to them as well. Pauline doesn't see them moving
around the set but only moving within their permanent shapes,
or the one comforting hug of Shawn. The gesture to comfort
Shawn is potentially the biggest move they make. A useful
reference point might be the living sculptures seen around
London in tourist hot-spots. The world of the living and the
world of the dead should be treated as equal: they co-exist and
neither must have power over the other. Jonathan suggests
going to a graveyard to be inspired.

Directors should note that it isn't necessary to go down the
classical route of the 'scary graveyard'.

DESIGN EXERCISE 2

The group is split up again, four ways this time, and each is
told they are only allowed to use the following design element
and nothing else, then asked how they would approach the
play:

- *Only with sound*   Some of the ideas included having extra
  angels onstage with musical instruments (trumpets?);
  playing with natural sound and recorded sound; microphones
  for the angels.

- *Only with light*   Using gobos for specific realistic effects;
  using torches. Can lighting distinguish the ethereal from the
  real? The kids from the angels? While keeping them in the
  same space?

- *Only with movement*   Each character has a different
  physicality. For instance, Joe moves like a robot and loosens
  over the course of the play.

- *Only using an empty warehouse*   And you can only alter the relationship between the performers and the audience, nothing else: try to discover communal moments. For instance, when Shawn is comforted by the angels, could the entire audience be part of that?

The configuration of the space is of course largely defined by the venue in which you present the play, but if you do have a choice as to how your audience is positioned, try to create an intimate relationship between them and the performers.

The play takes place over thirty-six hours. Try to find the fluidity of the action rather than seeing the scenes as separate set-pieces.

Music

It is very important that the songs within the play are integrated into the action so they don't feel like numbers in a musical. The angel songs are designed to have a beauty to them and should fit organically with the action but the songs sung by the kids can be treated with more freedom. Sometimes a song has been chosen to shift the tone of the play. As long as the production stays true to this tone or atmosphere, you can play around with harmony and instrumentation. The ending should feel like an exclamation not a 'final number'.

Analysing the script: facts and questions

Each person takes a page of the script (depending on how many people there are in the group) and then makes two columns, one for facts and one for questions.

Within the world of the play, list the FACTS and list the QUESTIONS (note that someone saying something does not constitute a fact). For instance, from page one:

FACT   There are three angels that are speaking.
QUESTION   Are we joining them in mid-conversation?

One of the key questions to address during rehearsals is: who are the characters' parents? It would be useful to fill in their back stories, using evidence from the play.

Anything extra

When approaching casting it can be helpful to choose, in certain cases, people who already display certain character traits; for instance the performer that plays Dan should have the essence of a stand-up already. To have the ability to show off already will be very useful as it is hard to instil in someone.

The genders of the parts can be interchangeable but it is important that in turning Lola and Sue into boys they don't become caricatures because the dialogue is quite specifically geared towards girls.

The word 'fucking' can be changed to an alternative but it must make rhythmical sense – for instance 'un-be-bloody-lievable'.

Pauline says the only rule is that Robbie Williams' song 'Angels' is *not* included! An important reference point for Pauline was the film *The Breakfast Club* (1985).

Glossary

A 'hedge party' is a kind of gathering of people drinking together outside.

A 'noticebox' is an attention seeker.

Hearts

by Luke Norris

Luke Norris is from Romford, Essex. His professional debut, *Goodbye to All That*, premiered at the Royal Court Theatre in March 2012. His other plays include: *A Puzzle* (short, Royal Court Theatre), *MacDonald and Son* (ATC) and *Borough Market* (Pleasance Dome). Short films include: *Sparks* (NFTS) and *Night of the Foxes*. He is developing his first feature film, *Jesus and the Jetpack*, with director Lucy Tcherniak. Luke Norris is also an actor whose recent work includes *As You Like It* and *Hamlet* (RSC); *Orpheus Descending* (Royal Exchange Theatre); and *Antigone* (National Theatre).

Characters

THE BOYS

Pie
Harry
Reedy
Langers
Mary
TJ
Leon
Blackhall

THE GIRLS

Bella
Simone
Jade
Jo
Tiff
Becky

The characters we see are all about fifteen years old.

All action occurs in the same place over the course of one football season.

One

The ramshackle changing room of Sacred Heart Football Club (on a sign somewhere). An exit to the showers on one side of the room, a toilet door and the entrance from outside on the other.

A tall, black, 'no hot ashes'-type bin stands in a corner, and one holdall hangs from a hook. Otherwise, the room is empty.

Voices from off:

Pie   It's too early!

Harry   It's nearly ten o'clock!

Pie   Exactly!

Harry *enters with* **Pie** *behind him. They both have kitbags.* **Harry** *also has the team kitbag containing eleven shirts and a couple of footballs.* **Pie** *looks like he's just woken up.*

Harry   D'you think Joe Hart stays in bed till lunchtime?

Pie   Probably not but –

Harry   No.

Pie   He gets paid.

Harry   Yeah, because he's good – now get your gloves on.

Pie   Can we sit down for a minute?

Harry   Do you want to play this season or not?

Pie   Well, yeah but –

Harry   Well then.

Pie   I will now Freeman's gone anyway.

Harry   That doesn't mean you can just turn up – you need the practice.

Pie   It's over an hour till kick-off!

Harry's *mobile starts ringing and he digs it out of his pocket.*

Harry   I don't care, get yourself sorted and let's go out.

Pie   But the ground's all dry and hard.

Harry   So what?

Pie   It'll hurt.

Harry   You are unbelievable.

He answers his phone:

Harry   Morning, mate.

Pie   If I get injured . . .

Harry   Hang on – I'm in the changing room – no signal.

He goes out.

Pie *unzips his bag, takes out a pair of goalkeeping gloves and begins to put them on.*

He yawns . . .

Then the lid of the bin flips off and **Reedy** *appears from inside it, shouting:*

Reedy   Aaaaaaghh!

Pie *jumps out of his skin and screams.* **Reedy** *falls about with laughter.*

Pie   What are you doing?!

Reedy   I was hiding in the bin.

Pie   What for?

Reedy   To scare you.

Pie   What for?!

Reedy   Because it's funny.

Pie   No it's not!

Reedy   It is for me.

Pie   Who let you in?

Reedy   Mick.

Pie   Who?

Reedy   Mick on the bar. Your face.

Pie   You never got me.

Reedy   Yeah I did!

Pie   Whatever.

Reedy   Why are you here so early anyway?

Pie   Why are you?

Reedy   I dropped my sister at swimming. I've been here ages.

Pie   In the bin?

Reedy   Don't be stupid, I just saw you coming. Where's H?

Pie   On the phone.

Reedy   So why are you here?

Pie   I'm warming up.

Reedy   What for?

Pie   For practice?

Reedy   But you're a sub.

Pie   Not any more.

Reedy   Freeman's the keeper.

Pie   Was.

Reedy   He's good.

Pie   He's gone.

Reedy   He's what?

Pie   To Brentfield.

Reedy   Ah no, not him as well!

Pie   Twenty quid a week. And a bonus if he keeps a clean sheet.

Reedy   Mate . . . do they need a left back?

Harry *returns.*

Harry   That was Deano. Morning, Reed.

Reedy   Alright H?

Pie   What did he say?

Harry   He's gone.

Pie   He's . . . ?

Harry   Yeah. Brentfield.

Reedy   Not him as well? It's the first day of the season!

Harry   Yeah, I know.

Pie   Why didn't he say before?

Harry   He's only just decided.

Reedy   Oh good.

Pie   So have we got a team?

Harry   Yeah, we must have. I'll ring round.

Reedy   Does your dad know?

Harry   Stepdad.

Reedy   Yeah.

Harry   Not yet. And don't tell him if you go out there.

Reedy   Why not?

Harry   Because he'll cancel the game or something.

Pie   We could have stayed in bed.

Harry   No, we'll have enough.

Pie   We better.

Harry   How come you're here so early?

Reedy   I dropped my sister at swimming.

Harry   She's still doing that?

Reedy   Yeah?

Harry   Didn't she get a bit fat?

Reedy   That's why my mum still makes her go. She won't win any races any more, but at least she can't eat while she's in the pool.

Pie   Fair enough.

Langers *sticks his head through the door.*

Langers   Reed, you got any fags?

Reedy   No.

Langers   Right.

He disappears again.

Harry   Langers is here, then.

Reedy   Him and Ash stayed out last night.

Harry   Out where?

Reedy   In the park.

Harry   What for?

Reedy   Something to do? Ash's dad's a gypsy.

Harry   What?

Reedy   That's why he can do what he wants all the time.

Harry   Is that true?

Pie   I wish my dad was a gypsy.

Reedy   He is a bit.

Pie   But an actual gypsy. So I could stay out and that.

Harry   You stayed at mine last night.

Pie   No, but in the park though.

Harry   What for?

Pie   To get closer to nature?

Harry   You hate nature.

Pie   Yeah I know.

Reedy   But you could get the girls to go and do stuff with them.

Pie   Exactly.

Harry   Right. Whatever, look: I need to ring and make sure everyone else is coming. Can you warm him up?

Pie   Wait, I need a poo.

Harry   Go after.

Pie   It's an emergency. His fault.

He exits to the toilet.

Harry   Why's it your fault?

Reedy   For jumping out of the bin.

Harry   For what?

Reedy   I was hiding in the bin.

Harry   What for?

Reedy   To jump out.

Harry   OK.

Reedy   Can't we just borrow a couple of players if we need them?

Harry   We're not under-twelves.

Reedy   Who are we playing?

Harry   Westow Park.

Reedy   Are they the ones with the flash minibus?

Harry *nods.*

Reedy   And Pie's in goal?

Harry   Yep.

Reedy   Cancel it, we don't stand a chance.

Harry   I'm not cancelling.

He searches for a number in his phone as **Mary** *enters.*

Mary   Morning boys.

Harry   Mary.

Mary   Don't call me that.

Harry *exits, phone to ear.*

Reedy   Mary.

Mary   Stop it.

Reedy   It's your name though.

Mary   Why? I'm not the only one who hasn't . . .

Reedy   You're the only one here.

Mary   Harry doesn't count – he's been going out with Becky for about a year.

Reedy   Three months.

Mary   Same thing.

Reedy   I haven't got a girlfriend and –

Mary   Simone doesn't count.

Reedy   Why not?

Mary   Everyone's had a go.

Reedy   You haven't.

Mary   I wouldn't want to, I don't know where she's been.

Reedy   I know where she hasn't been.

Mary   Whatever. It won't be long till I get some now anyway.

Reedy   You reckon?

Mary *grins.*

Beat.

Reedy   What are you doing?

Mary   What do you mean?

Reedy   Your face. Why are you doing that?

Mary   I'm smiling.

Reedy   Yeah. What for?

Mary   My braces?

Reedy   What?

Mary   I've had my braces off.

Reedy   Oh yeah.

Mary   So what d'you think?

He grins again, showing off his teeth.

Reedy   Have you always had that many teeth?

Mary   Yeah?

Reedy   Were they always that big?

Mary   Shut up.

Reedy   They look massive.

Mary   I've only just had it done, that's why.

Reedy   Are they swollen, then?

Mary My teeth?

Reedy Yeah.

Mary Teeth can't be swollen.

Reedy How do you know?

Mary Because they're teeth. They don't swell.

Reedy Then why are yours so big?

Mary They're not big!

Reedy They are, mate.

Mary They're just different.

Reedy Yeah. Bigger.

Mary Shut up.

Reedy Just telling the truth.

Mary Well don't. Why are you here anyway? You never warm up.

Reedy I dropped my sister at swimming.

Mary Your sister goes swimming?

Reedy Yeah, what?

Mary Is she an inflatable for the other kids to jump on?

Reedy Shut up, it's a glandular thing.

Mary Yeah, right.

Reedy It's serious actually, mate. She's only got a year to live.

Mary Really?

Reedy *nods solemnly.*

Mary Sorry mate.

Reedy I'm only joking, you div, she just eats like a pig.

Mary   You are really, really horrible.

Reedy   Thanks, mate.

Mary *tries the locked toilet door.*

Reedy   Pie's having a poo.

Mary   Oh nice.

Reedy   You doing number ones or twos?

Mary   Just a wee.

Reedy   Go in the showers.

Mary   What?

Reedy   What.

Mary   I'm not going in the showers!

Reedy   Suit yourself.

Mary   Do you?

Reedy   What?

Mary   Go in the showers?

Reedy   No . . .

Mary   Do you?

Reedy   Sometimes.

Mary   You dirty . . .

Reedy   I go straight down the drain.

Mary   I'm going outside.

Reedy   Watch out for that bloke with the dog.

Mary   Is he there again? He is definitely a perv.

Reedy   He won't see anything with you, will he?

Mary   Ask your mum.

Reedy   Leave my mum out of this and I'll leave this out of your mum.

Mary   You're a div.

Reedy   And you're a virgin.

Langers *crosses* **Mary** *as he leaves.*

Langers   Mary.

Mary   Stop calling me that!

And he's gone.

Langers   What's the matter with him?

Reedy   He's got massive teeth.

Langers   Alright. *Donde esta el capitán?*

Reedy   You what?

Langers   Where's H?

Reedy   Since when do you speak Spanish?

Langers   Since they got a fit teacher.

Reedy   We all have to do French with Miss Bass.

Langers   That's 'cause your school's crap.

Reedy   *Merde.*

Langers   What?

Reedy   It's French for crap.

Langers   Right.

Reedy   What's the Spanish for crap?

Langers   I dunno, they don't teach swearing at my school.

Reedy   They don't teach it at ours. My dad taught me that.

Langers   That explains a lot.

Reedy   Where've you just been?

Langers   Having a fag.

Reedy   I thought you didn't have any?

Langers   No, I just wanted one of yours.

Reedy   You pikey!

Langers   I'm skint. And subs have gone up.

Reedy   Blame Harry's dad.

Langers   Stepdad.

Reedy   Who cares? Can I have one?

Langers   Get your own.

Harry *reappears in the doorway.*

Harry   Have either of you got Paulo's number?

Langers   Yeah, hang on.

He gets his mobile out and scrolls for the number.

Reedy   I dropped my phone in the pond. I was trying to kick a duck.

Harry   Serves you right. Is Pie still in there?

Reedy   Yeah. I think he might've fallen in.

Harry *knocks on the toilet door.*

Harry   What are you doing?

Langers   H.

Harry   What? Oh, cheers.

Harry *takes* **Langers**' *phone, copies the number and calls.*

Langers   He's probably touching himself.

Reedy   He probably is as well, the little perv.

Harry   He better not be.

Langers   You'll go blind!

Harry   Where's Ash?

Langers   He went back to get his kit.

Reedy   To his caravan.

Harry   He's coming though, yeah?

Langers   Yeah, we stayed out, that's all.

Harry   Reed said. Did you get *any* sleep?

Langers   Not really.

Harry   Great.

Reedy   Any girls go?

Langers   No. Simone, but she doesn't really count.

Reedy   She does!

Langers   And Ash was on her anyway.

Reedy   Are they coming today? The girls.

Langers   Jade'll probably come to watch Leon. Or pretend to.

Reedy   Is Becky watching?

Harry   Yeah.

Reedy   You two are well loved-up.

Harry   So what?

Reedy   Bit gay.

Langers   Try not to be a turd then, eh?

Harry   That's the least of my worries mate – (*Into phone.*) Paulo!

He leaves, phone to ear.

Langers   What's he mean by that?

Reedy   We might not have a team yet.

Langers   Why not?

Reedy   Deano.

Langers   What about him?

Reedy   Gone.

Langers   Shut up!

Reedy   And Pie's in goal.

Langers   Why? He's the sub.

Reedy   That's what I said.

Langers   Freeman's the keeper.

Reedy   Exactly what I said. Gone as well.

Langers   Freeman? For good?

Reedy   Looks like it. Twenty quid a week.

Langers   That's everyone. Literally all our best players.

Reedy   I'm still here.

Langers   Point proved.

Reedy   So are you.

Langers   That's different.

Reedy   How?

Langers   I can't believe it. Big John, Gay John, Deano *and* Freeman.

Reedy   Yep.

Langers   Is Leon coming though, yeah?

Reedy   I hope so.

Langers   If he's not, I'm walking.

Harry *returns.*

Harry   Paulo and Titch are getting a lift with Titch's dad.

Langers   In his crappy little Fiesta? Gutted.

Reedy   Did you warn him about the bloke with the dog?

Harry   Who?

Reedy   Paulo.

Harry   No?

Reedy   He's scared of it.

Harry   Since when is Paulo scared of dogs?

Reedy   He's not. Just that one. He says it looks at him funny.

Harry   He'll be fine.

Reedy   If you say so.

Langers   Is Leon coming?

Harry   I can't get through to him.

Langers   Is it true that Pie's in goal?

Harry   He's all we've got.

Langers   But he's useless.

Harry   He'll be alright.

Langers   No he won't. I like him and that, but he's about as agile as my nan and she's got no legs.

Mary *comes back in with* **TJ**.

Mary   Look what I found.

Harry   TJ.

Reedy   Lang . . .

Harry   Well done.

TJ   Morning, girls.

Harry   How many's that?

He starts counting players on his fingers . . .

Reedy   Langers . . .

Langers   Where have you been for the whole of pre-season?

TJ   Holidays.

Reedy   Lang . . .

Langers   Yeah?

Mary   Where'd you go again?

Reedy   Has your nan really got no legs?

TJ   Tenerife.

Langers   What?

TJ   Sun, sea, sand.

Langers   No, you div.

Mary   And . . . ?

Langers   She's got both her legs.

TJ   And what?

Mary   Sex?

Langers   What? She's my nan.

Mary   Not you.

TJ   I don't kiss and tell.

Mary   That's a no.

TJ   No, I just don't talk about it.

Mary   A definite no.

TJ   As if. What would you know about it anyway?

Mary   I've been not getting girls long enough to know what failure looks like.

Reedy   Gutted.

TJ   Are you proud of that?

Reedy   What's the Spanish for sad little virgin boy?

Mary   Shut up.

Langers   I don't know.

Reedy   They don't teach you anything good.

Langers   They don't teach you *anything* at your school.

TJ   Where's the others?

Harry   Titch and Paulo are on their way. Ash is coming . . . Who am I missing? Me, you (**TJ**), Langers, Reedy, Mary . . .

Mary   Stop it!

Harry   Shush, I'm trying to count.

Pie *emerges from the toilet.*

Reedy   Here he is.

Harry   Pie . . .

Reedy   The poomeistergeneral.

Harry   Titch, Paulo and Ash . . .

Pie   What time is it? I fell asleep.

Reedy   In the middle of a poo?

Langers   It must have been massive.

Pie   I hadn't even started.

TJ   Amazing.

Pie   TJ.

TJ   Pie.

Pie   Where have you been?

Mary   We've done all that.

Langers   While you were touching yourself.

Pie   I fell asleep!

Harry   That's still only nine.

Leon (*voice from off*)   Miss you.

Harry   Leon.

Leon   Bye then. Bye. Bye.

Leon *enters, hanging up a phone call.*

Harry   That's ten.

Leon   Yo.

Harry   Morning.

Mary   Who was that on the phone?

Leon   None of your business.

Harry   Who else . . . ?

He starts scrolling through his phone again.

Mary   Was it Jade?

Leon   What did I just say?

Mary   Er, that you miss someone?

Leon   Shut up.

Mary   I never had you down as whipped.

Leon   What would you know about it, virgin?

TJ   That reminds me . . . check this out

Harry *heads outside to call another number as* **TJ** *opens his bag.*

Leon   Check what out?

TJ   Here.

He pulls out fistfuls of condoms.

Langers   Why have you got all them?

Leon   What are you doing, man?

TJ   My mum gave them to me.

Langers   Your mum?

Leon   What? Why?

Reedy   His mum's fit.

TJ   Shut up.

Reedy   She is.

Pie   She is though.

Leon   So what? Why's she giving out johnnies for?

Langers   Why d'you think?

Leon   That's wrong, man.

TJ   She works in a clinic. She gets loads.

Reedy   Yeah, I bet she does.

TJ   Mug. If you don't want them I'll take them back.

Mary   I'll have some.

Reedy   Like you're gonna need them!

Mary   I'll need them sooner than you.

Reedy   Keep dreaming.

Mary   I'm telling you, with these babies I'm in.

He points to his teeth.

Leon   What are you chatting about?

Reedy   Mary's got new teeth.

Mary   They're not new.

Leon   Are they real?

Mary   Yeah.

Leon   Mate . . .

Langers   Gimme some then.

Pie   Yeah, can I have some?

TJ   They'll go out of date before you use them . . .

Leon   Blatantly.

TJ   But if you want. Take some for H – he might actually need them.

Langers   With a vicar's daughter? Definitely.

Reedy   Is her dad a vicar?

Langers   Yeah.

Mary   Filth.

Pie   Yeah . . .

He puts some condoms into his bag and the side pocket of **Harry***'s bag.*

TJ   Where's everyone else?

Mary   Brentfield.

Langers   Both Johns, Freeman and Deano.

Mary   Deano?

Reedy   He phoned Harry this morning.

TJ   They're all gone?

Pie   Yep.

TJ   Didn't they ask you?

Leon   Why would I want to play for those fools?

Langers   Exactly.

Mary   Fifty quid a week?

Reedy   It's only twenty.

Leon   I don't need their money, man. I've got my own.

Mary   So what? Theo Walcott's on a hundred grand a week to stay at Arsenal.

Leon   And?

Mary   I'm just saying you can always be richer.

Leon   You want me to go play for Brentfield?

Reedy   I would if I was offered.

TJ   Would you?

Reedy   Yeah?

Mary   Me too.

TJ   What about us?

Mary   What?

Reedy   What about you?

TJ   Don't you wanna play with your mates?

Mary   I'd buy new mates.

Pie   I'll be your mate for a tenner a week.

Langers   No one's ever gonna pay you to play football.

Leon   No one's gonna pay *you* (**Pie**) to be their mate.

Mary   No one's paying you either.

Langers   Yeah, but I don't care.

TJ   That's not the point, is it?

Pie   Well . . .

Mary   What's the point then?

TJ   There is no point. That's the point.

Mary   What?

TJ   Yeah, I mean . . . it's a laugh. It's not an exam you've gotta pass or a class you've got go to. It's just . . . fun.

Langers   If you win.

TJ   I'm not really that bothered.

Leon   You don't care if we win?

TJ   What difference does it make in the end?

Leon   You look like a mug?

TJ   It'll take more than that to make me look like a mug.

Mary   Your ears make you look like an actual mug.

TJ   Whatever. I'm just saying it's supposed to be a laugh, that's all.

Langers   Don't let Harry hear you say that.

Just then **Harry** *enters.*

Harry   Don't let me hear you say what?

Langers   Nothing.

TJ   Half of this lot are talking about leaving.

Harry   What?

Pie   Not really.

Harry   If anyone else even thinks about leaving I will hunt you down and kill you in your sleep.

Leon   They're not going anywhere.

Pie   Sleep . . .

Leon   No one wants them.

TJ   Have we got a valuables bag?

Reedy   Have we got a team?

Harry   Nearly.

Reedy   No then.

Harry   No, but . . .

Mary   What?

Langers   So . . .

Harry   Has anyone got a mate who wants to play?

Mary   We can't even make eleven any more?

Harry   We're only short by one. Someone must have someone?

The boys all look back at him blankly.

Harry   No one?!

Langers   No.

Mary   No.

Pie   Everyone I know's already here.

Harry   What's the matter with you all?

Reedy   We'll have to borrow one from them.

Harry   I'm not doing that.

Leon   No, that's embarrassing, man.

TJ   Just tell your dad we'll play with ten.

Harry   Stepdad.

TJ   Whatever.

Harry   He won't let us. He'll borrow.

Leon   I'm not playing with one of theirs.

Mary   So we have to cancel the game?

Pie   We could go back to bed.

Harry   We're not cancelling

Langers   What choice have we got?

Reedy   What about that kid with the skin thing?

Harry   That was meningitis.

Reedy   So?

Harry   He had a leg cut off.

Reedy   Shut up.

Langers   Yeah he did.

Reedy   Mate . . .

Mary   So what are we gonna do?

Harry *shakes his head. Shrugs.*

Harry   Basically we need a miracle . . .

Just then, **Blackhall** *walks in wearing a smart-looking tracksuit, with an even smarter pair of boots hanging from his fingers. Everyone stares at him.*

Harry   Are you looking for a game?

Two

The same place, a few months later. The room full of kitbags and clothes. Some tinsel dotted around.

Bella *is sitting in the middle of the room in a Santa hat.* **Simone** *and* **Jade** *stand nearby,* **Tiff** *and* **Jo** *at a distance. They all stare at her.*

Silence.

For a while.

Bella *squirms.*

Jade   Stay still.

She does. They look at her a bit longer.

Until:

Jade   I give up.

Simone   I'll have a go.

Jade   Good luck.

Bella   I think I might be okay actually.

Jade   Er, you're not.

Simone   No you're not, to be fair.

Bella   Okay.

Tiff   Don't be mean.

Jade   Who is?

Simone   No one's being mean.

Jade   We're just trying to help.

Tiff   She might not want to wear make-up.

Jade   She does though.

Simone   Yeah, of course she does.

Tiff   Do you?

Bella *shrugs.*

Bella   I don't mind.

Simone   See?

Tiff   See what?

Jade   She needs it anyway if she's coming tonight.

Simone   Exactly. Now you've got to stay still while I do this, alright?

Tiff *goes back to what she's been doing before the scene: searching through the pockets of the assorted clothes and bags. Meanwhile,* **Jo** *begins waving her phone around to try and get a signal. Meanwhile:*

Jade   And no talking.

Simone   No talking.

Jade   Or eating.

Bella   Okay.

Tiff   That *is* mean.

Jade   It's for her own good!

Bella   I don't mind.

Jade   See? It's fine.

Simone   Right. Concealer . . .

She rummages through her make-up bag.

Jade   Have you got enough?

Simone   I just bought a new one.

Jade   What *are* all those red patches?

Bella   Um . . .

Jade   Is it eczema or something?

Bella   No.

Simone   Is it? Have you got eczema? Because I don't want to touch you if you have.

Bella   I don't think so.

Simone   Is that a yes or a no?

Bella   I think I'm just a bit hot from coming in.

Simone   What, if it's what that boy had?

Tiff   It's not.

Simone   How do you know, though? I've got good legs, I'm not having one cut off.

Tiff   It's not meningitis.

Bella   And I don't think eczema's contagious anyway.

Jade   How do you know if you haven't got it?

Bella   I just – I think it's like an allergic reaction.

Simone   To what?

Tiff   Make-up probably.

Bella   I'm not sure.

Jade   You're gonna have to take the risk; she can't come to the party like that.

Simone   Alright. But if you feel yourself eczema-ing up or meningitising or whatever just say and I'll stop before you flake on me.

Bella   Okay. Can I take the hat off now?

Simone   For God's sake yes.

Jo *gives up on her phone:*

Jo   Has anyone got signal?

Everyone gets a mobile phone out.

Jade   No.

Simone   Me neither.

Tiff   I have. One bar. No.

Jo   What about you?

Tiff   Gone.

Bella   Um . . .

Tiff   Back.

Simone   Don't move.

Tiff   Gone again.

Bella   Not sure.

Jo   Check your phone.

Bella   It's in my coat, I think.

Simone   Stop talking.

Bella   Sorry.

Jo   Is this yours?

Bella *daren't answer.*

Jo   Is it yours, this one here?

Still no answer.

Is this coat yours or not?

Bella   Yep.

Simone   What did I just say?

Jade   Why do you need a signal? Everyone who likes you is here.

Jo   I've got to get my sister's ID off her.

Simone   What for?

Jo   The wine.

Jade   I thought they served you in the Co-op?

Jo   Yeah, they do when I've got her ID.

Jade   So I've given you money and you can't even buy it?

Simone   And me!

Jo   No I can, I just need her ID.

Jade   And where's that?

Jo   In her purse?

Jade   And where's that?

Jo   Wherever she is.

Jade   Where's that?

Jo   I don't know, that's why I need to call her.

Simone   Just go back outside then.

Jo   I'm not standing in the rain.

Tiff   You can't phone her yet anyway.

Jade   Why not?

Tiff   I haven't found any money.

Jade   Hurry up then.

Tiff   I'm trying – no one's got anything.

Jo   Someone must have.

Tiff   Twenty p in a shoe, that's it.

Simone   Shame.

Jade   What a bunch of little gyppos.

Jo   You can't say that.

Jade   Why not?

Jo   Because Ashley McCann is one.

Simone   What, a gypsy?

Jade   Oh yeah.

Tiff   No he's not.

Jo   Yeah he is.

Jade   I forgot.

Simone   An actual gypsy?

Jo   Yeah, he lives in a caravan.

Simone   What, an actual caravan?

Jade   Yep.

Simone   Like an actual gypsy?

Jo   Yeah.

Tiff   No he doesn't.

Jade   He does.

Jo   Yeah he does.

Simone   That is rank.

Tiff   His dad works in B&Q.

Jo   So what?

Jade   Yeah and?

Tiff   He sold us our bath.

Jo   He's still a gypsy.

Jade   I heard he went to prison for killing someone.

Simone   Who, Ashley McCann?

Jade   No, his dad. In a fight.

Simone   Oh my God.

Tiff   Who told you that?

Jo   Yeah, that's true as well, apparently.

Simone   Weird.

Tiff   Before he worked at B&Q?

Jade   Must've been.

Tiff   What a load of rubbish.

Jade   Ask him then.

Tiff   I'm not going to ask him.

Jo   Why not?

Jade   Because you know it's true.

Tiff   Because it's stupid.

Jade   Ask him.

Tiff   No.

Simone   Imagine if you killed someone in a fight.

Tiff   It never happened!

Jo   Ask him.

Simone   You'd feel well bad.

Jade   Remember when you beat up Kelly Skelton?

Jo   I didn't beat her up.

Jade   You did.

Simone   Oh my God, yes you did.

Jo   Not really.

Tiff   You sort of did.

Jo   I gave her a black eye, that's all.

Jade   And a nosebleed.

Jo   She deserved it though.

Tiff   I've never had a black eye.

Jo   She was bullying Karen with the limp.

Simone   Aww.

Tiff   I think I might sort of want one.

Jade   You want a black eye?

Tiff   Maybe.

Simone   Why would you want a black eye?

Tiff   Just to see what it's like. Boys look good a bit roughed up, maybe I would too.

Jade   Jo'll give you one.

Jo   What? No I won't.

Jade   But she wants one.

Jo   Not really though.

Tiff   Yeah maybe though.

Jade   Go on.

Jo   What, now?

Jade   It'll be funny.

Jo   Why will it?

Jade   You can tell people you two had a fight.

Simone   Or you can say you got mugged and then someone might give you some money for booze.

Jade   Yeah, exactly.

Tiff   Who?

Jade   One of the boys.

Simone   Go on, do it.

Jade   You can't be the only one not drinking.

Joe (*of* **Bella**)   She's not drinking.

Jade   Yeah, but she doesn't count. No offence.

Bella   Mmm-hmm. (*The word 'okay' with her mouth closed.*)

Simone   Shush.

Tiff   Go on then.

Jo   No!

Jade   Why?

Jo   I don't want to punch her.

Simone   You've got to though, or she can't have a drink.

Tiff   Just do it lightly.

Jo   You want me to punch you in the face?

Tiff   Gently, yeah.

Jade   It'll have to be a little bit hard to give you a black eye.

Simone   Or you could just do a few little ones.

Jade   I suppose. If you get her on the bone.

Tiff   I don't like the sound of that.

Jade   It won't bruise otherwise.

Jo   I'm not doing it! Can't one of you lot just lend her some money?

Jade   You've already got all of mine.

Simone   Yeah, and mine.

Jo   You've still got a fiver in your bag.

Simone   I'm saving that for a taxi.

Jo   We can walk.

Simone   Er, no thanks.

Jade   And turn up soaking wet? Yeah, no thanks.

Tiff   Don't worry about it, I'll keep looking through the stuff.

Jo   Have you got any?

Bella   Nn-nn.

Jo   Nothing?

Bella   Nn.

Simone   Stop talking, I'm trying to solve your face.

Tiff   Err!

She has discovered a fistful of condoms in the side pocket of one of the kitbags.

Simone   Oh my God.

Jo   Whose are they?

Tiff   I don't know.

Jade   Whose *are* they?

Simone   Whose bag's that?

Tiff   Doesn't say.

Simone   Is it Leon's?

Jade   No!

Tiff   Is it?

Jade   It better not be. No, that one's Leon's.

Simone   Whose is that then?

Tiff   Hang on . . .

Jo   What else is in there?

Jade   Whose jacket's that?

Simone   Is it Harry's?

Jo   Is it?

Tiff   No idea.

Simone   Yeah, looks like it.

Jade   How do you know?

Jo   Check the pockets.

Tiff   No, it's his.

Simone   See, I told you.

Tiff   Check these out.

She throws a pair of pants out of the bag to **Jo**.

Jo   I don't want them!

She quickly throws them at **Jade**, *who doesn't catch them but lets them fall on the ground.*

Jade   Er, what are you doing?!

Tiff   Have a look inside.

Jade   No!

Tiff Go on.

Jade Why?

Tiff They've got his name in.

Jo Why's his name in his pants?

Tiff His mum must sew it in his clothes.

Jade That is tragic.

Jo Tradge.

Simone I can't believe that.

Jade What?

Simone Him and what's-her-name.

Jo Who?

Simone What's-her-name in the rain.

Tiff You know her name.

Simone Er, no I don't.

Tiff Yes you do.

Simone Becky, is it?

Jade Oh, her.

Tiff See?

Simone Whatever.

Jo They obviously are.

Tiff Yeah, and loads by the look of it.

Simone What a slut.

Tiff They are going out.

Simone So?

Tiff For nearly like nine months.

Simone   She pretends she's all pure and that.

Tiff   Does she?

Simone   Yeah, she's all like: 'Oh my dad's a vicar. My boyfriend's the captain.'

Tiff   Are you jealous?

Simone   Er, as if I'd be jealous of that skank!

Jo   That's her best mate you're talking about.

Simone   Not any more. She's with us now, aren't you?

Jo   You can't just make her choose.

Simone   Why not?

Jo   Because we're not eleven?

Jade   She's already chosen anyway.

Simone   Yeah she chose us when she came inside.

Tiff   Only because it's pouring down.

Jo   And you invited her out.

Simone   I didn't.

Jade   I did.

Tiff   It's not up to us anyway, it's Leon's party.

Jade   He invites who I tell him.

Simone   Make sure she can't come. Becky slutface.

Jo   Why?

Simone   Why not?

Tiff   You're jealous!

Simone   No I'm not. I just don't like her.

Tiff   What has she done to you?

Simone   Nothing, I just don't like her, is that alright with you?

Beat. **Tiff** *puts the condoms back and carries on looking through the stuff.*

Jo   What time does it start?

Jade   Whenever I get there.

Jo   When does it actually start?

Tiff   Not for ages yet.

Jo   I want a drink.

Jade   They'll all be crying for hours about losing first.

Simone   They must be used to it by now.

Jo   What's the score?

Simone   Who cares?

Tiff   Is it seven?

Jo   Seven–nil? It was only two when we came in!

Tiff   Not the score, the party.

Jo   Oh.

Tiff   Is it seven o' clock?

Jo   Is it?

Jade   Why are you asking me?

Jo   He's your boyfriend.

Jade   He's not my boyfriend.

Jo   Yes he is.

Jade   No he's not, I'm just seeing him.

Jo   That's the same thing.

Jade   Simone?

Simone   No it's not.

Tiff   I thought you were going out with him?

Jade   Not any more.

Tiff   Since when?

Jade   Since ages ago.

Simone   Since he started being rubbish.

Tiff   At what?

Jade   He hasn't scored a goal in about six weeks.

Simone   Seven weeks.

Tiff   So?

Jade   I'm not being funny, but I'm not going out with someone rubbish.

Simone   Blatantly.

Jo   But you can be seeing someone rubbish?

Jade   Yeah, because then I can see someone else if I want.

Jo   Does he know that?

Jade   No, he still thinks we're going out.

Tiff   Shouldn't you tell him then?

Jade   What for? He's not allowed to see anyone else.

Simone   Like he would anyway. He's well loved-up.

Jade   I know, he keeps telling me he misses me.

Simone   When they've just seen each other.

Jade   He's basically in love with me.

Simone   Embarrassing.

Jade   He was talking about baby names last week.

Simone   Oh my God, what?

Tiff   Leon?

Jo   Baby names?

Simone   As if though!

Jade   I know. He wants a boy called Rex because he says it means 'king'.

Jo   That's a dog's name.

Simone   Imagine having a baby now.

Jade   I know. I'd rather eat my own face.

Tiff   Like Stevie Blunden.

Simone   What?

Tiff   Having a baby.

Simone   Oh yeah. I thought you meant . . .

Jo   I'm never having one.

Jade   Me neither.

Jo   I'll just borrow other people's for the day.

Tiff   I want one.

Jo   You've got to have sex first.

Tiff   Shut up!

Simone   I'm gonna be a midwife.

Tiff   *You?*

Simone   Yeah?

Jade   That is rank.

Simone   Why is it?

Jade   Haven't you seen that programme?

Simone   Yeah?

Tiff   Which one?

Jade They're all there with their boyfriend or their mum or whatever

Tiff Oh that one.

Jade And they're all like screaming and swearing and that.

Tiff I like that programme.

Jo And then baby comes out covered in poo.

Simone Er, shut up!

Jo They do though.

Simone That's disgusting!

Jade That's what I'm saying – why would you want to see that every day?

Simone You see babies as well – it's not all just poo.

Jo Any poo is too much if you ask me.

Simone Can we stop talking about poo?

Jo I'm just saying.

Simone I don't care, I still wanna be a midwife.

Jade I hate kids.

Tiff Don't you want to be a teacher?

Jade Yeah?

Tiff Then don't you have to like kids then?

Jade No! Do you think the teachers like you?

Tiff Yeah?

Jade No! Mrs Welsh hates you, for a start.

Simone And Mr Peavoy does.

Tiff Mr Peavoy hates everyone.

Jade Exactly.

Simone   Especially you though.

Tiff   Mr Thompson likes me.

Jade   Mr Thompson fancies you – there's a difference.

Tiff   No he doesn't.

Jade   Yes he does!

Tiff   He fancies *you*.

Jade   And you.

Simone   And me.

Tiff   You most.

Jade   Probably.

Simone   You could have Mr Thompson's babies.

Jade   Shut up! He's about thirty!

Jo   And he's ugly.

Jade   Yeah, and he's ugly. No thanks.

Tiff   Who's that teacher at your school who got the sack for taking tools out of the technology workshop?

Bella   Mr Tate.

Simone   Shush.

Jade   What for?

Bella   He said he was building a kennel.

Simone   Are you deaf?

Bella   But he hasn't got a dog, so –

Simone   Right, that's it.

Tiff   I give up.

Simone   Me too.

Bella   Sorry.

Simone   Too late.

She puts her make-up away and **Tiff** *finally gives up searching through the boys' stuff.*

Jo   I'm going to phone my sister then.

Bella   Am I finished?

Tiff   Can I just have some of yours?

Simone   No . . .

Jo   No.

Simone   But you keep on talking so I'm done.

Tiff   Will you give me a bit of your drink?

Jade   No.

Bella   Does it look alright?

Simone   Not really.

Jade   Punch her.

Simone   But it's not my problem.

Jo   I'm not punching her.

Jade   Go on.

Jo   No.

Simone   Go on – if you punch her I'll give her my fiver.

Tiff   Really?

Simone   Yeah.

Tiff   Will you?

Simone   Yeah.

Tiff   Go on then.

Jo   What?

Tiff   Punch me.

Jade   Go on.

Simone   Go on.

Tiff   I want you to. It's the only way.

Jo *considers.*

Jo   Alright. But I'm not doing it hard.

Simone   You have to give her a black eye or she doesn't get anything.

Tiff   Come on then. Where do you want me?

Jo   Just . . .

She positions her where she wants her. The other girls gather round excitedly. Except **Bella***, who is left at a distance, her face half made-up (she should look a bit ridiculous with a tide-mark around her chin, or an overdone 'Scouse brow', or something).*

Jo *is poised with her fist raised over* **Tiff***'s face.*

Jo   Don't move.

Then **Becky** *enters, dripping wet and holding a drawstring bag in her hand.*

Becky   What's going on?

They turn and look at her.

Are you . . . ?

Jade   She's being punched in the face.

Becky   Why?

Jo   It was her idea.

Simone   And it's none of your business.

Jade   I thought you were staying out to watch?

Becky   Yeah, I was.

Simone   Did it get a bit wet? Shame.

Becky   It's finished.

Tiff   Already?

Jo   So are the boys coming in?

Simone   Desperate.

Jo   I'm just asking.

Becky   Not yet, they're celebrating.

Jade   What?

Tiff   What was the final score?

Becky   What's that all over your face?

Bella   Simone did it.

Simone   It's for Leon's Christmas party. You're not invited.

Becky   Is it fancy dress?

Simone   What did you just say?

Tiff   Did you say they're celebrating?

Becky   They won three–two.

Tiff   What?

Jade   Really?

Becky   Harry scored, then Danny Blackhall got the other two.

Jade   The new boy?

Jo   He's not that new any more.

Simone   Harry Harry Harry . . .

Jade   Did Leon score?

Becky   No.

Jade   Eugh.

Jo   Does it matter?

Jade Er, yes?

Simone He said you're filthy, by the way.

Becky What?

Simone Harry said you're dirt.

Jo Whoa.

Tiff Hang on.

Becky What?!

Simone Didn't he?

Jade What? Yeah.

Simone Just so you know.

Becky What are you talking about?

Tiff Simone . . .

Simone That's what he said.

Becky When?

Simone When I saw him earlier.

Becky You're making it up.

Simone Am I?

Becky Yeah.

Jade Didn't he show you his pants?

Simone Oh yeah, his pants with his name in? Cute. And he showed us his supplies. Have a look.

Becky What 'supplies'?

Simone Show her.

Tiff Leave me out of it.

Simone Don't drink later then.

Jade Show her.

Tiff   No.

Jo   This is . . .

Simone   Don't you start.

Jo   What's the point though?

Simone   Shush.

Jade   Here.

She opens the condom-filled pocket of **Harry***'s bag.*

Simone   So are they all for you? Or is there someone else?

Becky *doesn't know what to say. She looks across to* **Bella***, who just avoids her eyes.*

Simone   What's the matter? You don't fancy it now?

Becky *drops the bag in her hand and storms out.*

Jo   That was like . . .

Tiff   What was that for?

Simone   I don't like her, I told you.

Tiff   There was no need for that though.

Simone   It's not my fault she's frigid.

Jade   She didn't have to get all whingey about it.

Simone   And anyway I've done you a favour.

She goes and picks up the bag **Becky** *dropped.*

Tiff   How?

Simone   Have a look.

She throws the bag to **Tiff***, who opens it and looks inside.*

Jo   Is that the valuables bag?

Simone   Don't say I never do anything for you.

Jade   Phone your sister and let's get drinking.

Tiff   Alright, but I'm giving it back later.

Jade   Who cares?

Simone   Get some for her as well.

Bella   No, I'm fine.

Simone   No you're not. If you don't drink you're on your own.

Bella   Okay.

Jade   So let's do this. Merry Christmas us.

Three

The same. A few months later. A summery night.

Loud chart music seeps dully through the wall from the clubhouse bar.

Jade *enters the dark room. Like everyone, she's dressed for summer.*

Jade (*to herself*)   Perfect.

She turns back to the door.

(*In a half whisper.*) Come on then.

Blackhall *comes in. She takes him by the hand. He is holding a plastic trophy of some sort in his other hand.*

She leads him off into the showers.

A moment later the toilet flushes and **Langers** *emerges through the toilet door. The look on his face tells us he's just done the smelliest poo known to man.*

Langers (*to himself*)   I should be illegal.

He shuts the toilet door behind him. **Leon** *enters and switches on the light. He also has a trophy of some sort. Seeing* **Langers:**

Leon   Why are you standing in the dark?

Langers I'm not.

Leon Whatever. Have you seen Jade?

Langers Seen Jade?

Leon Yeah, what, is there an echo?

Langers Echo echo . . .

Leon *just stares at him.*

Langers Sorry.

Leon Have you seen her or not, man?

Langers No.

Leon She came this way.

Langers I haven't seen her.

Leon You sure?

Langers Yeah, why?

Leon *looks at him suspiciously. He opens the toilet door to check for her in there. Nothing.*

Leon Oh Jesus!

Langers Yeah, I wouldn't go in there.

Leon What's wrong with you?

Langers It was like that when I got here.

Leon Whatever, man.

Langers It was.

Leon Go see a doctor.

He makes to leave.

Langers You got a fag, Lee?

Leon Lee?

Langers Leon.

Leon   I don't smoke, you joker.

Langers   Alright.

Leon   You see Jade, you tell me. I'm going outside.

He goes. **Langers** *takes a cigarette from his shirt pocket or somewhere.*

Langers   'Please' would have been nice.

He pats himself down for a lighter but doesn't have one.

Simone *enters.*

Simone   Is Jade in here?

Langers   No.

Simone   You sure?

Langers   Why's everyone asking me that?

Simone   Oh my God . . .

Langers   What?

Simone   What is that smell?

Langers   The drains are broken.

Simone   It smells like something died.

Langers   Yeah, it might have. They get mice in here.

Simone   Mice?

Langers   Yeah.

Simone   That is rank.

She makes to leave.

Langers   Wait, have you got a lighter?

Simone   That depends.

Langers   On what?

Simone   If you've got a cigarette?

Langers   It's my last one.

Simone   I can see them in your pocket.

Langers *reluctantly offers her another cigarette from his pocket.*

Langers   Smokers die younger.

Simone   Good. Who wants to get old?

Langers   Good point. Go on then.

Simone   What?

Langers   Light me.

Simone   I haven't got one.

Langers   Gimme that then.

Simone   No.

Langers   Give.

Simone   No.

Langers   Give.

Simone   Come near me and I'll get Jo to break your face.

Langers   As if.

Simone   Have you seen Tiff?

Langers   Yeah?

Simone   Well then.

Reedy *runs in.*

Reedy   Quick, hide.

Langers   What?

Reedy   They're coming.

Langers   Who are?

Reedy   Quick!

Langers   What are you talking about?

Reedy *is climbing into the bin.*

Simone   What are you doing?

Reedy   Shh!

Simone   You are such a weirdo.

He replaces the lid. **Simone** *makes to leave.*

Langers   Give me my fag.

Simone   Make me.

She puts the cigarette behind her ear and goes.

Langers   She so wants me.

Pie *enters with* **Harry**, *mid-heated conversation.*

Pie   It's a fix!

Harry   It's not a fix.

Pie   It is, it's rigged!

Harry   Don't be stupid.

Langers   What's a fix?

Harry   Nothing.

Pie   How can Leon be most improved player?

Harry   He just is.

Pie   He's been rubbish!

Langers   Hang on . . .

Harry   He just won it, so.

Pie   Why?

Langers   Have I missed the presentations?

Pie   He scored twenty goals last year!

Harry   I know.

Pie   Twenty! This year he got two! That's not an improvement!

Harry   He's still been pretty good.

Pie   It's not the award for 'most pretty good player' though, is it? It's the 'most improved'. Which is me!

Langers   Except you haven't improved.

Pie   What?

Langers   You haven't. You're awful. No offence.

Pie   I saved the penalty that got us into the district quarter-final!

Langers   And then you let in six goals.

Pie   Only because Paulo got bit by that pervert's dog. We had one centre-back for the last half-an-hour!

Harry   You can't ask Leon to give you his trophy.

Pie   Watch me then. Where's he gone?

Langers   He went outside a minute ago.

Pie   I'm gonna find him.

Harry   Leave it.

Pie   When I've got my trophy.

He exits.

Harry   I've created a monster.

Langers   Was that your dad's idea?

Harry   Stepdad.

Langers   Yeah.

Harry   What?

Langers   To have Leon win player of the season?

Harry   Yeah. Blackhall got players' player.

Langers   Obviously.

Harry   So he said we had to give him something to stop him leaving.

Langers   Fair enough.

Harry   Poor old Pie.

Langers   There's always next year.

Beat.

Harry   What's that smell?

Langers   Dead mice.

Harry   What?

Langers   Dead mice, yeah.

Harry   Right.

Langers   They've got stuck and started to rot or something.

Harry   Nice.

Langers   Is Simone with anyone tonight? I might have a go.

Harry   Please do – she's been cracking on to me again, it's embarrassing.

Langers   Right, I'm having a beer, then I'm in.

Harry   Are you getting served?

Langers   No.

Harry   Mick won't serve the rest of us.

Langers   I said he wouldn't.

Harry   Where are you getting beer from, then?

Langers   Co-op. Jo got it with her sister's ID.

Harry   Can I have one?

Langers   No.

Harry   Don't be tight.

Langers   Get your dad to buy you one.

Harry   Stepdad. He won't.

Langers   Why not?

Harry   Because Titch's dad's here.

Langers   So?

Harry   He teaches me Maths.

Langers   Get Jo to go back to the Co-op.

Harry   Have you seen her? She's not going anywhere.

Reedy *jumps out of the bin.*

Reedy   Raaaaaaaah!

Neither **Langers** *nor* **Harry** *flinches. They just look at him.*

Beat.

Reedy   Where's Pie?

Langers   He's gone looking for Leon.

Reedy   Gutted.

TJ *runs in and straight into the toilet, locking the door behind him.*

Langers   I wouldn't go in there. The mice.

Harry   He must be desperate to put up with that.

Langers   Right, beer o'clock.

Harry   Where have you put them?

Langers   Well, if I told you that then they wouldn't be hidden.

He exits as **Mary** *runs in. His mouth is bleeding.*

Mary   Where is he?

Harry   Who?

Mary   Where's he gone?

Harry   TJ?

Reedy   Your mouth's bleeding.

Mary   I'm gonna kill him.

Harry   What happened?

Mary   Where is he?

He makes towards the showers.

Reedy   He's in there.

Mary *comes back and shouts at the toilet door.*

Mary   Come out now!

No response.

TJ!

Harry   What's happened?

Mary   Teej!

TJ *(from off)*   It was an accident!

Mary   I don't care, come out.

TJ   No!

Reedy   What did he do?

TJ   It stinks in here!

Harry   What happened?

Mary *gives them a grin. One of his front teeth is missing.*

Harry   Oh, mate . . .

Reedy   Have you lost a tooth?

Mary   I haven't 'lost' it, no, I know exactly where it is.

He produces a tooth from his pocket.

Mary   He knocked it out.

Reedy   What for?

Mary   TJ!

TJ   I said I'm sorry!

Mary   I don't care.

Harry   How did it happen?

Mary   He was dancing like a mug and elbowed me.

Harry   So it was an accident?

Mary   Simone was giving me the eyes before that.

TJ   I don't think she was, mate.

Tiff *(calling from off)*   This way!

Tiff, *sporting a black eye, rushes in and shoves* **Mary**.

Tiff   Move!

Mary   Oi!

She tries the toilet door.

Tiff   Who's in here?

Harry   TJ.

She bangs on the door.

Tiff   Tony!

Reedy   Tony?

Tiff   Quickly!

TJ   Go away!

Reedy   Is that his name?

Mary   TJ!

Tiff   Jo needs it!

TJ   She'll have to wait!

Pie (*calling from off*)   Leon!

Reedy *ducks back down in the bin, pulling the lid across just before* **Pie** *appears in the doorway.*

Pie   Is he in here?

Harry   No.

Pie   Where's he gone?

Jo *groans, then staggers in, white as a sheet.*

Tiff   You're gonna have to go outside.

Jo   No I'm . . .

Tiff   He won't come out.

Jo   No time . . .

She retches and puts her hand to her mouth.

Tiff   Oh no.

Harry   No.

Pie   Ah!

Tiff   Tony!

Mary   TJ!

Harry   Not in here.

Tiff   Tony!

Jo *runs through them, lifts the lid of the bin –*

Harry   No don't!

– and she's promptly sick all over **Reedy**. *They all make gross-out noises . . . except* **Reedy**, *who just stands there in the bin, stunned and covered in vomit.*

Jo *curls up in a ball on the floor.*

Leon *enters, trophy still in hand, and surveys the scene. He sees* **Reedy***. And just laughs.*

Reedy *says nothing: he just climbs out of the bin and walks slowly and silently across the room into the showers.*

Leon   Oh, shame.

The sound of a shower running begins offstage and **Jade** *hurries out. She stops at the sight of everyone.*

Leon   What are you doing in there?

Blackhall *emerges from the showers behind her.*

Pie   No way . . .

Harry   Oi.

He shushes him. **Leon** *addresses* **Blackhall**.

Leon   Man, you better explain yourself.

Jade   What for?

Bella *enters, fully made-up and overdressed. A moment as she takes in the atmosphere.*

Bella   What's going on?

Jade   We're out of here.

Bella   Okay . . .

Leon   Whoa.

Jade   What?

Leon   Where are you going?

Jade   Anywhere you're not?

With that she exits, taking **Bella** *with her.* **Leon** *just watches her go. Then he turns back to* **Blackhall**.

Leon   You got something to say?

Blackhall *shrugs, not bothered.*

Leon   What?!

They look at each other. Then **Blackhall** *smiles a winning smile.*

Leon   Right: outside, you fool.

He puts down his trophy, takes his jacket/hoodie off, and leaves.

(*Shouting from off.*) Come on!

The others look at **Blackhall***. He stands there a moment. Then, still seemingly nonplussed, he puts his trophy down and walks out after him.*

Harry   Blackhall . . .

But he just carries on out of the door.

Oh no.

Pie   I've got to see this.

He heads out, followed by **Harry** *and* **Tiff***.* **Mary** *calls through the toilet door as he leaves:*

Mary   I'm coming back!

He exits. A moment, then **Pie** *returns and picks up* **Leon***'s trophy.*

Pie   I'll have that.

And he goes again, leaving **Jo** *on her own on the floor.*

She stirs and crawls drunkenly towards the toilet door. When she finally gets there, she knocks feebly upon it and props herself up against it.

TJ   Who is it?

Jo *doesn't have the energy to answer. Beat.*

What do you want?

Still nothing. Beat.

Is that Mary?

She tries to speak. And fails. Beat.

Is he still there?

Long beat. **Jo** *is almost asleep when the door tentatively unlocks.* **TJ** *opens the door . . .*

And **Jo** *falls through it, so she's laid out flat.*

TJ   Sorry about that.

He looks cautiously around the room. No sight of **Mary**.

TJ   I would stay and help you out, but . . .

He hesitates a moment . . .

Sorry.

Then he pegs it out while he's got the chance. **Jo** *drags herself into the toilet and locks the door.*

Then **Simone** *enters, leading* **Langers** *by the hand. She tries the toilet door. Locked.*

Simone   Eugh.

Langers   What about just in here?

Simone   What if someone comes in?

Langers *shrugs.*

Simone   No offence but I don't really want anyone to see me with you.

Langers   Right. That's a bit . . .

Simone   I know, but . . .

Beat.

Alright.

She concedes and turns out the lights.

That'll do.

They move towards each other and just as they're about to kiss the lights flick on again, revealing **Becky** *in the doorway.*

Langers   Oh for –

Simone   Er, do you mind?

Becky   Sorry. I was looking for Jo.

Simone   Well she's not in here.

Becky   I think she might be.

Simone   Eugh.

She sweeps past **Becky** *and out of the door. Beat.*

Langers   We were just . . .

Simone *sticks her head back round the door.*

Simone   Are you coming or what?

And she's gone again.

Langers (*to* **Becky**)   I'll see you later.

Becky   Yeah.

Langers *goes and* **Becky** *moves to the toilet door.*

Becky   Are you alright in there?

Harry *walks in and sees her.*

Harry   Hello.

Becky   Jo?

Harry   She's smashed.

Becky   I know.

Harry   I thought you might have just been seeing how her wee was going.

She just looks at him a beat.

Joke.

Becky   Good one.

Harry   Yeah, sorry.

Beat.

So. Are you having a good night?

Becky   Not really.

She knocks on the toilet door.

Jo!

Jo *mumbles something faintly through the door.*

Becky   Are you still being sick?

Harry   I think she's probably empty.

Jo *heaves. The sound of vomit on toilet.*

Harry   Maybe not.

Becky   Can I come in?

Harry   I wouldn't if I were you.

Becky   I don't really care what you'd do.

Harry   I can't believe you're still angry with me.

Becky   I'm not.

Harry   Simone made it up!

Becky   What for?

Harry   I dunno! Why would I tell them we were, like . . . when we weren't?

Becky   Because you're an idiot?

Harry   Right, I'm gonna prove it once and for all.

Becky   I don't care.

Harry   I do.

Jo *unlocks the toilet door*

Harry   Stay there.

Jo *crawls out on her hands and knees as* **Harry** *exits.*

Jo   I'm never drinking again.

Becky   You've got some sick in your hair.

Jo   Oh God!

She gets a bit weepy.

Becky   You'll be alright.

Jo   When?

Becky   Not sure. It's sports day Monday, so…

Jo *puffs her cheeks out at the thought.*

Becky   Your mum's on her way.

Jo   Mmm?

Becky   Your mum. She's coming to pick you up.

Jo   Oh no . . .

Becky   It's alright, I'll talk to her.

Jo   She's just got a new car. It smells like melted plastic.

Becky   Do you want to stand up?

Jo   Not yet. Where is everyone?

Becky   Outside.

Jo   What for?

Becky   Leon's fighting Danny Blackhall.

Jo   Why?

Becky   Because they're boys.

Jo   I hate fighting. It makes me want to cry.

Becky   Didn't you punch Tiff earlier on?

Jo   She needed money.

Becky   What?

Jo   She . . . I don't know . . . Money. Ask Simone.

Becky   Can you smell that?

Jo *nods.*

Becky   What is it?

Jo   I don't want to talk about it.

Reedy *returns from the showers, dripping wet.*

Becky   What happened to you?

Reedy *doesn't answer, but walks to the exit. Just before he leaves:*

Jo   Sorry, Reed.

He turns to face her.

Reedy   Just so you know . . . that's the worst thing that's ever happened. To anyone. Ever. And I'm including 9/11 in that.

He leaves. **Becky** *looks to* **Jo**.

Jo   I was sick in his face.

Becky   Wow.

Beat.

Have you seen his sister lately?

Jo   Yeah. Massive.

Harry *returns, pushing* **Bella** *ahead of him. She's over-made-up and in a really awful, ill-fitting outfit.*

Harry   Right, go on then –

Becky   Leave it.

Bella   I don't really know what to say.

Harry   The truth?

Bella   It's not really my business.

Harry   Listen: do you want me to spend the rest of my life paying for something that someone else made up? No.

Becky   'The rest of your life'?

Harry   Maybe. We could've been supposed to get married or something.

Becky   We were only going out for eight months.

Harry   Only? That's . . . I can't work it out but that's – as a fraction – that's a big part of my life.

Bella   Simone would kill me. And this is her dress.

Harry   See? Simone.

Becky   What about Simone?

Bella   No, I don't . . .

Becky   Bella.

Bella   She found condoms.

Harry   What?

Bella   She just found them in your bag and pretended you'd been saying –

Harry   TJ put them in there! I didn't know anything about them until about a week ago – I never check that pocket.

Becky   Why should I believe you?

Harry   Because it's true!

Bella   And there was a pair of pants with your name in.

Harry   My mum did that in Year 7! I don't wear them!

Becky   It doesn't matter anyway.

Harry   Why doesn't it matter?

Becky   I'm not going back to standing around here every week while they slag me off and steal my best mates.

Bella   Your best mate?

Becky   Not any more.

Harry   You won't have to.

Becky   Are you going to stop playing then?

Harry   No, but . . .

Becky   Well then.

He thinks about saying something. Then, to **Bella***:*

Harry   Can you go now?

Bella   Okay. Sorry.

She makes to leave. Turns to **Becky***.*

Bella   I don't really like what I'm wearing, by the way.

She leaves.

Harry   What was that?

Becky   I used to dress her.

Harry   Right. Listen –

He looks to **Jo***.*

Harry   Is she . . . ?

Becky   I think she's asleep.

Harry   Good. I want to tell you something. And I've never said this to anyone else . . .

Beat.

I'm leaving Hearts.

Becky   You're what?

Harry   I'm going to Brentfield. They've made me an offer. So you won't have to come back here.

Becky   What about the rest of them?

Harry *shrugs.*

Harry   We're done anyway.

Becky   What do you mean, you're done?

Harry   Our only striker just punched our only good player in the face, Paulo won't come near the place because of the dog, Mary wants to kill TJ, and no one's spoken to Ash since Christmas.

Becky   Why not?

Harry   He took money out of the valuables bag.

Becky   Ashley?

Harry   Yeah.

Becky   Why would he do that?

Harry   He's a gypsy.

Becky   No he's not.

Harry   Yeah, he lives in a caravan.

Becky   He doesn't. He lives at the top of my road. They've got a double garage.

Harry   What?

Becky   His dad works in B&Q.

Harry   I knew it!

Jo   Tiff took it.

Harry   Tiff?

Becky   Tiff?

Jo   Yeah.

Harry   What for?

She can't bring herself to say 'booze'.

Harry   What for?

Jo *gags.*

Harry   What?

Jo *scrambles back through the toilet door, closing it behind her.*

Harry   Did you know?

Becky   No, of course I didn't.

Just then **Tiff** *walks in leading* **Mary** *by the hand. She stops at the sight of everyone.*

Tiff   Alright?

Harry   Did you steal from the valuables bag?

Tiff   Bye then.

She walks out, leaving **Mary**.

Mary   Oh, thanks a lot – I was on to a winner there. This night just keeps getting worse . . .

And he leaves, grumbling under his breath.

Becky   So that's it? You think the team will fold?

Harry   Yeah. Unless we get some sort of miracle . . .

He looks to the door, waiting.

Becky   What are you doing?

Harry   Nothing, just . . . Last time that worked. Doesn't matter.

Becky   What are you going to tell your stepdad?

Harry (*shrugs*)   There's more important things than this place.

Becky   Are you feeling alright?

Harry   I will be. If you go out with me again.

Becky   You're not drunk, are you?

Harry   I wish!

The sound of vomit on toilet from **Jo**.

Harry   Not *that* drunk, obviously.

Becky *grimaces/smiles.*

Harry   So what do you reckon? Do you want to be on my team again?

A car horn beeps outside.

Becky   I'll think about it.

Harry   Is that it?

Jo, *finally standing, emerges from the toilet.* **Becky** *looks to her.*

Becky   Ready?

Jo *nods.*

She makes her way gingerly to the door.

Sec you, Harry.

Harry   Yeah, bye.

Jo   Good luck.

And she's gone.

Becky   I'll see you then.

Harry   Will you?

Becky *smiles.*

Becky   Why do you think I came tonight, you idiot?

She exits, leaving **Harry** *alone.*

He grins to himself. Looks around the changing room, taking it in.

Beat.

He smells the smell again –

Harry   Dead mice . . .

– and shakes his head in disbelief.

Goes to the door, finger poised on the light switch.

One last look . . . and he switches out the light.

Blackout.

Hearts

BY LUKE NORRIS

*Notes on rehearsal and staging, drawn from a workshop
with the writer held at the National Theatre, November 2013*

Workshop led by Maria Aberg with notes by Phil Sheppard

How the writer came to write the play

Having read a lot of Connections plays over the last few years,
I was very keen to write something that sat on the 'light' end
of the spectrum: a play that contained no strong social or
political commentary, acts of violence or deep emotional
traumas. A play that allowed young people to enjoy, rather
than eviscerate, themselves.

Much of the play is anecdotal. I spent a lot of my youth hanging
around changing rooms, not doing much. And I loved it. It's
only now looking back that I realise that this seemingly wasted
time was just as important as the big 'events' of my adolescence.
N.B. I played rugby, but chose to write about football for a
couple of reasons: mainly because it's our 'national game' and
so feels farther-reaching, and less class- or region-specific than
rugby, but also because David Storey has already given us *The
Changing Room*, a wonderful play to which I owe a huge nod.

My hope is that the experience of rehearsing and performing
Hearts will reflect its content and my own experience . . . That
on the face of it all, there's no real 'point'. It's fun. It won't
topple governments or make people think differently about
recycling. But it will be fun. And one day, with any luck,
people involved in its staging will look back and realise the
time they spent together in doing so was full, invaluable and
a luxury rarely afforded in later life.

Luke Norris, 2014

Structure and story: exercises for rehearsals

Below are a number of exercises that focus on work that can
be done with your cast early on in the rehearsal process. These
exercises are directly linked to the text and are designed to
help keep characters and action specific and vibrant, and
avoid generalisation.

PREVIOUS CIRCUMSTANCE INVESTIGATION

Maria Aberg asked the group to list the key events that
happened leading up to the play's three scenes. Finding some
clarity with the previous circumstances will help to inform
the present onstage. To begin with, these facts should all be
found in the text and not elaborated on, yet.

Key events before Scene One

- Ash and Langers were out all night.
- Pie stayed over at Harry's.
- Reedy dropped his sister off at swimming.
- Mick on the bar let Reedy in.
- Reedy got in the bin.
- TJ went to Tenerife and missed pre-season training.
- TJ's mum gave him some condoms.
- Mary had his braces removed.

Key events before Scene Two

- It has started to rain.
- Becky has stayed outside to watch the game.
- Becky has been given the valuables bag to look after.
- The other girls have decided to move inside.
- Bella has allowed Simone to do her make-up.
- The girls have been invited to Leon's party.
- Jade is no longer going out with Leon, but merely 'seeing him'.
- Blackhall is now on the team.
- Leon has had a slump of form.

- The team haven't won a game yet.
- Harry hasn't removed his Year 7 pants from his bag – why?

Key events before Scene Three
- The team has had some success.
- There has been an awards ceremony.
- Becky and Harry have fallen out.
- A disco has been set up.
- Tiff is still after a black eye.
- Harry has decided to leave the team.

It would be interesting for the actor playing Harry to decide when he makes the decision to leave the team: is it a spur-of-the-moment resolution or has he given it some considered thought and is choosing this moment to announce it?

Try putting the key events into chronological order, to see if you can draw up a timeline of action and events leading up to the opening lines of the play. These could be the subject of improvised scenarios such as how did the falling out happen between Harry and Becky, setting up the disco, Jo eventually punching Tiff, the improvement of the football team, an outdoor park sleepover with Ash and Langers or the awards ceremony.

Encourage your actors to flesh-out characters who aren't seen in the play, like Ash, Harry's stepdad or TJ's mum; bring in photos of what they might look like and examine the text to see what details you can find out about them, improvise scenes that include them (TJ's mum gives him the condoms, Harry and his stepdad discuss another humiliating loss) so there is a shared perception of these characters among the group.

Units

The workshop participants discussed and established the beginning and end of units. Units are the building blocks of the action (some directors call them episodes), and the end of a unit is where the action or focus of the scene palpably changes;

This process, though time-consuming, will help to focus the intentions of the actors into bite-sized chunks. Rather than trying to tackle the thought processes for a character throughout an entire scene, it might be helpful to regard units as scenes within scenes.

The participants read through the scene and discussed when the unit came to an end. After establishing the changes of unit, each unit was then given a title; these titles, simply, and without using flamboyant language, should describe what is happening in that unit.

For UNIT ONE the title 'Pie becomes goalkeeper' was agreed on. The unit runs from the opening until:

> **Pie** *unzips his bag and takes out a pair of goalkeeping gloves and begins to put them on.*
>
> *He yawns . . .*

The next task is to establish psychological actions within each unit: what are the characters trying to do to one another, what do they want to achieve?

In the first unit the directors debated whether Harry was bullying or trying to boost Pie's confidence and deciding intimidation techniques wouldn't work on him, and also perhaps didn't suit Harry's character; Harry trying to enthuse and motivate a reluctant Pie who wants to be motivated and reassured would be a better tack to take. The participants re-read the first unit with the characters' psychological actions in mind and the scene changed considerably. Harry was milder, softer, more patriarchal and Pie much more sympathetic. Decide what it is that makes Pie change his mind: where in the first unit is his 'tipping-point', when and why is he persuaded that goalkeeping might be for him?

In the workshop UNIT TWO was decided as going as far as:

> **Harry** *returns.*

The character's intentions were decided as Reedy wanting to amuse himself and Pie wanting to be accepted as goalkeeper, using Freeman's move to Brentfield as ammunition.

UNIT THREE, titled as 'Harry starts Plan B', was decided as reaching:

Pie   Fair enough.

The character actions discussed were Harry's attempt to sort everything out, Pie wanting the game to take place and Reedy being more than happy to be a pain in the proverbial.

UNIT FOUR was decided to be from

Langers *sticks his head through the door.*

to

Pie *exits to the toilet.*

Harry's action is still to get things sorted, Pie's has become trying to stall and Reedy is still trying to entertain (mostly himself). What does Pie the poo-crastinator do in the toilet? Does he really fall asleep or is he panicking and buying himself some time?

UNIT FIVE was taken as far as:

Harry   I'm not cancelling.

This short but economic unit shows the struggle that Harry is having to get the game sorted and Reedy's persistent banter. The action decided for Harry was 'I'm not giving up', and for Reedy 'Don't panic, let's have some fun.'

UNIT SIX is a long one and could go as far as:

Mary   Stop calling me that!

As Harry exits and Mary enters, the adult authority in the guise of Harry leaves the room and the children are left alone and a tangle ensues. The directors were encouraged to look for more than conflict in this unit, altercations are easier to find and portray so what could be an alternative format for this dialogue? Does it have to be combative?

Maria advised the directors to stay away from malice as it might be more fruitful to try different manners of contest than aggression: perhaps a gag-battle, trying to unseat each other

with humour rather than pugnacity would help to establish
some of the team banter that is pervasive through the play,
and would be more interesting to watch than a fight.

Language

Luke is happy for companies to change the names of places,
football teams and players mentioned in the play.

Characters and characterisation

CHARACTER EXERCISE 1: CHARACTER LISTS

Paying close attention to the script, draw up some character
lists (it might be useful to do this in pairs or small groups to
allow for discussion). The first list should contain the facts
about the chosen character; these should be irrefutable truths
and not conjectures. The second list should contain everything
other characters say about them and the third list should
contain everything the character says about themselves.

Fleshing out characters and creating character histories or
back stories can risk indulging in elaboration that doesn't link
directly to the text and the given facts and circumstances in
the play; using this technique will directly bind the inception
of the character-building process to the text.

For this exercise in the workshop the participants worked on
the same character in pairs. Below are some of the discoveries
made in the workshop.

HARRY   He's captain of the team, he has the team's shirts,
he's on time, he doesn't want to cancel the game, he owns a
mobile phone and calls the other players with it and he has a
stepdad who is the team manager. He likes Becky and has
been going out with her for three months. He has pants with
his name in his bag that he's had since Year 7 (why?). These
are all actualities in the play and should be the foundations of
building a character; get the actors used to evolving characters
based on fact and then extrapolate and move to discussion of
what these facts might say about the character. If you knew

only these facts and nothing more, what kind of person would you say he might be?

Similarly, consider things the other characters say about him. For example:

Langers   Don't let Harry hear you say that.

Just then **Harry** *enters.*

Harry   Don't let me hear you say what?

Langers   Nothing.

TJ   Half of this lot are talking about leaving.

What might Langers' concern about Harry hearing this conversation indicate about Harry? That he has a temper? That he takes it all too seriously? Does the comment come from care, respect or fear?

Working from the evidence in the script the group concluded that Harry is a mature and respected leader. He takes responsibility seriously and leads by example with deeds and actions; when it seems that the match may be in jeopardy, Harry (not, his stepfather, the team manager) takes the initiative to call around. There was discussion of whether Harry may have 'issues' with his stepfather, that Harry doesn't want him to manage the problem, that he would rather deal with the pressure and inconvenience of taking the helm rather than entrust it to his stepdad. Harry is also very quick to correct people when they refer to his stepfather as his 'dad', and the four times it happens in the text he corrects them immediately. Is he doing this in order to 'distance' himself from his stepfather, making sure that his friends are quite clear that he is not a blood relation and that for him there is a distinction between stepdad and dad?

MARY   He's had his braces removed and is delighted with the result, he talks tirelessly about girls and sex, he's first to try and grab some of TJ's condoms stash. He's convinced that the days of his virginal status are numbered now that he has new teeth and a fistful of johnnies. Mary seems to be the butt of everyone's jokes but it doesn't really seem to bother him, only his mates' persistence in naming him after the Virgin Mary really seems to irritate him; he recognises his place in the pecking order and rides the ribaldry and teasing and gives as good as he gets. For Luke, this banter and piss-taking is an integral part of the camaraderie and he's keen to stress that no one should be wounded – it's not vindictive, no one is singled out: 'It's important to me that there are no victims . . . Everyone's fair game.'

When the team is together they can generate an *esprit de corps* that they all enjoy – a sense of belonging and community that allows them the freedom to ridicule themselves as well as each other. This is Mary talking about his current ranking as sexual underachiever:

> **Mary** I've been not getting girls long enough to know what failure looks like.

Comments like this could only really be made in a 'safe' group environment where no one intends to maltreat or harm.

TJ   His name is Tony, he's missed pre-season training as he's been in Tenerife; it is an undisputed fact in the play and everyone agrees that he has a fit mum. TJ's mum gives him condoms – what might this say about his home life? He's not bothered if the team wins or loses, he runs away (through guilt, fear or both?) when he knocks out Mary's tooth as he's dancing (might this mean he's a clumsily awful or crazily brilliant dancer, or was he drunk?) and Mary says he has ears like an actual mug. Of himself, TJ says 'I don't kiss and tell.' In discussion the workshop group agreed that TJ seems a reliable and trustworthy character, loyal and with a possible hint of hero worship of Harry. He speaks on impulse and perhaps doesn't consider his thoughts before voicing them.

SIMONE   The group decided that she is 'in charge'; she is a disciple of make-up and believes everyone else should be too; she's a little squeamish – she finds the idea of eczema and skin problems somewhat disconcerting and certainly is not interested in talking about poo. She wants to be a midwife and really doesn't like Becky. The workshop participants thought this had a lot to do with jealousy and that Simone might see Becky as a threat to her 'authority'. Becky is going out with the team captain after all.

Significant things said about Simone by others:

Mary   Simone doesn't count.

Reedy   Why not?

Mary   Everyone's had a go.

Is Simone's 'reputation' something she has willingly cultivated herself or something that has been imposed upon her? Does this renown upset her or does it make her a celebrity? Is her seeming willingness to get intimate with the boys a manifestation of low self-esteem? She confronts Becky when she has an audience and urges the other girls to get involved and to back her up. She is somewhat obsessed with how others perceive her and is swift to criticise others and herself, but isn't adverse to recognising and broadcasting her qualities ('I've got good legs'). She's snogged a few of the boys – she certainly snogged Ash the night before the play opens – but Luke was keen to point out 'She hasn't slept with any of them.' While discussing Simone's character, Maria alerted the group to the dangers of being judgemental when doing these exercises as it can lead to creating caricatures – of the 'Bad Girl', the 'Bully', the 'Goody Two-Shoes' – and in order to avoid stock characters the roles should be discussed in neutral teams and always linked to the facts in the play. Find sympathetic elements in every character and try to steer clear of moral evaluation.

TIFF   When we first see her she is rummaging through bags and coats in the changing room; she always seems to be without money and wants cash to buy booze. She takes money from the team's valuables bag (accidentally left behind by Becky) and does not return what she takes despite saying 'I'm giving it back later.' She wants to have a baby; she also wants a black eye and sports one in the final scene. She says that 'boys look good a bit roughed up' and nearly gets intimate with the absent-toothed Mary. She doesn't want to get involved with Simone's baiting of Becky and is confident enough to tell her to 'Leave me out of it' and repeat her suspicion that Simone is jealous of Becky. The group discussed the possibility that Tiff doesn't have that much respect for the petty politics and power games within her group of friends – she's a bit of a radical and thinks differently from the others.

BECKY   She is the daughter of a vicar – how religious is she? By the end of the play she's being going out with Harry for approximately nine months. She lives on the same road as Ashley, she used to 'dress' Bella, and she watches Harry playing football even in the rain. She's not been invited to Leon's party (so Simone says) and is good friends with Bella who is somewhere near the base of the girls' status tower. Simone has no shortage of things to say about her: 'Becky Slutface', 'skank', 'what a slut', 'filthy' and 'dirt' are all levelled at Becky, said both in and out of her presence. Becky has a maturity, a self-assuredness and self-awareness that many of the other characters lack, and is sufficiently confident to break the mould and move on: 'I'm not going back to standing around here every week while they slag me off and steal my best mates.'

CHARACTER EXERCISE 2: WANTS

The first thing the participants were asked to decide upon was 'What does your character most want in the play?' The next task was to establish 'What do they do to get what they want?' and finally 'What is at stake if they don't get what they want?' The participants again worked in pairs and investigated the same characters.

HARRY   The primary 'want' initially discussed for Harry was his desire to impress his stepdad, but it was argued that there was something more and the group settled on his want for a successful team so the friends could stay together. In order to achieve this, Harry willingly took on the necessary practical responsibilities of running and keeping the team together – phoning round, being in charge of the kit and equipment, ensuring Pie got to the game by having him stay over at his house – but he keeps struggling to hold the team together though it's crumbling around him.

Without the team, Harry may lose contact with his friends, and as no longer the captain of a team, might Becky lose interest? The team is something the boys have all chosen to be part of; they are not obliged to show up and join in, their participation has not been prescribed by school or parents, it's a choice they have made together and Harry wants to make that affinity work.

MARY   Mary is preoccupied with sex; he talks about it at every opportunity and now he has his braces out it seems that it is prime time for his first sexual experience. He tries extremely hard to get what he wants and just when he may be getting close it goes wrong.

The group discussed in considerable detail what Mary's obsession with sex might mean. Is there something beyond that? What does it represent? Is it that he doesn't want to get left behind or be the odd one out, or some kind of self-affirmation? Maria encouraged the directors to investigate the possible roots of the characters' wants as even though the characters might not know what they ultimately want, the actors playing them should.

TJ   TJ wants to be part of the team; as he expresses early in the play, the winning isn't important, it's being with his mates that's paramount:

> **TJ**   There is no point, that's the point.
> **Mary**   What?
> **TJ**   Yeah, I mean . . . it's a laugh. It's not an exam you've gotta pass or a class you've got go to. It's just . . . fun.
> **Langers**   If you win.
> **TJ**   I'm not really that bothered.

He's happy to play with ten men, he wants to avoid any acrimony or antagonism in the team but feels compelled to let the others know when he feels the team is beginning to fall apart. 'Without the team,' Luke concluded, 'TJ would be bereft.'

SIMONE   Her primary wants are to be in control, to be needed and to be and feel special. In order to achieve this she is happy to manipulate and lie, as without a sense of being exceptional and particular she may be overlooked, alone, ignored and forgotten. She is prepared to fight hard to make sure that doesn't happen.

TIFF   The group discussed whether the desire for security, a place, stability, affection and somewhere to fit in were integral to understanding Tiff. She's prepared to steal to avoid being left out, to get a black eye based on the conviction it might get her a boyfriend and almost gets intimate with desperate Mary just before her pilfering is revealed. If she doesn't try to fit in and achieve the prerequisites for membership she risks being out of the group.

It is interesting to note that the conclusions about Tiff drawn from this exercise almost contradict many inferences about her made in the character list exercise.

BECKY   Becky wants happiness, but happiness begot of decency not manipulation or deceit. Integrity, truth and blemish-free reputation are important. She is earning her probity by living it; she doesn't stoop to playing wily power games and, unlike many of the other characters, has some patience. She doesn't chase after Harry but allows him time to fix things; her maturity could conversely jeopardise their relationship if Harry weren't as sensible and level-headed as he turns out to be.

CHARACTER EXERCISE 3: DIAGNOSTICS

Using a row of chairs numbered one to ten with chair ten representing 'absolutely, definitely, one hundred per cent, yes' and chair one representing 'completely not, zero per cent, terrible, awful, no', the actors should position themselves in front of the relevant chair in response to questions about their characters.

Avoid choosing yes/no answers; aim for responses that can be measured or quantified in some way. But try to urge actors not consistently to hover around the middle of the scale; they must feel strongly about something. Similarly be wary of characters who are always placing themselves at the extremes, always all or nothing. Try not to rush this exercise and encourage your actors to be considered and precise, the choices are not absolute and may modulate so try the exercise at intervals during rehearsals.

Questions tried out during the workshop were:

- How confident is your character?
- How confident would they like to appear to be?
- How sexually active are they?
- How sexually active would they like to be?
- At school, how well do they perform academically?
- How comfortable are they with being alone?
- How comfortable are they in the company of members of their own sex?
- How comfortable are they in the company of members of the opposite sex?
- How aggressive are they?
- How vain are they?
- How critical of themselves are they?
- How critical of others are they?

Develop other questions to fill in any gaps. What else might be helpful to know? How religious, sporty or fashion-conscious? How well do they get on with their parents or guardians?

CHARACTER EXERCISE 4: STATUS

Without discussion, each participant chose a number from
one to ten to represent their 'status'. The concept of 'status'
wasn't discussed and each participant interpreted it in their
own way. In their new-found status everyone greeted one
another and were encouraged to go to extremes with the
physical manifestation of their prestige.

The participants were then asked to hide their status, to mask it,
carry it internally rather than broadcast it; they were then
asked to experiment with how their 'characters' might move,
sit, stand, lie and make themselves comfortable. How did they
deal with and relate to the space and people around them?
How easy was making and sustaining eye contact?

Each participant then chose another number from one to ten,
this time to represent how drunk they were and imagine that
this was the best night they'd ever had. (It's probably advisable
to get young actors to choose a number first before telling
them they're going to play drunk or you'll most likely get a
room of top-of-the-scale boozers. To ensure a good numeric
spread you could use playing cards ace to ten and distribute
them among your actors.) Then the participants were asked
to hide their drunkenness or sobriety; the intoxicated were to
try and appear temperate and the sober to project the persona
of someone well-fuddled.

Finally, keeping their characters, the actors were to imagine
they were in a desperate hurry to get somewhere important.

Maria suggested that these and similar exercises might help
free up your actors, giving them something else to focus on, a
point of concentration other than words. Try giving the actors
mini-tasks to achieve in the course of a scene or improvisation.
Examples given were to try and touch as many surfaces as
possible or to always support, stay close to or far away from a
specific character. These can be a playful ways of developing
interesting and creative dynamics during the scene-study work.

Production, staging and design

When writing the play, Luke had a clear image of the changing room he used to use when he played rugby. See if you can make decisions about staging quite early on in your rehearsal process so everyone is familiar with the geography of the scene. Some companies were considering rehearsing in their school changing rooms, then aiming to replicate the significant topography onstage. Play around with how benches could be configured and how bags and coats could be hung to create barriers and partitions.

Don't forget the other senses. What sounds might there be from outside? Is a road or playground nearby, how close is the football pitch? What does the changing room smell like? (Testosterone, Lynx, Deep Heat, chlorine and socks were the most prevalent olfactory memories of changing rooms.)

When considering staging don't forget the characters are getting ready to play in the first scene. What rituals might they go through? What business might there be: boot cleaning, stretching, deodorant spraying, keepy-uppies, etc.?

Vomit
Through trial and error in previous productions, Maria suggested orange juice and crushed digestive biscuits as the most successful and least unpleasant option when wanting to create upchuck. This could already be in Jo's mouth – she has two short lines just before ejection that will need to be considered, or the vomit could be in a tightly sealed clingfilm bag held in her hand (there should be no air pockets in the bag though or it won't burst), or the actor playing Reedy could cover himself in fake spew while he is in the bin, which would mean having Jo puke with her back to the audience or masked some other way. If you can, make sure you dedicate adequate time to investigating the alternatives for this unappetising but memorable moment.

The bin
Give suitable consideration to the safety implications of having someone in a bin for a protracted period, particularly if you're

thinking of having the actor playing Reedy in there as the audience come in. Find ways of making it safe – using a backless bin or drilling ventilation holes may be the easiest solutions.

Scene changes
The directors were encouraged to animate the transitions if possible, somehow marking the passage of time. Changes of graffiti, decoration and scrawlings on the changing-room walls were discussed as economic but effective ways of registering time passing during the two scene changes.

Style and technique
Luke said that he was aiming for theatrical realism in his play. The performances shouldn't be burlesques, parodies or character types.

He chose not to use overlaps in order to keep the text clean on the page but the dialogue should be pacey and lines should follow fast upon one another's heels. Before building pace, ensure the actors know exactly who they are speaking to and why, especially when there is more than one conversation taking place at a time, and do this work early on in your rehearsal process.

Make sure you find an effective balance between light and shade, allowing the play to breathe and marking significant moments – don't just aim for pace.

Pronoun

by Evan Placey

For Danny

Evan Placey is a Canadian-British playwright who grew up in Toronto and now lives in London. His plays include *Mother of Him* (Courtyard Theatre; King's Cross Award for New Writing, UK; RBC National Playwriting Competition, Canada; and the Samuel French Canadian Play Contest, US), *Banana Boys* (Hampstead Theatre), *Suicide(s) in Vegas* (Canadian tour, Centaur Theatre Award nomination), *Scarberia* (Forward Theatre Project/ York Theatre Royal), *How Was It for You?* (Unicorn Theatre); *Girls Like That* (Birmingham Rep/Theatre Royal Plymouth/West Yorkshire Playhouse) and *Holloway Jones* (Synergy Theatre Project, schools tour and Unicorn Theatre; Brian Way Award 2012 for Best Play for Young People; Writers' Guild Award nomination). For radio: *Mother of Him* (BBC Radio 3/Little Brother Productions). Evan Placey is a Creative Fellow and Lecturer at the University of Southampton, and also teaches playwriting to young people for various theatres, and also in prisons.

Acknowledgements

Anthony Banks, Rob Watt, Lucy Deere, Paula Hamilton, Tom Lyons, and all the staff at the National Theatre. James Grieve and Michael Fentiman.

Tanya Tillett at the Knight Hall Agency.

The staff and young people at Gendered Intelligence. Also the brilliant resources on their website, particularly 'A Guide for Parents and Family Members of Trans People Living in the UK' and 'A Guide for Young Trans People in the UK'.

Jamie, for the insight, openness and anecdotes.

Rebel Without a Cause by Steward Stern, Irving Shulman and Nicholas Ray from whom I have quoted lines. And the screenplay for *Breakfast at Tiffany's* by George Axelrod, based on the book by Truman Capote, for the same reason.

The many young people who took part in the premiere productions of this play. You give me hope for the future.

E.P.

A note on casting

This play could have a cast size of anywhere from seven to any number of actors. There should be a heightened awareness in the case of the adult characters that these are young actors playing adults – that this is performance: when they first appear, we watch an actor put on an apron to become Mum, an actor put on a doctor's coat, etc. But once they're 'dressed', they needn't worry about playing the gender or age of their character, merely the truth of that moment.

Dean is a transgender male – meaning Dean was born a girl, and is biologically female, but identifies as male, and is in transition to becoming male. In the stage directions Dean is referred to as *he* as this is the pronoun that Dean, if he were real and not in a play, would go by and identify with. The role should be played by a female actor.

A note on punctuation:

A slash (/) denotes a line that is interrupted, and the point of interruption.

A dash (–) indicates a cut-off, sometimes of one's own thought with a different thought (not a pause or beat).

An ellipsis (. . .) is a loss/search for words.

Absence of punctuation at the end of a line means the next line comes right in.

Square brackets [ ] suggest words that are not spoken, but will help to clarify a line's meaning.

Characters

THE TEENS

Dean, *transgender male (female-to-male), played by a female actor*
Josh, *male*
Kyle, *male*
Amy, *female*
Laura, *female*
Dani, *female*
James Dean, *male. as in the movie star,* Rebel Without a Cause *mid-1950s teenage look: blue jeans, white T-shirt, red jacket. Speaks with an American accent.*

THE ADULTS

Mum, *forties, played by a young male*
Dad, *forties, played by a young female*
Senior Management Team (*SMT*), *played by two to four actors*
Doctors (**Monroe**, **Bogart**, **Brando**), *played by three actors*
Private Doctor

The characters we see are all about sixteen years old.

Set

It is supposed that somewhere on stage (or maybe occupying the whole stage) is a closet/wardrobe/clothing rack or maybe a dressing-up chest – somewhere from which the actors get items of clothing on stage to become the adult characters.

Also on stage is a large poster of James Dean from Rebel Without a Cause.

The play takes place from May until June the following year.

Scene One

Amy's bedroom. **Josh** *wears a dress. He looks in a full-length mirror.*

Kyle What the fuck?

Josh For nothing in the world.

Kyle What?

Josh For nothing in the world, will I swear not to arm myself.

Kyle What?

Josh Will I swear not to arm myself and put on a man's dress.

Kyle Josh.

Josh Who said that?

Kyle What?

Josh Who said that?

Kyle Said what? Josh, why are you –

Josh For nothing in the world, will I swear not to arm myself and put on a man's dress. Who said it?

Kyle Rihanna?

Josh Joan of Arc.

Kyle . . . Okay.

Josh But in history, sir overlooked that bit, why she was actually condemned to death, y'know.

Kyle Josh?

Josh Yeah?

Kyle You're wearing a dress.

Josh Yeah.

Kyle   Okay.

Josh   Yeah.

Kyle   So you're aware, you're aware, that you're wearing –
I thought maybe.

Josh   No. I'm aware.

Kyle   Right.

Josh   Amy rang when you were downstairs. They're out of
pineapple so she's replaced it with mushrooms, which in my
mind isn't really a comparable replacement, one's a fruit and
the other's – And she's got it without cheese, which actually
entirely defeats the purpose of ordering a pizza if you ask me.

Kyle   Dude, why the fuck are you wearing a dress?

Josh   I dunno. I thought. Thought it would help. Understand,
y'know.

Kyle   And?

Josh   Nothing.

Kyle   At least you look pretty.

Josh   You think?

Kyle   Shows off your legs.

Josh   Thought somehow, if I, like, there'd be this moment,
it would just click, that I'd feel how she, how he . . . but I just
feel like a boy in a dress.

Kyle   You used to wear eye-liner and mascara.

Josh   For like a week.

Kyle   Three as I recall.

Josh   That's not the same.

Kyle   Your emo days.

Josh   It's not the – this isn't how it was supposed to go. This wasn't part of the plan.

Kyle   Every plan has variables, mate.

Josh   You go away for a shitty two-week holiday for Easter with your annoying family to some three-star shithole in Benidorm, you expect to come home with a sunburn, you expect to come home with diarrhoea, you expect to come home with a pen that has a picture of a woman on it whose clothes fall off everytime you click it – what you do not expect when you come home is to find your sixteen-year-old best friend engaged and that your girlfriend is . . .

Kyle   Come here.

Josh   No. What are you –

Kyle   It'll help.

He puts eyeliner on **Josh**.

Josh   We were supposed to – there were so many things we were supposed to do, that we'd planned to do. After next year, gonna spend our gap year together. Travel Thailand.

Kyle   You still can.

He gets lipstick, starts to put it on **Josh**.

Josh   How are we –

Kyle   Stop talking.

Push your lips together.

Josh *looks in mirror.*

Kyle   Anything?

Josh   No.

Kyle *gets on one knee. Holds out a ring box.*

Josh   The fuck you doing?

Kyle   Joshua Robbins.

Josh   Kyle.

Kyle   We've known each other a long time now.

Josh   Kyle, get up.

Kyle   Ever since I first spotted you having pissed your pants by the sandpit in nursery, I knew. I knew then you were the one. Joshua Michael Robbins, make me the happiest groom and be my best man?

Opens box, it's a Haribo sweet. **Josh** *takes it, eats it.*

Kyle   Is that a yes?

Josh   I love you, man.

Kyle *picks up* **Josh***, spins him around whooping.*

Kyle   It's gonna be ace. Here. (*Envelope.*)

Josh   What's this?

Kyle   Your duties as best man. I've put a tick-list in.

Josh   . . . Terrific.

He gets distracted by himself in the mirror again.

Kyle   It'll be alright, man.

Josh   It'll be great.

Kyle   I meant about.

Josh   Oh.

Kyle   Josh?

Josh   Yeah.

Kyle   Amy'll be back any minute, and [if] she finds you in her room she'll castrate you with her bare teeth. Trust me, I've got the teethmarks. It still hurts when I pee.

He exits.

The song 'Everyday' by Buddy Holly begins to play.

Josh *takes off the dress. On the other side of the mirror (i.e. somewhere else)* **Dean** *enters in boxers and a sports bra/vest top, faces himself in the mirror. By this point* **Josh** *too is in his underwear, and the effect is that the two of them are looking at one another through the mirror.*

Beat.

Josh *exits.*

Scene Two

Continuous from Scene One.

Dean'*s bedroom. A large poster of James Dean from* Rebel Without a Cause *on the wall.*

Dean *retrieves a needle. Fills it with liquid from a small tube. Squirts the end of the needle gently. And reaches round and confidently injects himself in his bum cheek.*

He then wraps a large roll of bandage around his chest, binding his breasts so they're flat. Puts a T-shirt on. Looks in mirror.

Puts another T-shirt on top of the first.

Gets a sock. Puts it in his underwear, adjusts it.

Puts on some skinny jeans and Converse.

Hair product in his short hair.

Douses himself in Lynx. The ritual is complete.

James Dean *appears. The music stops.*

James Dean   Hey kid.

Dean   I look crap.

James Dean   Take it easy.

Dean   Do I look crap?

James Dean   You look swell.

Dean   Fuck off swell.

James Dean   You look a bit like me, kid.

Dean *looks at the poster of James Dean, then at the* **James Dean** *standing there.*

Dean   You're totally Photoshopped.

James Dean   There was no such thing then. It's all me. C'mon. It's time for your jab, buddy.

Draping arm around him, the two looking in the mirror. **Dean** *throws off his arm, feeling insecure when looking at them side by side.*

Dean   I already took it. Buddy.

James   Whoa. I'm not the enemy, Dean.

Dean   No, you're just some dumb dead guy I talk to.

James Dean   No need to get personal 'bout it.

Shouting is heard.

James Dean   What's that?

Dean, *unhappy with his appearance, changes the top T-shirt for a button-down shirt.*

Dean   *That* is why no one should get married. *That* is why some people shouldn't be allowed to have children. *That* is the alien life forms also known as Mum and Dad.

James Dean   'She, she says one thing, he says another, and everybody changes back again', right?

Dean   Some things haven't changed.

He is looking at himself in profile again.

James Dean   Too big.

Dean   What do you know?

James Dean   Well, I've got one for a start.

Dean   You're not even here.

James Dean   You're the one talking to me.

Dean   It's the T. It's messing with my head.

Beat.

He takes out the sock from his trousers.

James Dean   Told you.

Dean (*throws it to him*)   Put a sock in it, will you?

James Dean   Touché.

Dean *puts a smaller sock in.* **James Dean** *lights a cigarette.*

Dean   Don't you know smoking can kill you?

James Dean *laughs.* ['*I'm already dead.*']

Dean   Touché.

James Dean *joins him at the mirror. Side by side they both check themselves out in profile. Fix their shirts.*

Dani *enters. She stands there for a moment watching before* **Dean** *notices her.*

Beat. **James Dean** *watches the rest of the scene unseen by* **Dani**.

Dani   They're shouting as per usual.

'Once upon a time'

This is clearly a game they used to play / story they used to tell as kids.

Dean   'There were two kids who learned they were in fact royalty'

Dani   'Who were in fact abducted by the people they thought were Mum and Dad'

Dean   'So they left their screaming parents and went to live in the castle'

Dean *and* **Dani**   'And lived happily ever after.'

Beat. **Dani** *still lingers in the doorway.*

Dean   You can come in.

Dani   Can I?

Dean   You've always been –

Dani   It's different now.

Dean   . . . No.

Dani   Yes.

Dean   . . . Yes.

Dani   Looks good. The shirt.

Dean   You think?

Dani   Matches your eyes.

Dean   / Thanks

Dani   / Almost wouldn't know.

Almost.

Doesn't it bother you?

Dean   . . . No.

Dani   No. You don't even know what I'm asking. *No.* Some things don't change. *No.* You were always scared of me. Meant to be the other way around. You're the older one. And even now.

Dean   What do you want, Dani?

Dani   Doesn't it bother you? How everyone's chatting shit about you?

Dean   No.

Dani   No?

Dean   I couldn't give a damn.

Dani   *Couldn't give a damn.* You're so goddamn *American* sometimes.

Dean   I don't care.

Dani   Well I do. I give a damn. You remember at primary. When people were chatting shit about you. Saying about you and what's his name, Brad, douchbag, saying how you'd – and I stood up for you. Even though you were the older one. When they were saying 'Hear your big sister's a right – ' I stood up for you, fought for you. No one said nothing to me 'bout you after that, once I told 'em what's what, showed 'em what's what.

Dean   Okay.

Dani   But now I can't say nothing. 'Cause this time the shit they're talking's true.

Dean   I'm sorry that you're . . . I'd never want you to . . . because of me.

Dani   . . . I know. (*Pause.*) Let's have a look at you then.

Are you happy?

Dean   Yeah. I am. I'm. Getting there.

Dani   Okay.

Goes to leave. Changes her mind. Turns back.

Dean?

Dean   Yeah?

Dani   You can pretend all you want, but you'll never have a dick.

Scene Three

Mum *and* **Dad** *appear. We watch as a male actor puts one thing on from the closet (e.g. an apron) to become* **Mum**, *and a female actor puts one thing on (e.g. tie or hat) to become* **Dad**. *They speak to the audience.*

Mum   Once upon a time there was a girl.

Dad   We'd read to her every night.

Mum   Once upon a time there was a little girl who lived in a house.

Dad   She'd cry all the time. Nights, days, you name it.

Mum   Isn't anything else to name. Nights and days. That's everything.

Dad   She cried all the time.

Mum   First day wouldn't stop crying, in the hospital. Nurse said, I remember, she said, 'Think this is bad, wait till she's a teenager.'

Dad   Slamming doors.

Mum   You have hopes for your child.

Dad   Headphones attached to her ears.

Mum   Dreams for your child.

Dad   Don't even know what her ears look like any more.

Mum   Big plans for your child.

Dad   Weeks without saying a word to us.

Mum   And you plan for all that other stuff, the awkward years they want nothing to do with you, but this.

Dad   Silence.

Mum   This you don't plan for. This is not in the handbook.

Dad   Can't remember the last time you actually saw her.

Mum   It's not even in the secondary reading.

Dad   Maybe she was never there.

Mum   After the incident. When she was thirteen. We went on this course.

Dad   It was counselling.

Mum   To try to understand why she tried to . . . well . . .

Beat. This is uncomfortable for them.

Dad   We all went. The whole family. To Dr Learner.

Mum   She wasn't a doctor.

Dad   She had a PhD.

Mum   In anthropology.

Dad   Sociology.

Mum   She sent us on this course. They may as well have called it the Centre for Failed Parents, the sorry lot of us, doing role-plays.

Dad   As I recall you refused to take part.

Mum   I am forty years old – I think it's a bit ridiculous I should have to prance around finding my inner teen. This is the best part, they had these situations, and I had to play my daughter while some of out-of-work actor gets trolleyed in to play me. Show me how to communicate with my child. Girl's half my age, can't even get a walk-on part in *Hollyoaks* and she's telling me how to be a mother.

Dad   The point is

Mum   The point is *this* was not covered on the course. Not even mentioned. I should go ask for a refund.

Dad   It's not like we knew then anyway that's what this was all about, why she – he, he. I find the pronouns so confusing. Spend half the day practising, in my head, so I don't get it wrong.

Mum   Once upon a time there was a girl. She was breastfed and burped and rocked to sleep and everything the manual tells you to do. And she grew up and became a princess.

Dad *gives her a look.*

Mum   What?

Scene Four

Glastonbury Festival. **Dean** *and* **Laura** *by a tent. Shorts, hoodies, and wellies.* **Amy** *returns with beers. She wears leather boots.*

Amy   Think I just saw Sir.

Laura   Is that one of the bands? Are they cute?

Amy   As in Sir sir. As in Mr Woolner.

Laura   Eww, isn't that like, isn't there like an age limit? To ban teachers' entry? It's not on seeing teachers in the summer hols. Glastonbury should be off-limits.

Dean   How'd you get beers?

Laura   Last thing I want to see in my hols is Mr Woolner putting on Factor 45 in a vest top.

Amy   Sister's ID. I think he's kinda cute.

Laura (*fixes hair, looking round*)   Who?

Amy   Mr Woolner.

Dean   Gross.

Laura   Mega-gross. And you're not allowed to say stuff like that – you're engaged.

Amy   He was wearing a motorbike jacket.

Laura   Ew, literally mid-life crisis. When I reach middle age, I'm going to embrace it. Start wearing polo necks, and my hair in a bun, and big pants.

Amy   God, I'd rather die.

Laura   No you wouldn't.

Amy   I would. Literally.

Laura   No. Not literally.

Amy   Literally. I'm gonna die young, for ever remembered like this, never age, like all the greats – Buddy Holly, Kurt Cobain, James Dean. For ever young and beautiful.

Laura   Yeah, but those are all guys. Can you think of one famous girl who went young?

Amy   Amy Winehouse.

Laura   Yeah, but do you really, I mean honestly, Amy Winehouse? Do you really wanna go out like her?

Amy   Thanks, Laura, I'm now destined to a long, unhappy future growing old. At least I'll age gracefully. No big pants for me.

Laura   No, sorry. Men age like red wine. Women age like milk.

Amy   Did you actually just – you can't say things like that any more, this isn't 1950.

Laura   Speaking of which we've thought of the perfect theme for your wedding.

Dean   We have?

Amy   There's a theme?

Laura   As your maids of honour

Amy   Maid and male of honour

Laura   We thought that

Dean   We haven't actually discussed this actually.

Amy   I don't know that I want a theme.

Laura   You *have* to have a theme. Literally everyone has one. Everyone.

Amy   Maybe we should check with Kyle. The wedding's all kind of his thing, you know.

Laura   But you're the bride – when will he be here?

Dean   Kyle's coming?

Amy   Didn't I say? They got last-minute tickets.

Dean   They? Who's they?

Pause.

Fuck you, Amy.

Amy   I could've sworn I told you.

Dean   Fuck you, Amy.

Amy   Can't we all be grown-ups. I mean I'm getting married for God's sake.

Dean   Good for you. You grow up then.

Amy   Shit. I'm getting married. Bit scary when you say it out loud.

Dean   You could've warned me, Amy.

Amy   Shit.

Laura   You literally haven't talked to each other in months. You gonna spend the last year of college ignoring each other? Speaking for myself, just me, it's a bit awkward for the rest of us, don't you think, Amy?

Amy   I'm gonna be a wife.

Laura   I'm happy to be the mediator. My mum's a psychologist y'know.

Dean   I remember. She came in to give us all counselling in Year 10 when the Science teacher ran off with that Year 11 girl.

Amy   Whatever happened to her?

Laura   She became a Scientologist. Had twins.

Dean   How do you know this?

Laura   My mum counselled the teacher.

Amy   I thought he's in prison.

Laura   No, he's in Slough.

Kyle *and* **Josh** *enter with bags of food.*

Kyle   If food be the music of love, eat on.

Amy   Thank God, I'm starving.

Josh   We've got Tesco's finest breadsticks, falafel and humous.

Laura   Didn't you bring any real food?

Josh   Oh. Hi.

Dean   Oh. Hi.

Awkward pause. **Amy** *has already dug into the humous.*

Amy   Humous anyone?

No?

Laura   Did you bring any sausage rolls?

Kyle   Amy's a vegan.

Amy   Sweetie, I'm not *a* vegan. I'm vegan.

Kyle   Well yeah.

Amy   Well no. It's derogatory. You don't say *a* black, *a* gay.

Kyle   I do actually.

Laura   Oh my God, the wedding's not going to be vegan, is it?

Amy   Yes.

Kyle (*simultaneously*)   No.

Laura   It doesn't really fit with the theme though.

Kyle   What theme?

Amy   So, what, we're going to have dead animals on every table, are we?

Kyle   My mum just wants roast chicken, you make it sound like we're gonna have some taxidermy centrepieces.

Josh   That'd be pretty cool actually. (*Off* **Amy***'s 'kill you' look.*) Or not.

Laura   We were thinking it could be

Dean   Again there's no 'we'

Laura   Like a *Grease* wedding.

Josh   As in a fry-up?

Laura   As in the musical.

Kyle   I hate musicals. There's just so much . . . singing.

Laura   Well it could just be like a fifties theme.

Amy   You just want to wear that stupid poodle skirt you bought and can't wear.

Laura   They were supposed to make a comeback.

Dean   Fifties, I like it.

Kyle   We could get like a fifties band.

Amy   Or maybe you could just get some battery hens and force them to play the bongos with their broken beaks and I can wear a piglet-skin dress with leather shoes!

Laura   You're actually wearing leather shoes. Literally. Like right now.

Kyle   You actually are though, babe.

Amy   I had them before, okay! God! I'm not marrying you!

She stomps off.

Kyle   Wait. Was she being serious? Shit. Babes!

He goes after her.

Laura   I hope they're okay. The venue's non-refundable is all. And I've already cut the price tag off my skirt.

Dean   People get married for less.

Laura   I better go mediate.

She exits.

Josh *attempts to set up the tent. He quickly becomes exasperated with it and its lack of cooperation. He beats the tent with one of the poles.*

Josh   Dumb-ass piece of . . . piece of . . . plastic, piece of carrier bag!

Dean   Easy, cowboy, or someone's gonna call a hotline for victims of tent abuse.

Josh   She was asking for it, your honour. She'd unzip the door to anyone.

Sorry, not funny.

Dean   No.

It's inside out.

Josh   How do you mean?

Dean   The bit that's currently on the inside should be on the outside.

Josh   Oh.

He begins to put it up. Still struggling. **Dean** *wordlessly assists him, and together they quickly put it up.*

Josh   Thanks. I would have managed eventually y'know?

Dean   No. You forget we've been camping before.

Beat.

Josh   So you're talking to me?

Dean   So you're talking to me?

Josh   I never stopped talking to you.

Dean   I never stopped talking to you.

Josh   Then why weren't you talking to me?

Dean   Cos you weren't talking to me.

Josh   Only cos I thought you weren't talking to me.

Dean   Why would you think that?

Josh   Cos you sent a text and that was it.

Dean   That was it cos you never wrote back.

Josh   What was I meant to write?

Pause.

Dean   You're staring. What?

Josh   Spent the last few months avoiding eye contact that I've not properly got to really . . . You've got the same eyes.

Dean   No shit, Josh.

Josh   The rest of you, it's you, but not. But you still look . . . still look –

Dean (*defensive*)   *Look* what?

Josh   Look fit. You still look fit. But as a boy. You're a fit boy.

Beat.

I'm not gay.

Dean   I know.

Josh   Just saying, cos don't want you to think

Dean   I know, Josh. I know.

Josh   I know you do.

I bloody hate festivals. Buncha smelly muddy piss-heads in wellies pretending to have a good time.

Dean   So why'd you come?

Beat. [Because I knew you'd be here.]

Dean   Your tent's a bit crap. Sure it's gonna keep you dry?

Josh   Got nowhere else to sleep. Do I?

He looks to his tent.

Is that you? Inside out? Outside in?

Dean   Maybe.

Josh   I'm trying here, Izz – Dean. I'm trying. Cos I don't, you don't just wake up one morning and . . . !

Dean   I did. I did just wake up one morning and.

Josh   Well that's that then.

Dean   I don't have to explain myself to you.

Josh   No. But you should. You should want to. As your, as your former

Dean   As the artist formerly known as boyfriend.

Josh   Do you always have to make a joke of everything? If you were gonna change something, couldn't it at least have been your sarcasm?

Why are you smiling? It's not funny.

Dean   It is. Us. Here. This. I dunno.

Josh   Right. Well you have a little laugh. I'm gonna join the others.

*He goes to leave, but stops when **Dean** starts speaking.*

Dean   I woke up.

I woke up. I showered.

I woke up. I showered. And then the mirror was just there. Suddenly there. Only it had always been there, but I'd, somehow, I'd managed to never look. To never really look. Little tricks to avoid myself. But this day, I was there

reflecting back, naked. And it took a minute, prolly only
seconds, but felt like ages before I realised it was me. My
body. And without even thinking I crossed my arms, have
you ever noticed – how I always do that? For as long as I can
remember I've always been doing that. And I tried to make
them go away. I tried to look away. Because I'd never really
looked. But I couldn't. This was me. And I hated it. Because
it wasn't me. Do you understand? My little cousin Adam, you
met him at my aunt's wedding, and she's always complaining
because Adam won't leave it alone – he's five and he won't
stop playing with his willy. Always investigating. I never did.
Never investigated my own body. Why? Why is that? I'm
standing in front of this mirror, the steam fading away,
making the image clearer and clearer, this girl, this woman
staring back at me. And it was like everything clicked into
place. People say your life flashes before your eyes before you
die, well, I wasn't dying but suddenly everything in my life
was playing back.

Mum *and* **Dad** *appear, speak to audience. They can't be seen by*
Dean *or* **Josh**.

Mum   My mother gave her a doll for her sixth birthday, the
one, what's the one, everyone had it, everyone had it but it
was hard to get, but my mother had gone all over town just to
get one, and she opened it up and started screaming: 'I don't
want a doll! I don't want a doll!' Threw it at Granny. It
landed in the lasagne. We laughed about it the next day. But.
Well, the lasagne was ruined.

Dad   When she was five, I took her to the toilets, at a fair,
into the men's, cos Mum wasn't there. At first she tried to use
the urinal. A week later she asked: 'Daddy, when am I going
to grow a willy?'

Mum *and* **Dad** *disappear again.*

Dean   And in the mirror it all just suddenly made sense.
Why I'd always felt a bit . . . wrong. And suddenly in my

head, everything was . . . right. I'd never investigated, because I knew I wouldn't like what I found.

Music can be heard distantly. **Josh** *suddenly does an impromptu dance move – cartwheel, flip, weird dance?*

Dean   What was that?

Josh   Dunno. Couldn't think of what to say . . .

Dean   I can't believe they're getting married. Christ. They should be locked up.

Josh   Both their parents are letting them.

Dean   They should be locked up too.

Josh   I'm still in love with you.

Pause.

Then thunder. Rain starts to piss down.

Shit.

They go into their respective tents.

Shit, there's a – I'm getting – there's a bloody hole.

Dean   It's just water.

Josh   This is a new shirt. It's a bloody bathtub in here.

Dean   If you're gonna be a girl about it. Just come here.

Josh *goes and sits in* **Dean***'s tent. They're close together. Their legs touching.*

Josh   You've got leg hair. Is that the um, the hormones?

Dean   I've always had leg hair, douchbag. I just used to shave it.

Josh   Right. Yeah.

They watch the rain.

Josh *watches* **Dean***.*

Dean   What?

Josh   I bloody hate festivals.

Dean   Yeah. Me too.

Scene Five

*Some actors enter the stage. Put on suit jackets or ties or something smart.
This is the school's* **Senior Management Team**. *Divide the
lines amongst actors as desired.*

Senior Management Team   We the school
We the SMT of the school
must tell you
want to tell you
that we one-hundred-per-cent support you
one hundred per cent of the way.

We the SMT
need to stress
want to stress
that we are a very tolerant school
meaning we will show no tolerance
for those who are not tolerant
meaning we're tolerant of everyone
except those who aren't tolerant.
Meaning we the SMT
and you
we're all going to go through this together.
It's a first for all of us.
We're all transitioning together.
Well not literally.
Not literally, no, we won't actually
my wife wouldn't . . .
Not actually
not literally
but in a manner of speaking.

What we mean
the key
yes the key. This is a key
to the staff toilets
should you
if you feel
if you'd like to use those
if it would make you more comfortable.
It's up to you.
Absolutely. We're not saying
we're definitely not saying you can't use the student loos
definitely not
meaning where you pee is up to you
where you pee is your business
pee where you like.
Within reason.
Within reason.
Pee wherever suits you.
Not literally. You can't actually start peeing in the corridor.
What it boils down to
what it comes down to is . . .

Ofsted are coming.
Literally.
Actually.
Sometime in the next school year.
And there'll be an assembly for them.
Not *for*, just while they're here.
For the students, we don't do things just for Ofsted.
About diversity, and inclusivity, and tolerance.
And we, the SMT, would like you, Dean, to make a speech.

What do you say?

Scene Six

Boys' toilets at school. **Dean** *pees at a urinal.* **Josh** *watches.* **Dean** *finishes, and turns around.*

Dean   How long have you been standing there?

Josh   Why are you avoiding me?

Dean   Were you watching me? That's a bit –

Josh   Been trying to speak to you all week, you haven't answered my texts, I have to follow you into the boys' toilets to actually get to you talk to me.

Dean   That's a bit

Josh   Determined.

Dean   I was gonna go with stalkerish.

Josh   Ever since the festival

Dean   There's never any soap in here.

Josh   I thought it was good, I thought we were

Dean   Why is there never any soap?

Josh   And then in the morning you went all

Dean   You don't have any hand sanitiser, do you?

Josh   Do you have to be such a dick about it?

You just gonna pretend nothing happened? That we didn't – ?

Dean   Yes that's exactly what I'm going to do.

Josh   I don't get you Dean.

Dean   Sometimes I don't get me either, alright.

Can you move please? I have class.

Josh   No. Not until we – you don't get to just, just make all the decisions. You don't get to pretend it didn't happen. I, I am part of that decision.

Dean   Josh, move.

Josh   No.

Dean   You gonna trap me in here?

Josh   Yes. Yes that's exactly what I'm going to do. (*He stands in a pose as barrier, re-poses to something tougher – hands on hips?, re-poses again, can't quite get it right.*)

Dean *laughs.*

Josh   Don't laugh. This is serious. This is, this is kidnapping, this is illegal, this is this is, this is fucking *no one's leaving this fucking toilet till I get some answers!*

Beat. He realises how ridiculous he is.

Josh   Christ, I can't even pull off a takeover in the school toilets. How am I ever going to be a detective?

Your fly.

Dean*'s fly is undone.*

Dean   Thanks Miss Marple. (*Re. crotch/peeing.*) It's a tube thing before you ask. That's how.

Josh   I wasn't going to ask.

Dean   Yes you were.

Josh   No.

Dean   You were thinking it.

Josh   I was thinking it, but I wasn't going to ask.

Beat. They smile.

Dean *takes an audition poster off the wall / stall door.*

Dean   The Year 9s are doing *Twelfth Night* again.

Woolner has a limited repertoire.

Josh   Worked for us, didn't it?

'Want me to help you practise your lines?'

Dean   You're such a cheeseball.

Josh   Rehearsed it the whole night before. Couldn't even look at you. 'Want me to help you practise your lines?'

Dean   You're an idiot.

Josh
'What a deal of scorn looks beautiful
In the contempt and anger of his lip!'

Dean
'We men may say more, swear more, but indeed
Our shows are more than will, for still we prove
Much in our vows, but little in our love.'

Josh   I thought we were good.

Dean   Your acting was a bit ropey.

Josh   At the festival. I thought we were back on track. When we

Dean   I'd been drinking.

Josh   You invited me to sleep in your tent.

Dean   Yours had turned into a wading pool.

Josh   You said, after, you said how we'd still go away gap year. 'Course,' you said. Go to Thailand like we planned. Bum around on the beach, get shitfaced, bathe in the sea, go see the ladyboys of Bangkok, / swim in the

Dean   / I definitely never said anything about the ladyboys of / Bangkok

Josh   / and then we get back to school and you go all –

I won't just pretend it didn't happen. The festival.

Dean   But you want to pretend it's the same as before. Like nothing's changed.

Josh   That's not true.

Dean   You're not gay, Josh. You said it yourself.

Josh   So?

Dean   So! What do you mean 'so'?

Josh   I mean so. Why do you have to put a label on everything? I want you. What does the rest of it matter?

Dean   It just. It matters.

Josh   What are you so afraid of?

Dean   I don't know. I don't . . .

I hated *Twelfth Night* you know.

Josh   What?

Dean   I'm just saying.

Everyone all happy, getting married, just hated it. And that line. When Viola says: 'Conceal me what I am.' I always thought it should be: Conceal me what I'm not. Conceal me what I'm not.

This is who I am, Josh. It can't be like before. I'm trying to protect you.

Josh   From what?

Dean   Me. Them. It'll be worse for you, Josh. Worse for you than me. They'll give you a harder time than me.

Josh   Fuck 'em. Fuck 'em.

Dean   And if it's not them, it'll be me. The hormones, they're, I'm moody, and tired, and my sex drive is out of control –

Josh   I can cope with that.

Dean   And I'm, emotionally, I'm on a fucking other planet, I'm a concrete wall, and when I'm not, I'm a goddamn waterfall, I just start, out of nowhere, and I've got like a hundred doctors, and my fucking parents, and my fucking sister, and the fucking school and their fucking equality policies they want *me* to update, and I'm a complete – like you said, I'm a complete dick. Okay? Right now, I'm just a, a complete fucking dick.

Josh Well, be my fucking dick. Be my dick, Dean.

Beat. **Dean** *takes* **Josh**'s *hands. They're back together.*

Josh Some stories have a happy ending, Dean. You're allowed to give yourself a happy ending.

Scene Seven

Mum *and* **Dad**.

Dad I bought lots of books.

Mum I read her lots of books.

Dad I like to read up on things to really understand, what's what – I'm a scientist, how my brain works.

Mum You're not a – you work in computers.

Dad Need to understand the logic. The whys and wherefores. Only no one really knows.

Mum There's no science.

Dad There are theories that it's the shape of the brain. The bed nucleus of the *stria terminalis*. Or could just be her environment. How she was nurtured.

Mum No, we did everything by the book.

Dad I've read every book on the subject. And you know what I learned in the end?

Mum Once upon a time, there was a girl. The girl was given everything she was supposed to. Pretty dresses, and pretty toys, and pretty ballet slippers. And pink wallpaper.

Dad   Left her alone for a day, seven hours, she was ten. Walked to B&Q and back. We came home. She'd painted over all the wallpaper. She'd painted her room black.

Mum   Ballet class and gymnastics and horseback riding – we signed her up for everything, so don't give me your nurture bullshit. She sucked at my nipples for eighteen months. What the hell did you do?

Dad   There was a point I thought she might be – it crosses your mind as a parent – I thought she might be a lesbian.

Mum   We both did.

Dad   She was never a girly girl.

Mum   They were playing classics at the Picturehouse. She was thirteen, just after she – around the time of the counselling.

Dad   Dr Learner.

Mum   And so we made an effort. A family trip. *Rebel Without a Cause*. And she fell in love. Poster on her wall of James Dean. And I thought, yes, yes! Normal. This is what normal teenage girls do – they put posters on their wall.

Dad   Arrived one day. In the post. An A1 James Dean.

Mum   We followed the books and we succeeded.

Dad   Two months earlier she'd tried to kill herself. I think she'd self-harmed before, but we didn't know.

Pause.

Mum   Once upon a time . . .

Once upon . . .

There's a line in the film. *Rebel Without a Cause*. The dad of the girl says: 'All of a sudden she's a problem.' And she, the wife, says: 'She'll outgrow it dear, it's just the age. It's just the age where nothing fits.'

I've only seen the film once. But I still remember that line.

Scene Eight

Split scene: **Dean***'s room and various doctors' offices. We watch three actors put on doctors' coats to become* **Doctors Monroe**, **Bogart** *and* **Brando***. The scene should become more and more physical and surreal as it goes on. It should feel by the end that* **Dean** *is engaged in a workout.*

Monroe   Diagnosis is important, to get access to treatment

Bogart   Transgender, Gender Dysphoria

Brando   Gender Identity Disorder

Monroe   Gender nonconformity.

Bogart   Assessments:

Monroe   Psychodiagnostic and psychiatric

Bogart   Social

Brando   Physical.

Monroe   To prepare you for

Bogart   Full transition

Monroe   Treatment

Brando   Surgery.

Bogart   Take a seat

Monroe   Take a seat

Brando   Take a seat.

James Dean   Look how you're sitting. Lean back. Like you own the place. More.

But don't slouch.

Put an arm on the back of the chair.

Let your wrist flop. Not that much.

Open your legs. Guys take up a lot of room.

Yeah. Sorta. Look, watch me, kid.

Your turn.

Dean *copies his sit.*

James Dean   You look like you're constipated.

Dean   It's easy for you, alright. It's natural. You don't need to think about it.

James Dean   You think this is natural? It's all performance, kid. I learned it. Now try again.

Monroe   When did you first have dysphoric feelings?

Bogart   Will your parents be coming to any appointments? It would be useful to speak to them as well.

Monroe   Are you in a relationship? Girlfriend? Boyfriend?

Brando   I'll refer you to Dr Monroe

Monroe   I'll refer you to Dr Bogart

Bogart   I'll refer you to Dr Brando

Brando   It'll be just fine, Dean. Just breathe.

James Dean   Breathe deep. Gotta speak from the back of your throat, your chest.

Hum down, head down, then bring your head up.

Again.

Again.

Really open your throat.

Monroe   Need you to open up. Need to ask how it felt? How it feels?

James Dean   'Boy, if I had one day when I didn't have to be all confused and I didn't have to feel ashamed of everything. I felt that I belonged someplace, you know?'

Dean   That's my favourite part of the film.

James Dean   Your turn.

Dean (*American accent*)   Boy, if I had one day

James Dean   Not in my accent, crazy.

Dean (*back in own accent*)   Boy, if I had one day

James Dean   Lower.

Dean   Boy, if I had one day

James Dean   Lower

Dean   Boy, if I had

James Dean   Guys got less inflection. More monotone.

Dean   Boy, if I had one day when I didn't have to be all confused and I didn't have to feel ashamed of everything. I felt that I belonged someplace, you know?

Monroe   I do. Yeah.

James Dean   Yeah. We're getting there.

Monroe   Dean. Can I ask about the scars on your arms?

Dean *standing.* **Brando** *measures his chest.*

James Dean   What you doin' with your arms?

Dean   I dunno!

James Dean   Monotone.

Dean   I dunno.

James Dean   Well, gotta put 'em somewhere. Put your hands in your pocket. Walk.

Not so straight, your hips'll sway. Imagine an invisible line.

Doctors *roll out the measuring tape on the floor.*

James Dean   You wanna be walking a foot either side of that.

Dean *does.*

Brando   Keep the partying to a minimum. Drugs, alcohol – they can mess with your testosterone.

James Dean   T-time.

Hands needle. **Dean** *injects.*

Brando   Some of it's irreversible. You can expect

Doctors   Body-hair growth

Scalpel-hair loss

Increased muscle mass

Body-fat redistribution

Skin oiliness

Clitoral enlargement

James Dean   Lean back.

Doctors   Body-hair growth

James Dean   Hum down

Doctors   Scalpel-hair loss

James Dean   Monotone

Doctors   Increased muscle mass

James Dean   Pocket

Doctors   Body-fat redistribution

James Dean   Invisible line

Doctors   Skin oiliness

James Dean   Lower

Doctors   Clitoral enlargement

James Dean   Again.

Lean back

Doctors   Body-hair growth

James Dean   Hum down

Doctors   Scalpel-hair loss

James Dean   Monotone

Doctors   Increased muscle mass

James Dean   Pocket

Doctors   Body-fat redistribution

James Dean   Invisible line

Doctors   Skin oiliness

James Dean   Lower

Doctors   Clitoral enlargement

James Dean   Again.

Bogart   Have you seen Dr Monroe yet?

Laura *and* **Josh** *appear.*

James Dean (*keeps repeating underneath* **Laura**, **Josh** *and* **Doctors**)   Invisible, Pocket, Mono, Lean, Low, Hum, T, Again.

Laura   Don't forget to bring a naughty parcel for the hen-do. I've got her this hilarious penis-hat to wear all evening. It's gonna be a riot.

Josh   Don't forget to bring booze for the stag. We've got him a naughty nurse's outfit he's got to wear all evening. And a fourteen-stone stripper. Gonna be brilliant.

Brando   For you it would be a bilateral mastectomy.

Bogart   Horizontal incisions across each breast.

Monroe   Peel skin

Brando   Remove mammary glands and fatty tissue

Bogart   Remove the areola, nipples

Monroe   Trim

Bogart   Then regraft them on to the chest in a male position

Brando   And you'll be home in time for supper.

Monroe   How does that sound?

James Dean *and* **Doctors** *(can be divided up or in unison)*
Skin, trim, hair, T, lean, line, low, again.

Skin, trim, hair, T, lean, low, again.

Brando   I can schedule the chest surgery for 12th June.

Dean   Perfect. I've got a wedding late June.

Brando   Haha. No, not this June. 2016.

Dean   Two years?

Brando   See you then.

Things speed up.

James Dean, Doctors, Laura *and* **Josh** *(can be divided up or in unison)*   Skin, trim, hair, T, lean, line, low, penis-hat, stripper, again.

Skin, trim, hair, 'T', lean, line, low, penis-hat, stripper, again.

Again. Again. Again. Again. Again.

Dean *emerges, stands calmly, collected. At ease with his male self.*

Dean   I felt that I belonged someplace, you know?

Beat.

James Dean, Doctors, Laura *and* **Josh** *all disappear and are replaced with* **Mum, Dad** *and* **Private Doctor**.

Mum   We agreed to go along

Dad   Dean had found a doctor, a private doctor.

Mum   She was very nice. I don't know what I was expecting. Frankenstein or something.

Private Doctor Lots of people go private for the same reason. Shorter wait times.

Dad She explained the procedure.

Mum She *was* very nice.

Private Doctor 30th August of this year, okay Dean?

Don't forget, you'll need to pay by the 29th.

Five thousand nine hundred twenty-five pounds.

Mum Once upon a time there was a witch who could turn the princess into anything.

Dad Photos. What it would look like after. Without . . .

Mum And I'm sorry. If that's what she wants to do. If she wants to mutilate her – then that's her prerogative. But we're certainly not going to bankroll it. When Sharon's daughter got a tattoo, do you think she paid for it?

Dad This isn't a tattoo.

Mum No. It's worse.

Dad And these photos. All these *after* photos. And I thought

Mum I'm sorry.

Dad All these daughters. All these. Not just ours.

Scene Nine

Dean's *room.* **Dani** *is in there.* **Dean** *has just entered.*

Dean Dani.

Dani They're fighting again.

Dean What are you doing?

Dani Nothing. Just, y'know. Looking.

Dean Don't look through my stuff, alright?

Dani   I'm your younger sister. I'm meant to look through your stuff. I've done it for years.

Dean   Well, stop.

Dani   I thought maybe I could have your old clothes.

Dean   I got rid of them already.

Dani   I noticed.

Dean   Well . . . can you get out of here then?

Beat.

Dani *holds up a pair of boxer briefs.*

Dani   Where did you get these?

Dean   It's weird you going through my underwear.

Dani   *I'm* weird?

Dean   Don't go through my stuff.

Dani   Where'd you get them?

Dean   Why?

Dani   Topman. Says so on the price tag.

Why'd you steal them?

Dean   What?

Dani   'Cause they're expensive, these. Especially when you only get six-fifty an hour at Tesco. Expensive when you're saving up for an operation that costs six grand. Heard Dad say. Should buy your underwear from M&S. Much better value for money. Then you wouldn't have to steal.

Dean   I don't know what you're talking about.

Dani *produces a security tag from her pocket.*

Dani   The security tag was on it.

Dean   What do you want?

Dani   Why'd you steal them?

Dean   I didn't.

Dani   You used to tell me stuff. But now you . . .

Fine. I'll just tell Mum and Dad and you can tell them why.

She goes to leave.

Dean   I panicked. I just . . . panicked. I was going to the till, and all these young men behind with their biceps, and rolled-up sleeves with bits of armpit hair sticking out, and designer beards, and the line of hair below their belly button when they absently start scratching, the band of their own Calvin Kleins and what if I get up there to pay and they . . .

Dani   And they know.

Beat. **Dani** *hands* **Dean** *the underwear.*

Dani   I stole a dress last month 'cause it was ridiculously overpriced and I just wanted to see if I could. My friend taught me how to get the security tag off.

She hands **Dean** *the security tag.*

Dani   So we're not that different, you and me. (*Of poster.*) You sort of look like him.

Dean   You think?

Dani   Sort of. Not really.

You remember when we all went to see that film altogether? Don't think we've done anything altogether since. Don't think we've been happy since.

I found this hidden in your wardrobe. (*Photo album.*) The trip to the south of France when I was nine. Spent every day swimming. Look. We even had matching swimsuits. Do you remember? 'Cause if Mum bought it for you, she had to buy it for me. Do you remember? (*Laughs.*) And those hideous polkadot long-sleeve dresses. So we cut the sleeves off – Mum was so angry. (*Laughs harder.*) Remember?

Look.

Dean   I don't want to.

Dani   We were happy then.

Dean   I wasn't. I wasn't happy then.

Dani   You were.

Dean   No.

Dani   I was there. There are pictures! Look! We're smiling.

Dean   Still

Dani   Not still. I was there!

Dean   It wasn't the same for me.

Dani   You can't just change everything! You can't just change history, Izzy.

Dean   Don't call me that.

Dani   They're my memories too. It's my life too. You can't just say it wasn't what it was and that's that – it's not some fucking video game you can just start again, new character, like none of it ever happened.

Dean   I'm not saying it didn't happen. I'm just saying it wasn't the same for me.

Dani   That's not fair.

Dean   No. But it's true.

Dani   We had matching swimsuits. We were a pair. The Cheeky Girls we called ourselves. (*Sings.*) 'We are the cheeky girls, we are the cheeky girls, you are the – '

Dean   I hated that swimsuit.

Dani   We cut the sleeves off our dresses. Mum was so –

Dean   I wished I could've cut the whole thing up.

Dani   No. No, Izzy.

Dean   Stop calling me that.

Dani   I have pictures, Izzy. We're smiling.

Dean   Don't call me that.

Dani   Izzy, Izzy, Dizzy Izzy, Isabella!

Dean *grabs the photo album. Rips a page from it. Scrunches/rips it up.*

Dani   Stop it! Stop it!

But **Dean** *is on a mission.*

He grabs the James Dean poster. Rips it down the middle. Runs out.

He stops himself crying by focusing on mantra.

Dean   Invisible. Pocket. Mono. Lean. Low. Hum. T. Again.

He calmly gets some scissors and cuts Izzy out of one of the photos as he repeats his mantra.

Invisible. Pocket. Mono. Lean. Low. Hum. T. Again.

Scene Ten

Later. **Josh** *has just entered. Cut-up photos are all over the floor.*

Dean   What's five thousand nine hundred and twenty-five divided by two?

Josh   Why does it look like Instagram vomited all over your room? I got you something.

Dean   That's like . . . that's like three thousand a month, which is . . .

Josh   A present.

Dean   Fifteen hundred a week.

Josh   Here.

Dean   Which is like, with my six-fifty a Tesco hour, that's like, that's like

Josh   Over two hundred hours.

Dean   Two hundred hours. How the hell am I gonna work two hundred hours a week?

Josh   You're not. There aren't two hundred hours in a week.

Dean   What the hell am I meant to do?

Josh   Are you not going to open my present?

Dean   I could buy lottery tickets.

Josh   Dean.

Dean   No you're right, that's completely, the odds are against me. Something less risky.

I could rob a bank.

Josh   That's a brilliant idea.

Dean   I could start an online business, and sell, sell – I could sell my old underwear. People pay big money for that you know.

Josh   Dean, that's weird. Would you just open

Dean   Yes, Yes, I'll open the damn –

Josh   There's a card.

Dean (*opens it*)   *Happy Anniversary*. Shit. Sorry. Shit.

Josh   I don't care.

Dean   I've just been completely wrapped up in

Josh   I know. Honestly, I don't care.

Dean (*opens gift*)   Lonely Planet Thailand.

Sorry, I didn't . . . Sorry. I'm crap.

Josh (*affectionately*)   I know. But you're my crap.

Look, they've got a whole chapter just on beaches. I thought we could start planning, y'know. Make it like a thing. A date. Each week we read one of the chapters, plan stuff.

Dean That sounds great. Though at this rate I won't be going.

Josh What do you mean?

Dean Well the tiny bit I've saved so far now's gotta go to the surgery, right? And if I can't get the money together by August, might have to have the surgery in the autumn or the winter.

Josh But we're leaving 1 September. That was the plan.

Dean Plan might have to change.

Josh You can have the surgery when you get back.

Dean That's not an option.

Josh I don't get what the hurry is.

Dean The hurry is I've already spent more than seventeen years like this.

Josh So what's one more year?

Dean . . . What?

Josh Maybe there's a reason the other wait list is two years, maybe you should just wait, you're meant to wait, and when we come back then you can see if you still . . .

Dean Still what?

Josh . . . There's nothing wrong with the way you are now.

Dean Oh my God. What you think – have you been hoping all this time I'd suddenly – what – that this is a phase or something?

Josh No.

Dean Oh, I've seen sense, pass me the dress and make-up!

Josh No! That's not fair Dean!

Dean What's not fair is having to wake up with these every day.

Josh I'm just saying how it is now is fine, you don't need to

Dean Fine for who?

Josh I'm trying here, Dean.

Dean Try harder.

Josh I have, I have, I have . . . Well, I've done loads, haven't I? I'm here, aren't I?

This affects both of us.

Dean This?

Josh And I'm sorry, okay, but the thought of you, I'm okay with this, I love this, but the thought of you . . . mutilating your body . . . the thought of you without . . . it just, it just . . . freaks me out a bit.

Pause.

Dean

Dean Get out.

Josh Don't be

Dean Get out, Josh.

Josh Let's talk about this. We'll figure something out.

Dean Stay away from me.

Josh I love you, Dean.

Dean (*grabs scissors, holds out*)   I said stay the fuck away from me.

Get out. (*Holds scissors to breasts.*) Or I'll cut them off myself.

Josh *exits.*

Dean *drops the scissors, starts crying. Sorts himself out in the mirror repeating mantra quietly to himself. Puts on some music. Buddy Holly's 'Everyday' like at the start. Gels his hair. Sprays some Lynx. Grabs a box/piggy bank. Takes a handful of cash from it.*

Scene Eleven

Voicemail.

Senior Management Team   Dean, we're just checking in
checking up really
making sure you're alright
making sure everything's alright
'cause you've been absent for the past three weeks
so we wanted to make sure everything's okay . . .

And to inform you that the warning came
the call came
they're coming. Ofsted.
Which means the assembly
and you haven't given us your speech
which is fine
we totally trust you
absolutely
we just want to double-check you're still game
still on board
still alive and well.

And getting better.

Get well soon.

And if you could get better by Monday at two p.m. well then
all the better.

Scene Twelve

Dean*'s bedroom.* **Dean** *looks a bit worse for wear. He's been
partying hard the last couple weeks.* **Laura***'s just entered.*

Laura   What happened to your sick poster? I wanted to
borrow it.

Dean   What for?

Laura   For the wedding. Would work brilliantly with the decor. We could tape it.

Dean   Um. Maybe.

Laura   Who have you been out partying with?

Dean   No one. I haven't.

Laura   Sorry to just like, but I've left you like, literally a hundred messages. And no one's seen you. And you've missed a bunch of Tesco shifts.

Dean   I've been here studying.

Laura   Then why are you like dressed? Who have you been out with?

Dean   I've been here.

Laura   Dean.

Dean   No one, Laura.

Laura   Well, you look a bit like a Pete Doherty–Amy Winehouse love child.

So. Anyway. It's a bit awkward, but it's just best to come right out and say it. I'm a bit concerned about you and Josh.

Dean   Oh. Thanks. But you don't need to be.

Laura   But I do. Literally. 'Cause you're meant to be partners, walking back up the aisle after. And I'm concerned really, that your not talking could affect the dynamic.

Dean   I'm not gonna get back together just for the sake of a wedding march.

Laura   No. Course. That would be. Just. It might ruin the wedding. And I wouldn't want you to feel guilty, to feel responsible for ruining the most important day of their lives, that's all.

Dean   I won't.

Laura   Good, no. I just don't – like if it ends in divorce, don't want you to feel that you could've prevented it.

Dean   Laura, I'm sure I can walk down the aisle with Josh, smiles and all.

Laura   Good. Well that is a re-lief.

Dean   Is that why you came over?

Laura   No. I came. To show you . . . this! (*Pulls out poodle skirt and bow.*) What do you think?

Dean   Yeah. You'll look great in it.

Laura   Aww. Actually. It's not for me.

Dean   Who's it for?

Laura   Um. Well.

Pause.

Look Dean. We all support you one hundred per cent. Really. But this is their wedding day and I was chatting with Amy's mum and we both agree that, well, it could take the attention away from Amy and Kyle. Steal the limelight. You understand.

Dean   I'm not wearing a skirt.

Laura   It's just for one day.

Dean   Do you know what you're asking me?

Laura   Definitely. I definitely do. And I wouldn't if it were any other day.

Dean   Does Amy know about this?

Laura   She's got enough to worry about.

Dean   I can't. No.

Laura   Sure. I understand. It's just. Her mum said. Dean, you can't come to the wedding then. I'm really sorry.

I'll just. (*Leaves outfit.*) It's just one day, right?

She exits.

Dean *takes more money from his piggy bank / box.*

James Dean *appears.*

James Dean   I thought you were saving that money.

Dean   I thought you were dead.

James Dean   Why? 'Cause she ripped the poster? I'm James Dean, buddy. I don't die. Not really.

Where are you going?

Dean   I'm not.

James Dean   Who are you going with?

Dean   What are you – my mum? If I'd wanted a mother figure I'd have dreamt up Audrey Hepburn or someone instead of you.

James Dean *(impersonating Hepburn)*   'I don't want to own anything until I find a place where me and things go together. I'm not sure where that is but I know what it is like. It's like Tiffany's.'

Dean   You weren't even alive any more when that came out.

James Dean   Ouch. So why are you ignoring them? Your friends?

Dean   I'm not ig – It's complicated. You wouldn't understand.

James Dean   Try me.

Dean   . . . I just went in. I don't know what I was planning.

Sound / light from the bar / memory filters through, so it's like **Dean***'s there.*

To get shit-faced and forget him and snog some random maybe. But I . . . walked in, started talking to these young guys and they went to buy me a drink. And so I stood alone waiting in some crappy disco lights in a place that smelled of sweat and piss and farts, and I realised: they don't know anything about me. No one here does.

The disco light/sound goes, so we're back in the bedroom.

When I'm with them I feel like . . . I can forget.

James Dean   So you're just gonna cut off your friends? Forget them?

Dean   But that's just it. Maybe they're not my friends. Maybe they're her friends.

Scene Thirteen

Men's toilets at a bar. **Dean** *turns around from a urinal to find* **Kyle** *standing there.*

Kyle (*speaking into mobile phone as if it's a walkie talkie*)   Got him. Read: Subject has been located.

Dean   Kyle, what are you doing here?

Amy *enters.*

Kyle (*speaks into mobile*)   Subject identified.

Amy   You don't need to talk into your phone, I'm right here.

Dean   Amy? You know you're in the men's toilets.

Amy   You know you haven't returned my calls or texts. Literally not a single one.

Dean   Sorry, I've been . . . busy.

Amy   Is it drugs? Alcohol?

Dean   What?

Amy   Well, there must be some teenage cliché going on, which has forced us to stage an intervention.

Dean   Oh. Is that what this is? How'd you find me?

Amy   Let's just say we have our ways, we know people.

Kyle   Your dad told us. Maybe we should go outside.

Amy   I'm not letting him out of my sight.

Kyle   But we're not really supposed to be in here. It's a bar.

Amy   What kind of bar has board games by the way?
People getting pissed playing Connect 4.

Kyle   Just, if we get caught . . . I mean we're – (*whispering*)
under age.

Amy   We're GETTING MARRIED, for God's sake.

Kyle   And if you're caught in the gents, you could get
arrested.

Amy   Well, at least if I'm in prison I can stop talking about
bloody table decorations. (*To* **Dean**.) What's going on, Dean?
You and Josh break up and then you stop talking to all of us,
just disappear for like weeks and now Laura tells you you
might not come to the wedding? We miss you, Dean.

Dean   . . . I miss you guys too.

Kyle   Great. Sorted. Can we go? We're meant to be at an
hors d'oeuvres tasting in like five minutes. (*To* **Dean**.) We've
been here like an hour. Amy didn't want to cause a scene in
front of your new friends. So I've been waiting in here ages.
One guy even called the manager to say there was a perv just
sitting eating crisps in the toilets.

Amy   So who are they? That guy in the coveralls –

Dean   Bart.

Amy   – is he your boyfriend?

Dean   I guess he's . . .

Josh *jumps out of one of the stalls (or wherever he's hidden).*

Josh   That hipster-douche is your boyfriend?

Dean   What the hell?

Amy   How long have you been hiding in there?

Kyle?

Kyle   I wanted someone to keep me company. (*To* **Josh**.) You promised not to come out, mate.

Amy   I cannot believe you. I actually cannot like literally look at you right now, Kyle.

Kyle   You are looking at me.

Amy   It's a mirror. It doesn't count.

Josh   Bart? Bart? As in Simpson?

Dean   As in the Apostle actually. Bartholomew.

Josh   You dumped me for a guy in a farmer's dungarees!

Dean   Just because I find someone who's funny and chilled out and nice to me and doesn't hide in toilets –

Josh   Does he know?

Dean   Does he know what?

Josh   Think if I go and tell him he'll still be so nice and funny and chilled out?

Dean   Do you always have to be such a douche? All of the time?

Josh   *I'm* a douche? I was peering at that guy for like the last hour. *He's* the douche. The king of douchebags. The *apostle* of douchebags.

Kyle   We should probably go, Amy.

Amy   I said I'm not looking at you.

Kyle   Yeah, but you can still hear me right?

Amy   If I hear the words 'seat-cover' or 'party favours' once more, I swear to God I will divorce you before the wedding. Dean, can I ring you tonight? Will you pick up?

Dean   Yeah. Yeah.

Kyle   Later, guys.

Amy *and* **Kyle** *exit.*

Josh   We should talk.

Dean   Ever noticed how your talks always need to happen in toilets? A metaphor for how piss-poor your talking is and the crap that comes out of your mouth. You're one of those turds that just won't go down. No matter how many times I flush you away, you magically keep reappearing.

Josh   I still care about you, Dean.

Dean   Well, stop. Hiding? Spying on me? What is wrong with you?

Josh   What is wrong with *you*? You don't even know this guy.

Dean   It has nothing to do with you, Josh.

Josh   He could be a . . . proper mental case, kill you in the night.

Dean   Well, he hasn't killed me in the night yet.

Josh   You've spent the night with him?

Dean   What do you want, Josh?

Josh   He could be part of some crazy paedophile ring.

Dean   He's fifteen!

Josh   What kind of name is Bartholomew anyway? What is he, a pirate?

Dean   Yeah, he's a pirate.

Josh   Really?

Dean   No, Josh. Now please just go home and leave us alone.

Josh   Us? So you're an us?

Dean   You know what, I don't care, stay here. Stay in the toilets. Write poetry about your genitals on the wall.

He goes to leave.

Josh   The plane tickets came.

Dean   What?

Josh   Thailand. Ordered them months ago. Well, they arrived.

Dean   No, no, you don't get to – this is what you do. I sort things out, I finally get shit in my life together and then you come along and fuck everything up again.

Josh   I haven't – I'm just telling you the tickets arrived. And I don't know what to do. Tell me what to do, Dean.

Dean   Sometimes you need to figure out what to do for yourself.

Josh   Yeah. Yeah. I know. So I researched, I went online, and they say . . . it's normal.

Beat.

That I'm normal . . .

Dean   You're . . . ?

Josh   How I reacted. And they . . . I think you need to be more patient with me.

I was, I was, all things considered, quite patient with you. And you were quite . . . selfish. So.

Pause.

And I think I've been, all things considered, I was, I've been a really tolerant person. So . . . yeah.

Pause. **Dean** *moves slowly towards* **Josh***, stands close. Looks him in the eye.* **Josh** *(and we) think* **Dean** *might even hug him, or kiss him.*

But then **Dean** *punches* **Josh** *in the chest.*

Josh   Ow.

Dean *hits* **Josh** *again.*

Josh   Dean, that really hurts.

Dean *hits him again.*

Dean   Hit me.

Josh   What?

Dean   You wanna sort this out? Is that why you came here?

Josh   I guess I –

Dean   Is it?

Josh   I s'pose.

Dean   Then let's sort this out. Hit me.

Josh   I'm not gonna –

Dean *hits* **Josh** *again.*

Dean   What? Not gonna fight back? Be a man, Josh.

He hits **Josh** *again.*

Josh   Ow, I'm not gonna

Dean *hits* **Josh** *again.*

Dean   You wanna sort this out? Keep your *tolerance* and fight back.

He hits **Josh** *again.*

Dean   Fight.

And again.

Back.

Josh   Stop! I'm not gonna hit a . . .

Dean   A what? A what, Josh?

Hits again.

Say it! Say it!

Hits again.

Josh   Stop it!

Dean   I dare you. Say it!

Hits again.

Josh   Stop it!

Dean   Or (*hits*) hit me! (*Keeps hitting.*) 'I'm not gonna hit a – ' say it!

Josh   Stop it!

Josh *punches* **Dean** *in the face.* **Josh** *is as shocked as* **Dean** *is.*

Josh   Shit. Sorry, sorry.

Pause.

Dean (*genuine*)   Thank you.

Josh *goes.*

Scene Fourteen

School assembly. **Dean** *has a black eye.*

Dean   Good afternoon students, teachers, and visitors from Ofsted.

Our school prides itself on tolerance. You can be who you want to be and we will tolerate you. It says so in a policy document in a drawer somewhere.

We learn in history about a black woman who decided one day to sit where she wanted to on a bus.

We learn about another woman who chained herself to parliament.

We learn about some angry drag queens in a bar who fought back one night.

We learn that to be tolerant of every person is what we should aspire to. A badge of honour we can wear. *I am a tolerant person.*

Fuck tolerance.

Those people – the black lady on the bus, the woman in chains, those men in heels. They weren't fighting for tolerance. To be tolerated.
Because tolerance is horseshit.

Tolerance is the emptiest word in the dictionary.

Tolerate is what you do when someone's playing their music loudly on the bus.
Tolerate is what you do when someone's texting next to you in the cinema.
I don't want to be tolerated.

I want to be admired.
I want to be envied.
I want to be . . . loved.

Love me.

And if that's too much to ask. Then hate me.
But don't tolerate me.
Because tolerance means sweet fuck all.

Scene Fifteen

Amy's *bedroom.* **Kyle** *wears a wedding dress.*

Josh   What the fuck?

Kyle   The band cancelled. Lead singer's getting a hip replacement.

Josh   You're wearing a dress.

Kyle   Yeah.

Josh   Okay.

Kyle   Yeah. So we've had to get a new band.

Josh   Guess that's what happens when you get a band who were actually playing in the 1950s.

Kyle   So we've had to get impersonators. Buddy Hollister and the Abercrombies. Who were only born in like 1992 . . . so just not as authentic. Like what will these kids actually know?

Josh   Why are you wearing a wedding dress?

Kyle   I don't like surprises. Couldn't leave it to chance.

Josh   Oh. But why'd you put it on?

Kyle   Not sure.

Josh   I thought it's bad luck to see the dress before.

Kyle   No, bad luck to see the bride *in* the dress.

Josh   Groom in the dress is alright then.

Kyle *puts on the veil.*

Josh   Amy could walk in any second.

Kyle   No, she's watching *Don't Tell the Bride*, analysing all the things that could go wrong.

Josh   Gonna be perfect.

Kyle   No surprise punches.

Josh   There won't be.

Kyle   I mean you and Dean. Walking down the aisle.

Lift up the veil for me.

He does.

Is it easy?

Josh   What?

Kyle   The lifting. What if it gets stuck?

Josh It won't.

Kyle Gets caught in my cufflink and I can't raise it up?

Josh It's gonna be perfect. (*Starts to cry.*)

Kyle Save it for the day, mate. Tears look great on camera.

Josh I fucked up. I royally – I always thought we'd get married. One day. Maybe after Thailand, uni. Find a flat, move in together. Grow old together. That was the plan. And I fucked it up.

Kyle If you have a plan, you could make it happen.

Josh Sorry to break it to you, Kyle, but sometimes plans don't go to plan. Sometimes, no matter what you wish for or plan for, what you get . . . you just get a shit fifties knock-off band.

There are days when I'm like, I can do this. It's all normal. It's just a pronoun. And then suddenly I think it's all – and I think about Izzy and what we – and I don't know if I can handle it.

Dean *appears on the other side of the mirror.*

Kyle Do you love him?

Josh . . . Yeah. Yeah.

Kyle Then unfuck it up.

Beat as **Dean** *and* **Josh** *stare at each other through the mirror. Then* **Josh** *and* **Kyle** *go.*

Scene Sixteen

Dean's *bedroom.*

Dean *holds up the poodle skirt and bow in front of himself in the mirror.* **James Dean** *appears.*

James Dean You know that skirt is so last century, right?

Dean (*in an American accent*)   'Y'know. I bet you're a real yoyo.'

James Dean   'I love you too.'

I saw your little speech.

Dean   What'd you think?

James Dean   You've got balls. I'm proud of you, kid.

Dean   It just sorta came out . . . the words.

Both   But it felt . . . I felt . . . for the first time I was really . . . me.

James Dean   Gimme those.

Dean   I haven't got anything else to wear to the wedding.

James Dean (*takes off his jacket*)   Here.

Dean   What will you wear?

James Dean (*takes skirt and bow*)   These.

He puts on the skirt, puts the bow in his hair. **Dean** *puts on the jacket.*

Dean   Are you coming?

James Dean   Think I'll pass.

Dean   Will you be here when I get back?

Pause.

James Dean   You'll be alright, kid. I think you'll be just fine.

Goodbye, Dean.

Dean   Goodbye, Izzy.

Dean *finds a dollar bill in the jacket pocket. Turns to give it to* **James Dean** *but he's gone. He puts the bill in his now-empty piggy bank/box. A new start.*

Scene Seventeen

Dad   Dani's not coping very well. So. She'll go live with her mother. She found a place not far. She didn't want the house.

Mum   She cut up all the photos. One night when everyone was sleeping. Cut herself out of all of them. If she was in the middle, if it was like a group photo, a family photo, she just cut out her head. Frame after frame after frame of . . . space. The space where my child used to be.

Dad   Book after book after book. And you know what I learned in the end?

Mum   But she missed one. (*Holds photo.*) Forgot to check my wallet. My baby. My baby girl.

Dad   I learned nothing. 'Cause no one has an explanation. But who needs an explanation? He's my . . . my . . .

Mum   My . . .

They switch clothes. So the female actor now plays **Mum**, *the male actor* **Dad**.

Dad   My . . . I still struggle saying *son*. When she was pregnant, I hoped it was a boy. I know you're not supposed to say that. But I did.

Mum   Once upon a time there was a girl. And then there wasn't.

Dad   He's my child. And I love him.

Mum   The guidebooks don't –

When a child dies you mourn. They say losing a child is the hardest of all deaths. They describe the feeling as – the noun they use is loss. Mourning. And when a child goes missing and is never found, you feel you're never able to rest, to properly just live. The noun they use is restlessness.

She starts to cry softly.

My daughter is not dead. My daughter is not missing. But she is gone. And so I don't have the language to describe what I'm feeling. It's not in any of the books. There's no noun for that.

Dad   We went out for dinner the other day, the two of us, and the waiter comes over and he says: 'What can I get you lads to drink?' Two lads. Out for a drink.

Mum   There's a line in the film when she says: 'She'll outgrow it, dear. It's just the age when nothing fits.'

I think that's a lie. 'Cause sometimes you turn forty-one, and still nothing fits like it's supposed to.

I hope . . . I hope he does. I hope Dean . . . fits.

Scene Eighteen

Wedding reception. Everyone wears 50s outfits. **Dean** *looks like James Dean.*

Josh   Nice jacket.

Dean   You think?

Josh   I think.

Dean   Amy's mum was giving me evils.

Josh   No, it suits you. And the colour distracts from your eye.

Dean   Is that meant to be funny?

Josh   Yeah. No. I'm not sure.

Dean   You're useless.

Josh   I know. I'm sorry. 'Bout the eye.

Dean   I asked for it. Literally.

Josh   I'm still sorry. If it's any consolation, my chest still hurts like a bitch. That's some fist.

I liked your speech, by the way.

Dean   Laura wrote most of it. A speech to the tune of 'Summer Lovin'' certainly wasn't my idea.

Josh   I meant your speech at school.

Dean   Oh. Got me two weeks' suspension.

Josh   Still. It was kick-ass.

Dean   Yeah.

Josh   Bartholomew here? Or is he on a ship with a parrot looking for gold?

Dean   I wouldn't know. Call me jean-ophobic but I just couldn't see a future with someone who wears dungarees.

Josh   Here. (*Hands gift bag.*)

Dean   Meant to get a gift for the bride and groom.

Josh   Just open it.

He does. It's a McDonald's Happy Meal box.

Dean   Uhh . . . thanks . . . not sure weddings are really 'bring your own meal'.

Josh   No, inside.

Dean *opens the Happy Meal box. There's lots of money inside.*

Dean   . . .

Josh   Ever since that date we had at McDonald's a couple years ago, when we first talked about spending our gap year together, I kept the box, to remind me. And whenever I could, I'd put savings in there, for our trip. Took it out in cash, put it under my bed, make sure I didn't spend it. There's about three and a half grand. It's over two grand short, but it's all I have.

Dean   Josh.

Josh   And before you even say it, you have to. Okay? You have to take it. 30th August.

Dean   But Thailand.

Josh   Thailand can wait.

Music lingers through from the dancefloor. 'Teenager in Love' by Dion and the Belmonts.

Dean   Josh, I don't know what to . . .

Josh   One last dance?

Dean   You're so melodramatic.

Josh   Just shut up and dance with me.

Dean *approaches. They're unsure where to put their hands . . . who's the boy in the dance? They try a couple of things out and dance.*

Josh   I always thought Olivia should've married Viola, and Sebastian should've married Orsino . . . don't you think?

They keep dancing. The song comes to an end and changes to some cheesy wedding music.

Josh   I fucking hate weddings.

Dean   Me too.

*They stand close. Are about to kiss. When **Amy** runs on in her wedding dress.*

Amy   Save me. If I have to smile for one more photo, I swear to God I'm gonna be the first bride to go berserk and murder all her guests on her wedding day. Kyle's made a spreadsheet of every photo that needs to be taken today. And who thought it would be a good idea to have a five-kilo wedding dress?

Dean   At least you look beautiful.

Amy   I look like a Tinkerbell on steroids.

Josh   Well, at least you look better in it than Kyle.

Amy   What?

Are you eating McDonald's at my wedding?

Kyle *enters, with a clipboard.* **Laura** *follows.*

Kyle   There you are. We're like eleven minutes behind. We're meant to have already cut the tofu cheesecake.

Laura   And everyone's waiting for you to throw the bouquet.

Amy   I can barely lift my arms in this.

Kyle   Oh come on, my little soy-chocolate button. I'll help you.

Kyle *leads here off,* **Amy** *mouths 'Help' behind her.*

Josh   I like your skirt, Laura.

Laura   Thanks. You look good too. You both do. Really.

Don't want to miss the bouquet! (*Exits.*)

Josh   Coming? It'll be fun.

Dean   I'd rather spend eternity eating tofu cheesecake.

Josh   Fair enough.

Josh *exits. Pause.* **Dean** *alone. Distant wedding sounds.*

Dean   Once upon a time.

Josh *runs back in.*

Dean   Josh.

Josh?

Josh *grabs* **Dean***. Kisses him passionately.*

He runs back off. Before he's quite off:

Dean   Josh?

Josh   Yes Dean?

Dean   . . . Catch that bouquet and I'll kill you.

Josh *smiles. And exits.*

Dean   Once upon a time there was a boy.

Pronoun

BY EVAN PLACEY

Notes on rehearsal and staging, drawn from workshops led by two directors and the writer, held at the National Theatre, November 2013

Workshops led by Michael Fentiman and James Grieve with notes by Jane Fallowfield and Pia Furtado

How the writer came to write the play

Evan Placey set out with the intention of writing a play about a transgender teenager. He felt that this story had not yet been told in any plays for young people – or for mainstream audiences – and he wanted to address this.

In researching the play, Evan ran workshops with young people, including a youth group in Ipswich which he turned up to in make-up to get the discussion started! He also went along to a group set up for transgender teens called Gendered Intelligence who begin each session with a 'pronoun circle' when each person in the group introduces themselves and says what pronoun they would like you to use. One boy's story became a particular inspiration for the character of Dean.

Evan didn't want the play to be simply a 'coming out' story. He chose to set the play after Dean had made the decision to identify himself as male and explore what happens next. He also wanted to tell a story about teenage love, which is so potent but often so easily dismissed.

James Dean is a sort of fairy godmother in the play. Evan was interested in asking, where do we learn what we become? James Dean is interesting because he is a figure of rebellion and he is also a bit camp or feminine; it's important that Dean does not aspire to be the butchest boy on the block but instead finds his own masculinity.

At our workshop, Evan urged the directors to focus more on the artistic than the educational aspects of the piece, to strive for truthful and honest storytelling and to try to make the audience root for Josh and Dean to get together.

Themes

You don't need to be an expert on transgender issues to do the play. The actors' experiences of falling in love, arguing with friends and family will all inform their performances. Any research the company do into transgender issues should be focused on the characters and the story rather than giving the production any educational quality.

Evan strongly agrees with Dean's speech about tolerance. It is not enough just to tolerate those around you; this is not the sort of society he wants to live in.

Evan wanted to give 'the queer kid a happy ending'. A transgender teen should be able to have a rom com, they should not have to sacrifice love in return for being happy with who they are. However, there are tragic elements to the ending. Dean's transition has brought about the break-up of his parents, and his mum and sister never come round to his male identity.

Structure

The opening of the play should trick the audience. who are coming in with preconceptions of what the play will be about. They might presume that this boy in the dress is the transgender character but we want to surprise them by revealing that he is just trying to get a feeling of what it must be like for Dean.

Language

Punctuation is important to this play. Often the writer intends for there to be a pacey rhythm to the dialogue. When there is a slash (/) or a dash (−) it should be a tight interruption, which is different to when there is an ellipsis (. . .). These have been used sparingly, so do not allow them to creep in where they are not written.

In the Senior Managment Team scenes, a new line means a new voice.

It is fine to be playful with the awkwardness around referring to Dean as male and to show the characters worrying about whether they have used the right pronoun. This is part of the comedy of the piece.

Evan was asked if the students could alter the language in the play to fit with their young people and the way they express themselves. His response was to try to make it work with the words that are written (douche, hipsters, prolly) – try to develop a character that would speak like this. If that takes you away from who you are as an actor, all the better.

Characters and characterisation

DEAN   Dean has already realised that he wants to identify as male. He has started hormone treatment (the needle in the play is his testosterone jab). When he explains to Josh how he feels, he is not struggling for words, he is absolutely certain that he is making the right decision. Before the play begins, Dean had self-harmed out of confusion and feeling that his life was a mess. His transition is a liberation from this.

JOSH   Josh is a trying to understand what Dean is going through. When Dean accuses him of thinking he is just going through a phase, this is not true. Josh is just freaked out and not sure what to do as Dean gets to the next stage of the transition.

JAMES DEAN   James Dean might be a figment of Dean's imagination, a representation of his male self, a ghost, or all these things. The writer imagines him as a fairy godmother, guiding Dean through.

MUM AND DAD   When they see the photos of the girls who have been through what Dean is going through, Dean's dad is relieved rather than horrified because he realises it is not just their daughter this is happening to. The fractures in Mum and Dad's relationship get bigger at this point.

Casting

There is the potential to use a chorus of actors, most obviously for the Senior Managment Team and Doctors, but you might also consider having several characters playing James Dean or Mum and Dad if you have a large cast. Other moments which lend themselves to ensemble work are Glastonbury, the club and the wedding.

If you need to cast against gender due to the make-up of your group, make sure this doesn't confuse Dean's journey. You could either change the gender of the character (e.g. Laura becomes Lorne) or make sure that the character is not performing their gender in the same way as Dean is; they must seem to inhabit it totally naturally.

Production, staging and design

When the actors are transforming into the adult characters such as Mum, Dad and the Doctors, they should put on one simple item of costume and then forget the fact that they are playing grown-ups and focus instead on the emotional truth of the scene.

The play lends itself to a simple and fluid design. Don't feel that you have to create every location. The set should be kept as fluid as possible, so that it doesn't get in the way of the pace or the emotions of the drama.

James Grieve suggested that when you are thinking about design, consider what motifs are in the play. For example, the photographs that are cut up might lead you to having fragments of pictures on the set, or re-creating a camera flash with the lighting.

Michael Fentiman suggested conceiving three different visual worlds that the play could live in – Political, Poetical and Personal – then exploring what connections and repetitions arise that could be carried into the production. Don't get too caught up in theme, unless that theme can be experienced visually. In Rupert Goold's *Romeo and Juliet*, for example, they looked at Castile in 1548 and the tension between Catholics and North African Moors in the area (Political); the 'POV love' in a psych ward (Poetical); and images from press clippings of a series of emo suicides in UK graveyards in the early 2000s (Personal). These provided specific images and ideas that could play against and with each other.

EXAMPLES OF IMAGES IN THE PLAY

- Traditional top of a wedding cake, idealised picture of a hetero-relationship.
- Photos (Dean cutting them up and Dad seeing the photos of the other transgender teens).
- Mirrors and self-reflection.
- Transformations, dressing-up and artifice.
- 2-D *versus* 3-D versions of people. Photos are 2-D. The difference between looking and being.

Style and technique

The style of the play is not always naturalistic. It is full of emotional truth but it also contains some more challenging, non-naturalistic moments. In James's workshop we highlighted two of these moments:

- The moment when Josh and Dean mirror each other shows the audience that Josh is thinking about what Dean is going through. It also suggests that what Dean sees in the mirror is a boy's body, which is how he envisages himself.
- Scene Eight is like a theatrical version of a film montage. It allows you to show what is happening to Dean over a period of time. It shows all the pressures he's under and it reveals the process of his performance, how he is going to pull off being a guy. It's like a 'work-out' or a 'boot camp' of masculinity.

Three key things to remember about this story are: it is a love story, it has lots of comedy and it has a happy ending.

Other points of contrast to discuss: What is male and what is female? Childhood/adulthood. Teen idol fantasy/SMT mundane. Daughters and sons opposition. Support and lack of support.

Exercises for use in rehearsals

On the first day of rehearsals, read through the play pulling out all facts and questions. Write the questions up and try to answer them during the rest of the rehearsal process. Create timelines for each of the characters. Give the actors practical tasks such as 'Bring in three YouTube clips of James Dean', 'Bring in a playlist of songs from the fifties'.

James looked closely at the Mum and Dad scenes, as some of the directors were anxious about how the gender swap would work. He encouraged them not to worry too much about it, and to investigate instead the feelings, relationship and wants of the characters; then the gender swap will not be an issue. Try getting the actors to do a scene several times, riffing on different versions of it. For example, try it as if they are having a session with a marriage counsellor; or try it with them not looking at each other until the final line . . .

Michael suggested some exercises to unlock the text by enabling the actor to respond to the punctuation in the script:

- When you see a full stop, jump.
  (Reminder of what full stop means: the end of a thought.)
- When you see a comma, click.
  (A comma is a development, a muscle, an energy within the thought.)
- When you see a slash, physicalise a cutting action.
- When you see a dot, dot, dot, wave your arms.
- When you see a question mark, leap forward.

In the workshop we practised this using a Dean speech. Making physical the distinction in the punctuation makes you

appreciate it without intellectualising it and starts to unlock
the specific thought music for the characters. This is also
useful because it can be common in duologues for two people
to end up playing each other's rhythms.

THOUGHT-LADDERS

In performance words can sometimes get thrown away with
the acting layered *on top* of the words rather than through
them. When we speak, we do so to be understood by the other
person. Thought-ladders help us see the language as a means
of being understood.

• Walk around the room but take each word as a footstep on
  a new square on the floor. Land the words on a square,
  then also add the punctuation elements. Don't let it be
  stated – discover it. Don't fear frustration and confusion as
  it may lead to a useful character truth.

FIGHTS

Below are notes based on a workshop led by Alison de Burgh.
They are not meant to be used as a substitute for professional
tuition. NB: all watches and jewellery off!

• Turn and face a partner. Label yourselves 'A' and 'B'.

• 'A' will be the attacker first. With your non-hitting hand
  (i.e. left if you are right-handed) grab 'B' by the shoulder.
  This is how close you have to be to land a punch.

• You can either punch by not hitting someone or by hitting
  someone. Major muscle groups can take impact so it is
  useful to know where you can safely make contact.

• First, take a step back so you can't reach one another.

• Whichever hand is your punching hand, take that foot back
  so that your toe is in line with the heel of your other foot
  and bend your knees.

• How low do you bend your knees? Silly-cowboy low!

- When you make a fist make sure your thumb is closed over both fingers, across your joints, then relax your hand. (If your hand is too tense – you'll hurt yourself.)

- Line up the back of your hand with your forearm. If it is not straight, the reflex action can snap your wrist.

- The best option is to stage a *jab*, as it is the easiest and looks the most effective.

    To jab:

- Turn your palm towards the ceiling. Pull your hand back (pressed into side of the body, no chicken wings!). With your other hand, point at your victim letting your pointing finger emerge from your own solar plexus. Your fist is going to come in to replace your finger, which at the last moment will pull back.

- Your pointy finger is going to make the impact noise, using your chest as a drum with a relaxed hand so you get a good noise.

- The speed of your arm pulling back will sell the jab!

- Start practising jabs by punching chests. It also helps to make noises to punctuate your hits.

You all know what a good punch looks like. These need to be practised in front of a mirror with the important moments being the beginning and the end (the reaction), so start the fist well back and end it well back. Most importantly, make sure you are not going to reach your victim. As you get better you can get closer! The safest thing is to make contact with the clothing and not the person. Baggy shirts are great for this purpose.

If you are going to make contact, allow it to be the sides of the torso and *never* the stomach. The fist travels towards the belly button and flicks the oblique muscles with back of the hand.

Upper arms can also take impact. To look like you are giving a dead arm, keep the elbow up and let the outside of the fist hit the arm.

You can also hit the top of bum cheeks! To do this reaction take your knees to *side* (disco knees) when you have felt the contact on your bottom. If you bend them straight down, you can damage your back.

Finally the hook/John Wayne/roundhouse smack around the jaw:

- First, swing around to make sure you have space without hitting your partner!

- Arms should be arced with the opposite hand pointing a finger at the solar plexus.

- Pull your swinging hand back, and at the point of contact with the jaw you can hit your upper chest with your punching arm to get impact noise. *Or* keep the punching arm going around (right around to the back foot).

NB: fights need to be rehearsed *a lot*! Actors need to be able to know them off by heart like choreography to be safe.

Timeline of the play

Scenes One and Two   April/May

Scene Four   Late June

Scenes Five and Six   July

Scene Eight   A montage that lasts from summer to May the following year

Scenes Nine and Ten   Late May

Scenes Eleven, Twelve, Thirteen and Fourteen   June

Tomorrow

by Simon Vinnicombe

Simon Vinnicombe began his career when he was invited to join the Royal Court Theatre in a 'Super Group' within the Young Writers Programme. His first two plays, *Year 10* (2005) and *Cradle Me* (2008), opened at the Finborough Theatre. *Year 10* was named *Time Out* Critics' Choice and subsequently transferred to the BAC and the Festival Premieres second edition, a festival by the Théâtre National de Strasbourg and Le Maillon, and as part of the Brittany International Theatre Festival in 2006. Both *Year 10* and *Cradle Me* have been performed across Europe in several different languages. Simon Vinnicombe was part of the BBC Writers' Academy 2010 for television and has subsequently written for both TV and film. He won the Pearson Award for playwriting in the same year. His play *City Love* was performed at the Bussey Building in September 2013. His other work has been produced at the Bush, Union Theatre, Edinburgh Festival, Southwark Playhouse, the Old Vic, the Manhattan Theatre Club, New York City, and on BBC Radio 4.

Characters

Peter *is a boy without a peer group, yet to find his niche. He is never comfortable within a group and this manifests itself in his tentative physical movements. He works very hard for his successes.*

Lana *is acutely shy. She is desperate to be hidden from the world. Incredibly clever and very kind but without any of the social skills to go with it. An A* student in every subject.*

Zak *is a massive presence in the room. He can switch from being warm to ferocious in a moment but has a natural charisma. When he is up, the sun shines on everyone.*

Naomi *has an odd maturity which doesn't match her outward appearance. She's fiercely intelligent, and is constantly battling to hide any of her vulnerabilities. She does her best to hide her prettiness.*

Kelly *is a ball of anxiety. She feels the full force of external pressure to succeed and is on the edge of exhaustion. She is kind and open and genuinely loves being at school. Constantly worried as to whether or not others like her.*

Billy *is full of artificial confidence. His every movement is dictated by his desire to be liked. A ball of energy. He has a quick wit and a desperate need to be approved of.*

Shulay *tries to be brash and loud in an attempt to hide her lack of confidence.*

Shadia *is extremely bright and ambitious. She is loyal and fiercely protective of those close to her. She has a maternal nature about her which belies her years.*

Benni *oozes confidence. He speaks with a calmness that communicates he is utterly untroubled by whether or not he is liked. He is well dressed and effortlessly cool.*

Sam *is a scruffy, clumsy mess of limbs. It's as if he has not grown into his body yet. He is always in the immediate, always upbeat. A loyal, huge-hearted boy.*

Cox *is a fifteen-year-old in a fifty-year-old's body. He worships his dad and unwittingly mimics him in his movements. He is very clever but extremely anxious. Has never learnt how to be a teenager.*

Matt *is an athlete and moves with the casual confidence of a sportsman. He is less comfortable in the classroom and gets frustrated with his inability to articulate himself. An odd mixture of confidence and insecurity. A good-looking young man.*

Chloe *has a quiet confidence born of years of popularity. She has a restlessness about her, as if her anger is about to bubble over. She is naturally pretty and takes great care over her appearance.*

Act One

Peter *and* *Lana* *are sitting alone in the school hall.*

There is a stage at the end of the room with some mops and buckets scattered around. There is also a stuffed dog, a curly red wig, a top hat lying on the stage.

There are a few desks and chairs scattered around but the room is clearly not used for lessons.

It's quiet. Very quiet.

Lana *has her head arched down into her chest, making every effort not to make any eye contact.*

Peter *tries to grab* *Lana's* *attention. He's fidgety, looking for the right words.*

He gazes at something high up on the wall.

Peter   Look at the detail of the gold lettering. It's pretty magnificent, that.

Imagine your name up there?

'Lana Buckley 2014'.

Immortalised. Never to be forgotten.

He looks to *Lana*. *Nothing.*

Peter   My brother says that school is the only time of your life where you can't choose your friends. And attendance is enforceable by law.

Unless you go to prison of course.

He also reckons that the people who are kings at school . . . in five years' time . . . are stood outside job centres, with angry dogs and bottles of Special K. While the losers, the tripped-up
He looks pleased with his joke. Until he sees that *Lana* *is less than impressed.*

Peter   Frank Healey was a right geek in my brother's year and he's still eating his own snot outside the Tesco Metro in Winchmore Hill.

There are some people that I never ever want to see again. Gotta be honest.

Are you going to the prom?

Are you?

I hope you are.

Lana *searches for salvation in her bag.*

Peter   Are you nervous about the exams?

You shouldn't be. Aced your mocks, didn't you?

Just let me pass them. Please God. C and above and I'm back in September.

It'll be better then. The mad fuckers will leave, won't they?

Fucking exhausting trying not to look people in the eye. Worrying about who or what will be waiting for you at the school gates.

Silence

I'm sorry about what you did.

Maybe you thought you had no one to talk to.

You can talk to me. Any time.

I know I'm not. And that no one thinks I'm. You know. I'm not.

I might not understand. But I would listen.

Lana *is almost covering her ears now.*

Peter   I just can't help but think about your mum.

Silence

Lana *looks at* **Peter**. *A moment when she might be about to speak.*

Naomi *and* **Kelly** *enter noisily,* **Peter** *scurries back to his seat.*
Lana *folds her head back into her chest and does her best to shrink.*
The girls sit down. They are not together and sit separately.

Silence.

Naomi *leans back on her chair, chewing gum.*

She lets out a moan. She slumps forward in her chair and lets her head hit the desk.

Naomi   No more, no more, no more.

Peter *looks to* **Naomi**. *He tries to respond. He can't.*

Kelly *looks annoyed that her concentration is temporarily broken.*

Naomi *lets out a groan of frustration.* **Kelly** *puts her earphones in.*
Peter *stands. He sits. He stands.* **Naomi** *watches him, bemused.*

Naomi   What are you doing?

Peter   . . . Nothing.

Naomi   How can you take it?

How can you just sit there all . . . ?

For God's sake, Peter. Don't you just want to stand up and scream?

Peter *shrugs.* **Naomi** *slumps down into her chair.*

Billy *enters. He drops his bag to the floor. He kicks it across the room.*

Billy   Nooo!

No. No. No. No. No!

Naomi   I know.

Billy   Baaaaaassssssstards!

Naomi   I know.

Billy   I can't do it no more.

'Maths in the hall.' I thought, 'Yeah, yeah, stroll the fuck on', they're letting us go.

Back at yard having a toke up in time for *Jeremy Kyle USA*.

They've seriously put desks out an' everything.

Naomi   Calm down.

Billy   You do know it's a Friday? They always tell you to do one by lunch cos they ring your mum or your old man. (*Patronisingly, to* **Peter**.) Or your 'carer', Pete, and they tell 'em you're home that day.

Naomi   Is that true?

Peter   It is always a Friday.

Kelly *yanks out her earphones, annoyed at the distraction.*

Kelly   You'll get a bit more work done then won't you, Billy?

Billy   I don't like to get violent but I will cut you.

Shadia *and* **Shulay** *saunter into the room.*

Shulay   Chatting some rubbish again, Billy?

Benni *follows, earphones in, extremely relaxed. He finds a desk and rests his head on it. He may or may not have gone straight to sleep.*

Shadia   Where is he then?

Kelly   Nobody knows.

Shulay   We heard he was going massive for last day.

Naomi   He's going to look a right knobhead if he's here for another week.

Billy   Zak Knight never get caught. Man is Teflon.

The ping of a PA announcement. A muffled crackle. They all freeze, straining to listen . . .

PA 'Could Peter Dubury of 11JA report to reception, please. Peter Dubury of 11JA to reception, please.'

Billy Got yourself in some shit, Dubury?

Peter (*worried*) I ain't done nothing.

Billy (*enjoying it*) Oh dear, oh dear. Always the quiet ones.

Peter I swear.

Billy (*laughs*) Off you go, little man.

A terrified-looking **Peter** *creeps out of the room.*

Kelly Maybe they're letting us go one by one.

Naomi Yeah, right.

Kelly That's how you get your results.

Naomi No you don't.

Kelly True. Tash said. Alphabetical order. All lined up outside Science block.

Shadia That is so wrong.

Kelly Said it's like waiting to get shot.

Billy I don't care about exams. I just want to be told I'm going home. And I want to be told today.

Kelly They don't want anyone vandalising or doing crazy stuff. That's all it is.

Billy Nah, nah, nah. They just want to mess with our minds.

Kelly The teachers don't even get told.

Shulay That's gotta be a lie.

Billy I've got no interest in setting the school on fire.

I just want to leave.

Lie in my bed.

Stroke my beast 'least four time before breakfast.

Kelly   Revising. You're supposed to be revising.

It's called study leave for a reason.

Billy   Ohmydays, your thing ain't never gonna get no air, is it?

Kelly   Shut up you. I hate you. Just.

Billy   Why, do they think we're going to shit under the desks and piss on the chairs?

I'm sixteen. I can leave home! Get a job! Get my National Insurance. Get a passport!

Naomi   You've never stepped foot past Winchmore Shopping Centre.

Billy   I could have a drink in a restaurant with a meal. Get married. Shag. Untold. Bitches / so why would I want to fuck with . . .

Naomi   'Could' is a very big word for you. Billy.

Billy   'Low it now, emo. I just don't put my piece in the pond. I like to cast out to the sea. Get me?

Shadia *and* **Shulay** *laugh at him.*

Kelly   What is he talking about?

Billy   All the girls here been tainted by some other yute in this place.

Kelly   I haven't!

A breathless **Peter** *re-enters. He's holding a piece of paper. They look to him.*

Billy   What *did* you do, numptie? Been bumming the Year Sevens round the back of Albury again?

Peter *looks at* **Billy**. *He slips the piece of paper into his pocket.*

Peter   Naomi?

Naomi   What do they want with me?

I haven't done anything!

Peter   Nothing. No.

(*Quietly.*) I . . . It's just. I wanted a word with . . . I . . .

Naomi   What is it?

Peter   Alone. It's about.

It's urgent.

Sam *charges in. He is covered in sweat. Very flustered.* **Peter** *recoils from the smell of him.*

Shulay   Can you get a wash?

Shadia   Seriously.

Get out.

Sam   What?

Naomi   Peter? What's the matter?

Peter   I just need to . . . talk to you . . .

Peter *beckons* **Naomi** *away from the others.*

Billy   Dubury wants to beat on the emo!

Naomi   Shut it, Billy. I've warned you. I'm about three seconds from telling everyone that you're hung like an oven chip.

Laughter from the others. **Peter** *and* **Naomi** *are now downstage. He moves in close to* **Naomi***.*

Peter (*almost a whisper*)   Naomi . . .

Naomi   What have I done?

Peter   . . . They just asked . . . if you were staying . . . for sixth form. Or if you. If you were leaving.

Naomi   For God's sake!

Peter   They really want you to stay on.

Naomi   Why can't they just leave me alone? I told them
I am gone.

Peter   Where will you go?

Naomi   Dunno. Kayleigh College probably. Depends on
results, doesn't it?

Peter   It'll be good here. It'll be different.

Naomi   It'll still be here though, won't it?

She walks back to her desk.

Shulay   Why do boys think it's alright to bomb about
playing football for an hour and then come in here and stink
the place out?

Sam *smells himself.*

Sam   That's pheromones, that's what that is.

Shulay   No. You just stink.

Sam   Pheromones set off a chemical reaction in the ladies.
It's what attracts them to the opposite sex.

Shulay   You definitely just stink –

Sam   Raw. Manly. Sweat.

Shadia *gips.*

Sam   What's happening here is that you two are totally
aroused and you can't stand it.

Kelly   No, no, no.

You completely hum and you are making me want to vom.

Sam   It's hot out there. I could barely find the strength to
get a hat-trick.

Benni (*barely lifting his head from his desk*)   Please, boy! They
made you play in goal again didn't they?

Sam *drops his head. He retreats a little. Laughter from the others.*

Sam   You should have seen Knighty on the roof!
It's definitely big.

Shadia   You lying?

Sam   Fielding blowing a whistle at him to get off and Zak just dropped his trousers and gave him a moon. And a bit of sun.

Benni   Boooyyy!

Sam   I thought Fielding was going to have a heart attack.

Shulay (*shocked*)   Shut. Up. Really?

Cox *enters. Books under his arm. He looks like a picture from the school website. Pristine. Professorial.*

Cox   That is correct. Got a picture on my phone if you want a look?

He holds out his phone and shows them all. Laughter.

Lana, Kelly *and* **Naomi** *don't look.*

Sam   You should see what me and the guys have got hatching.

Benni (*makes a face*)   'Guys'?

Cox   Can barely contain myself.

Sam   Got nine big tubs of Vaseline. Gonna do all the banisters in Oak House.

Benni (*sarcastic*)   'Wacky'!

Sam   I've got thirty packs of Durex.

Shulay   Posh wanking again, Sammy?

Sam   Sean's old man. Run's a florist's. Got his own helium tank. Fill the johnnies with helium, set 'em off in the playground.

Cox   That, I quite like.

Sam   And. And. We're still working on this but . . .

Three pigs. Paint a number on 'em. One, Two and Four.

Let 'em loose round the school. Staff round 'em up eventually. Then they do their nut looking for Number Three. Genius bit is . . . there is no Number Three!

Peter   Where will you get the pigs?

Sam   Thought we'd just nick 'em out of Andy Mace's petting zoo. There's a gate down the bottom of the recycling centre, you can get through.

Shulay   Doesn't Wayne Clarkson work down there?

He'll sort you out.

Kelly   Wayne Clarkson?!

Shadia   Ohmygod, boy was so fine!

Shulay   Well, he's shovelling Alpaca shit in 'Andy's Andes' now.

Sam   Padlocking all the Year 7 lockers? Flash mob in the middle of assembly?

He can see that he's drowning. Speeds up, a little desperate.

Fish slapping. Giant great fish. Take it round school hitting people with it.

Kelly   Stop, Samuel. I'm embarrassed for you.

Sam   I heard right. And I've got this on good authority, right. And this is genius. Right. I've bought all the stuff. And. Don't go telling no one neither. Right. I've let you in on this. Right?

Shulay   Does he take pills for what he's got?

Sam   Nine batteries.

Four hundred grams of salt.

In the bog.

When someone goes for a piss it sends an electric bolt up their old boy!

Silence

Benni   There must be someone you can ring.

The ping of the PA system. The muffle and the crackle. All stop still to listen . . .

PA   Could a Miss Hugh Jarse report to Miss Phelps in the staff room, please.

Silence for a moment. Followed by laughter.

Benni   No way!

Billy   Zak!

PA   Could Hugh Jarse, Anna Rack and Mike Hunt all report to Miss Phelps in the staff room immediately.

Laughter.

Cox   Now. That. Is funny.

Beat

Sam   Could have been a genuine announcement.

Matt and **Chloe** *enter, laughing. They are holding hands.*

Matt   Teachers running round doing their nuts out there. That boy is a genius!

Benni   'Genuine' my arse, stinky. Knighty, all day long.

Matt (*double-take at* **Sam**)   How are you still sweating? You were only in goal.

Benni *roars with laughter.* **Sam** *looks devastated.*

Shadia   Do you reckon he does know we're done?

Peter   I know.

Cox   Dubury. You wouldn't know your penis if it smacked you in the face.

Peter   I'm telling you, I know.

Cox   I heard he was going for something big at the Prom. Then he knows they can't pull him from the exams.

Kelly   He's not going to ruin it?

Cox   You don't actually leave until that last exam paper's handed over.

Kelly   No, no, no and no. He can't.

I got my dress like, eleven months ago.

Shadia   You lying? Your tits have gone up, like, two sizes this year.

Kelly (*embarrassed*)   Shut up.

Shulay   Enjoy them. I would.

Kelly   Ain't two sizes.

Cox   I'd say a good three.

Kelly *explodes, stands and hurtles a compass from her pencil case at* **Cox** *in one quick motion.*

Cox   What the fuck?!

Just heard your – (*very deliberately points to his private area*) hasn't seen the light for a while. Thought I could help?

Naomi   Do you want to know what it feels like to have one of your textbooks shoved up your rear funnel?

Silence. Awkward. **Peter** *tries to release the tension in the room . . .*

Peter   Is it true you're DJing the prom, Billy?

Billy   . . . They can't afford me.

Cox   I heard you begged Phelps for the gig.

Billy   I'm gonna fucking hang you by that stupid tie, Cox, I wear down.

Cox *immerses himself back in his book.*

Kelly   Got a really cool live band apparently. Professional.

Naomi   Not a live band!

It'll be some old git who dresses like my dad. Playing lame stuff like Bruno Mars and expect us to explode into a mosh pit of joy and togetherness. I'd rather die.

Billy   Should've paid Billy B's booking fee then, shouldn't they?

Chloe   You don't get rappers in Winchmore Hill.

Billy   R&B artist. And I came from the streets, thank you. Not Winchmore.

Naomi (*laughs*)   Streets?! . . . You're white. You live in a semi with hedges sculpted in the shape of animals. And your dad has a garage.

Billy   They're not animals. They're –

Naomi   Your mum plays badminton in the church hall. There is not an R&B bone in your body.

Billy   You listen to the music of the self-harmers!

Kelly   If you were any good at music you would have been in *Annie* this year.

Billy   A musical? I'm straight.

Sam   *Annie*? Which one is *Annie*? What happens in that?

Kelly   Why do they have to do *Annie* when I'm doing my GCSEs?

Naomi   You seriously want to be in that?

Kelly   I would have made an amazing Miss Hannigan. I could sing all the words to 'Little Girls' when I was four.

Billy   Up you get then. Gives us a song.

Kelly   Er . . . I . . .

She's thinking about it.

I'm not warmed up.

Billy   Ohmydays.

Peter   Has everyone got their tickets?

Billy   Fifty pound to listen to their 'live band'. Disgusting.

Cox   It's for the hotel apparently. It's like, £350 a room.

Kelly   You can all just come to prom. Bloody well be there.

You boys. And dress nicely.

And dance.

Shadia   Damn right. Gonna be awesome.

Kelly   Why do boys always try and be above these things?

Peter   I'm looking forward to it.

Billy (*slaps own forehead in dismay*)   So gay, Dubury. So gay.

Peter   Speeches. Prizes. Prom King. Prom Queen. Dancing. Food. Music.

Great.

Billy   Where is your penis?

Sam   No, Peter's right. Everyone looking their best. Last goodbyes under the hotel chandeliers.

Like a fairy tale.

I'm hoping to say a few words.

Cox   Like any teacher is going to let you near a microphone!

Sam   They should. I bet I could make everyone cry.

Matt   That's why you ain't allowed. Supposed to be funny.

Danny Hart did an impression of all the teachers as if they were on speed for his year. It was amazing apparently.

Shulay   It will be a little bit sad I suppose.

Shadia   You been looking forward to it since Year 7, Billy boy. I bet you had your little suit picked out for time.

Probably gonna make your play for my girl here after too many WKDs too.

Billy *and* **Shulay**   Shut up!

Kelly   I'd love to win a prize.

Never won anything in my life.

Shadia   You better all vote for me for queen. Remember what a good friend I've been to all of you.

Naomi *snorts.*

Shadia   It must be hard work being that miserable. There's nothing wrong with smiling, just occasionally you know?

Naomi   What's to smile about?

The two of them glare at one another. **Peter** *quickly interjects in a bid to calm the mood.*

Peter   Zuk will get Prom King, won't he?

Naomi   You're supposed to like the person you're voting for.

Cox   Come on. All you girls wanna get on him.

Naomi   He's repugnant.

Shadia   Just hurting cos he don't want you no more.

Bless.

Kelly (*in a world of her own*)   Best hair. Best smile. Best couple?

Shadia   Need yourself a mans first.

Sam   I am yet to come to a decision as to who I may be escorting on the evening in question.

Shadia   Oi Lana! Time get some, girl. You've found your match.

Shulay   You two should definitely get it together. Jacamo rubbing up on Jacamo.

Billy   Is it true that Holly's dad is getting them a helicopter to arrive in?

Shadia   You lying?

Cox   All the coupley lot are doing it. Costing them £200 each. Landing in the hotel gardens.

Shulay   Definitely worth it. Imagine everyone's faces when you step out of that thing in your dress.

Cox   It is quite cool I suppose.

Peter   Are you supposed to come as a couple?

Naomi   Only Justin and Selina.

Chloe   Jealousy. There's loads of us.

Matt   Just cos none of you lot have the maturity to stay with someone for longer than two minutes.

I'll wave to you from my helicopter.

Shulay   Please, boy. I know you haven't even put a lonely finger down there.

Chloe   Shut up!

Shulay   You didn't just tell me to shut up?

Matt   She did. You heard. Shut it.

Shulay   Last time I listen to you cry in the toilets about having no boobs.

Matt   Just leave it out! You don't know shit, Shulay Daniels.

Shulay (*mimics*)   'I just don't think he's attracted to me in that way.' Does it not work down there, Matthew?

Matt   You shut up! Just shut. Shut. Up!

Kelly   Can everyone just calm down!

Voice (*from off, singing*)   'The sun will come out, tomorrow, bet your bottom dollar that tomorrow . . . '

All turn to the stage. Nothing.

Cox   Who was that?

Shulay What the fuck?

Zak *enters. He is wearing a red curly wig and an orphan's apron over his uniform.*

Zak (*singing*) 'Tooooo-morrow, tomorrow, I love ya tomorrow, you're only a . . . daaaaay . . . aaaaa . . . waaaaay.'

Laughter from the others as **Zak** *hams up a bow and hurls his wig into the air.*

Where is she? Where's huge-arse?

Benni We thought you knew?

Zak I ain't heard nothing.

Billy What was all that stuff on the roof? And the Tannoy announcements?

Zak (*smiles*) I'm innocent.

Although if you have a look on Google Earth later on tonight there should be a giant painting of an ejaculating cock on top of the gym.

Benni I knew it blud!

Zak I hope they never send us home! They all look terrified. Every lesson. Waiting to be told.

I just locked half of Year 8 in the science block.

It's all too much fun, this.

Zak *and* **Benni** *bounce fists.*

Naomi They find out about any of it and you're gone.

Zak Never gonna happen.

Naomi (*smiles*) I heard something different.

Zak (*turns, aggressive*) Oh yeah? And what's that?

Peter . . . It's true.

Zak You what?

He charges towards **Peter** *as if he is about to attack. He stops near his face.* **Peter** *trembles with fear.*

Peter   Fielding . . . Fielding said at assembly on Monday. If any of us get caught we . . . we get pulled from the exams.

Beat.

Zak (*calms*)   They need my pretty arse to bring up the exam average. I'm their OFSTED banker.

Naomi   How did those mocks work out for you again?

Zak   I was too stoned to write my name, darlin'.

Sam   I'm predicted four 'A'-stars.

Cox   I'm predicted nine. Nine.

Send me home today. There is nothing more these idiots can teach me.

Kelly   What if they haven't covered the syllabus and they let us go?

Naomi   They're not going to do that –

Kelly   And there'll be stuff in that exam –

Cox   Calm down –

Kelly   – stuff that we don't know.

Cox   The government want you to get your five 'C's and above. The school want you to do your A-levels, more cash for them, new staff room. The government want you to spend even more at uni. Loans. Loans. Money. Money.

Everyone wants you to pass. Why do you even think General Studies was invented?

Sam   Got a D in General Studies in the mocks.

Cox   Shit the bed, Samuel. How?!

Sam   Fuck off, Cox. I will spark you out!

Cox   'Spark'? You been taking 'urban root' classes with MC Winchmore over there?

Silence. They look to **Billy**. *Waiting for him to bark. A smile slowly spreads across his face.*

Billy   You just keep talking, Cox. I wasn't gonna tell anyone that you look at your bumhole with a hand mirror, but as we're feeling a bit punchy . . .

Laughs from the others. **Zak** *gives* **Billy** *an approving 'fist touch'.* **Billy** *looks delighted by the recognition.*

Silence for a moment.

Kelly   I keep having dreams about ringing my mum on exam day.

And her crying down the phone. And telling me not to come home.

Zak   She ain't gonna do that. She's your mum.

Kelly   I just want to sleep. Just one good night's sleep.

Peter   My dad would tell me to leave.

Billy   My old man says I've got to get a job.

'Rent day starts on August 2nd, boy.'

Kelly   August 2nd? What's August 2nd?

Billy   My sixteenth birthday.

Kelly   What about your A-levels?

Billy *laughs at the absurdity of the suggestion.*

Billy   I ain't bothered. I'll be in the studio in a month.

Shadia   You'll be in the petting zoo with Clarkson more like!

Kelly   It's not funny!

Aren't you even worried?

Every day of our lives for the past eleven years has been about those exams. And every day after will be about what happens in those exams.

It's not a fucking joke!

Silence. A long silence. Her words seem to have affected the group . . .

Zak   Jesus. Your thing really does need to get some air.

Some laughter. Brief silence.

Kelly   I've got a date for prom night actually.

Silence. No one is quite sure that they heard this.

Going out with Lex, aren't I?

He's taking me to a jazz bar. In a hotel.

Make the night really special.

Naomi   Oh dear lord.

Kelly   He's driving us.

He has his own car, Billy. Not one on his X-Box. A real car.

Billy   He says it's his. Blate'rs it's his mum's.

Kelly   You sound jealous.

Billy   A Ford Focus?

When I'm his age you will see me. Audi 3 series.

Matt black.

Shadia   Petting zoo pays three-sixty an hour, you mug.

Billy   I ain't gonna be working in no petting zoo!

And I ain't gonna be livin' with my mum neither.

Kelly   We'll see.

Billy   If I'm livin' round these ends in five years' time you have my permission to shoot me down.

Kelly   Lex said he got 'A'-stars for everything 'cept English.

Zak   He is a mug though, Kel. No offence.

But he bowls about in his brother's suit and sunglasses in his hair.

He sells, like, insurance upgrades on the phones above Primark on Leonards.

Billy   Gotta wonder why he's still driving up the school five years after he left.

Chatting to barely legals about 'jazz bars'.

Kelly   You're barely legal.

Zak   Maybe we need to make our night 'special', Shar. What do you reckon?

He strolls over to **Shadia** *with a smirk on his face.*

Shadia   I need more than some foolishness in the school office if you wanna get with this prom night, Zachary.

Zak   Look at me, Shar. Just look at me.

He is close to her now. He moves in, almost as to kiss her. **Shadia** *invites this.*

Zak   Do you remember? First assembly in here? Five years . . . (*Closes his eyes, wistful.*) Red ribbons in your hair, Shar. Still remember red ribbons.

Shadia *melts. She waits for the kiss.*

Zak *suddenly turns his head from* **Shadia**. *He pins his eyes on* **Matt**.

Zak   Matty geez'? How gorgeous is your girlfriend looking this afternoon?

Matt   Err . . . thanks.

Zak   Doing something special for the big night?

Matt   We're with Holly's old man. In the. In . . . helicopter.

Zak   What a beautiful thing. That'll be amazing.

Good for you.

Matt   . . . Cheers.

Benni   I hope you've got yourself ready, mate. A girl expects things on prom night.

Naomi   Shut up, Benni.

Benni   A night for dreams to become reality.

Laughter.

(*To* **Chloe**.)   You know where to find me don't you, darlin'?

Zak   Benni! Leave her alone.

Benni *is a little shocked by the remonstration. He visibly shrinks.*

Zak (*to* **Chloe**)   Don't listen to him. He's out of order.

Chloe *storms out.* **Matt** *hurries after her.*

Silence.

Zak   Come on, people. Why all the sad faces? We're on the edge of something here.

Dubury? You look like someone's about to die.

Peter   I'm nervous.

Zak   I'm fucking buzzing!

Kelly   We're waiting for Miss Phelps and Maths class. What do you suppose we do?

Zak   You're nearly free and out of here and you're letting them own you.

Go out in style. Give those morons something to remember us by.

Kelly   I can't get in trouble. Not now.

Zak   They can't touch you. Don't you see?

Those teachers are all bored out of their minds. Flapping about whether to have the fish and chips or the ploughman's in the Railway. That's as good as it gets for them. They want us to fuck things up a bit.

Sam   He's right, you know. He's right.

Zak   I don't mean writing some rude words on your shirt. Or thieving from your mum and dad's spirit cupboard. Do something that scares the shit out of people. Best of all. Make sure it scares the shit out of you.

What are you scared of, Kelly Larkin?

Kelly   Nothing.

Zak (*smiles*)   Then why are you shaking?

He leans over and kisses **Shadia**.

Stunned laughs from the others.

Shulay   Oi, oi!

Zak   Come on now, people. Roll up! Roll up!

Let's get this thing started.

He moves to the wall and hits the fire alarm. A modern siren sound blasts out.

He kicks over chairs, desks, anything he can get near. **Benni** *cheers.*

Zak *moves to* **Sam**. *He dummies to punch* **Sam**. **Sam** *flinches terribly. He dummies to hit him again.* **Sam** *flinches horribly again.*

Zak *laughs.*

Zak   Jokes. Just jokes.

Sam   Yeah . . . yeah . . . (*Tries to laugh along.*) Course.

Zak *pulls a fish out of his jacket and smacks* **Sam** *around the face. Laughs from all.*

Zak *runs round behind* **Peter**, *yanks down his trousers to expose his underwear. He pushes him.* **Peter** *trips over his tousers and falls to the floor.*

Huge laughs from **Billy** *and* **Benni**.

Zak   Now's the time to scratch that itch.

The siren rings out. No one says a thing.

Tell Phelps I'm all done.

Going for a smoke.

He leaves.

Kelly *finally gets up to go and help* **Peter**.

Peter *rises before she can reach him. He desperately tries to pull up his trousers. Mortified.*

He moves to the front of the room. He wearily stands on a chair.

They all watch and wait.

Peter *lifts his head.*

Peter   Miss Phelps told me to read this . . . this . . . message.

He takes a piece of paper from his pocket.

(*Reads.*) 'Today is your last day at school. You are all to leave immediately and return for examinations. Please head straight home and begin your study leave. Anyone causing any disturbance to the other pupils remaining at school today will be severely punished. Wishing you every success with your exams. Study hard! Miss Phelps.'

The siren continues to ring out.

Siren stops suddenly.

Lights.

Act Two

The blare of music rings out in the darkness – Bruno Mars or something similar. The music suddenly stops. A light on the stage. An eerie hush.

Kelly   Sorry to interrupt this wonderful evening. It's nearly time for us all to say goodnight and . . . Miss Phelps asked me to say something to mark the night. To acknowledge what's happening this evening.

Beat. She composes herself.

To the Year 11s of 2014 I say thank you.

To every last one of you.

Five years . . . don't they go by in a whisper?

Not for me.

I won't forget a single second.

Mum taking my picture on my first day in the hall. And crying that she'd 'lost me'.

Smell of my uniform and my shiny new shoes.

Miss Ainslie reading out my name in registration.

Mufti days, sports days, trips and outings. All.

More the everyday though. Walking through those gates. Coming here to learn and grow. And knowing that . . . knowing that . . . we're all growing together as we make our way towards adulthood.

Make our way into the world to achieve all of our dreams.

Fighting back tears. More breathing.

Tonight's not the night for goodbye but good luck. A time for celebration.

I'd like to raise a glass.

Year 11s, 2014.

Some applause and some cheers.

Now. As a special treat to play us out for this wonderful night. Please welcome back some brilliantly talented old friends of ours . . .

She hurries off.

Music kicks in . . .

Two sorry-looking seventeen-year-olds are on the stage. One keyboard. One guitar player. They look apologetic rather than confident as they play the opening bars of PM Dawn's 'Set Adrift on Memory Bliss'.

The keyboard player and guitarist double as backing singers, delivering the 'huh, huh, huh, haah, haa' opening with as much enthusiasm as they can muster. Finally the lead singer struts towards the mic, all forced swagger and faux pop star 'edge'. He begins to sing.

The lights gradually brighten . . .

A mirror ball, disco lights . . .

A large banner hangs across the hall, reading 'Winchmore Prom 2014'.

There are large headshots of each student hanging from the string of the banner. They have their statements beneath them. These should be a few lines of thanks and memories from each student of their time and school. They are often followed by a quote. I would encourage each actor to write the statement for the character they are playing. It's your choice how visible these should be. The headshots should be your typically posed 'school mugshots'.

It's the school hall.

A large trestle table across the back of the room with paper cups and a big bowl of pink-coloured punch. Chairs surround the dance floor.

Matt, **Chloe**, **Sam**, **Kelly** and **Cox** *are on the dance floor.* **Sam** *is in a sixties-style suit that is so big it looks like it's eating him. He's dancing with* **Kelly** *without dancing 'with' her.* **Sam** *is doing his best but it remains very awkward.*

Cox *is dressed smartly in a suit with a bow tie. He saunters across the dance floor. He is alone.*

Naomi *sits on the fringes.* **Lana** *and* **Peter***, just a few seats away from her, are watching the action.* **Zak** *and* **Benni** *hover by the trestle table, intermittently downing glasses of the punch.* **Zak** *is wearing the 'Prom King' crown.*

Chloe *is wearing the 'Prom Queen' crown and looks like a perfect Disney princess, while* **Matt** *looks every inch the non-league footballer with his waistcoat and extremely thin tie.* **Chloe** *has her arms draped around* **Matt***'s neck while he holds her waist. They move slowly around the floor with only eyes for one another.*

Kelly *is watching the happy couple dance.*

Kelly (*shouts over the music to* **Sam**)   They're actually perfect for each other. Don't you think?

Sam   Yeah. Definitely.

They'll get married.

Kelly   Amazing.

Sam   Amazing.

Kelly   So beautiful!

Sam *wants to say more but he can't think.* **Kelly** *is dancing in a world of happiness and oblivious to* **Sam***'s struggle. A short time passes.*

Sam   It's a great dress.

Kelly   . . . What?!

Sam (*shouts over music*)   I said you should have won 'best dressed'!

Kelly   Thank you!

More dancing. They're not looking at each other.

Sam   It's a shame about the hotel, isn't it?

Kelly   I dunno. I think it's quite fitting. Being here.

Even more emotional.

You could be my Daddy Warbucks in that suit!

Sam (*smiles*)   Yeah? He's in *Annie*, right? Isn't he the old bloke?

Kelly   But he's very cool. And he's a great dancer.

And rich!

Sam   Oh! Cheers.

Kelly   Do you think 'best smile' is like, some sort of merit award?

Sam   No way.

It's cos you've got a lovely smile.

Kelly (*smiles*)   I've never won a prize, you know?

Sam *smiles. More dancing. They're not looking at each other.*

Kelly   I love you, you know. I do. I love everyone.

Going to miss you!

She tries to hug **Sam**. *It's not logistically possible with her dress. They manage an awkward embrace.* **Cox** *looks over to them.*

Cox (*pulls* **Sam** *aside*)   You're in there!

Sam   Don't be stupid.

Cox   She's emotional. Vulnerable. Time to strike.

Sam   You are a bit rapey, Cox.

Cox   Just trying to help you seal the deal.

Sam   Look. I'm just having a great night. And so is she.

And all I was doing was complimenting her on her dress.

Cox   Didn't mean it though, did you?

It doesn't even fit her.

Sam   Don't be a dick. Try just once. Not being a dick.

Cox   What's the matter with you?

Sam   She should have won 'best dressed'.

Cox   Who did?

Sam *looks across the room for the winner. His eyes stop wondering. He nods his head in the direction of . . .*

Shadia *and* **Shulay** *entering.*

Shadia *is in a bright pink meringue, every inch the 'gypsy wedding' ensemble, body covered in diamantes and a tiara.* **Shulay** *wears a similar, if slightly less flamboyant dress. But she is immaculately put together.*

Shadia *clutches her prize in one hand.*

Shadia   What is this music?

Shulay   That's James and Tim Avery and Tyrell Cummings.

Shadia   I thought they moved into town.

Shulay   Left two years ago to go to music college. Dropped out already.

Shadia   James?

Shulay   James does front desk at his mum's nail place, Tim cleans pots in the Carvery and Tyrell . . . Tyrell just tokes as far as I know.

Shadia   Are they wearing make-up?

The band are into the 'rap' section of the song. It's not going well.

Billy *charges into the room. He does not look happy. He is making his way towards the stage when* **Shadia** *grabs him by the shoulder.* **Billy** *is clearly very drunk.*

Shadia   Oi, oi, slow down Billy boy.

Billy   Enough's enough.

Shulay   What's the matter? Calm yourself down.

Billy   Heard this shit from the car park?!

Do you understand what I could do for this party if they let me near the decks?

Shulay   What you doing in the car park?

Billy *is embarrassed.*

Shadia   You didn't vom did you?

Billy   I only had a can before I come.

Shulay   Bless you, Billy.

I am definitely going to miss you.

Billy   Cheers. Respect.

Shulay   You gotta stop with the awful 'street talk' though, little man.

Billy   What you chatting about?

Shadia   Honestly, Bill. When I met you, you was listening to Bieber and wearing cardigans.

Billy   A man can change.

Shadia   Don't change too much will you, Billy?

She suddenly hugs him. **Billy** *looks delighted. Doesn't know what to do.*

Billy   Yeah. Well. Yeah.

This party might die if I don't do something.

Shulay   You go, Bill!

Billy *turns to charge towards the stage. He gets around five paces before suddenly clutching his stomach and desperately running out of the room holding his breath.*

Shadia   Ohmydays.

Matt *has grown in confidence on the dance floor. He manages to 'dip'* **Chloe** *as part of their dance. The move receives some whoops of encouragement from the rest of the dance floor.* **Chloe** *lets out a loud giggle.*

Shadia (*glowering at* **Chloe** *on the dance floor*)   Who voted for that?

Shulay   All the boys wanna put their thing in the virgin innit?

Shadia   She goes near my man and she won't have a face any more.

Shulay   I bet you can't wait for later? I'm so jealous.

Shadia   Does he like me? Really?

Shulay   Have you seen yourself tonight?

Every boy in this place wants you.

Shadia   But it'll be just me. And him.

And sometimes I just don't know.

Shulay   What you wanted for time.

Get over there and get your man.

Shadia   In a minute.

Shulay   He's coming over.

Shadia   I can't.

Not yet. I can't.

She runs out. **Shulay** *hurries after her.*

Zak *and* **Benni** *see them leave. They are too late.* **Benni** *moves to hurry after them.* **Zak** *pulls him back.*

Benni   Where's she going?

Zak   I don't know why you want to get on that anyway.

Benni   Sometimes man just has to take one for the team.

Zak (*looks around him*)   This is a piss-take. No way hotel got double-booked. We're paying for the teachers end-of-year piss-up.

Benni   Fifty large to be patted on the head and told to go away.

Zak   We're gonna have to raise it then, aren't we, bruv?

Benni   What you thinking?

Zak   It's a ceremony. As your king I promise you something special Ben.

They cut me down on the last day but they ain't doing it now.

Make way for the king!

Benni *cackles with delight.* **Zak** *beckons him away.* **Peter** *bumps into them. He spills his drink down himself.*

Benni   Watch where you're fuckin' going!

Zak *bends down and picks up* **Peter***'s cup. He hands it to* **Peter**.

Zak   My bad.

Peter   . . . 'S alright.

Zak   Not leaving, are you?

Peter   Just gonna get some air.

Silence

Zak   Sorry about before.

Not personal.

Jokes.

You having a good time?

Peter   . . . It's good. Yeah.

Zak   Who you reckon's the hottest girl here?

Peter   . . . Dunno . . . Chloe?

Zak   Want me to sort it out?

Peter   . . . No. Thanks. She's with Matt.

Zak   And? I need to be making sure you have a great night, mate.

Peter   Why?

Zak   I'm your king.

Peter   I didn't vote for you.

Zak (*half laugh*)   You what?

Peter   I voted for Sam.

Zak   Is that right, Dubury?

Why's that then?

Peter   I think they're nice people.

Benni (*half laugh*)   Ohhh! You're a madman, Dubury.

Zak   You don't think I'm 'nice'?

Peter *shrugs.* **Zak** *fixes* **Peter** *with a stare. He suddenly breaks into a smile.*

Zak   I fucking hope not.

Peter   I need to get some more punch.

Zak   Alright, man. Bless.

Peter *goes.* **Zak** *watches him go.*

Benni *strolls away. He looks back to* **Zak***, who is lost in thought.*

Benni   Come on, bruv. Ain't got long.

Zak   Yeah, yeah. Coming.

He and **Benni** *hurry away.*

Cox *intercepts* **Peter***.*

Cox   What's going down?

Are you in on it?

Peter   What are you talking about?

Cox   It's definitely gonna go off, isn't it?

Peter   I don't really care.

Cox   He made a mess of you, didn't he?

Peter (*walking away*)   Bye, Cox.

Have a great life.

Cox   Wait!

Dubury.

I saw you leave early in English exam. Did you fuck it up?

Peter (*shrugs*)   Couldn't think of anything else to write. And I didn't wanna stay there.

Cos I was just going over it and over it. I dunno.

You coming in to get your results?

Cox   Yeah. Might do. My dad's going to take me out after though. Going shooting with his mates.

Peter (*starting to walk away*)   Good for you.

Cox (*hurries after* **Peter**)   It's networking really. Cos you can get headhunted way before uni these days.

Peter   . . . Good luck.

Cox   Staying here, aren't you?

Peter   Five 'C' and above. Please God.

Cox   Then what? What are you going to do with your life?

Peter   Haven't got a clue.

Cox   Jesus, Dubury!

Nearly last dance. Time to be getting some my friend!

He chuckles and races back on to the dance floor.

The music plays for a time. **Peter** *lost in thought. He fixes his eyes on* **Naomi**, *still sitting in one of the chairs. Straightens himself out. Tidies his hair.*

Peter   Would you like me to get you some punch?

Naomi   No. Thank you.

That idiot has poured half a bottle of ouzo in there.

Peter   You should have a dance. Never know when you'll see everyone again.

Naomi   I've got no intention of seeing any of them ever again.

Peter   . . . Well. You never know how your exams went.

I'm sure they went brilliantly.

Naomi   It doesn't matter, does it?

I shouldn't have bothered coming here.

Peter (*frustrated*)   Why are you like this?

Naomi   Look.

In twenty-three years I'm going to be my mum.

It was all decided a long time ago. Before I even stepped foot in this place. Kind of job I can get, the house I'll live in, the man I'll marry.

Peter   For God's sake.

Naomi   He'll take too long proposing to me.

Cos he'll still be looking for something better.

He'll talk about getting dancing lessons for our first dance.

And losing weight for the wedding.

And none of it will happen.

And he'll watch sport endlessly on the TV with one hand in his pants.

And stop talking to me within a year.

He'll be my dad.

Peter (*riled*)   It doesn't have to be like that!

Naomi   Look around you . . . Billy and his music career?
Cox the king of Canary Wharf. Supernanny Shadia . . . Can
you really see any of it happening?

Peter   Why not?

You can always look a bit further than that idiot careers
officer tells you to.

Did you even look at his shoes? Never trust a man with tassels
on his shoes.

Naomi   You're weird.

I'm not sure if I like it.

Peter *sits next to her. They survey the dance floor for a moment.*

Peter   Who'd you vote for on Prom King?

Naomi   Not Zachary Knight. That is sure as shit.

Peter   Did anything ever happen . . . ?

With you and . . . ?

Naomi   He's a thug, a bully and a moron, Peter. What do
you think?

Peter   Everyone here thinks he's a legend.

Naomi   He's already been told that they will keep him back
a year for retakes if he fucks up.

Peter   Really?

Naomi   His mum would never let him leave here with
nothing.

He's not what you think he is.

Peter   Apparently he went into Northborough last week
and challenged all of their hardest boys to a fight.

He was on his own and they all backed off. Gave his number to one of the girls on the way out.

Naomi   And . . . ?

Peter   Well. That's pretty cool, isn't it?

Naomi   That'll impress them in the job centre, won't it?

School's out, Peter.

Silence

Peter   You should have at least one dance, you know.

Naomi   I don't do dancing. I don't do public displays of enthusiasm in any shape or form.

She stands, starts to leave.

Peter   Don't go.

Please.

Billy *staggers on to the stage and grabs the mic off the band, before they can finish their song. He starts to beat box. Not very well.*

Billy *(raps the following between beat boxing)*
   Ahhh yeah . . . people I know you feel me, another year in this yard gonna kill me, you can't cage me, can't contain me, future burn so bright that I can't even see. Love me, or hate me, you can't never forget me, I'm lyrically blessed, my rhymes possess, no stress, I digress cos I'm the yute at the top of the tree, ah yeah, ah yeah . . . I'm Billy B.

He holds his arms aloft waiting for applause. There is nothing but a stunned silence. He drops the mic, it makes a loud piercing noise as it hits the floor. **Zak** *and* **Benni** *enter and holler in approval.* **Billy** *runs off.*

Naomi *is looking at* **Zak** *and* **Benni**.

Music starts up again from an iPod.

The band leave, defeated.

Naomi *(to* **Peter***)*   Always know when to leave the party.

Naomi *goes to leave.*

Peter   Please don't go.

Wait!

Zak *blocks* **Naomi**'*s exit.*

Naomi   Get out of my way.

Zak   Frightened about having a good time?

Naomi   Not a chance of that with you here.

Zak   I remember when you wrote my name on your pencil case.

Naomi   It was a joke.

Zak   What can I say?

She gave out more than you.

Naomi   Shut up.

Zak   Still hurts, does it?

Naomi *(tries to sidestep him, he blocks her)*   Just go away.

Zak   You know what fucks you off the most?

For the rest of your life.

You'll think about me.

Naomi   You're wrong.

Zak *(moves close to* **Naomi***, sniffs his finger)*   I think about you.

Naomi *looks as if she might cry. She runs out.* **Peter** *looks at* **Zak***.*

Zak   Problem, little man?

Peter *lowers his eyes and makes his way to the door.*

Benni *clucks after him, his best chicken impression.* **Peter** *goes.*

Benni *erupts in laughter. He looks for* **Zak**'*s approval but* **Zak** *is headed for the dance floor. Eyes focused.*

Matt *and* **Chloe** *are slow dancing, close.* **Zak** *approaches them.*

Zak   It's almost lights up.

Time for a dance with my queen.

He puts his crown on.

Matt   Not last dance yet. They'll announce it.

Zak   I need a bit of practice. Need to look the part, don't we, my queen?

Chloe *lowers her head, embarrassed.*

Zak   She's been eye-shagging me all night, mate.

Walk.

He smiles, gives **Matt** *a dismissive wave.*

Matt *looks at* **Chloe**. *She doesn't look up.* **Zak** *is now glowering at* **Matt**.

Matt *runs off.*

Zak   Sorry about that.

Breaks my heart to watch you though.

He doesn't even know how to look at you, let alone how to touch you.

Chloe   Don't.

Zak   I see the way he puts his arm round you as you stroll about school.

Clinging on for dear life, isn't he?

Chloe *tries to break off from the dance.*

Zak   Hey, hey, hey.

I don't mean any harm.

Zak *pulls* **Chloe** *back. They're dancing again.* **Zak** *gently brushes the hair away from* **Chloe**'s *face.*

Zak   You look beautiful tonight.

Really.

Chloe   . . . Thanks.

I should –

Zak   Leave him. He needs to come back himself, doesn't he?

Chloe   He's my boyfriend.

Zak   How long are you going to keep telling him how to behave?

Right now he's a nice boy who looks pretty in his Fred Perry's.

What's he going to be to you in a couple of years?

Chloe   We're going to try and go to the same college. Stick together.

Zak   Did you just hear that?

Chloe   Don't.

Zak   He's nice. He really is.

You like his family. They like you. Feel safe. Comfortable. You know exactly what you're going to get for the rest of time. That's a nice feeling, isn't it?

Chloe   . . . Yes.

Zak   Do you have any idea how happy you should be?

Chloe   . . . Stop it.

Zak   Look at me. Look into my eyes.

Do you know what you're gonna get from me?

Chloe   Five years, Zak. We've been together for . . .

Zak   He's a boy.

And look at you. Just look at you.

Chloe *looks down. Embarrassed.* **Zak** *gently lifts her chin and kisses her.* **Chloe** *kisses him back.*

Zak *breaks the kiss suddenly.*

Chloe   What's the matter?

Zak   Nothing.

Chloe   Good. I thought it was –

Zak   No. I mean I felt nothing. Not a thing.

Dead down there.

Chloe   What?

Zak   This definitely ain't gonna work out.

Chloe   How could you . . .

Zak   Nah, nah, nah.

I need a bit more punch. Not sure the virgin Mary's gonna do it for me.

Chloe   You. Horrible.

Zak   You better run after that faggot after all.

I need to get find me a proper prom queen.

Chloe *runs before she can cry.* **Zak** *laughs.*

Zak *moves from the dance floor and high-fives* **Benni**.

The rest of the dance floor are looking at them.

Kelly *takes to the stage. She approaches the mic.*

Kelly   Ladies and gentlemen! Please gather on the dance floor.

Winchmore High 2014!

It's the last dance!

Some muted applause. All gather on the dance floor.

Even **Lana** *stands and moves on.*

Shadia and **Shulay** *rush back into the hall as the music begins.*

It's 'Lifetime' by Emeli Sandé or something similar.

They all begin to dance.

Kelly *dances with* **Sam**. *All others do their best not to look as if they are dancing alone.*

Shadia *goes to* **Zak**.

Shadia   You alright?

What's going on?

Zak   Nothing much.

Waiting for you.

Shadia   You gonna ask me to dance then?

Zak   Maybe. Depends if she'll hook up with my boy.

Shadia *looks over to* **Shulay**, *imploring*. **Shulay** *gives a very reluctant nod.*

Benni *takes* **Shulay** *by the hand. They head on to the dance floor.*

Shadia *puts her arms around* **Zak**'s *neck. They begin to dance.*

Shadia   I ain't seen you all night.

Zak   Gotta stick with my boy.

Shadia   I wanted to be with you.

Zak   Other people need me.

Shadia   Thought tonight was going to be special.

Zak   We can do that.

Shadia   Yeah?

Zak   Right here. Right now.

If you want to.

Zak *looks up to the stage suggestively.*

Shadia   What?

Zak   Behind the curtain.

Come on. Be legendary.

Shadia   Can't you take me home?

Zak   And have breakfast with Mummy in the morning?

Matt *storms into the hall and heads for* **Zak***. He stops suddenly, just a few yards from him.*

Zak *breaks from* **Shadia***.*

Zak   What?

Matt *is breathing heavily. He points at* **Zak***.*

Zak   Someone's had a drink. Very careful now.

Matt   You . . . you . . .

Zak   Come on. Come on. Come on!

Shadia   What's going on?

Zak *moves closer to* **Matt***. They are almost nose to nose.* **Zak** *tilts his head from side to side. Enjoying it.*

Zak   Come on, boy, I'd fucking love to.

Matt   You stay away from my girlfriend.

Shadia   What's he talking about?

Zak (*turns to* **Shadia**)   Oh, fuck off. Seriously.

You honestly think I wanna get on you? Rather stick it in a barb-wire fence.

Shadia   What?

Zak   You must know . . .

You look like a ten-euro hooker.

Shadia *is too upset to speak. She hides her face, runs off.*

Matt   You're out of order.

Zak   Let's have it then, you mug.

Zak *charges to* **Matt** *and punches him to the floor. He kicks him when he's down.*

Peter *rushes over to them and lies over the body of* **Matt**. *The kicks are now hitting* **Peter** *with savage ferocity.* **Zak** *begins to lose his breath with the effort of it all.*

The ping of the PA announcer rings out. **Zak** *stops kicking and reels back from* **Peter**.

The music stops.

All stop to listen.

Naomi (*over PA*)   Pupils of Winchmore High 2014.

Pupils of Winchmore High 2014.

This is a message for Zachary Knight. A message for Zachary Knight.

Silence.

Who once tried to kiss me in the gymnasium.

I said no.

And then he begged me to kiss him. And I said no.

And then he grabbed my hair and forced his tongue down my throat and he grabbed at me.

And I was still saying no when my head hit the floor . . .

Beat.

You should all know that he cried. And he cried. And he cried.

And begged me never to tell anyone what he did.

Beat.

Zak Knight is king of the cowards.

And he will never do anything with his shitty little life.

Coward. Coward. Coward. Coward. Coward. Coward.

Silence

Miss Phelps is on her way to make sure you never set foot in this school again.

Silence. A long time. **Zak** *looks around. All eyes are on him. No one else dares take another breath.*

All the lights suddenly come up. Balloons fall from the ceiling.

Silence for a moment.

Zak *looks around him. No one dares say a word.*

Zak   What? What are you all looking at?

What?

Benni   Come on, mate, we better get out of here.

He tries to guide **Zak** *away.*

Zak *shrugs him off.*

Zak   I'm not going anywhere.

Looks at the stunned faces around him.

What?

Lana *moves over to check on* **Peter**.

Zak   Stay where you are. You stay where you are!

Cut down, not across and next time you'll finish the job.

Benni   We need to go mate. Teachers –

Zak   Mate? I'm not your fucking mate.

Benni   What?

Zak   Move! Get away from me.

The door opens.

Naomi *enters.*

All look to her for a moment.

A beat. **Zak** *is boiling.*

He begins to move towards her.

Benni   No. No. Don't! Phelps is –

Faster.

Don't!

Zak *keeps on moving, faster and faster, about to explode.*

Zak   Bitch!

Benni *moves to stop him. He's pushed aside.*

Zak *is almost at* **Naomi**.

Benni   NO!

The door swings open.

Blackout.

In the blackout we hear the sound of all the balloons quickly being popped.

Act Three

The now empty school hall.

There is a banner with a new message which reads 'Winchmore School Sixth Form, the path to a better future'. Still some debris from the school play and the prom scattered on the floor: ticker tape, bust balloons, etc.

After a short time, **Peter** *enters. He is looking almost healed. He wears a plaster over the bridge of his nose and hobbles ever so slightly. He carries an A4 envelope. He looks around him for a moment. He checks the time.*

He suddenly breaks into a bizarre sort of 'victory dance'. He's in full flow when the door opens. He stops dancing suddenly. Tries to quickly transform to 'casual' stillness.

Lana *creeps into the room cuddling her envelope to her chest as if it were the most delicate and priceless of objects. She heads towards the door to leave.*

Peter   Wait!

How did you go?

Lana *hesitates. Then suddenly breaks into a smile.*

Peter *(smiles)*   Of course you did. Brilliant!

Lana *shrugs, embarrassed. She goes to leave again.*

Peter   Lana!

Aren't you gonna wait for the others?

Lana *shrugs. She doesn't know where to go.*

Peter   Don't have to. It's just.

You won't see some of them. Ever again. And.

Cox *enters without his envelope. He looks blankly at* **Peter**.

Silence

Peter *(fit to burst)*   Well . . . ? How'd you go?

Cox *(bored)*   What do you think?

Peter   Ten 'A'-stars probably?

Cox   Was it ever in doubt?

Peter   You should ring your mum.

Cox   She knew it was going to happen. So . . .

What about you?

Peter   Fuck yeah. I even rang my aunt in the Isle of Wight.

Cox   You did alright then?

Peter   Four 'A's, three 'B's and a 'C'.

They'll let me back in come September.

Cox   I'm out of here, mate.

Embarrassing watching them beg me to stay. Phelps was shouting at me to enrol for next year.

Peter   Isn't your dad taking you out?

Silence.

Cox *nods. And keeps nodding as he tries to stop himself from crying.*

Peter   . . . Cox?

Are you alright?

Cox?

Cox *nods several times.*

Peter   What happened?

Cox   . . . They . . . I . . .

The questions. Were all. Wrong.

All of them. Wrong!

Peter   You can ask to be re-marked.

I'm sure you can. If.

Cox   It's fine. It's fine. It's . . .

Doesn't matter. It's just. It's just.

Peter   It's going to be alright.

Cox (*turns suddenly to* **Lana**)   Don't you fucking say anything!

Not a fucking word!

Peter   Cox!

Silence. **Cox** *breathes deep and heavy in a bid to calm himself. He holds a hand up by way of a limp apology to* **Lana**. *The two boys look at one another. Neither is sure what to say.*

Cox   Isn't he coming?

Peter   I was told he wasn't allowed to sit any of his exams.

Cox   Aren't you shitting yourself?

Peter *shrugs.*

Cox   I don't know why he . . .

I thought he was going to do something funny. I thought he'd do something unforgettable.

Peter   Well. You could call it that I s'pose.

Cox   I wish I was hard. If I was hard I would have.

Would have.

Peter   It's alright.

Cox   I'm not hard.

And he's Zak Knight isn't he?

Peter   It's alright.

Cox   People are saying his cousins are going to come after you.

They know where you live, Dubury.

Peter   Well . . .

He does his best to shrug. Clearly very nervous.

Silence.

The door opens. **Peter** *and* **Cox** *jump a little.*

It's **Matt** *and* **Chloe**.

Matt *still has some bruises on his face.*

Silence

Peter   Alright?

Chloe   Hi.

Peter   Everything . . . ?

Chloe   Yeah.

She smiles, looks to **Matt**.

Chloe   You can re-take Maths.

Matt *nods sadly.*

Peter   Only Maths. Fuck Maths.

Get a calculator.

Matt   I ain't bothered about Maths, am I?

Chloe   Matt?

Silence. **Chloe** *tries to take* **Matt** *by the hand. He shrugs her off.*

Chloe   He got an 'A'-star in General Studies!

Peter   Nice one, mate.

Cox   You are kidding me –

Peter   Shut it, Cox. Actually fucking shut it.

A scream from off. They all jump, turn to the door.

Shadia *bolts into the room, runs a full lap of the hall screeching with delight.*

She looks around the room.

Sorry. I'm just. I'm buzzing. I'm.

Shulay *enters.*

Silence as they wait for her to speak.

Shadia   Well . . . ?

Shulay   I can't open it.

Shadia   Open it!

Shulay   I might puke.

Shadia   Ohmygod, you've got to open it!

Shulay   Can't do it in front of everyone.

Shadia   I'll do it for you.

*She moves to **Shulay** and tries to take the envelope. **Shulay** hurries away from her.*

Shadia (*softly*)   Gonna be alright. I swear.

Shulay *slowly relents. Opens the envelope. Her eyes hurry down the paper. Breath quickens.*

Shadia   What you get? What you get? What you get?

Shulay *continues to read the paper over and over. Her eyes begin to widen.*

Shulay *sits on the ground.*

Shadia   What? What?

Shulay (*clutches the paper to her chest, closes her eyes*)   Oh thank God. Thank God. Thank God. Thank God.

Shadia   No way!

Shulay *nods.* **Shadia** *sprints to her. She looks at her paper.* **Shadia** *embraces **Shulay** a little too hard. They tumble on the ground.*

Peter   Shadia?

Have you . . .

Shadia (*stands, shakes her head*)   . . . No.

Cox   Did he sit any . . .

Shulay   He weren't in Geography. Weren't in History.

Shadia   Hope I never see him again.

The door goes. All jump a little.

It's **Benni**, *with a disconsolate looking* **Billy**.

Shulay   . . . Oh Bill. That bad?

Billy   Fuck.

Shadia   Sorry, Billy.

Billy   Fuck. Fuck. Fuck.

Shulay   It'll be alright.

Benni   Only exams, bruv.

Shulay   A piece of paper at the end of the day.

Billy (*heartbroken*)   My dad, my dad, my dad . . .

Shadia   Just ring him.

Billy   Can't. Can't –

Shadia   Text him.

Shulay   Thought he told you to get a job anyway.

Billy   . . .

Shadia   You can do them again?

Billy *shakes his head over and over again.*

Shadia *goes to him and hugs him.*

A smiling **Sam** *enters with* **Kelly**.

Sam   Are you alright, Billy?

Shadia *shakes her head.*

Sam   . . . Sorry mate.

Cox   What about you? How did you . . .

Sam *nods modestly, aware of* **Billy***'s struggle.* **Kelly** *can't keep the grin off her face.*

Cox   . . . Well done.

I do mean it.

Kelly   Does anyone want to come to the Railway?

No real response.

Kelly   I've got some great pictures of the Prom.

Everyone looks like a fairy tale.

Silence.

Sam   Come on guys.

Just go in the garden.

Cox always gets served.

Shulay   That blazer does have its uses.

Shadia   I'll come.

Shulay   Yeah. Why not?

Sam   Pete?

Peter   I was gonna hang on for a bit.

Ring Mum and Dad and. You know.

Sam   He's here you know.

Beat.

His mum brought him up here.

Peter   Right. Well.

Kelly   He's not allowed in here. I saw Phelps talking to his mum.

Shulay   Just come with us, Pete.

Peter   Waiting for someone.

Sam   I'll get you one in.

Come on, you lot . . .

Kelly   We gotta go this way. I ain't walking past him.

Benni   He's a fucking loser.

Shadia   Happy hour in the Railway.

There's a breezer with my name on it.

Billy   Can't. Gotta go. I . . .

Sam (*to* **Peter**)   Who you waiting for?

Peter   I just want a second.

Shadia   Stay away from him, Pete.

Just stay away from him.

They all begin to leave.

Shulay (*to* **Kelly**)   So then? Tell us, Larkin?

How was Lex and the back of his Ford Focus?

Laughter.

Kelly   If you must know. Sam walked me home.

Sam (*proudly*)   I did indeed.

Some 'whoos' and more laughter.

They are gone.

Lana *is still standing waiting, looking at* **Peter**.

Peter   You not going too?

Lana *looks at him.*

Peter   You alright?

Lana   Thank you.

Peter   Haven't done anything.

Lana   You will stay away from that boy, won't you?

Peter   You aced it, didn't you? You totally aced it.

It can all change now. Can't it? If you want it to?

Lana *nods.*

Peter (*points up to the Head Boy and Head Girl board*)   Chloe Simms? Head girl? Prom Queen? That has to be some kind of a joke, doesn't it?

I voted for you on both, you know.

Lana *smiles. She leaves.*

Peter *is alone. He looks at his watch. He looks towards the door. Paces a little. Waiting.*

Zak   So. You're coming back here then?

Peter *nods.*

Peter *turns to see* **Zak**. *He freezes for a moment.* **Zak** *looks smaller, softer. The fight has gone, his body draped over his bones, he barely lifts his head to make eye contact with* **Peter**.

Zak   You remember your first day?

Peter *looks at him. Doesn't respond.*

Zak   I do.

I remember walking in and seeing all the girls. Checking 'em out and them smiling back. I remember we played footy at lunch and I took on four players and scored. Kenny and his boys in Year 10 came over and asked me to play with them. And I went home buzzing.

Peter   I can't really remember my first day.

Zak   I remember my first row that week. Michael Davey started givin' it biggun in the corridor about my cousin. And I stepped to him and put him down. He fell in half. Couldn't breathe.

And the sound of everyone shouting 'Fight, fight, fight . . . '

And they laughed at him when he ran down the stairs.

And they cheered for me.

I ask Carly Haze out. She said yes. Kissed her behind the labs.

It was so hot that day.

By the end of the day everyone knew my name.

Peter   I remember being scared on my first day. All looked so bloody big.

Zak *nods. He walks around the room. Taking it in.* **Peter** *watches him.*

Zak   My dad used to say that life is about being harder than the next bloke. That's all it is.

What do you think?

Peter *shrugs.*

Zak   I'm not like that. I'm not what Naomi said. Not . . .

He looks up the board on the wall. Recovers his composure.

Matt Phillips head boy?

My arse, mate.

I owned this place. I was the fucking king.

He struts towards the exit. He stops near the door. Turns back to **Peter**.

Zak   Do you like me, Pete?

Did you ever like me?

Peter *merely looks at* **Zak**.

Zak   They're keeping me back a year.

Putting me in with the Year 10s.

Peter   What?

Zak   I'll be on my own.

Peter   You'll be here.

Zak   They'll laugh at me.

I'll be a joke.

(*Cracking.*) I'm a knight.

Silence. He is struggling to remain composed.

I don't think I can do it.

Peter   I'm sorry.

Zak   Be alright though, won't it? Will be alright?

Zak *looks at* **Peter**, *who doesn't respond.* **Zak** *looks up to the ceiling. He leaves.*

Peter *is alone. He looks up to the Head Boy and Head Girl roll of honour on the wall.*

Naomi *enters behind him. She hurls her envelope across the school floor.*

Naomi   This building stinks. The floor makes me want to puke. The smell. Goes right down my gullet and smacks my stomach like a brick.

When I get in I take all my clothes off.

Peter *nearly falls over.*

Naomi   I throw them in the washing machine.

I jump in the shower.

And I still can't shake the stink.

Tomorrow it all begins.

I can be who I want. With whoever I want.

I can taste the air. Can't you?

Peter *nods sadly.*

Peter   What happened. Did you . . . ?

Peter *nods to* **Naomi**'s *discarded envelope.*

Naomi Yeah, yeah. I'm off go college.

(*Fakes enthusiasm.*) 'Whoop, whoop!' or whatever you're supposed to say.

Peter Right.

Naomi See you later, alligator.

Peter I need to talk to you. I need to . . .

Naomi Why so serious?

Peter Because it's important.

Because I've needed to say it for . . .

For . . .

F – I . . .

Silence. **Peter** *can't bring himself to say it.*

Naomi Jesus. You'll die, you know? One day you'll die.

Goodbye, Peter.

There's a word.

Goodbye.

And good riddance to these four walls.

I'm out of here.

Peter But . . . But . . .

She's gone.

Because I've been completely haunted by you for three and a half years. Eight hundred and fifty-nine days since Miss Parker introduced you to 2JA. And you walked to the back of the class. And your smell.

You looked at me. You looked at *me*.

And I've never ever been that happy before or since. Wednesday January 5th 2011.

Remember when Miss Davies told us off for not paying attention in General Studies? You probably don't.

She said our name in the same sentence. She said Peter Dubury and Naomi Keys, and it made me giddy.

And I can't stand the idea that there'll never be another Monday. I'll never get to see your face again.

I think you are beautiful from right inside to out. The most beautiful girl I've seen in my life.

So I thought. You know. I thought. Maybe. Maybe we could go out. Maybe we could. Could . . .

Fuck it. Fuck it.

Prick. Prick. Prick.

He sinks down. He picks up a discarded red Annie *wig from the floor. He puts it in his pocket.*

He goes to leave.

The shuffle of shoes from off. **Peter** *turns.*

Naomi *is standing there. Nothing is said for some time.*

She walks towards **Peter** *and straight past him. She picks up her jumper.*

Naomi   Forgot my jumper.

Was never any good at making an exit.

Later.

She walks away.

She stops. She turns to **Peter***.*

Naomi   Why do you pick up the wig?

Peter   Memento. Never did get my shirt signed. I thought it was a good show.

Naomi   I was in it at primary school.

Peter   You're a dark horse.

I liked the songs. But I don't get the ending. Annie ends up with the rich bloke Warbucks. And the President says he's going to end the depression and all that. But what happens to all the other orphans?

Naomi   Back to the orphanage.

Peter   That'll be me. I've got 'orphan' written all over me.

Which part did you play?

Naomi   Annie.

Peter   Well. You'll be alright then, won't you? Sorted.

Naomi (*smiles, she sings*)
>   So maybe now it's time
>   And maybe when I wake
>   They'll be there calling me 'baby'
>   Maybe.

Peter   Bloody hell. You can sing. That was . . .

Naomi *takes this in. She pulls a pen out of her bag and goes to* **Peter**. *She grabs the bottom of his shirt and pulls him towards her. He freezes.*

She writes her name on his shirt.

Naomi   I remember that. I remember getting told off by Miss Davies.

Peter   Really?

Naomi   'Beautiful'? Really?

Peter *nods.*

Naomi *smiles. She grabs* **Peter** *by the shirt again. She writes her phone number on the shirt.*

Naomi   You should ring me. We should go out.

Tomorrow.

If you want?

Peter (*breathless*)   . . . Yeah.

Naomi *locks her fingers with* **Peter**. *She leans in. She stops. She removes the gum from her mouth and kisses him gently on the lips.*

Naomi   Later. Peter Dubury.

She skips off.

Peter *is alone. He looks elated.*

He starts to whistle the tune of 'Tomorrow' from Annie *as he leaves.*

Lights fade down . . .

Tomorrow

BY SIMON VINNICOMBE

*Notes on rehearsal and staging drawn from a workshop
with the writer held at the National Theatre, November 2013*

*Workshop led by Clare Lizzimore, with combat work
led by Alison de Burgh and notes by Dan Bird*

How the writer came to write the play

The play was developed with students from Simon Vinnicombe's old school in London. One of his earliest memories of his time at that school was on the first day seeing three people have their heads pushed through windows. At the time this seemed so different to fights at primary school, where you could see the fear in other people's faces – this was violence as second nature. The school is very different now, and there are elements of the play inspired by events and experiences from both then and now. Zac is based on a real classmate, a boxer, who because his cousins were feared throughout the school had a great pressure to behave a certain way. If you're feared you therefore don't fear anything, and if you're part of that world then your life will improve – for him being at school was heaven. But as Simon learned later, the classmate only had that in his life, and as the end of school got nearer, he got more and more terrified. Simon's dad used to say 'You have a time in your life when you're at your best, and the rest of your life you're trying to get back there. It's terrifying for those who have that early on.' All of that said, it important that Zac is an enjoyable part to play, constantly using manipulation and charm – no one who is a villain thinks they're a villain, so be careful not to judge the characters. When working with the group to develop the play Simon was struck by how the parents (or their lack) were very noticeable in the kids – through things they said or particular ways of thinking about things – and this has affected the portrayal of several of the characters.

Simon's writing has been very influenced by the time he has spent at the Royal Court and his characters are rigorously driven by a few simple 'rules'. What do they want? What's stopping them getting what they want? What do they do in order to get what they want? Do they achieve it? Scene by scene this is always very specific and therefore it's really useful to bear this in mind continuously while you're working through the play.

Simon is happy for groups to change references to locations and places and the types of exams to fit their geography.

Approaching the play

When you read a play you are its first audience – you have your own personal and specific reaction to it – and therefore part of what you're trying to do is re-create that connection for the audience that will see the production. So think about how *you* connect with the material. We're all human beings who've had experiences – it's your world, and therefore it doesn't need to feel complicated. Clare Lizzimore asked the questions: 'What school did you go to?', 'Who was your first crush?', and 'What was your proudest exam result?', and noted the number of interesting stories and shared or similar experiences.

Directing new plays is about how you connect to the play and then how you translate that connection with the young people you're working with, and the audience. You could talk with the group about finding contemporary real-life examples of the characters – but there should obviously be sensitivity not to 'name and shame' other students. It might be as simple as recognising specific traits in film or music stars – what are the sensibilities of these characters?

To help get your head round this you could start by simply pooling what's *in* the play – it doesn't need to be complicated or rational, simply what strikes *you* about the play. Some suggestions from the workshop:

THEMES   What we use as our 'shield' – control of things we're going through; sex and sexuality used as a weapon to protect ourselves; survival; school as a horrible melting pot; growing up; rites of passage and self-discovery; expectations of the future; pressure to perform: five years' work compressed into a two-and-a-half-hour exam; kings and underdogs; boredom; youth; manipulation; institutionalism; fear; losing your virginity; sexual playfulness: 'Will you? Have you? Why aren't you?'; a waiting room for the future; revenge; relationships: first girlfriend/boyfriend, friendships, parents and teachers, alpha males and females; positivity *versus* negativity; losers ending as winners – a just ending; kissing, fighting, dancing, couples arguing; hierarchy and labelling; argumentative flirting.

REALITY   A microcosm of a real school; recognisable and familiar characters; it relates to real students; smells – school and the memories you associate with it, sweat and cheap perfume; sounds – the rhythm of the play is punctuated with highs and lows; the memory of a school hall – it transforms from a communal space to a space where you're on your own sitting an exam.

TEXT   A world with its own language; humour; fast-paced dialogue – a 'pinball' effect; a gentle intro into chaos; character wants; tone; theatricality; intervals; banter; naturalism; a long timeline with three very clear parts – beginning, middle and end – structured around key calendar moments: study leave, prom, exam results; fights; live band; bold costume and scene changes; we never see any adults.

Exercises for use in rehearsal

How do you access all of these themes *practically*? How do you enable your actors to embrace everything above? How can you get actors to really understand who they are within the world and also what's affecting them? Particularly when your actors ask, 'What do I actually *do*?'

To start with, you don't need to feel like you have to do everything at once. It can be useful to establish a common *language* in rehearsal so you can guide the actors with both broad and specific detail. To get to truth and authenticity, sometimes it's helpful to explode things first – so the following exercises are ways of exploring the idea of character through practical and tangible means.

STATES OF TENSION

Have the actors walk through the space and encourage them to physically embody the following states of tension, one by one:

1 Exhausted/catatonic: a jellyfish, no tension in the body at all.

2 Californian: laid-back, cool, relaxed, casual.

3 Neutral: efficient – nothing more, nothing less.

4 Alert/curious: interested in things, more purpose to what you're doing.

5 Reactive: edgy, concentrated, reacting to everyone and everything.

6 Passionate: convinced, embracing life, melodramatic.

7 Tragic: an extreme level of tension, absolutely petrified.

As the actors are walking round, talk them through what each state might mean using evocative words and encourage them to really commit to finding the state in their body. Take your time in each state to get a really clear sense about what the difference between each state is, and find the muscle memory so the cast can re-create it easily and naturally. It's also really useful to encourage the actors to vocalise their state of tension so that later it can inform their delivery of lines. Once they're comfortable with the seven states, get the actors to jump between states to recognise the differences between them.

Status

Characters (like real people) have different statuses with a larger group. Give each member of the group a playing card: the number on the card is their level of status. Walk around the space embodying that status – how does it change your behaviour and thoughts and physicality? Begin to be more aware of other people and see how your sense of their different status affects your behaviour and your interaction with them. See if the group can line themselves up in order of status simply by the impression they get of how they interact. You could then start combining levels of status and tension – what happens if (for example) a character with eight- or nine-level status has a Californian level of tension?

Giving the cast a clear sense of their characters through these levels mean they can own the characters themselves and creatively interpret, rather than waiting to be told what to do. They have concrete things to play – they inhabit each character and you can direct/shape it.

You can also guide those choices for particular moments in the play; for example you might suggest that someone plays something as an eight-level, but if for your taste it's too much you can scale it down using a language that everyone understands – it's a practical code to activate the drama that's going on underneath it all. Also, in drama, as in life, status and tension continually change depending on which group you're in, so how do the levels of each character change when they're in different groups or with different people? Those moments when status and tension change are the interesting events of the play – it's how you communicate a story, it's how the drama in the play *changes*.

Super-objectives

To help give a clear journey for each character you should consider what *drives* them – what they *want* or *need* – you could call it a super-objective. Simon described it as the end of school being a light at the end of a tunnel. All the characters are moving towards it but they each have different feelings about it; for example, Peter is looking towards it, or Zac is terrified of it, walks into the light and explodes. Some characters have a super-objective about the future outside, some have a super-objective that just operates within the school. It can be a difficult thing for actors to play but it's important they know their super-objective.

Characters

Using the exercises above you could go through the list of characters and decide what their super-objective, and natural levels of status and tension are. Some suggestions from Simon, Clare and the workshop group:

PETER   Wants to go out with Naomi. He starts as a 1, ends up near a 10. Peter wants to delay the end of school so he can ask Naomi out.

ZAC   Wants to be king. He's a 10 at the start but by the end he's a 2 or 3. You could build Zac's status by him being outside of the room – maybe on his own he's a 3, but when he gets into the room he explodes into a 10.

NAOMI   Wants to get out. Her status is probably a 6 – she's not necessarily liked but everyone listens to her. She has a level of maturity and a confidence to be herself, but she's also got a vulnerability in that she can be crushed. Simon imagined her as having courage through stillness.

KELLY   Wants to succeed/pass. Her status is around a 4 – she's crippled by her own anxiety, not interested in popularity, but can still be crushed.

BILLY   Wants to be remembered. He thinks he's a 10 but other people perceive him as a 5.

LANA   is a 1 or even a zero at the beginning of the play. She's lost in self-loathing and wants to disappear. By the end of the play she climbs to a 5 or a 6. She is recovering. She can see the light of change and realises that she is genuinely cared about by someone in Peter.

SHULAY   Wants to impress her peers. She's got support from Shadia and is probably around a 6.

SHADIA   Wants to make her family proud. An 8 – she's got strength to fight for herself and other people. She's got a higher status that Shulay but without her would probably be lower. Even though she's big, bubbly and brutal she should be a highly entertaining and big presence.

BENNY   Wants his life to move on. He has a high status (9?) because of his relationship with Zac but doesn't seem to worry about it too much. Maybe he's got a high status but Californian tension.

SAM   Hard to say what his super-objective is because he can't see past five minutes – he moves as the play moves. He's trying really hard to project an 8 but is probably more like a 4. Everyone knocks him down and can see straight through him.

COX   Wants to be his father. His status is around 7 because of his relation to Sam and he has a level of self-confidence. He is his father and has a 'posh confidence' – 'I am therefore I will.'

MATT   Wants Chloe. He has a high status of maybe 8 because of his sporting ability and because he's going out with Chloe. You could explore the competition between him and Zac.

CHLOE   Wants to be queen. She's a desirable person with a status of around 8, but her status plummets after kissing Zac.

A simple approach to the first rehearsal

It can be very daunting at a first rehearsal, and the play has a joyful challenge of finding the difference between delicacy and boldness. A suggestion of how you could begin to explore this under very little pressure is to read the scene (or even the entire play) aloud including stage directions and dialogue, and record it. Give enough time to allow stage directions to occur. Then set up the playing space roughly as it'll be and play the recording back – ask the actors simply to listen and re-create what they're hearing. In this way you can work through the entire play and stage it really simply, giving the cast an understanding of the simple things they need to do. After that first rehearsal you'll have done the whole play – it's just a starting point, but it will reveal very simple things about what's happening in each moment and throughout the action. On one hand it's a bit anxious-making, but it also means you don't have to over-think anything. If you like it, you can go

back and record again – actors will start making new choices
and finessing and self-directing.

BREAKING UP THE ACTION TO WORK ON IT

Read through the scene and when something *changes* (topic,
atmosphere, tone, decision) draw a line under it – this creates
a section that is a beat of action. Title the beat to describe
what's happening, and who's driving it. For example in the
first scene:

1 Lana wants to be invisible.

2 Peter wants to be noticed.

3 Peter wants to break the silence.

4 Peter wants to encourage her.

You could go one stage further and explore 'actions'. These
are transitive verbs (verbs you can do *to* someone) that you
can attach to each line or different sections. Give a line a
particular action: say, *inspire*. Announce the action by saying
'I inspire you' and make sure the delivery is imbued with the
quality of the verb (e.g. it's inspiring); then say the line in the
same way so it also has that quality.

Get a pad of Post-It notes and read the scene. For each thought
stick a note on to the other person in the manner of the
intention (in a funny way, or an insistent way, or a protective
way, etc.). Or throw a tennis ball to your partner for each
thought, giving the thought a pressure and firmness. It can
help the actors explore how they're interacting physically and
instinctively rather than intellectually. Then when it's put back
into the actual setting, what nuances does the delivery retain?

Fights

During the workshop Alison de Burgh worked through some
suggestions for how to approach the fights in the play. Below
are notes as a reminder for the participants – they are not
meant to be used as a substitute for appropriate professional
tuition.

FIGHTING DISTANCE   In pairs, A and B stand opposite each other. A puts hand on B's shoulder with a straight arm – that's a real fighting distance, how close you are to 'land' a blow; a step back to enlarge the distance means a hit can have body weight behind it; any closer and all you can really do is head-butt. In order to create the right level of tension or threat between characters it's important that you consider distance.

SPIN   B turns around. A moves slightly to the left, lining their right foot with B's left foot. A's left hand on B's right shoulder. A gives a squeeze-signal and B pivots on left foot to spin round clockwise – looking like A has grabbed them round. The more slick B's spin, the greater A's apparent aggression.

JAB   Relax your stance and sink your centre by bending your knees, take right foot back so toes level with left heel – this is a basic fighting stance for any unarmed combat. Make a fist with your right hand, with the thumb across the middle joints. Make sure the fist isn't tight, and level the back of the hand in line with your forearm. Pull your fist back to your waist, palm up. Point your left-hand index finger forward, level with the middle of your chest – the solar plexus – elbow just touching chest. With your right arm close to your body, move the fist forward towards the pointed finger (twisting fist as reaches tip of finger) then back to get the action of the jab. At the same time, your left hand hits the meat of your right chest with a relaxed open hand. Your two hands should move in opposition – left hand pointing, hitting chest and back again, right hand jabbing in and back – both go together. Checklist: low centre; finger pointing to solar plexus; punching elbow just touching you; fist is way back; elbow stays behind the fist as punch, twists at the last minute and then returns. Do not 'chicken wing'.

WITH A PARTNER   Stand in fighting distance and now step back so that your punching hand can't reach; or, to be really safe, stretch straight arm just away from victim's nose, then take a big step back so there can't be any contact. A, practise jabbing B as above. The most important person is the victim (B) – it's their response that will sell the impact. When the jab 'lands' B must throw their bum back and swing their arms round like they're doing butterfly stroke, which will send them back like you've been punched (think of the shape of someone being punched in a movie).

HOOK   Start as with the jab and lift your right elbow away from your body – this punch will hook across your partner. Pull back before you punch (like you would a tennis serve) so you have more power – it also gives a visual cue to your partner. Spiral all the way round to you don't end up punching your own chest.

UPPERCUT   Same principle as above but your punch will go straight up rather than round – so drop your right knee and pull your left arm down after the 'nap'.

SLAP   Look your partner in the eye, prep your arm back like a tennis serve and then slap down like you're hitting an 'ace' – it's a diagonal movement across their face. The victim makes the nap – the side of face that's hit, that hand face down, the other facing up. To make the sound, clap your hands so they swap and then grab the face with the hand that travelled up.

KICK   Practise trying to not kick an object like a water bottle. Kick from your knee not your waist to maintain your balance – it's the jerk backwards that does it, just like the jab. The nap can be really simple by just slapping your thigh or bum. Don't kick the back of your other leg or skid your foot along the floor – if you must hit the floor then make it a tap into the floor like a foot-pump action. And you can sell the reaction by moving back after the hit.

CONTACT PUNCH   Go to punch your partner but, instead of punching, flick your fingers out to tap the side of their stomach (oblique muscles) with the back of your fingers. Break it down slowly first – aim, relax, flick, close, back – then build it up to speed. Be careful to keep the line of your arm accurate, otherwise it'll lose visual impact.

PROTECTION   This moment came from a real incident and led to the image of one character lying on the other to protect them. Crucially, Simon is interested in it being a beautiful image on stage, rather than the realism of a brutal moment of violence. However, it should be as savage an attack as possible. Most of the effect will come from the reactions of the victims and the psychological conviction of the aggressor. Ideally help disguise it using costume or staging to create spaces to kick-jab the foot in.

FLINCHING   It might be a good idea that the 'flinch' punch is less convincing (i.e. the punching hand stays outstretched) so that the actual punch looks different – keep your best moves for the end. It's also more about status – the idea that Zac could punch you at any time, rather than the actual act of threatening. Similarly, when rushing people use your leg as a break so emphasise the near impact.

WRITING A FIGHT   A column for each character in the fight. List each move going down the page, putting them into the correct character column, leaving horizontal gaps between moves so that they're clearly distinct. Include any reactions to be played. You can also add dialogue cues and so on.

SOME GENERAL THOUGHTS   Practise in front of a mirror and you'll soon see what's wrong. It'll take *at least* fifty practices before you're even close to getting it right. Never use the same move more than once because the audience will suss it. You'll need to find a justified reason for why your hands can be in the right positions – and think of them really early on so the cast can *practise*. To sink your centre pretend you're a comedy cowboy with low-slung hips from being on a horse all day. Think about how characters can retain status. Eye contact is key to everything as it can signal status and conviction as well as giving you safety and timing. When using knee-pads, make sure the fight is safe and you're not just relying on the padding.

Participating Companies

360 Youth Theatre
ACT Aberdeen
Actors Centre Theatre Company
Alderbrook School
Alnwick Playhouse Youth Theatre
Artemis Studios – Medusa Teen
    Theatre Company
artsdepot young company
Artsed Sixth Form
Ascendance Theatre Arts
Ayrshire College
BACStage
Badenoch and Strathspey Youth
    Theatre
Barbara Priestman Academy
Barnwell School
Bedford College
Belgrade Theatre
Berzerk Productions
Birmingham Metropolitan College
Bishops High School
Blatchington Mill School
Bodens Youth Theatre
Borders Youth Theatre (BYT)
Bounce Theatre
Brampton Manor Academy
Brannel Theatre Company
Brewery Youth Theatre
Bridgend College
Bridgwater College Drama Academy
Bromsgrove School
Calday Grange Grammar School
Calderdale Theatre School
Cardinal Wiseman School
Carshalton High School for Girls
CASTEnsemble
Castleford Academy
Chapter 4 (Mansfield Palace Youth
    Theatre)
Chichester Festival Youth Theatre

Christ's College Guildford
Churston Ferrers Grammar School
Cockburn School
Colchester Royal Grammar School
Coopers College
Cornwall College – St Austell
Coulsdon Sixth Form College
Court Fields Community School
Crosskeys College Drama Group
De Warenne Academy
definate
Dig Theatre
Drama Lab
Dumfries Youth Theatre
Dumont High School Youth
    Theatre
East Berkshire College
Eastside Young Leaders' Academy
Easy Street Theatre Company
Eden Court Young Company
Electric Youth Theatre
Everyman Youth Theatre
Felixstowe Academy
Flying High Theatre Company
Fowey Community College
Free Spirits
Front Row Theatre
Generator
George Greens School
Glebe School
Glenwood High School
Great Baddow High School
Group 64
Gulbenkian Youth Theatre
Halesowen College
Heaton Manor Theatre Project
Hemsworth Arts and Community
    College
High Jinks
Hive Youth Performance Group

Hope Academy
Hove Park School
Hunterhouse College
Immediate Theatre
InterACT Youth Theatre
Invicta Grammar School
John Cabot Academy
John Spence Community High
    School
Junk Shop Theatre Company
JWC Theatre Company
Kildare Youth Theatre
King's Company
King's Lynn Academy
King's Theatre Company
Kirkcaldy High School
KPAC
Leigh Technology Academy
Llanelli Youth Theatre
Lochaber Youth Theatre
London Bubble Theatre Company
Longley Park Sixth Form College
Lostleters
Lowton C of E High School
LVS Ascot
Lyceum Youth Theatre
Lymm High School
LYTX
Maidstone Grammar School for Girls
Mess Up The Mess Theatre
    Company
Monkeywrench
Montage Theatre Arts
Morpeth School
Morphic Young People's Theatre
Nairn Youth Theatre
New College Nottingham
New College, Swindon
New South Wales Public Schools
    Drama Company
Newcastle College
North Durham Academy
Northampton High School
Northern Stage Young Company

Norwich Theatre Royal Youth
    Theatre Company
Oasis Academy Hadley Senior
    Drama Company
OP and MCS Young Company
Orange Tree Youth Theatre
Oxford Actors Company
PACE Youth Theatre
Pangbourne College
Parabola Arts Centre Youth
    Theatre (PAC YT)
Perfect Circle Youth Theatre
Perpich Center for Arts Education
Perth Youth Theatre
Phoenix
Playhouse Youth Theatre
Portal Theatre Company
Portsmouth High School
Queens Theatre Hornchurch
RAaW YPTC
RAPA Youth
RAW Academy
Retford Post 16 Centre
Rising Stars Youth Theatre
Rokeby School
Rotherham College of Arts and
    Technology
Roundwood Park School
Royal & Derngate Youth Theatre
Salisbury Playhouse BTEC
    Company
Samuel Whitbread Academy
Scarborough Youth Theatre
Sgioba Dràma Òigridh Inbhir Nis
Sheffield Theatres
Shenley Triple Threats
Sherman Cymru
Shotton Hall Theatre School
Something Wicked This Way Comes
South Downs College Theatre
    Company
South Wirral High School
Spotlight UK
St Anselm's College Drama Group

St Catherine's Catholic School
St Catherine's School
St Dominic's
St Joseph's RC High School, Newport
St Mark's Catholic School
St Mary's Catholic School
St Monica's Theatre Company
St Olave's
St Swithun's School
Stafford Gatehouse Youth Theatre
Stage by Stage
Stage Door 1 Youth Theatre
Stage Stars Theatre Academy
Stagecoach East Kilbride
Stage-Fright
Stephen Joseph Youth Theatre
Stockton Riverside College
Stokesley School Drama Group
Stopsley High School
Strode's College
Strood Academy Drama (SAD)
Suffolk New College Performing Arts
Surbiton High School
Tanbridge House School
Thame Youth Theatre
The Arnewood School
The Becket School
The Berry Youth Theatre
The Blue Coat School
The Boswells Academy
The Castle School
The Churchill Young Company
The Crestwood School
The Customs House Youth Theatre
The de Ferrers Academy
The Fallibroome Academy
The Garage
The Green School
The Kings School – Peterborough
The Lincoln Young Company
The Lowry B
The Lowry Young Actors Company

The Marist Senior School
The Marlowe Youth Theatre
The Nuffield Youth Theatre Company
The Petchey Academy
The Playing Space
The Priory City of Lincoln Academy
The Regis
The Savvy Young Company
The St Marylebone Theatre Company
The Warwick Arts Centre Connections Company
The Young Theatre
Theatre in Transit
Theatre Royal Plymouth Young Company
Theatreworx
Thurso High School
Tomorrow's Talent
Tricycle Young Company
Trinity Youth Theatre Company
Tyne Valley Youth Theatre
UpStageRight: Nescot Performing Arts
Urock Youth Theatre
Uxbridge College
Valentines High School
Walton Girls High School
West Thames College
Winstanley College
Winterhill School
Wirral Grammar Girls
Woolwich Polytechnic School
Worthing College
Wychwood Theatre Company
Yew Tree Youth Theatre
Young and Unique Theatre Company
Young Dramatic Arts Theatre Company
Young Peoples Theatre
Ysgol Aberconwy

Partner Theatres

artsdepot, London
Brewery Arts Centre, Kendal
Bristol Old Vic
Chichester Festival Theatre/The Capitol, Horsham
Derby Theatre
Eden Court, Inverness
Greenwich Theatre, London
Lyceum, Edinburgh
Marlowe Theatre, Canterbury
Northern Stage, Newcastle
Norwich Playhouse
Royal & Derngate, Northampton
Salisbury Playhouse
Sheffield Theatres
Sherman Cymru, Cardiff
Soho Theatre, London
Stephen Joseph Theatre, Scarborough
The Bush, London
The Garage, Norwich
The Lowry Centre, Salford
The Lyric Theatre, Belfast
The North Wall, Oxford
Theatre Royal Plymouth
Tricycle Theatre, London
Warwick Arts Centre, Coventry
West Yorkshire Playhouse, Leeds

Performing Rights

Applications for permission to perform, etc. should be made, before rehearsals begin, to the following representatives:

For *A Letter to Lacey*, *Hearts*, *Horizon* and *Tomorrow*
The Agency (London) Ltd
24 Pottery Lane
Holland Park, London W11 4LZ

For *Angels*
Lisa Richards Agency
108 Upper Leeson Street
Dublin 4
Ireland

For *A Shop Selling Speech* and *Heritage*
Curtis Brown Group
Haymarket House
28–29 Haymarket, London SW1 4SP

For *Pronoun*
Knight Hall Agency Ltd
Lower Ground Floor
7 Mallow Street, London EC1Y 8RQ

For *Same*
United Agents
12–26 Lexington Street, London W1F OLE

For *The Wardrobe*
Casarotto Ramsay
Waverley House
7–12 Noel Street, ondon W1F 8GQ

Applications for performance of *Pronoun*, *Same* and *The Wardrobe*,
including readings and excerpts, by amateurs in English
should be addressed in the first instance to
The Performing Rights Manager, Nick Hern Books Ltd,
The Glasshouse, 49a Goldhawk Road,
London W12 8QP
(*tel* +44 (0)20 8749 4953
email info@nickhernbooks.co.uk

National Theatre Connections 2014 Team

Alice King-Farlow	*Director of Learning*
Rob Watt	*Connections Producer*
Anthony Banks	*Associate Director, NT Learning*
Lucy Deere	*Connections Assistant Producer*
Paula Hamilton	*Head of Programmes, NT Learning*
Katie Town	*General Manager, NT Learning*
Tom Lyons	*Associate Literary Manager*

The National Theatre

National Theatre
Upper Ground
London SE1 9PX

Registered charity no: 224223

Director of the National Theatre
Nicholas Hytner

Executive Director
Nick Starr

Chief Operating Officer
Lisa Burger